DATE DUE

DEMCO 38-296

LORD BURLINGTON:

ARCHITECTURE, ART AND LIFE

LORD BURLINGTON

———

ARCHITECTURE, ART AND LIFE

EDITED BY

TOBY BARNARD AND JANE CLARK

THE HAMBLEDON PRESS

LONDON AND RIO GRANDE

995
102 Gloucester Avenue, London NW1 8HX (U.K.)
P.O. Box 162, Rio Grande, Ohio 45674 (U.S.A.)

ISBN 1 85285 094 9

A description of this book is available from
the British Library and from the Library of Congress

Typeset by York House Typographic Ltd
Printed on acid-free paper and bound in
Great Britain by Cambridge University Press

Contents

Illustrations

Preface

Burlington is a household word. Quite apart from Burlington House, home of the Royal Academy of Arts, the number of streets and businesses in London and the provinces, not to mention towns in the United States of America, called after this great eighteenth-century figure testify to the universal renown of Richard Boyle, 3rd earl of Burlington. Yet there is no biography. His few remaining architectural exercises, the most important of these being Chiswick House, have been discussed in endless detail but even here the international scope of his influence has not been recognised; still less has the message his buildings conveyed been explored. An acute awareness of the mysteries surrounding this man whose architectural influence is to be seen the world over, mysteries which make a study of his life a tremendous challenge to scholars of all disciplines, have prompted this book. It is the result of what is merely the beginning of a study that must, as it progresses, cause a reassessment of many aspects of eighteenth-century life and thought.

This publication has been undertaken with the help and support of English Heritage and Chiswick House Friends. The editors would also like to thank Howard Colvin for writing an introduction, Valerie Kemp and Anthony O'Connor for their considerable labours on the index and Martin Sheppard for his patience. We also express our gratitude to the Duke and Duchess of Devonshire, the Trustees of the Chatsworth Settlement and to Peter Day and the archivists at Chatsworth.

Toby Barnard   Jane Clark

Acknowledgements

The editors, contributors and publisher are most grateful to the following for permission to reproduce illustrations:

The Trustees of the Chatsworth Settlement 4a, 5a, 12d, 14a, 15b, 22b, 26b, 27a, 31a, 37a, 42b, 43b, 44b, 44c, 45f, 46b, 50a, 50b, 61, 67, 68, 69

Chiswick Public Library 47d

English Heritage 1a, 1b, 2, 3a, 6a, 8a, 9a, 9b, 12a, 13a, 15a, 16a, 16b, 16c, 16h, 17a, 19a, 20a, 21a, 22a, 23a, 24a, 25a, 26a, 27a, 27b, 28a, 29a, 32, 33a, 33c, 35a, 39, 41a, 42a, 44a, 45a, 46a, 47a, 47b, 47c, 49a, 49b, 49c, 49d, 51, 52a, 52b, 53, 55, 56, 57, 58, 59, 60

Harris Museum and Art Collection, Preston 70

Richard Hewlings 47d

The Trustees of the Lismore Estate 72

National Portrait Gallery 71

National Trust 68

RCHME 18d, 18e, 40

RIBA 3b, 4c, 7, 8b, 9b, 14b, 16d, 16e, 16f, 16g, 16i, 16j, 27c, 33b, 38, 40, 45b, 45e, 48a, 48b, 49e, 49f, 49g, 49h

Victoria and Albert Museum 63a, 64, 65

Contributors

Toby Barnard	Hertford College, Oxford
Jane Clark	London
Howard Colvin	St John's College, Oxford
Eveline Cruickshanks	Formerly History of Parliament, London; University of Versailles
Howard Erskine-Hill	Pembroke College, Cambridge
Richard Hewlings	English Heritage
Edward McParland	Trinity College, Dublin
Murray Pittcock	University of Edinburgh

Abbreviations

BL	British Library
CSPD	*Calendar of State Papers Domestic*
HMC	Historical Manuscripts Commission
NLI	National Library of Ireland, Dublin
PRO	Public Record Office
RA, SP	Royal Archives, State Papers
RCHME	Royal Commission on the Historical Monuments of England
RIBA	Royal Institute of British Architects
SRO	Scottish Record Office
TCD	Trinity College, Dublin
VCH	Victoria County History

Introduction

Howard Colvin

Lord Burlington's place in the history of English architecture is assured. It was under his direction that Palladianism became the national style of Georgian England, triumphing over the insular Baroque of Wren and Vanbrugh to give Europe an equally insular premonition of that neo-classicism that was eventually to prevail everywhere over the Baroque and the Rococo. Taking an initiative that in any other European state would have been the prerogative of the ruler, he was able both to fill the Office of the King's Works with his nominees and to build up a circle of like-minded gentry who propagated his architectural gospel in the country. By the time of his death in 1753, what for him had been a highly intellectual interpretation of the architecture of classical antiquity, studied largely through the drawings of Palladio, had become a vernacular style easily recognisable by such clichés as the 'Venetian' window or the corner towers from Wilton House.

All this is well enough known.[1] What has not been so well known is the political stance from which Burlington accomplished his architectural revolution. As a major landowner both in England and in Ireland Burlington could hardly be politically neutral in a country as deeply divided between Whigs and Tories as early Georgian England. Many of the political dilemmas that faced his ancestor the first earl of Burlington and second earl of Cork must have faced him too, but his political record is too enigmatic to make his response clear.[2] To all appearances he was a confirmed Whig, and up to the age of thirty-nine his career was that of a great Whig nobleman:

1 See R. Wittkower, *Palladio and Palladianism* (London 1974), John Summerson, *Architecture in Britain, 1530-1830* (Harmondsworth, 1991), part 4, and John Harris, *The Palladians*, RIBA Drawings Series (London, 1981). For Burlington and the Office of Works, see H. Colvin in *Lord Burlington and his Circle* (Georgian Group Symposium 1982), pp. 97-101.

2 See T.C. Barnard, 'Land and the Limits of Loyalty: The Second Earl of Cork and the First Earl of Burlington (1612-98)', below, pp. 167-99.

lord lieutenant of the East and West Ridings of Yorkshire (1715), a member
of the privy council (1729), a knight of the Garter (1730), and captain of the
Gentlemen Pensioners, a body of privileged men in personal attendance on
the king (1731). He could hardly have infiltrated the Office of Works in the
way he did unless he had been on good terms with Walpole, and the year-
by-year record of his political activity set out by Eveline Cruickshanks
shows that when the Whig party split in 1717, he adhered to Walpole and
Townshend against Sunderland and Stanhope.[3] Moreover, on five occasions between 1723 and 1732 he was invited to pre-sessional meetings of
court lords. With rank and political conformity went influence: in 1722
Burlington was able not only to obtain for his protégé William Kent the job
of decorating the state apartment in Kensington Palace in the face of Sir
James Thornhill, the established court painter, but to get a special post of
Surveyor or Inspector of Paintings in the Royal Palaces created for his
benefit (1728).[4] In 1726 he had already got Kent onto the Board of Works,
and in the same year another of his architectural protégés, Henry Flitcroft,
was appointed to the key Clerkship of the Works at Whitehall, Westminster
and St James's. Two years later Daniel Garrett, a man of whom Burlington
was reported to have a higher opinion than of anyone else except Kent
himself, was appointed to a salaried post at Richmond. It was no
coincidence that the Surveyor of the King's Works at this time was the Hon.
Richard Arundell, a life-long friend of Burlington, whose architectural
tastes he shared and who made him his executor and trustee. A friend of
Walpole, Pelham and Newcastle, Arundell was a loyal Whig who was in
high favour at Court and who held office as a lord of the treasury in
Pelham's administration of 1744. He was of course a Member of Parliament
and he owed his election to Knaresborough in 1720 to the influence of
Burlington, who had the chief interest in one of the town's two seats, the
other being in the hands of the Tory Slingsbys.[5]

In May 1733 Burlington's career as a courtier came abruptly to an end. He
resigned all his offices at court, ostensibly because the king had failed to
honour a promise to give him the next 'white staff' (a symbol of high office
at court) that fell vacant. What lay behind this breach between king and
courtier we do not know, but according to Lord Hervey (vice-chamberlain

3 See Eveline Cruickshanks, 'The Political
  Career of the Third Earl of Burlington',
  below, pp. 201-15.
4 George Vertue specifically states that
  Kent was given this post 'by the interest

of Lord Burlington his Patron', *Walpole
Society*, 22, p. 55.
5 R. Sedgwick, *The House of Commons,
1715-1754*, (History of Parliament), i
(1970), pp. 360, 421.

of the Household) Burlington went out of his way to deny that it arose from any dissatisfaction with Walpole's regime.[6] Nevertheless, the breach of 1733 was to some extent a political as well as a personal one. Thereafter Burlington used his considerable influence in Yorkshire to support a Tory and an independent Whig for the two county seats, while continuing to secure Arundell's return to Knaresborough whenever it was necessary (as it was on seven occasions between 1733 and 1748). Up to 1733 the record is one of unbroken support for Walpole and the Whig party, after 1733 one of opposition tempered by personal loyalties.

It is therefore a shock to read Jane Clark's contribution to this volume.[7] For her carefully argued case, based on Burlington's own papers as well as on other contemporary records, is that throughout his life he was a Jacobite: not just a Jacobite sympathiser or one of those (of whom there were many) who made occasional gestures of friendship in the direction of the Stuart court just in case the King of England should one day be named James rather than George, but an active conspirator whose foreign tours were dictated as much by the need to make contact with Jacobite exiles as by the wish to study Palladian architecture, and whose notorious debts were caused by his lavish contributions to the Jacobite cause rather than by any architectural extravagance: in other words an eighteenth-century Anthony Blunt, masquerading as a loyal courtier while concealing a record of treasonable activity. The parallel is, of course, not quite exact, for it would no doubt have been rather less disreputable to be an active Jacobite at the court of George II than it was to be an ex-Communist spy at that of Elizabeth II; still, the conflict of loyalties involved in being captain of the Gentlemen Pensioners of George II while placing one's fortune at the disposal of his rival would have been acute. Can it in fact have been to resolve that conflict that Burlington resigned his offices in 1733?

If Burlington was an active Jacobite, it is natural to inquire how he behaved in the three great crises that confronted the English Jacobites in the course of his life: the invasions of 1715 and 1745 and the trial of Bishop Atterbury for treasonable conspiracy in 1723. In 1715, as Lord Lieutenant of the East and West Ridings, Burlington was in a key position to assist any Jacobite force that might penetrate the northern counties of England after crossing the Border. In 1715 the army led by Lords Derwentwater and

6 *Lord Hervey's Memoirs*, ed. R. Sedgwick, i (London, 1931), p. 188.

7 See Jane Clark, ' "Lord Burlington is Here" ', below, pp. 251-310.

Widdrington got no farther than Preston, where it was defeated by Stanhope's generals Wills and Carpenter. Wherever his private loyalties may have lain, Burlington is included by the contemporary chronicler of events, Abel Boyer, among those whose resolute measures contributed to the defeat of the rebels. 'We must take notice', he wrote, 'that the Earl of Warrington did . . . exert his Zeal for the King's Service at this critical Juncture *in Cheshire*; as did in a most signal manner the Earl of *Burlington* in Yorkshire; the Earl of *Scarborough* and the Lord *Lumley* in Northumberland; and . . . the Earl of *Carlisle* and the Lord *Lonsdale* in Cumberland and *Westmoreland*.'[8] Coming from Boyer, a known Whig, this was a genuine tribute to Burlington's loyalty. Less certain is the testimony of the dedication to Burlington of Richard Graham's edition of Du Fresnoy's *Art of Painting*, as translated by Dryden (1716). It praises 'Your glorious Conduct in the *North*, upon the late unhappy Disturbances that threaten'd Your *Province*', and 'that exemplary Moderation and Generosity, which mov'd You to intercede for the Lives of *those*, against whom You stood prepar'd to hazard *Your* own'. This may have been the truth, but it was the truth as Burlington himself wished it to be read, for the editor of the book was none other than his own secretary, and the dedication was written with the assistance of Pope, who in a letter to Graham hopes that the reference to Burlington's magnanimity will be included, 'provided he allows it'.[9] Was Graham publicly crediting his patron with a generosity that was really covert help for fellow-Jacobites in trouble?

   In 1745, with no official responsibility for the defence of Yorkshire against invasion, Burlington waited at Londesborough for the outcome without giving any clear sign as to where his loyalties lay. His initial failure to join actively in the measures taken to oppose the rebels worried that zealous Whig Archbishop Herring and his colleagues at York, but in the end they were persuaded that he was 'a warm friend' and 'hearty' in the Hanoverian cause.[10] Their confidence in Burlington's loyalty may have been misplaced, but if his sympathies were really with the Pretender's army it is strange to find William Kent, his close friend and protégé, writing from London on 24 October 1745 to say that 'the best news I can tell you [is that]

---

8 A. Boyer, *Political State of Great Britain*, x (London, 1716), p. 488.

9 *The Correspondence of Alexander Pope*, ed. G. Sherborne, i (Oxford 1956), p. 334.

10 R. Garnett, 'Correspondence of Arch-bishop Herring and Lord Hardwicke during the Rebellion of 1745', *English Historical Review*, 19 (1904), pp. 536–38, 544, 547.

an exprise is come that Ld Albermarle & Troops are landed at Shields & Genl: Wade is on his March, so its hoped in a little time whe shall here the Ribels will be dispers'd or destroy'd. The zeal that is shewd in every county to raise men, makes me believe my Ld Ailesbury [Burlington's brother-in-law] will do the like & be a Capt:.'[11]

If Kent did not know that his patron was a secret Jacobite neither did that wayward supporter of the Pretender, the duke of Wharton, who did not include his name in a list of sixty-seven members of the English and Scottish peerage favourable to the Jacobite cause which he drew up in 1725.[12] This was, perhaps, hardly surprising after Burlington's conduct at Atterbury's trial in the House of Lords in 1723, when he failed to join with Wharton and thirty-nine other Tory peers in trying to save the bishop by a procedural protest. Their names are known and Burlington's is not among them. In fact it is far from certain that Burlington did not vote for the condemnation of the man for whom he had recently designed the Dormitory of Westminster School and with whom (if he really was a Jacobite) he must often have conferred about the state of the Stuart cause. On 15 May 1723 eighty-three peers voted for Atterbury's exile, forty-three for his acquittal.[13] Of the forty-three all but three are accounted for by the forty who signed the protest. Was Burlington one of the remaining three, or was he bound by his commitment to the government to join the majority?

The case for Burlington's Jacobitism is therefore not conclusive. The weight of circumstantial evidence assembled by Jane Clark is impressive, but proof of clandestine political activity is of its nature difficult to establish, and there are some episodes in Burlington's political career that point in the opposite direction. It is to be hoped that the publication of this volume will stimulate further research and discussion in the course of which fresh, and perhaps more decisive, evidence as to Burlington's true political loyalties will be brought to light.

Does it matter whether Burlington was a loyal subject of King George or a Jacobite? To the political historian it obviously matters if a great nobleman whose name has never hitherto been mentioned in Jacobite historical literature should turn out to have been a major supporter of the Stuart cause,

---

11 Letter at Chatsworth, reproduced in facsimile by J. Dixon Hunt, *William Kent: Landscape Garden Designer* (London, 1987), p. 14.

12 P.S. Fritz, *The English Ministers and Jacobitism between the Rebellions of 1715 and 1745* (Toronto, 1975), appendix 5.

13 *Journals of the House of Lords*, 22, pp. 199-201; Hansard, *Parliamentary History*, 8 (1811), pp. 347-51.

actively engaged in plotting the downfall of the Hanoverian regime and personally contributing large sums of money to the Pretender's coffers. But does it matter to the architectural historian? It matters for two reasons. The first is that if Burlington was a Jacobite it would finally dispose of the old idea (propagated by Christopher Hussey) that Palladianism was thought up by Lord Burlington in his private 'academy' as the architectural expression of a 'Whig Ideal' founded on Platonism and Protestantism.[14] More Palladian buildings were no doubt built by Whigs than by Tories or Jacobites, but that was due to the accident of political ascendancy rather than to any ideological commitment to the style. In fact the pioneers of Palladianism were an English Tory (Dean Aldrich) and a Scottish Jacobite (James Smith), and when Colen Campbell planned that manifesto of Palladianism, *Vitruvius Britannicus*, in 1714, he dedicated several of the plates in the first volume to prominent Tories, who happened to be the men in power at that date.[15] Other plates were prudently dedicated to equally prominent Whigs. In short, the book was addressed to the powers that be, irrespective of their political allegiances. As it was, Palladianism was inevitably associated with the long Whig ascendancy which lasted through-out the reigns of the first two Georges. But if the Stuarts had recovered their throne in 1715 or 1723 or even in 1745, who can doubt that a Jacobite Lord Burlington (if Jacobite he was) would have designed a new Palladian palace for James III with at least as much enthusiasm as he had helped Kent to design Palladian Houses of Parliament for Walpole's government? The rivalry that doubtless would have ensued between himself and that other aristocratic and indubitably Jacobite architect, the duke of Mar, who spent so much of his exile designing palaces for a restored Stuart monarch,[16] is one of the might-have-beens of British architectural history.

The other reason why the claim that Burlington was a Jacobite is important to the architectural historian lies in the Jacobite allusions that both Jane Clark and Richard Hewlings have detected in Burlington's villa at Chiswick. This involves some highly esoteric symbolism drawn either from Antiquity or from Freemasonry or both. The extent to which ancient literature could be made to yield a modern political message is illustrated by Murray Pittock's paper on the *Aeneid*, which makes it easier to accept the Jacobite interpretation with which Hewlings concludes his meticulous

14 C. Hussey, *English Country Houses: Early Georgian, 1715-1760* (London, 1955), pp. 10-11.

15 Notably the earl of Oxford, the earl of Mar and Dr George Clarke (then a lord of the Admiralty).

16 T. Friedman, 'A Palace Worthy of the Grandeur of the King: Lord Mar's Designs for the Old Pretender, 1728-30', *Architectural History*, 29 (1986).

analysis of the architectural sources of Burlington's villa.[17] Jane Clark's invitation to see Chiswick as a Jacobite shrine expressed in masonic terms is more disturbing. The notion of an architecture as lucid as that of Burlington's villa serving a political purpose by means as profoundly irrational as those proposed here is worrying. If she is right, Chiswick, so far from expressing the intellectual values of the dawning Age of Reason, is an exquisite reversion to the arcane world of symbolism exemplified by Sir Thomas Tresham and the Triangular Lodge at Rushton.

17 See Murray Pittock, 'The *Aeneid* in the Age of Burlington: A Jacobite Text?', below pp. 231-49; Richard Hewlings, 'Chiswick House and Gardens: Appearance and Meaning', below, pp. 1-149.

1

Chiswick House and Gardens: Appearance and Meaning

Richard Hewlings

Chiswick House is unique among Georgian noblemen's houses in having petrified architects in waiting at the perron step (Fig. 1a, b). It is unlikely to be a temple built in their honour: if so, their effigies would have been housed in a place of greater moment – indoors, or at least at a higher level (Fig.2). Instead the two architects, Palladio and Inigo Jones, are set at the door, more like house porters or city guides. Effigies at the door, if uncommon in eighteenth-century houses, were not uncommon in antiquity, the middle ages and the Renaissance. Above the first-century BC Porta Marzia of Perugia busts of the presiding deities, Jupiter and the Dioscuri, lean over an

Fig. 1a Statue by Michael Rysbrack of the architect Andrea Palladio, outside the south (main) elevation of Chiswick House (*English Heritage*)

Fig. 1b Statue by Michael Rysbrack of the architect Inigo Jones, outside the south (main) elevation of Chiswick House (*English Heritage*)

illusionist balcony,[1] not unlike the illusionist balcony painted by William
Kent around the King's Stair at Kensington Palace, over which peer
courtiers who are inquisitive, but by no means deterrent.[2] Medieval and
Renaissance versions in England were, as their situations demanded, either
threatening, re-assuring or welcoming. On the ramparts of the castles of
Alnwick,[3] Bothal,[4] Hylton[5] and Raby,[6] on Monk Bar and Micklegate Bar
at York,[7] on the bridge at Doncaster[8] and on the great hall of the Field of
Cloth of Gold,[9] the petrified retainers were armed and threatening.
Sculpted figures on the ramparts of Newcastle[10] and on those of Conway,[11]
Caernavon,[12] Chepstow[13] and Dalton Castles,[14] are either destroyed or too
eroded to proclaim their intended message. The gatehouse of Thornton
Abbey, however, a building which is at once sacred, ostentatious and
bellicose, was ornamented with figures which personify a wide range of
messages. Immediately above the door are figures of the Virgin, the Baptist,
one of the four Doctors, Christ blessing and an angel with a spear and
crown of thorns. On the battlements stood 'men with swords, shields, poll-
axes, etc, in their hands'. Elsewhere there were statues 'of astronomers,
others of carpenters, others of all trades and sciences'.[15] Equally, one of the
gates of Newcastle had a statue of King James I,[16] and Ludgate in London

1 E. Baldwin Smith, *Architectural Symbolism of Imperial Rome and the Middle Ages* (Princeton, 1956), p. 24 and fig. 3.
2 Edward Croft-Murray, *Decorative Painting in England*, ii (London, 1970), pp. 28, 234 and plate 43.
3 Christopher Hussey, 'Alnwick Castle – I, Northumberland', *Country Life*, 45, June 22 1929, p. 898 and figs 2, 11, 12, 14 and 15; David J. Cathcart King, *Castellarium anglicanum*, ii (Millwood, NY, 1983), p. 325.
4 John Grundy, Grace McCombie, Peter Ryder, Humphrey Welfare and Nikolaus Pevsner, *The Buildings of England, Northumberland* (Harmondsworth, 1992), p. 199; King, *Castellarium anglicanum*, ii, pp. 328-29.
5 Beric M. Morley, 'Hylton Castle', *Archaeological Journal*, 133, p. 120 and plates xv and xvi; Peter Leach, 'In the Gothick Vein . . . ', *Country Life*, 156, 26 September 1974, p. 835, fig. 6; King, *Castellarium anglicanum*, i, p. 136.
6 Alastair Rowan, 'Raby Castle, Co. Durham', *Country Life*, 146, 10 and 17 July 1969, p. 78, fig. 1, and p. 151, fig. 5; King, *Castellarium anglicanum*, i, p. 137.
7 Royal Commission on Historic Monuments for England, *City of York*, ii, *The Defences* (London, 1972), p. 130 and plates 36 and 38 (Monk Bar), and p. 96 and plate 22 (Micklegate Bar).
8 W.C. Lukis (ed.), 'The Family Memoirs of the Rev. William Stukeley M.D., and the Antiquarian and Other Correspondence of William Stukeley, Roger and Samuel Gale, etc.', *Surtees Society*, 80 (1885), p. 383.
9 Joycelyne G. Russell, *The Field of Cloth of Gold* (London, 1969), p. 38 and plate iii; Sydney Anglo, 'The Hampton Court Painting of the Field of Cloth of Gold Considered as a Historical Document', *Antiquaries Journal*, 46 (1966), ii, pp. 287-307.
10 Sheriton Holmes, 'The Walls of Newcastle upon Tyne', *Archaeologia Aeliana*, 2nd series, 18, (1896), p. 24.
11 A.J. Taylor, *Conwy Castle and Town Walls* (London, 1956); King, *Castellarium anglicanum*, i, p. 33.
12 A.J. Taylor, *Caernarvon Castle and Town Walls* (London, 1953), pp. 23-24; King, *Castellarium anglicanum*, i, p. 32.
13 John Clifford Perks, *Chepstow Castle, Monmouthshire*, (London, 1967), 9 and 23; King, *Castellarium anglicanum*, i, p. 282.
14 *Victoria History of the Counties of England, Lancashire*, viii (London, 1914), p. 309 and plate opposite p. 310; King, *Castellarium anglicanum*, i, p. 245.
15 Sir Alfred Clapham and P.K. Baillie Reynolds, *Thornton Abbey, Humberside* (London, 1951, 1993), p. 21.
16 Holmes, 'The Walls of Newcastle', pp. 15-16.

had a statue of Queen Elizabeth,[17] whose intention was not to deter, but to reassure the visitor that he entered a place whose liberties and privileges were well-founded. These statues intimated that the town's favoured position was embodied in statute; other statues might imply that it was established in antiquity. Ludgate's statue of Elizabeth was therefore paired with a statue of King Lud.[18] Bristol displayed statues of Brennus and Belinus,[19] York a statue of King Ebrauk,[20] and Chester a statue of Mars.[21] In other places the figures are positively benign: at Chillingham Castle the external stair within the courtyard is flanked by what appear to be the senior servants standing at the visitor's service. At Hazlewood Castle, men-at-arms knelt respectfully at the visitor's approach.[22] On Bootham Bar in York the apotropaic figures included a lord mayor flanked by a mason and a knight,[23] evidently courteous greeters rather than menacing defenders. At Chiswick, gesture suggests that Jones and Palladio are of this last type. They are there to guide the visitor, as Virgil guided Dante. At Chiswick, however, it is not the underworld to which they are the guide, but the ancient world.

In the absence of a statement of intent by its author, his objectives at Chiswick have to be assumed from the evidence of its individual parts. The first part of this essay identifies fifty individual features at Chiswick. Three of them, no more, may have been invented by Palladio. Another four are features which Palladio used, in common with other sixteenth-century architects, and which it would therefore be imprecise to call 'Palladian'. A further ten are features of sixteenth-century origin, which Palladio never used. The remaining thirty-three are features which Burlington knew had been used in ancient buildings. Of these thirty-three features, he copied nine from illustrations of ancient buildings in Palladio's book, and five from Palladio's record drawings. Thus an insignificant proportion (6 per cent) of the component features of Chiswick House and Garden are indebted to the creative efforts of Palladio, while just under one third (28 per cent) are

17 C.S. Cooper, *The Outdoor Monuments of London* (London, 1928), p. 33.
18 Ibid.; John Schofield, *The Building of London from the Conquest to the Great Fire* (London, 1984), p. 3, fig. 2.
19 William Barrett, *The History and Antiquities of the City of Bristol* (Bristol, 1789), p. 487.
20 Royal Commission on Historic Monuments for England, *City of York*, ii, *The Defences*, p. 55.
21 Ibid., citing no authority. Victoria History of the Counties of England, *Cheshire*, i (London, 1987), p. 129, however, describes an anony-

mous relief of the Roman period, obscured until the demolition of the gate in 1768 and subsequently lost.
22 'Chillingham Castle, Northumberland', *Country Life*, 30, 8 March 1913, p. 349. Arthur Oswald, 'Hazlewood Castle, Yorkshire - II, *Country Life*, 122, 26 December 1957, p. 1429, where the figures are shown in a more recent location and are described as praying.
23 Royal Commission on Historic Monuments for England, *City of York*, ii, *The Defences* (1972), p. 117 and plate 32.

indebted to Palladio's achievements as an archaeological draughtsman. Two thirds (66 per cent) represent Burlington's efforts to replicate ancient architecture. These figures suggest that the reproduction of ancient, not Palladian, architecture was Burlington's principal intention, although they also reveal his debt to Palladio as a guide to the ancient world.

The second part of this essay offers some explanation of why this might have been so.

Fig. 2 The south elevation of Chiswick House (*English Heritage*)

Fig. 3a The north elevation of Chiswick House (*English Heritage*)

Fig. 3b Drawing by Andrea Palladio of a villa (*RIBA*)

Part 1

Appearance

Burlington's archaistic intentions have been noted since 1927, and to that extent this essay only amplifies the original observations advanced then by Fiske Kimball.[24] But Kimball's evidence, when taken from Chiswick, returns some ambiguous answers. For instance, the intercolumniation of the portico is regular, following Palladio's observations that this was ancient practice. Kimball noted that, although Palladio made this observation, he did not always follow it himself. In these terms Burlington's architecture is more ancient than Palladio's. Kimball's conclusion cannot be reached, at least from this evidence, first because the columns of ancient porticos, like Palladio's, are not always regularly spaced, and secondly because Burlington's are not regularly spaced either. The portico of the ancient Temple of Jupiter at Baalbek, for instance, has a wider central space,[25] as does Burlington's proposed design for the Palace of Westminster.[26] Kimball also noted that one of Burlington's designs for a proposed Orangery at Chiswick is based upon the façade of Palladio's S. Giorgio Maggiore at Venice. The difference, he noted, was that the pilasters of Burlington's design stood on the ground in the ancient manner, whereas those in Palladio's stand on high pedestals in a modern manner. In fact numerous ancient pilasters stand on high pedestals, including famous and conspicuous examples such as the Arches of Septimius Severus and Constantine, and all the upper orders of the Colosseum.[27] And it happens that Burlington's design is, in this particular instance, copied from an alternative design by Palladio for S. Giorgio,[28] which omits the pedestals. Burlington owned this drawing, and

24 Fiske Kimball, 'Burlington Architectus', *Journal of the Royal Institute of British Architects*, 34, 15 October 1927, pp. 675-93.

25 John B. Ward-Perkins, *Roman Architecture* (Harmondsworth, 1979), p. 165, fig. 258; Axel Boethius and J.B. Ward-Perkins, *Etruscan and Roman Architecture* (Harmondsworth, 1970), pp. 419-20.

26 H.M. Colvin (ed.), *The History of the King's*

Works, v (London, 1976), plate 61, although there attributed to William Kent.

27 Boethius and Ward-Perkins, *Etruscan and Roman Architecture*, p. 275 and plate 104, p. 507 and plate 262, pp. 221-24 and plate 121.

28 London, British Architectural Library, Drawings Collection, Burlington-Devonshire Collection, xiv, 12.

it was the only design for S. Giorgio which Burlington knew, since none are included in Palladio's book. These features have therefore not contributed to the figures whose analysis appears above.

The evidence which follows, however, offers a conclusion similar, but not identical to Kimball's. Kimball's examples indicate that Burlington modelled his architecture primarily on Palladio's, though on occasion correcting it by reference to antiquity. This essay suggests instead that ancient architecture was Burlington's primary model, and that Palladio, together with other sixteenth-century architects to whose identities Burlington was largely indifferent, was only a source of information about it. Burlington's archaistic intentions had been unnoted until Kimball published his paper. This essay's conclusions therefore differ from Kimball's but only by advancing his position further in the same direction.

Features of Palladian Origin

There is only one feature of Palladian origin on or in the house itself. The north elevation has three *serlianas* with concentric relieving arches, alternating with niches (Fig. 3a). The history of *serlianas*, both with and without relieving arches, is outlined below (pp. 94-104), where it is suggested that Burlington chose to use them because he knew that they had been used by the ancient Romans. Ancient usage included *serlianas* with relieving arches, which he knew from his own collection of Palladio's record drawings of ancient baths.[29] But these drawings do not show the feature triplicated, and alternating with niches, as at Chiswick. It is possible that Burlington saw a drawing in the Office of Works for rebuilding Whitehall Palace, made between 1698 to 1702,[30] which includes three adjacent *serlianas* with relieving arches in an otherwise plain wall. But, even if he saw it, this drawing is not very close to the north elevation of Chiswick House: the building which it illustrates is much bigger, the *serlianas* are in the attic storey, their

29 London, British Architectural Library, Drawings Collection, Burlington-Devonshire Collection, iii, 7 (Baths of Nero); and v, 4, 5 (Baths of Diocletian).

30 Oxford, All Souls College, Architectural Drawings, ii, supplement no. 1. This drawing has been attributed to the 'Wren office' (presumably the Office of Works), Kerry Downes, *English Baroque Architecture* (London, 1966), plate 78; to Talman, Kerry Downes, *Wren* (1971), p. 102; to Wren, Colvin, *History of the* *King's Works*, v, p. 299; and to Hawksmoor, Giles Worsley, 'Nicholas Hawksmoor: A Pioneer Neo-Palladian?', *Architectural History*, 33 (1990), p. 66. Although it is less likely to have influenced the design of Chiswick than the drawing by Palladio cited below (n. 31), the latter, which in 1698-1702 belonged to John Oliver or William Talman, is likely to have been the source of both designs, Worsley, 'Nicholas Hawksmoor'.

Fig. 4a Drawing by Lord Burlington for a proposed orangery at Chiswick (*Chatsworth*)

Fig. 4b Illustration by Andrea Palladio of the Basilica of Maxentius, Rome

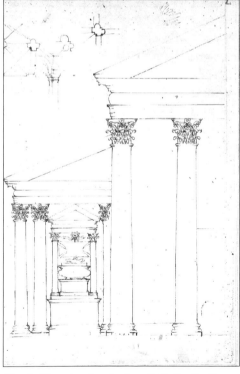

Fig. 4c Drawing by Andrea Palladio for S. Giorgio Maggiore, Venice (*RIBA*)

relieving arches are not concentric with the round arch of the centre light, but segmental, and no niches separate them. However, Burlington had in his own possession a design of Palladio's, which includes three *serlianas* in almost exactly the form which they possess at Chiswick (Fig. 3b).[31] Although the triplication of a motif in current use may hardly be regarded as creativity of a high order, Palladio was certainly responsible for it, and his drawing is self-evidently the prototype of the Chiswick elevation.

There were other features of Palladian origin on buildings in the garden. The Orangery design discussed by Kimball was made by 1736,[32] but was not executed (Fig. 4a). It consisted of an applied Corinthian tetrastyle portico, set between lower wings, each of which is surmounted by half a pediment. The distant ancestor of this design is the elevation of the Basilica of Maxentius, published in Palladio's book (Fig. 4b).[33] But the Basilica, a more complex design, has no order, and its pediments are supported by unadorned wall. The lower members of the two half pediments are continued across the whole elevation, below the central whole pediment. The central, pedimented part does not break forward. This was evidently not Burlington's inspiration; instead he followed Palladio's rationalised versions, the three Venetian church fronts.[34] His Orangery resembled S. Giorgio Maggiore, save in omitting the high pedestals; in this it resembled the Redentore. The conflation of the two churches was not without English precedent. Wren's chapel front at Emmanuel College, Cambridge, was a similar conflation, though omitting the half-pedimented wings.[35] Wren used these instead for the south front of the Sheldonian Theatre, Oxford.[36] Burlington was not, however, dependent on these for an immediate source, for he owned Palladio's alternative design for S. Giorgio,[37] omitting the pedestals, and thus offering him a conflation of S. Giorgio and the Redentore off the shelf (Fig. 4c).

The third instance of Burlington's use of a feature of Palladian origin is more hypothetical. It occurs on the Pagan Temple. The Pagan Temple, first

31 London, British Architectural Library, Drawings Collection, Burlington-Devonshire Collection, xvii, 15.
32 J. Badeslade and J. Rocque, *Vitruvius Britannicus* (sic), *Volume the Fourth* (London, 1739), plates 82–83, 'Plan du jardin et vue des maisons de Chiswick, 1736'.
33 Andrea Palladio, *I quattro libri del'architettura* (Venice, 1570), iv, plate 2.
34 Lionello Puppi, *Andrea Palladio* (London, 1975), pp. 178–79 (S. Giorgio Maggiore), 246 (Redentore) and 470–1 (S. Francesco della

Vigna).
35 Kerry Downes, *The Architecture of Wren* (London, 1982), plate 12; Robert Willis and John Willis Clark, *The Architectural History of the University of Cambridge*, ii (Cambridge, 1886), pp. 700–11.
36 Downes, *The Architecture of Wren*, plate 9; H.M. Colvin, *The Sheldonian Theatre and the Divinity School* (2nd edn, Oxford, 1975), passim.
37 See note 28.

Fig. 5a Painting by Pieter Andreas Rysbrack of
the Pagan Temple at Chiswick (*Chatsworth*)

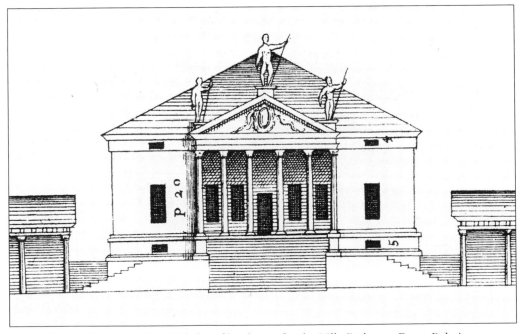

Fig. 5b Illustration by Andrea Palladio of his design for the Villa Badoer at Fratta Polesine

illustrated *c.* 1729-32 (Fig. 5a),[38] whose appearance is confirmed in illust-rations of 1733,[39] 1736[40] and 1753,[41] was demolished by 1784.[42] It is usually omitted from discussions of Burlington, in the unsubstantiated belief that it was designed by Gibbs.[43] Gibbs is alleged to have designed something at Chiswick,[44] and the Pagan Temple is alleged to have the character of his architecture.[45] Hence, and hence only, the connection. But it would be unwise to exclude the Pagan Temple from discussion of Burlington's style since there is equal stylistic evidence of his authorship. The Gibbs character has not been explained and is doubtless assumed to be self-evident; but it may rest on what appears, although only from the shadow it casts, to be a portico *in antis*, or partially *in antis*. Gibbs has some claim to be the portico *in antis* man of the hour, having designed at least five, probably six.[46] Burlington, however, designed seven porticos *in antis*, although they remained on paper only.[47] He too was evidently interested in this feature. The bay either side of the portico had festoons at capital level, evidently also a feature of interest to Burlington since he used it in three other designs besides the Orangery.[48] The portico *in antis* is often regarded as a character-istically Baroque feature. It was used by Archer twice,[49] by Hawksmoor,[50] Thornhill[51] and Galilei[52] once each. But the inspiration of these Baroque

38 John Harris, *The Artist and the Country House* (London, 1979), p. 158 and fig. 187f; R.T. Spence, 'Chiswick House and its Gardens, 1726-32', *Burlington Magazine*, 135, August 1993, p. 531, provides evidence for the date of these illustrations.
39 Jacques Carré, 'Through French Eyes: Rigaud's Drawings of Chiswick', *Journal of Garden History*, 2, no. 2, p. 133 and fig. 5.
40 Badeslade and Rocque, *Vitruvius Britannicus*, iv.
41 Michael Symes, 'John Donowell's Views of Chiswick and Other Gardens', *Journal of Garden History*, 7, no. 1, p. 48, fig 5.
42 Chatsworth, Devonshire Collection, 35, box 114, plan of Chiswick Garden by Samuel Lapidge, October 1784, which shows an open space on the site of the Pagan Temple.
43 John Harris, *The Palladians* (London, 1981), pp. 18, 75.
44 Terry Friedman, *James Gibbs* (London, 1984), p. 315b.
45 Cinzia Maria Sicca, 'Lord Burlington at Chis-wick: Architecture and Landscape', *Garden History*, 10, no. 1 (Spring, 1982), p. 38.
46 At Sudbrook in 1715, James Gibbs, *A Book of Architecture* (London, 1728), plate 40; Witham, *c.* 1716, Colen Campbell, *Vitruvius Britannicus*, ii (1717), plates 91-92; probably Adderbury in 1717, Mary Cosh, 'Two Dukes and their Houses', *Country Life*, 152, 13 July 1972, p. 80;

Down Hall in 1720, Gibbs, *A Book of Architec-ture*, plate 55; Whitton, *c.* 1725, ibid., plates 59-60; and a house at Greenwich, before 1728, ibid., plates 46-47.
47 Chatsworth, Devonshire Collection, Lord Burlington's architectural drawings, Boy 32-34, Boy 42-43, Boy 21.
48 In York Assembly Rooms, Rudolf Witt-kower, 'Lord Burlington's Work at York', in idem, *Palladio and English Palladianism* (1974), fig, 168; and in two designs at Chatsworth, Devonshire Collection, Lord Burlington's architectural drawings, namely Boy 28, 2 and Boy 32.
49 At Heythrop in 1699, John Woolfe and James Gandon, *Vitruvius Britannicus*, v (London, 1771), plates 82 and 85; and at St John's Church, Smith Square, London, in 1713, W.A. Eden, 'Rebuilding a Masterpiece', *Country Life*, 131, 1 March 1962, p. 445, figs 1 and 2.
50 At St Alfege's Church, Greenwich, in 1712, Kerry Downes, *Hawksmoor* (London, 1959), pp. 167-70 and plates 53a.
51 At Luxborough House, Chigwell, *c.* 1716-20, Victoria History of the Counties of England, *Essex*, iv (London 1956), p. 30.
52 At Kimbolton, *c.* 1719, Arthur Oswald, 'Kim-bolton Castle, Huntingdonshire – IV', *Country Life*, 144, 26 December 1968, pp. 1696-98.

examples came from Palladio, who published eleven: two single-storeyed like the Pagan Temple (Fig. 5b) (at the villas Badoer at Fratta Polesine and Emo at Fanzolo); four giant (at the villas Ragona at Le Ghizzole, Thiene at Cicogna) and Thiene at Quinto, and the proposed Villa Mocenigo on the Brenta);[53] and five two-storeyed (at the villas Mocenigo at Marocco, Valmarana at Lisiera,[54] Sarego at La Miga, Torre at Della Bra, and the unfinished Villa Garzadore. If the Pagan Temple was designed by Burlington, his possession of twelve copies of Palladio's books make it probable that Palladio inspired his use of this feature.[55]

Features Used by Palladio, in Common with Other Sixteenth-Century Architects

There are four of these at Chiswick. It is not possible to tell whether Burlington was first acquainted with the Palladian instance of each of them, or with the other instances. But in all four cases the particular detailing was taken from buildings or drawings which are not by Palladio.

The most distinctive feature of Chiswick House is its plan (Fig. 6a), tirelessly compared with that of Palladio's Villa Almerico (the Rotonda) at Vicenza.[56] Palladio designed (and published) two similarly planned villas, the Villa Almerico and the Villa Trissino at Meledo.[57] But he did not invent the plan, whose prototype was Mantegna's house in Mantua,[58] its central court transformed into a double height room. Even the transformation was not made by Palladio, but by Falconetto, for the Odeo Cornaro in Padua of c. 1530.[59] Serlio published the Odeo Cornaro in his Book VII,[60] and four plans of his own based on it.[61] Scamozzi, however, designed more versions of it than anyone. He published four, the Rocca Pisani at Lonigo,[62] the Villas Bardellini at Asolo[63] and Molin at Padua,[64] and an anonymous villa on the Brenta.[65] In common with Chiswick, Palladio's two villas have a central room equivalent to two or three storeys in height, stairs formed in

53 Puppi, *Andrea Palladio*, plate 31.
54 Ibid., plate 38.
55 Philip Ayres, 'Burlington's Library at Chiswick', *Studies in Bibliogrpahy*, 45 (1992), pp. 117-18.
56 Puppi, *Andrea Palladio*, pp. 380-83 and plates 533-35; Palladio, *I quattro libri*, ii, plate 13.
57 Ibid., pp. 384-88 and plate 541; Palladio, *I quattro libri*, ii, p. 43.
58 E. Rosenthal, 'The House of Andrea Mantegna in Mantua', *Gazette des beaux arts*, 60

(1962), pp. 327-48.
59 Robert Tavernor, *Palladio and Palladianism* (London, 1991), p. 80 and plate 57.
60 Sebastiano Serlio, *Tutte l'opere d'architettura et prospettiva* (Venice, 1619), vii, p. 219.
61 Ibid., pp. 5, 17, 27 and 31.
62 Vincenzo Scamozzi, *L'idea dell'architettura universale*, i (Venice, 1615), p. 273.
63 Ibid., p. 279.
64 Ibid., p. 275.
65 Ibid., p. 277.

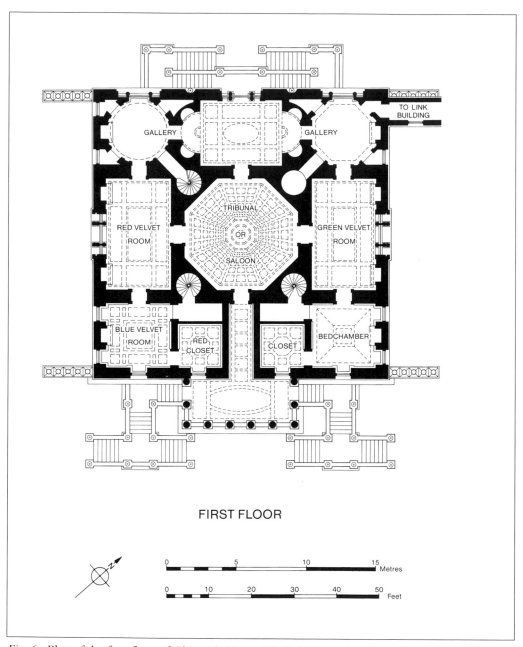

TO LINK
BUILDING

GALLERY

GALLERY

RED VELVET
ROOM

TRIBUNAL
OR
SALOON

GREEN VELVET
ROOM

BLUE VELVET
ROOM

RED
CLOSET

CLOSET

BEDCHAMBER

FIRST FLOOR

| 0 | 5 | 10 | 15 |
Metres

| 0 | 10 | 20 | 30 | 40 | 50 |
Feet

Fig. 6a Plan of the first floor of Chiswick House (*English Heritage*)

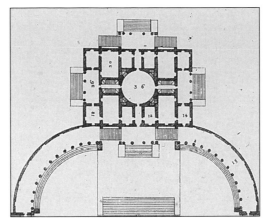

Fig. 6b Illustration by Andrea Palladio of his design for
the Villa Trissino at Meledo

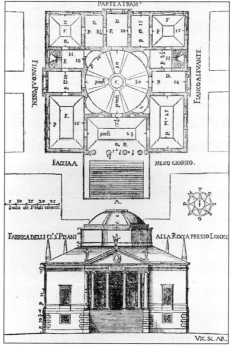

Fig. 6c Illustration by Vincenzo Scamozzi of his design for
the Rocca (or Villa) Pisani at Lonego

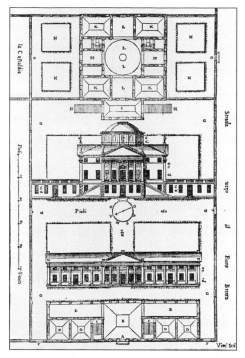

Fig. 6d Illustration by Vincenzo Scamozzi for his design
for a villa on the River Brenta

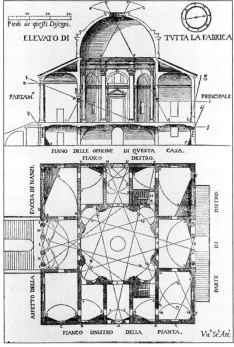

Fig. 6e Illustration by Vincenzo Scamozzi of his design for the Villa
Bardellini at Asolo

the spandrels at the corners of the central room, passages leading to it directly from the entrance, and projecting porticoes. The design for the Villa Trissino (which was never built) has, in addition, a drum, and a shallow dome of segmental profile (Fig. 6b); whereas the Villa Almerico has no drum and a steep hemispherical dome. Of these two the Villa Trissino, which Burlington only knew from Palladio's book, is closer to Chiswick than the Villa Almerica, which he visited.[66]

Three of the Scamozzi villas, however, are closer to Chiswick than either of Palladio's. (The Villa Molin has a square-planned central room with a pyramidal roof; at Chiswick the central room is an octagon with a domed roof, so the resemblance of this example is less close.) All three have drums and shallow domes with stepped profiles. The drums of the Rocca Pisani (Fig. 6c) and the villa on the Brenta (Fig. 6d) are octagonal, not circular, in plan. These two also have one portico each, instead of four, as at both Palladio's and Scamozzi's other examples. The Villa Bardellini, in common with the two villas by Palladio, has passages from the entrance to the central room, and its drum is pierced by Diocletian windows (Fig. 6e). The Rocca Pisani has chimneys in the form of obelisks. These features were followed at Chiswick. The Chiswick plan is evidently a conflation of these five Italian prototypes. Which of them first acquainted Burlington with the plan type depends on which book he saw first, or whether he saw either book before he visited the Villa Almerico, a fact which is not known. Without doubt, however, the detailed working out of the plan was based more closely on Scamozzi's three models than on Palladio's two. It was made possible by Burlington's possession of Scamozzi's *Idea dell'archittettura universale*, in which these designs were published.[67]

There are three internal stairs at Chiswick, formed in three of the triangular spaces left behind the ordinal walls of the central octagon (Fig. 6a). (The fourth is occupied by a void in the upper part and a straight flight from the ground floor to the cellar.) This is also the arrangement in the published plan of Palladio's Villa Almerico, which may have first acquainted Burlington with this arrangement. But it was not unique to Palladio. Burlington apparently used another sixteenth-century Italian example of it to help him with the detailed planning. At the Villa Almerico Palladio designed stairs on a triangular plan to fill the triangular spaces which result from the inscription of an octagon within a square. Burlington

66 Chatsworth, Devonshire Collection, Andrea
    Palladio, *I quattro libri dell'architettura* (1601 edi-
    tion), annotations by Lord Burlington oppo-
    site page 18.

67 Ayres, 'Burlington's Library at Chiswick', p.
    118.

possessed architect's drawings of the Villa Giulia (Fig. 7), outside Rome, which illustrate newel stairs in comparable positions.[68] Burlington, whose own drawings indicate an addiction to newels, possessed at least nine other drawings by architects other than Palladio, which include newels.[69] It is the newel, rather than the triangular, form which was followed at Chiswick. The architects of the Villa Giulia were successively Vignola, Vasari and Ammanati.[70] The newels occur in the part probably designed by Vignola. Even if this is not correct, it is certain that Burlington believed it to be, for the relevant drawing is captioned 'Vignola' in his hand.

One of the most conspicuous features at Chiswick is the wall whose two short lengths extend the front of the house on its entrance side. They are made noticeable by their position, their singularity (for they abut no other building and shield no other feature), and their unusual ornament of curved crenellation topped by ball finials (Fig. 8a). Burlington repeated the crenellation type on the short lengths of wall which flank the Inigo Jones gateway, which he bought from Sir Hans Sloane in 1738.[71] He placed more stone balls (without the curved crenellation) on the coping of the arched gateway at the south-west corner of the garden.[72] Similarly ornamented walls (with more evident purpose) flank the west front of Palladio's church of S. Giorgio Maggiore, in Venice, which Burlington visited.[73] Although Burlington owned one of Palladio's drawings for S. Giorgio, it did not include this feature. So, if S. Giorgio was his inspiration, he would have been obliged to memorise its details for up to eight years. Furthermore, it is unlikely that Burlington was so indifferent to the meaning of ornament that he was content to transfer a feature from surroundings which were sacred to surroundings which were profane. Alternatively he may have been inspired by seeing this ornament on a secular building, for it was not unique to S. Giorgio, nor even to Palladio. It may have originated as a variant of the

68 London, British Architectural Library, Drawings Collection, Burlington-Devonshire Collection, viii, 1-4.

69 Chatsworth, Devonshire Collection, Lord Burlington's architectural drawings, Boy 2, 3 and 4 (Chichester Council House), Boy 13, 1-3 (Richmond House Whitehall), Boy 18.8 and 18.14 (Tottenham Park), Boy 19 (Waldershare Belvedere), Boy 21.2 (York Assembly Rooms), Boy 28, Boy 35, Boy 41, Boy 43 and Boy Coll 11.4 (Raby Castle); London, Royal Institute of British Architects, Drawings Collection, Burlington-Devonshire Collection, vi, 3 (Pulteney House), and vi, 5 (General Wade's House). Chatsworth, Devonshire Collection, album 36, fos 3, 5r, 8, 10, 11a, 11c, 12b, 12c, 13.

70 Frances Land Moore, 'A Contribution to the Study of the Villa Giulia', *Römisches Jahrbuch für Kunstgeschichte*, 12 (1969), pp. 171-93.

71 Richard Hewlings, 'The Inigo Jones Gate', *Chiswick House Friends' Newsletter*, Summer 1990, p. 2.

72 John Dixon Hunt, *William Kent: Landscape Garden Designer*, (London, 1987), pp. 125, fig. 27, and 126, fig. 30; Chatsworth, Devonshire Collection, album 26a, fos 17 and 20.

73 Chatsworth, Devonshire Collection, Library, Andrea Palladio, *I quattro libri dell'architettura* (1601 edition), annotations by Lord Burlington, page following title-page.

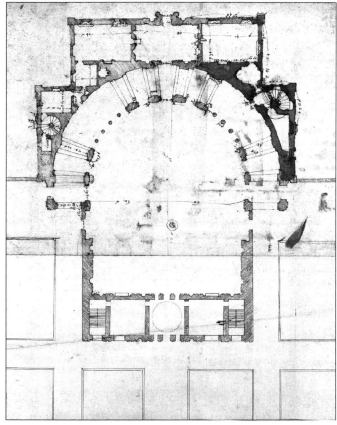

Fig. 7 Drawing of the plan of the Villa Giulia, Rome (*RIBA*)

Fig. 8a Wall flanking the south elevation of Chiswick House (*English Heritage*)

Fig. 8b Drawing by Inigo Jones for a proposed gateway at Oatlands Palace (*RIBA*)

Guelph and Ghibelline crenellations of late mediaeval Italy. That on Michelangelo's Porta Pia, Rome, begun in 1561,[74] is one version; like all travellers from the north, Burlington could not have avoided seeing this unless he entered Rome in the dark. Another version, which his 1714–15 account book positively indicates that he saw, is at the Villa Mondragone, Frascati.[75] Here the garden walls are not actually crenellated, but are topped by regularly spaced plinths, each crowned by a stone ball on a curved neck, similar to those at Chiswick.[76] The particular Chiswick crenellation type is peculiar to the Veneto. The earliest example of it may be Falconetto's, at the Villa dei Vescovi, Luvigliano, of 1529-35.[77] It was used again by Sansovino at the Villa Garzoni, Pontecasale, in about 1550.[78] Both these are without the finials. The garden wall of the Palazzo Benci in Venice, built between 1581 and 1621, also has the crenellation type, but with urns instead of balls.[79] Perhaps the Porta Pia or the Villa Mondragone suggested this addition. Palladio used it in a rustic form at the Villa Badoer, Fratta Polesine, in 1568-70.[80]

But Burlington saw none of these Venetan examples. His models were English. Probably the only English example of this ornament to be built before Chiswick was at John Webb's Gunnersbury House, dating from *c*.1658 and less than two miles away.[81] Even this was not the precise model. Webb's finials were widely spaced and the concave profiles of the wall-head between them were segmental; at Chiswick they are closely spaced and the arcs between them are semi-circular. The sources of the Chiswick profile would have been drawings. He may have seen drawings by Webb for walls with ball crenellation, for there were two in Dr Clarke's collection.[82] It is possible that he saw Talman's proposal drawing of a house for the Duke of Newcastle, done in 1703, which includes this detail.[83] It is certain that he saw drawings of the detail alone by Inigo Jones, since he owned four.[84] Jones' drawings are not unlike the S. Giorgio version, but differ in replacing

74 James S. Ackerman, *The Architecture of Michelangelo* (Harmondsworth, 1970), p. 244, fig. 123.

75 Chatsworth, Devonshire Collection, Lord Burlington's Grand Tour Account Book.

76 David R. Coffin, *Gardens and Gardening in Papal Rome* (Princeton, 1991), p. 50.

77 Giuseppe Mazzotti, *Palladian and Other Venetian Villas* (London, 1958), plate 108.

78 Ibid., plates 115-16.

79 Elena Bassi, *Palazzi di Venezia* (n.d., *c*. 1980), p. 311, fig. 410.

80 Puppi, *Andrea Palladio*, pp. 308-10 and plates 124 and 127.

81 London, Guildhall Library, extra-illustrated edition of Daniel Lysons, *The Environs of London* (London, 1813), ii, pt 2, water-colour drawing interleaved opposite p. 226.

82 John Harris and A.A. Tait, *Catalogue of the Drawings by Inigo Jones, John Webb and Isaac de Caus at Worcester College, Oxford* (Oxford, 1979), plate 118.

83 John Harris, *William Talman* (London, 1982), figs 62, 64-66.

84 John Harris and Gordon Higgott, *Inigo Jones: Complete Architectural Drawings* (New York, 1989), pp. 81, 133, 139, 141.

the latter's mellifluous interchange between crenellation and finial, with abrupt angles between curves and straight lines (Fig. 8b). It is possible that S. Giorgio Maggiore first gave Burlington the idea for this feature in its fully developed form; but it is certain that he was indebted to Jones for its detailed realisation.

North of the Orange Tree Garden, but on the same side of the River, there was an oblong piece of water with curved ends; on its east bank stood a pavilion (Fig. 9a). Water and pavilion were both in existence by *c.* 1729-32,[85] and were removed some time after 1784,[86] but before 1818.[87] The painting of *c.* 1729-32 renders the pavilion in a pale pink colour, presumably that of brick. It was five bays wide, had two storeys, of which the upper one was little more than half the height of the lower one, and was heated by stacks at each end. It was, in other words, habitable but reticent, like a service building, and consequently its only ornamental feature was in the Tuscan order. This feature was a projecting tetrastyle portico, painted white and therefore probably wooden, equivalent to one storey in height: the apex of its pediment lay just below the eaves of the pavilion. The pavilion's roof was of pyramidal shape.

Pyramidal roofs were a speciality of Palladio's. His predecessors in this area were few. Guiliano da Maiano's Poggio Reale at Naples, as represented by Serlio, had pyramidal roofs:[88] it had stood, however, since 1487-88.[89] Closer to Vicenza, Palladio knew Falconetto's Villa dei Vescovi at Luvigliano of *c.* 1535,[90] with a single pyramidal roof. Palladio's own pyramidal roofs covered the Villas Pojana,[91] Emo at Fanzolo,[92] Cornara at Piombino Dese,[93] Pisani at Montagnana,[94] Zeno at Cesalto,[95] Badoer at Fratta Polesine,[96] Pisani at Bagnolo,[97] in Vicenza the unbuilt Palazzi Capra[98] and

85 Richard Hewlings, *Chiswick House and Gardens* (London, 1991), pp. 42 and 44; Harris, *Artist and Country House*, p. 158 and fig. 187c; Badeslade and Rocque, *Vitruvius Britannicus*; for the dating, see Spence 'Chiswick House and Gardens', p. 531.

86 Chatsworth, Devonshire Collection, 35, box 114, Samuel Lapidge, plan of Chiswick Garden (1784).

87 London, Guildhall Library, map case 305, 'A Plan of the Mansion and Estate at Chiswick in the County of Middlesex Belonging to The Most Noble William Spencer Duke of Devonshire Surveyed by Peter Potter, Kentish Town, 1818'.

88 Sebastian Serly [Serlio], *The First Book of Architecture* (English edn, London, 1611), iii, p. 72.

89 George L. Hersey, *Alfonso II and the Artistic Renewal of Naples, 1485-1495* (New Haven, 1969), pp. 58-63.

90 Ludwig H. Heydenreich and Wolfgang Lotz, *Architecture in Italy, 1400 to 1600* (Harmondsworth, 1974), plate 220; G. Schweikhart, 'Studien zum Werk des Giovanni Maria Falconetto', *Bolletino del Museo Civico di Padova*, 57 (1968), pp. 35ff.

91 Puppi, *Andrea Palladio*, pp. 273-76 and plates 84-86.

92 Ibid., pp. 352-53 and plates 171 and 172.

93 Ibid., pp. 292-94 and plate 107.

94 Ibid., pp. 288-89 and plates 96-98.

95 Ibid., pp. 373-74, and plates 520 and 521.

96 Ibid., pp. 308-10, and plates 124 and 125.

97 Ibid., pp. 254-56 and plate 36.

98 Ibid., pp. 349-51 and plate 477.

Barbarano,[99] and in Udine the Palazzo Antonini.[100] All ten were published in his book,[101] plus four 'Inventions' of his own in Book 2, Chapter 17.[102]

Difficult as it may have been to overlook such determined propagation, Jones responded with only two drawings including this feature, of which probably one was realised. Both belonged to Burlington: one is a preliminary design for the Queen's House at Greenwich,[103] and the other is for a service building at Hassenbrook Hall, Essex.[104] Designs for the Queen's House, built for the queen to whom his title was due,[105] would have guaranteed his interest. The service building at Hassenbrook was comparable in character to the pavilion at Chiswick (Fig. 9b).

Of the ten Palladian pyramidal roofs, four also have one-storey tetrastyle porticos, the Villas Emo, Badoer and Pisani, and the Palazzo Capra. But only one of these has a portico which, like that of the pavilion at Chiswick, is entirely below the eaves of its host building; that is the Villa Pisani at Bagnolo (Fig. 9c), to which the Chiswick pavilion uncontestably has a distant general resemblance.

Both the Jones drawings have one-storey tetrastyle porticos. Burlington regarded that of the Queen's House proposal as sufficiently important to be redrawn for the engraver (Fig. 48b).[106] But the Hassenbrook Hall drawing, showing a Tuscan portico which projects (the Queen's House portico is Corinthian and applied), and a first storey less than half the height of the ground floor, is of all these precedents the closest to the Chiswick pavilion. Although Palladio's influence on this pavilion is undeniably apparent, it is clearly eclipsed by that of Inigo Jones.

Features of Sixteenth Century Origin Not Used by Palladio

Palladio's partial inspiration of the foregoing features cannot be entirely discounted, although the inspiration of Scamozzi, Vignola, Webb and Jones is clearer. They are nonetheless, the only features for which any Palladian inspiration can be shown. A further ten features at Chiswick were apparently inspired by other sixteenth-century (or early sixteenth-century) models.

99 Ibid., pp. 393-95 and plate 555.
100 Ibid., pp. 306-8 and plate 114.
101 Palladio, *I quattro libri*, ii, plates 1, 14, 15, 30, 31, 32, 35, 36, 38 and 41.
102 Ibid., ii, plates 52-55.
103 Harris and Higgott, *Inigo Jones: Complete Architectural Drawings*, pp. 68-69. Jones's drawing, in its present state, does not show the roof clearly. Flitcroft's copy, however, shows a pyramidal roof, indicating that Burlington believed this roof to have been intended.
104 Ibid., pp. 264-65.
105 See below.
106 London, Royal Institute of British Architects, Drawings Collection, Burlington-Devonshire Collection, vi, 15.

Fig. 9a Painting by Pieter Andreas Rysbrack of a pavilion by the water at Chiswick (*English Heritage*)

Fig. 9b Drawing by Inigo Jones for a proposed office building at Hassenbrook Hall, Essex (*RIBA*)

Fig. 9c Illustration by Andrea Palladio of his design for the Villa Pisani at Bagnolo

Of these the most conspicuous is the perron (Figs 2, 6a). It descends in two flights, one from each side of the portico, to a half-landing. Many perrons, Ancient, Renaissance or Baroque, are similarly designed, but in nearly all of them the lower flights either continue from the half-landing in the same direction as the upper flights, or return towards the centre. At Chiswick an intermediate flight descends at right angles to the upper ones to a second half-landing, from which two pairs of lower flights descent, one of each pair falling towards the periphery of the building, the other towards the centre. The precedents for this sumptuous arrangement are scarce. The single English precedent, however, was quite accessible (Fig. 10a). It occurs in the second volume of Colen Campbell's *Vitruvius Britannicus*, published in 1717, and is an elevation of High Meadow, a country house in the Forest of Dean, which in that year became the property of Thomas Gage. Campbell's third volume, published in 1725, illustrated the other elevation of High Meadow, with a different, but almost as splendid, perron. The second perron had been built only recently, as a view taken in the ownership of Gage's father-in-law, Benedict Hall (and thus before 1717) shows yet another perron. The recentness of the second perron, and the contrast between both the perrons illustrated by Campbell and the more provincial late seventeenth-century architecture of the body of the house, suggest that both perrons were added not long before Campbell illustrated them; or they could just have been proposals. The fact that Campbell illustrated this old-fashioned house twice suggests that he was a little partisan: could it be that he designed the perrons?[107]

If, so, Campbell's inspiration may have been Italian. In the mid seventeenth century, for instance, Orazio Spada designed a similar perron for a house intended probably at Castel Viscardo, near Orvieto.[108] Neither Campbell nor Burlington are likely to have known this. But they may have been aware of similar perrons in villas of the dukes of Savoy (from 1713 to 1720 king of Sicily, and from 1720 kings of Sardinia) within a few miles of Turin. One was at the castle of Carignano (Fig. 10b), built by Carlo Morello and Carlo di Castellamonte for Duke Carlo Emanuele in 1625-32;[109] another was on the garden front of Viboccone (Fig. 10c), built for Duke

107 Colen Campbell, *Vitruvius Britannicus*, ii (London, 1717), plate 40; Nicholas Kingsley, *The Country Houses of Gloucestershire*, ii, *1660-1830* (Chichester, 1992), p. 161; Campbell, *Vitruvius Britannicus*, iii (London, 1725), plate 62; Gloucester, Gloucestershire Record Office, GPS 227/2.
108 David Butler 'Orazio Spada and his Archi-

tects, *Journal of the Society of Architectural Historians*, 53 (1994), p. 64, figs 1 and 2.
109 Costanza Roggero Bardelli, Maria Grazia Vinardi and Vittorio Defabiani, *Ville Sabaude*, ii (Milan, 1990), pp. 58-59; Gian Tommaso Borgonio, *Theatrum Sabaudiae* (1682), plate 60.

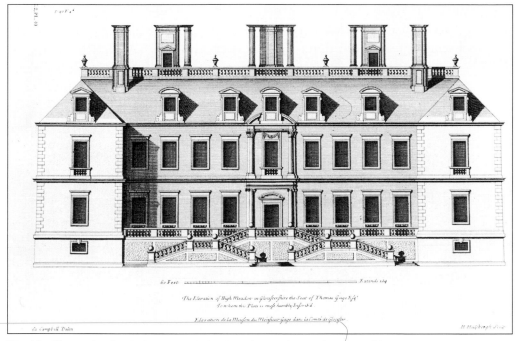

Fig. 10a Illustration by Colen Campbell of High Meadow, Gloucestershire

Fig. 10b Illustration by Gian Tommaso Borgonio of the castle of Carignano, near Turin

Fig. 10c Illustration by Gian Tommaso Borgonio of Viboccone, near Turin

Emanuele Filiberto by an unidentified architect between 1565 and 1572.[110] A design for a third, for the castle of Racconigi, presumably also of mid sixteenth-century date, remained on paper alone until its realisation in 1848.[111] One of them, or all three of them, inspired Juvarra (while in the service of King Vittorio Amedeo of Sardinia) to draw an architectural *capriccio* which included a rotunda with a perron of this type, in a sketch-book which he presented to Burlington.[112] But his drawing is dated 1729 and the sketchbook was presented to Burlington in 1730. The Chiswick perron was illustrated in Kent's *Designs of Inigo Jones* in 1727.[113] As Juvarra evidently knew about the perron type, presumably from his service in Turin, he may have introduced Burlington to it; but if so, it must have been at an earlier date than that of his *capriccio*, perhaps in 1720, when Juvarra visited London.[114] Burlington could have seen Carignano, which lies seven miles south of Turin, in 1719; nothing is known of that visit to the city save that he wrote a letter from there.[115] He could even have seen the drawing for Racconigi. But he could not have seen Viboccone, as it was destroyed in 1706 during the siege of Turin. However, he did not have to, as he owned a copy of Borgonio's *Theatrum Subaudiae*, which illustrates both Carignano and Viboccone.[116] Doubtless this was his means of introduction to the perron type. Unless the designer of the High Meadow perron had an independent (or different) introduction, it may have been his means of introduction also.

One of the queerest features of Chiswick is the position of the fireplaces on its outside walls (Fig. 3a). By the 1720s English houses of high status invariably had fireplaces on inside walls, freeing the outside walls for windows, and allowing an enfilade to be formed opposite the fireplaces, just within the perimeter of the house. Medieval English houses, on the other hand, and vernacular houses until well into the eighteenth century, had external chimneys, usually projecting from the wall plane to allow them to be constructed in a different, heat-resistant material.[117] The commonest

110 Borgonio, *Theatrum Sabaudiae*, plate 36; Nino Carboneri, *Ascanio Vitozzi* (Rome, 1966), p. 165.

111 Noemi Gabrielli, *Racconigi* (Turin, 1972), p. 26. Rudolf Wittkower, 'A Sketchbook of Filippo Juvarra at Chatsworth', in *Studies in the Italian Baroque* (London, 1975), p. 210, proposes Racconigi as the source of the perron, in the belief that 'Burlington would have seen the staircase' at Racconigi in 1714 or 1715. Wittkower evidently cannot have known that the perron at Racconigi was not built until 1848.

112 Wittkower, *Studies in Italian Baroque*, p. 210, and fig. 258; Chatsworth, Devonshire Collec-

tion, album 30, fol. 14.

113 William Kent, *The Designs of Inigo Jones* (London, 1727), p. 71.

114 Wittkower, *Studies in Italian Baroque*, p. 206.

115 Narford, Fountaine MSS, Letters, 6 November 1719.

116 Carboneri, *Ascanio Vitozzi*, p. 169 n. 20; Chatsworth, Devonshire Collection, Library, MS 'Catalogue of the Earl of Burlington's Library, at his Lordships Seat at Cheswick; January 1741/2', p. 4; Borgonio, *Theatrum Sabaudiae*, plates 36 and 60.

117 Maurice Barley, *Houses and History* (London, 1986), p. 69, fig. 32 illustrates one example.

English gentry house type of the sixteenth and seventeenth centuries had a hall and cross wings plan. Chimneys in the cross wings were usually sited on the external end walls.[118] As the hall and cross wings plan was absorbed by its successor type, the compact plan, it sometimes passed this arrangement on, although to achieve visual regularity the chimney breasts rarely projected.[119] This plan type with external chimneys in the side walls only, as at Chiswick, reached its highest social level at Coleshill.[120] Like Woolfe and Gandon, Burlington apparently believed Coleshill to be by Jones,[121] and thus a suitable model. But in house-keeping matters it was an old-fashioned one. Following Jones' Queen's House, almost all great English houses of the second half of the seventeenth century had internal chimneys. They reduced heat loss and, in centrally-planned houses, they had the added convenience of allowing all the flues to be clustered together. At Chiswick all these conveniences are sacrificed for an effect apparently of replicating a Jones cynosure.

However, Burlington appears to have made his first visit to Coleshill only in May 1730,[122] after Chiswick House was complete.[123] Nor were any illustrations of Coleshill published until 1771, so Burlington's inspiration may instead have been the domestic buildings of Venetia and the Po valley. There it is a vernacular and urban feature, although used without any obvious rationale in signorial houses also.[124] One of the consequences of its use is that Venetan houses have irregularly spaced windows. Burlington would have been easily reminded of this by consulting Scamozzi's book, where chimneys on the external walls of four houses are illustrated (Fig. 11a, b),[125] but not by consulting Palladio's, where they are not illustrated at all.

Still less forgettable are the chimney stacks, shaped like obelisks (Figs 3a, 12a). They are based upon a type peculiar to the Veneto and Lombardy, although used by many architects within that region. These included

118 Ibid., pp. 123, fig. 72, and 224, fig. 146, illustrate two examples.

119 Ibid., pp. 211, fig. 135, and 223, fig. 145 illustrate two examples.

120 H. Avray Tipping, 'Coleshill House, Berkshire', *Country Life*, 46, 26 July, 2 Aug 1919, pp. 108–16, 138–46.

121 J. Woolfe and J. Gandon, *Vitruvius Britannicus*, v, plates 86–87.

122 Chatsworth, Devonshire Collection, letter 162.3, Lord Bruce to Lord Burlington, 23 May 1730, giving him directions to reach Coleshill.

123 Hewlings, *Chiswick*, pp. 36–37; Spence, 'Chiswick House and Gardens, 1726-1732', pp. 525–31.

124 Mazzotti, *Palladian and Other Venetian Villas*, plates 5, 13, 84, 86, 115, 119, 129, 135, 136, 174, 180, 211, 218, 219, 220, 221, 227, 232, 244, 252, 256, 260, 261, 262, 292, 307, 311, 317, 320, 322, 323, 325, 326, 330, 335, 344, 345, 375, 376, 388, 390 and later examples; Richard J. Goy, *Venetian Vernacular Architecture* (Cambridge, 1989), plates 28–30, 80–81, 110 and 156.

125 Scamozzi, *L'idea dell'architettura universale*, i, pp. 273, 275, 279, 281, 287, 289, 291 and 293.

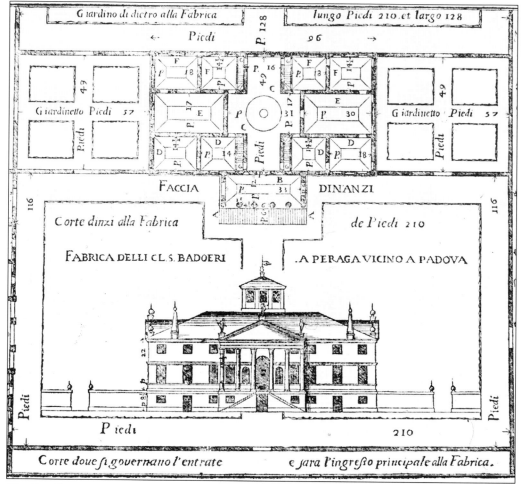

Fig. 11a Illustration by Vincenzo Scamozzi of his design for the Villa Badoer at Peraga

Fig. 11b Illustration by Vincenzo Scamozzi of his design for the Villa Contarini at Loregia

Fig. 12a Chimney stacks at Chiswick House
(*English Heritage*)

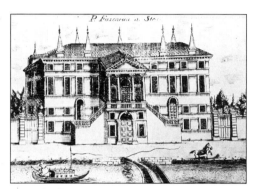

Fig. 12b Illustration by Coronelli of the Villa
Foscarini at Stra

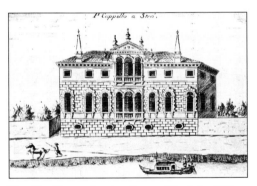

Fig. 12c Illustration by Coronelli of the Villa
Cappello at Stra

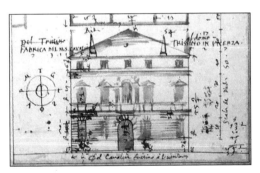

Fig. 12d Drawing by Vincenzo Scamozzi for
a proposed palace for Giovanni Francesco
Trissino in Vicenza (*Chatsworth*)

Palladio, who built obelisk chimneys at the Villa Cornaro at Piombino Dese.[126] Burlington did not visit this villa and, although it is illustrated in Palladio's book, the illustration omits the chimneys.[127] The vernacular Venetan chimney type emits smoke near its base, the superstructure acting as a baffle:[128] the obelisk was one of a number of baffle designs experimented with in the sixteenth century, probably resulting from a fusion of baffles with the obelisk finials with which Burlington would have been more familiar from, for example, Guidetto Guidetti's Sta Maria dell'Orto,[129] Giacomo del Duca's S. Maria in Trivio,[130] or Michelangelo's Porta Pia, all in Rome,[131] or Galeazzo Alessi's Sta Maria presso S. Celso in Milan[132] (where he was in 1715,[133] possibly revisiting in 1719), and from an illustration in Serlio's book.[134] The obelisk finial had reached Venice by 1537, when Sansovino used it on the Library of St Mark,[135] and it was used as a chimney at least by 1560 when it occurs as such on Giangiacomo dei Grigi's Palazzo Coccina Tiepolo.[136] By 1719 there were at least six patrician houses in Venice,[137] and at least fourteen on the *terraferma* with obelisk chimneys, mostly seventeenth century.[138] Burlington would have passed the Villas Foscarini (Fig. 12b), Capello (Fig. 12c) and Soranza at Stra, all visible from the Brenta (down which he travelled). The Venetian examples are all on the Grand Canal. Even if his concentration had wandered from these riparian sights, he could have refreshed his memory back home by opening Scamozzi's book at the illustrations of the Rocca Pisani at Lonigo,

126 Puppi, *Andrea Palladio*, pp. 292-94 and plates 102 and 104.
127 Palladio, *I quattro libri*, ii, plate 36.
128 Mazzotti, *Palladian and Other Venetian Villas*, plates 5, 13, 227, 232, 260, 261, 292, 307, 311, 344, 345, 375, 376.
129 Paolo Portoghesi, *Roma Barocca* (Rome, 1966), plates 317-21; F.R. Milone, 'La facciata di S. Maria dell'Orto', *Quaderni*, 22 (1976), p. 127; Anthony Blunt, *Guide to Baroque Rome* (London, 1982), p. 102, attributes the design of the façade to Vignola.
130 Sandro Benedetti, *Giacomo del Duca e l'architettura del Cinquecento* (1972), plates 123-24.
131 Ackerman, *The Architecture of Michelangelo*.
132 Heydenreich and Lotz, *Architecture in Italy*, plates 314-15.
133 Chatsworth, Devonshire Collection, Lord Burlington's Grand Tour Account Book.
134 Serlio, *Architecture*, iv, p. 55.
135 Deborah Howard, *Jacopo Sansovino: Architecture and Patronage in Renaissance Venice* (New Haven and London, 1975), plate 11.
136 Bassi, *Palazzi di Venezia*, pp. 140-45.
137 Palazzo Fontana, Palazzo Giustinian Lolin, Palazzo Caotorta Angaran, Palazzo Coccina Tiepolo, Palazzo Businello and Palazzo Belloni, all illustrated in a panorama of the Canal Grande by Antonio Quadri and Dionisio Moretti (engraver), 1828.
138 Villa Contarini at Este, Villa Ferretti Angeli at Dolo, Villa Soranza at Stra, Villa Giusti (now Griggio) at Vendre de Valpantena, Villa Marogna (now Romani) at Nogara, Villa Barbarigo Rezzonico at Noventa Vicentina, Villa Benzi at Caerano S. Marco, Villa Foscarini (now Negrelli) at Stra, Villa Cappello at Stra, Villa Trento (now Carli) at Costozza, Villa Mangilli at Marsura di Sotto, Villa Pellegrini at Salvaterra di Badia Polesine, Villa Cordellina (now Lombardi) at Montecchio Maggiore, Villa Deciani at Montegnacco de Cassacco and Villa Pasole Berton di Pedavena near Belluno, all illustrated in Mazzotti, *Palladian and Other Venetian Villas*, passim; and the Villa Repeta at Campiglia, illustrated in Puppi, *Andrea Palladio*, plates 418, 419 and 421.

the Villa Contarini at Loregia, and the Villa Badoer at Peraga.[139] He also knew that the illustrations in this book sometimes omitted these details, for he possessed Scamozzi's drawing for the plate illustrating the palace of the Cavaliere Giovanni Francesco Trissino in Vicenza.[140] The plate omits the chimneys, but Burlington's drawing includes them (Fig. 12d).

In 1732 (probably) Burlington decided to join his new house at Chiswick with the house which he had inherited, by a carefully and expensively styled passage, now known as the Link Building (Fig. 13a).[141] Its existence does not contribute to the theory that Burlington's architectural ideology was neo-Platonist, or neo-Pythagorean, based on symmetrically balanced figures such as circles or squares.[142] It does support the observation that Burlington composed buildings as visually distinguishable units.[143] He was doubtless encouraged to do so less by abstract theory than by princely precedent. The Great Palace in Constantinople, a labyrinth of rooms separated by courtyards,[144] had, among other link buildings, an important passage direct from the Chalke Gate to the south gallery of Hagia Sophia.[145] The *Regia* of Charlemagne at Aachen was linked to the palatine chapel by a *porticus*.[146] The palace of William II at Monreale was similarly linked to the *Capella Palatina*.[147] Henry VI linked the palace in the Upper Ward at Windsor to the donjon on the motte by a covered passage in 1439-40.[148] Henry VIII linked the two parts of his palace at Whitehall by the Holbein Gate, not a gate at all, but a bridge.[149] In Vienna the Hofburg was similarly linked in 1550, both to the Augustinierkirche and to the palace of the Archprince.[150] In Moscow the Kremlin was composed of separate units linked by passages, not unlike its Byzantine model.[151] Chiswick, although not royal, is evidently indebted to this tradition.

139 Scamozzi, *L'idea dell'architettura universale*, i, pp. 273, 289 and 291.

140 Chatsworth, Devonshire Collection, album 35, fo. 68.

141 Hewlings, *Chiswick*, p. 37; Spence, 'Chiswick House and Gardens', pp. 525-31.

142 Kerry Downes, 'Chiswick Villa', *Architectural Review*, 164 (1978), pp. 225-36.

143 Rudolf Wittkower, 'Lord Burlington and William Kent', in *Palladio and English Palladianism*, pp. 120, 122 and 132.

144 Richard Krautheimer, *Early Christian and Byzantine Architecture* (Harmondsworth, 1965), pp. 251-54.

145 C. Mango, *The Brazen House* (Copenhagen, 1959), pp. 87-92.

146 Kenneth John Conant, *Carolingian and Roman-

esque Architecture 800 to 1200* (Harmondsworth, 1959), pp. 14-16 and fig. 1; S. Buchkremer, 'Die Karolingische Porticus der Aachener Pfalz', *Bonner Jahrbucher*, 149 (1949), pp. 212-38.

147 E. Kitzinger, *I mosaici di Monreale* (Palermo, 1960), p. 24.

148 W. St John Hope, *Windsor Castle* (London, 1913), i, p. 230 and plate xviii.

149 London County Council, *Survey of London*, xiv, *The Parish of St Margaret, Westminster – Part III* (London, 1931), pp. 10-21.

150 Moriz Dreger, *Baugeschichte des K.K. Hofburg in Wien* (Vienna, 1914), pp. 104, 126 and figs 73 and 96.

151 William Craft Brumfield, *A History of Russian Architecture* (Cambridge, 1993), pp. 92-101.

Fig. 13a The Link Building at Chiswick House from the north (*English Heritage*)

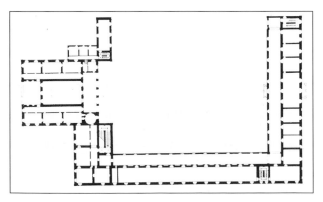

Fig. 13b Plan of the Villa Mondragone, Frascati, showing
the link (bottom) between the Villa (left) and the Palazzo
della Retirata (right)

Fig. 13c Illustration by Gian Tommaso Borgonio of the *galleria* linking the Castello (centre) to the Palazzo Reale (bottom right), Turin

Literary authority, both poetic and philosophical, could have encouraged him to overlook the requirements of symmetry. The *Aeneid* describes the private passages between the 'palace halls' of King Priam's family in Troy.[152] Alberti advised princes to provide passages 'by which, if need be, he may escape himself'.[153] Nero's Passage House (*Domus Transitoria*) linked the Palatine with the Gardens of Maecenas on the Esquiline.[154] Caligula linked the Palatine with the Capitol, bridging the Temple of Divus Augustus in the process.[155] Burlington could not have seen these two long-demolished passage buildings, but he could have read about both in the pages of Suetonius.[156] He could have seen Hadrian's Villa at Tivoli, composed (like the Byzantine Great Palace or the Moscow Kremlin) of discrete units linked by passages;[157] Kent, who visited Tivoli,[158] presumably did see it.

There were also princely passages of the Renaissance period conspicuous in the towns through which Burlington and Kent passed. In Mantua a passage linked the Duomo with the Palazzo Ducale,[159] itself composed of discrete units like Hadrian's Villa.[160] In Ferrara the Palazzo Estense was linked to the Castello,[161] as at Windsor. In Urbino the Palazzo Ducale, another building of discrete units and passage-galleries, had a passage of Chiswick proportion and comparably antique ornament which spanned the *giardino segreto*.[162] Most comparable, however, was the Villa Imperiale at Pesaro. Unlike the others, it was not its owner's principal palace but a *villa suburbana*. Around 1530, Duke Francesco Maria I della Rovere of Urbino added an entirely new villa, linking the two by a bridge-passage like the old and new houses at Chiswick.[163]

It is not known whether Burlington saw these five buildings, but some knowledge of them was at least available to him. On his way back from

152 Virgil, *The Aeneid*, trans. Robert Fitzgerald (Harmondsworth, 1983), p. 49; ii, pp. 453-57.
153 Leone Battista Alberti, *Ten Books on Architecture*, translated by James Leoni (London, 1726), v, pt 2, p. 84.
154 Boethius and Ward-Parkins, *Etruscan and Roman Architecture*, pp. 212-14 and figs 88 and 89.
155 Frank Sear, *Roman Architecture* (London, 1982), p. 92.
156 Gaius Suetonius Tranquillus, *The Twelve Caesars*, trans. Robert Graves (Harmondsworth, 1964), pp. 161 (Caligula's bridge) and 226 (Nero's passageway).
157 Boethius and Ward-Parkins, *Etruscan and Roman Architecture*, pp. 328-29 and fig. 127.
158 London, Victoria and Albert Museum, Department of Prints and Drawings, E 896,
1298, 'a view of Tivoli' signed 'Wm Kent'; reproduced in Michael I. Wilson, *William Kent* (London, 1984), p. 14, fig. 2.
159 Leon George Satkowski, *Studies on Vasari's Architecture* (New York, 1979), p. 254 n.35.
160 David Chambers and Jane Martineau, *The Splendours of the Gonzaga* (London, 1981), fig 3.
161 B. Zevi, *Biagio Rosetti, architetto Ferrarese* (Turin, 1960), pp. 350, 493.
162 Pasquale Rotondi, *The Ducal Palace of Urbino* (London, 1969), pp. 49, 97 and figs 49 and 50.
163 Craig Hugh Smyth, 'The Sunken Courts of the Villa Giulia and the Villa Imperiale', in *Essays in Memory of Karl Lehmann* (New York, 1964), pp. 306-9; Adolfo Venturi, *Storia dell'arte Italiana*, xi, pt 1 (Milan, 1938), p. 870, fig. 790.

Rome in 1715 he went via Bologna to Padua, and thus had to pass through Ferrara. Kent visited Mantua and made detailed observations there.[164] And it is likely that Kent at least passed through Urbino on his way to 'ye Bright Republick of San Marino' in 1714,[165] and possible that he visited Pesaro on the same journey.

The foregoing were short passages, as at Chiswick. Dissimilar by virtue of their great length, but for that reason more conspicuous, were those of Rome, Florence, Turin and Paris. The oldest was the *passeto*, built by Alexander VI (1492-1502) to link the Vatican to the Castel S. Angelo.[166] In 1505-6 the Vatican was linked to the Villa Belvedere by Bramante's corridor.[167] In 1537 the Belvedere Court was linked to *hortus conclusus* of Paul III by another passage (less conspicuous as part of it was underground).[168] The Palazzo Venezia was linked by Paul III (1534-49) to his villa adjacent to the monastery of Santa Maria d'Aracoeli on the Capitoline, to the design of that most antiquarian of architects, Pirro Ligorio;[169] no doubt he had Caligula's efforts in mind. In Florence the Palazzo Vecchio and Uffizi were linked to the Palazzo Pitti by the Corridoio, designed by Vasari in 1565.[170] In Turin there was a passage from the Palazzo Reale to the Castello, built by Duke Emanuele Filiberto in 1570 (Fig. 13c).[171] In Paris the Louvre was linked to the Tuileries by the Grande Galerie, begun in 1595.[172] Burlington could hardly have failed to notice the Corridoio, even though he only spent three days in Florence,[173] as it runs along the river and over the Ponte Vecchio. He spent three days in Turin in autumn 1714, and three more days there on his way back in 1715;[174] he was in Turin again in November 1719,[175] when the

164 Chatsworth, Devonshire Collection, Lord Burlington's Grand Tour Account Book; Cinzia Maria Sicca, 'On William Kent's Roman Sources', *Architectural History*, 29 (1986), pp. 137-38.

165 Lincoln, Lincolnshire Archives Office, 2MM/B19A, Kent to Massingberd, 24 November 1714.

166 G. Zaretti, 'Il passeto del Vaticano', *L'illustrazione Vaticana*, 4 (1933), pp. 841-43; E. Ponti, 'Il corridore', *Capitolium* (1934), pp. 243-56.

167 James S. Ackerman, *The Cortile del Belvedere* (Vatican City, 1954).

168 Coffin, *Gardens and Gardening in Papal Rome*, p. 15 and figs 6, 9 and 10.

169 David R. Coffin, 'Pirro Ligorio', in *Macmillan Encyclopedia of Architects* (London, 1982), iii, p. 10; Satkowski, *Studies on Vasari's Architecture*, figs 77 and 78; J. Hess, 'Die Papstliche Villa bei Aracoeli', *Miscellanea Biblioteca Hertziana* (1961), p. 239.

170 Satkowski, *Studies on Vasari's Architecture*, pp. 76-97, 195-99; J. del Badia, 'Il corridore dal Palazzo Vecchio al Palazzo Pitti', *Miscellanea Florentina*, i (1902), pp. 3-11.

171 Martha D. Pollak, *Turin, 1564-1680* (Chicago, 1991), pp. 41-44; Borgonio, *Theatrum Sabaudiae*, plate 13; A. Peyrot, *Torino nei secoli* (Turin, 1965), nos 9 and 10.

172 Louis Hautecoeur, *Historie du Louvre* (Paris, 1928), pp. 28-31; Rosalys Coope, *Salomon de Brosse* (London, 1972), pp. 34-35.

173 Chatsworth, Devonshire Collection, Lord Burlington's Grand Tour Account Book; see below.

174 Chatsworth, Devonshire Collection, Lord Burlington's Grand Tour Account Book; James Lees-Milne, *The Earls of Creation* (London, 1962), p. 90.

175 Narford, Fountaine MSS, letters, 6 November 1719.

passage to the Castello was either just demolished, or on the point of demolition, to make way for the Palazzo Madama.[176] In either circumstance he might have been particularly aware of it. He spent thirty-five days in Paris,[177] where the Grande Galerie, as in Florence, also ran along the river bank.

These link passages were all in the palaces of ruling princes. One of the few socially comparable examples to that at Chiswick was the link built between the Villa Mondragone at Frascati and the Palazzo della Ritirata by Cardinal Scipione Borghese, after 1613 (Fig. 13b).[178] This is a country house which Burlington visited in person.[179] Modern historians treat the Link Building at Chiswick with silent respect, perhaps embarrassed by its lack of conformity to Palladian norm. There were, however, enough predecessors, both socially and visually impressive, for Burlington to have felt no diffidence in using it to join his two houses. It is true, however, that none of these were Palladian.

When he built the Link room he also added a three-arched *loggia* at first-floor level to the west of the old house, looking across a small court to the *serliana* at the same level in the east-facing front of the new house (Fig. 14a). Behind the loggia there was apparently a semi-circular stair.[180] These features were not suggested by Palladio, but by similar arrangements in three other sixteenth-century Italian villas, the Palazzo Pitti in Florence (a villa only in comparison to the ruler's official residence in the Palazzo Vecchio), the Villa Imperiale, Pesaro, and the Villa Giulia, Rome.[181] All three are built on sloping sites; so their courtyards consist of three ranges of buildings fronting a garden at a higher level behind an architecturally ornamented retaining wall. Chiswick House is on a level site, so the retaining wall is omitted, giving only a three-sided courtyard opening southwards to the garden; but the sensation in the Italian examples of looking down into a sunken courtyard is maintained at Chiswick by the position of the principal rooms on the first floor. Two of them, the Villas Imperiale and Giulia, have three-arched loggias in the centre of the principal side of the courtyard. At the Villa Imperiale this is reached directly from the bridge linking the two parts of the complex, as at Chiswick. The Villa Giulia, like Chiswick, has its three-arched loggia on the first floor, with

176   A. Tellucini, *Il Palazzo Madama di Torino* (n.d. but 1928), p. 80.

177   Chatsworth, Devonshire Collection, Lord Burlington's Grand Tour Account Book; Lees-Milne, *The Earls of Creation*, p. 94.

178   Carl L. Franck, *The Villas of Frascati, 1550-1750* (London, 1966), p. 63 and fig. 57.

179   Chatsworth, Devonshire Collection, Lord Burlington's Grand Tour Account Book.

180   Chatsworth, Devonshire Collection, Lord Burlington's architectural drawings, Boy 8.28, is a plan of this feature as proposed. Proof of its execution is to be found in the report of archaeological excavations undertaken by the Museum of London for the Department of the Environment, 1982-83.

181   Smyth, 'The Sunken Courts of the Villa Giulia', p. 313.

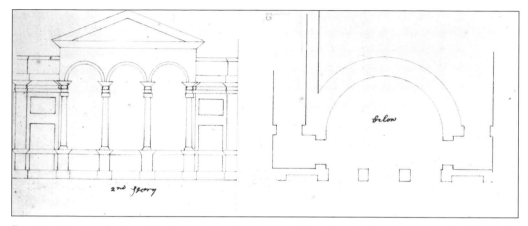

Fig. 14a Drawing by Lord Burlington for the proposed first floor *loggia* attached to old Chiswick House (*Chatsworth*)

Fig. 14b Drawing of the *loggia* of the Villa Giulia, Rome (*RIBA*)

Fig. 15a Ceiling of the Blue Velvet Room, Chiswick House (*English Heritage*)

Fig. 15b Drawing of a ceiling (*Chatsworth*)

access to the ground floor by a semi-circular stair (Fig. 14b). The point of difference is that in the Villa Giulia the semi-circular stair is placed in front of the arcade. This part of the Villa Giulia, of which Burlington possessed architect's drawings,[182] was designed by Ammanati.[183]

Within Chiswick House, the most distinctive room is the Blue Velvet Room, distinguished in particular by its extraordinary ceiling (Fig. 15a). The ceiling has two visually separable components, though the first is only explicable by the second. The first is the disproportionately large consoles. Consoles of this size can be seen beneath the cornice of Galeazzo Alessi's Palazzo Nicolo Grimaldi in Genoa.[184] The significance of Burlington's second visit to Genoa, and his evident recognition of the pronounced neo-antique taste of its sixteenth-century architecture has not been previously discussed. He had already spent six days there in 1714,[185] but in October

182 London, British Architectural Library, Drawings Collection, Burlington-Devonshire Collection, viii, 1-4.
183 Land Moore, 'Villa Giulia', pp. 188 and 190.

184 Ennio Poleggi, *Strada Nuova* (Genoa, 1972), plates 198-99.
185 Chatsworth, Devonshire Collection, Lord Burlington's Grand Tour Account Book.

Fig. 16a Chimneypiece in the Red Velvet Room, Chiswick House (*English Heritage*)

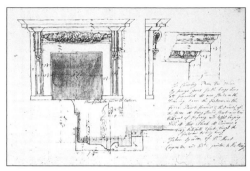

Fig. 16b Drawing by Samuel Savill of a chimneypiece in the Dining Room of the Queen's House, Greenwich (*English Heritage*)

Fig. 16c Chimneypiece and overmantel in the Round Room of the Gallery, Chiswick House (*English Heritage*)

Fig. 16d Drawing by Inigo Jones for the chimneypiece in 'the roome next the bac stairs above' in the Queen's House, Greenwich (*RIBA*)

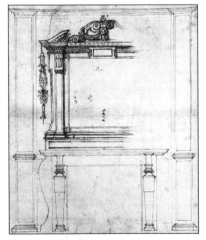

Fig. 16e Drawing by Inigo Jones for an overmantel in the Cross Gallery at Somerset House which also records the existing chimneypiece (*RIBA*)

Fig. 16f Drawing by Inigo Jones for a
chimneypiece and overmantel at Oatlands
Palace, Surrey (*RIBA*)

Fig. 16g Drawing by Inigo Jones for a
chimneypiece and overmantel at Oatlands
Palace, Surrey (*RIBA*)

Fig. 16h Chimneypiece and overmantel in the
Bedchamber, Chiswick House (*English
Heritage*)

Fig. 16i Drawing by Inigo Jones for a
chimneypiece and overmantel in the Cabinet
Room of the Queen's House, Greenwich
(*RIBA*)

Fig. 16j Drawing of an aedicule at the Villa
Giulia, Rome (*RIBA*)

1719, en route from London to Venice, he met William Kent there, en route from Rome to London. Kent, to whose account we are indebted for knowledge of the visit, was anxious to be on his way, but was delayed by Burlington's enthusiasm for 'tow [*sic*] fine Pallaces of Vetruvio a Genova that my Ld. carry'd me to see which he has order'd to be drawn'.[186] Kent did not identify the palaces 'of Vetruvio' but, as a large part of the neo-antique architecture of that town was designed by Galeazzo Alessi, Burlington may have been an admirer of that architect. Alessi would at least have indicated to him that consoles of such size were not absurd. Similar, but alternative, imagery might have been furnished by looking at Philibert de l'Orme's *Architecture* of 1567, which has two plates illustrating brackets of this size; one of them, significantly, illustrates de l'Orme's own house. De l'Orme's book was in his library.[187] But no doubt he would have been motivated more by a situation more comparable. The Blue Velvet Room was intended as a study, and it may have flattered him to give himself accommodation suitable for a humanist prince. He had not visited Mantua, but Kent had,[188] and could have told him about the second *studiolo* of Isabella d'Este in the Corte Vecchio of the Palazzo Ducale,[189] and about the room leading to the Appartamento dei Nani in the same building.[190] The Blue Velvet Room most resembles the latter.

The second component of the ceiling is the illusionistic effect of two ceilings, one above the other, in which the fictional lower ceiling is pierced by a large square hole through which the upper one is revealed. Such an illusion makes sense of the otherwise overlarge consoles, which assume the part of the required structural engineering for a *trompe l'oeil* balcony. The doubled ceiling concept may be French; Francois Mansart employed it at Ste Marie de la Visitation, Paris, in 1632-3,[191] and at Blois in 1635-8.[192] Burlington could have seen the former during his month in Paris in 1715,[193] or on his visits there in 1717[194] and 1726-7;[195] but there is no positive

186 Lincoln, Lincolnshire Archive Office, 2MM/B19A, William Kent to Burrell Massingberd, 15 November 1719; Michael I. Wilson, *William Kent*, p. 37.

187 Philibert de l'Orme, *Le premier tome de l'architecture* (Paris, 1567), 253v. Ayres, 'Burlington's Library at Chiswick', p. 118.

188 Sicca, 'Kent's Roman Sources', pp. 137-38.

189 Chambers and Martineau, *Splendours of the Gonzaga*, fig, 64; Clifford M. Brown, 'The *Grotta* of Isabella d'Este', *Gazette des beaux arts*, 6th series, 89 (1977), p. 158, fig. 2.

190 Sicca, 'Kent's Roman Sources', p. 139 and figs 2 and 3.

191 Anthony Blunt, *Art and Architecture in France, 1500 to 1700* (Harmondsworth, 1953), plate 167.

192 Alan Braham and Peter Smith, *François Mansart* (London, 1973), plate 180.

193 Chatsworth, Devonshire Collection, Lord Burlington's Grand Tour Account Book; see below Lees-Milne, *The Earls of Creation*, p. 94.

194 Jane Clark, 'For Kings and Senates Fit', *Georgian Group Report and Journal* (1989), p. 56; see also below.

195 Chatsworth, Devonshire Collection, Andrew Crotty's Account Book from 4 August 1725 to 24 October 1732, fo. 15 (16 Sept. 1726) and fo. 41 (30 Sept. 1727).

evidence that he did. However, France is a more plausible inspiration than Italy. Although the combination of large brackets and illusory upper ceiling also occurs in a room in the Palazzo Vizzani, Bologna,[196] which resembles the Blue Velvet Room more than any other, Burlington's brief visit to this city may not have included this private house.[197] He did, on the other hand, possess a large collection of seventeenth-century French ceiling designs,[198] one of which illustrates the same relationship of giant consoles and illusionist ceiling as in the Blue Velvet Room (Fig. 15b).[199] Whatever Burlington's sources may have been, one conclusion can be surely drawn from them: they do not include Palladio.

There are five chimneypiece types at Chiswick House. None are derived from Palladio. Palladio's book does not illustrate chimneypieces, and Burlington evidently possessed no record (either his own or anyone else's) of the chimneypieces in the only five heated Palladian buildings which he visited.[200] Nor does he appear to have relied on Kent as a source of information on Italian chimneys; nor (except in a general way) on Serlio's book, which illustrates eight splendid chimneypieces and a number of other features adaptable as chimneypieces. All five Chiswick examples are copied from chimneypieces designed by Inigo Jones. Burlington dispatched his clerk Samuel Savill to sketch one executed at the Queen's House, Greenwich (Fig. 16b), which he reproduced in the Red Velvet Room (Fig. 16a). He was able to copy the others from his own collection of Jones' drawings. Those in the Round and Octagonal Rooms of the Gallery (Fig. 16c) are copies of a design dated 1637 by Jones 'for the roome next the bac stairs above', at the Queen's House (Fig. 16d), and their overmantels are a conflation of three of Jones' drawings, all dated 1636, one for the Cross Gallery of Somerset House (Fig. 16e), and two for Oatlands Palace (Fig. 16f, g). The overmantel in the Bedchamber (Fig. 16h) is a version of a design by Jones for the Cabinet Room of the Queen's House, dated 1637 (Fig. 16i), itself a version of a design by an unidentified French architect. The chimneypiece below it is copied from the drawing of 1636 by Jones for

196 Peter Thornton, *Authentic Decor* (London, 1984), p. 74.
197 Chatsworth, Devonshire Collection, Lord Burlington's Grand Tour Account Book.
198 Chatsworth, Devonshire Collection, album 35, e.g. fos 4, 6, 8, 41, 43.
199 Ibid., fol. 6.
200 The Palazzi Chiericati, Iseppo de' Porti and Thiene in Vicenza, the Ville Almerico (the Rotonda) at Vicenza and Foscari at Malcontenta, as revealed in Lord Burlington's annotated edition of Palladio's *I quattro libri*, ii, chapter 3, interleaved pages opposite pp. 6, 7, 8, 14 and 18; chapter 13, interleaved page opposite p. 50.

the Cross Gallery at Somerset House (Fig. 16e).[201] Burlington failed to notice that this was only in part a proposal drawing; the other part was Jones' record of the existing chimneypiece of 1611 by Maximilian Colt. It is the latter which Burlington reproduced. Colt's pilasters, tapering towards their bases, are the most Mannerist element of all the chimneypieces at Chiswick. They were among a number of Renaissance and Mannerist examples, of which the two most famous were the window architraves in the *Ricetta* of Michelangelo's Laurentian Library in Florence. Burlington's drawings of the Villa Giulia (believed by him to be by Vignola) also illustrated downward tapering pilasters (Fig. 16j). No doubt this was Burlington's authority.[202]

With nearly fifty statues, three of them antique, and together constituting an apparently meaningful iconographic programme, the garden at Chiswick falls within the definition of a statue garden. Lord Burlington's gatepiers carried sphinxes, his forecourt was patrolled by herms, and architects flanked his steps. In the Grove beyond his house, wolf, boar, sphinx, lion, lioness, Samson, Philistine, athlete, philosopher and politician led the visitor to a trio of genuine antiques from Hadrian's villa at Tivoli.[203] Sixteenth- and seventeenth-century English gardens had statuary, but rarely more than four or six figures, each the centre of a grass plot. Only Chatsworth, Denham Place and Hampton Court had denser concentrations, and none included ancient pieces.[204] More, with more complete and self-evident iconographic programmes, were to be seen in Italy and France. Burlington visited the Villa Borghese in Rome,[205] the Villas Mondragone and Aldobrandini at Frascati,[206] and, in France, the Château de

201 Serlio, *Architecture*, iv, pp. 32, 33, 43, 44, 52, 58, 61 and 62; Chatsworth, Devonshire Collection, album 26a, fo. 27v; Harris and Higgott, *Inigo Jones: Complete Architectural Drawings*, p. 229; *Inigo Jones: Complete Architectural Drawings*, pp. 211; 221, 223; 233; 232, fig. 72; 211.

202 Colvin, *King's Works*, iv, p. 267; Ackerman, *The Architecture of Michelangelo*, plate 45; Giovanni Battista Montano, *Architettura con diversi ornamenti cavati dall'antico* (Rome, 1684), iv, p. 31. London, British Architectural Library, Drawings Collection, Burlington–Devonshire Collection viii, 1-4.

203 A Gentleman [Daniel Defoe], *A Tour thro' the Whole Island of Great Britain* (3rd edn, London, 1742), iii, p. 289; R. and J. Dodsley, *London and its Environs Described* (London, 1761), ii, p. 114.

204 Francis Thompson, *Chatsworth: A Short History* (London, 1951), pp. 31, 113; Harris, *Artist and the Country House*, plate xiv; A.J. van der Horst and David Jacques, *Gardens of Wil-*

liam and Mary (London, 1988), fig. 4.14 and plate 8.

205 Chatsworth, Devonshire Collection, Lord Burlington's Grand Tour Account Book; Lees-Milne, *The Earls of Creation*, p. 91; Coffin, *Gardens and Gardening in Papal Rome*, p. 148; C.H. Heilmann, 'Die Entstehungsgeschichte der Villa Borghese in Rom', *Münchner Jahrbuch der bildenden Kunst*, 3rd series, 24 (1973), pp. 97-158.

206 Chatsworth, Devonshire Collection, Lord Burlington's Grand Tour Account Book; Franck, *The Villas of Frascati*, pp. 57-72; Chatsworth, Devonshire Collection, Lord Burlington's Grand Tour Account Book; Franck, *The Villas of Frascati*, pp. 115-32; Howard Hibbard, *Carlo Maderno* (London, 1971), pp. 47-50, 131-33; Klaus Schwager, 'Kardinal Pietro Aldobrandinis Villa di Belvedere in Frascati', *Römisches Jahrbuch für Kunstgeschichte*, 9, 10 (1961-62), pp. 291-382.

Fig. 17a The Cascade, Chiswick (*English Heritage*)

Fig. 17b Illustration by Israel Silvestre of the grotto at the Château de Rueil

Versailles.[207] William Kent knew the statue garden of the Villa Ludovisi, where he worked as a painter in 1713 and 1715.[208] Both Burlington and Kent (who lived in Rome for ten years) may have known more. Whether either of them visited the two Renaissance gardens which were most crowded with emblematic ancient sculpture, the Cesi garden[209] and the garden which had belonged to Jacopo Galla,[210] is not known. But in this area Palladio, who is not known to have designed statue gardens, cannot have been an influence.

The largest surviving garden ornament is not a statue but the Cascade, south west of the house (Fig. 17a), added *c.* 1738.[211] Its name misleadingly suggests that it is one of the real cascades, or water staircases, derived from the Generalife at Granada,[212] which were the particular ornament of the Villas d'Este at Tivoli,[213] Lante at Bagnaia,[214] Farnese at Caprarola,[215] Ludovisi[216] and Aldobrandini at Frascati,[217] of the Château de Ruel in France,[218] of Chatsworth,[219] Dyrham,[220] Castle Howard,[221] Wentworth Castle,[222] Stanway,[223] Bramham,[224] and Corby Castle in England,[225] and of Drumlanrig in Scotland.[226] In fact the Chiswick geography conspired

207 Chatsworth, Devonshire Collection, Lord Burlington's Grand Tour Account Book; Lees-Milne, *The Earls of Creation*, p. 94; Alfred and Jeanne Marie, *Versailles au temps de Louis XIV*, iii (Paris, 1976), pp. 331-444.
208 Dixon Hunt, *William Kent*, 1987, p. 22 and fig. 11.
209 Phyllis Pray Bober and Ruth Rubinstein, *Renaissance Artists and Antique Sculpture* (London, 1986), p. 472; Elisabeth B. Mac-Dougall, 'L'Ingegnoso Artifizio: Sixteenth-Century Garden Fountains in Rome', in Elisabeth B. MacDougall (ed.), *Fons sapientiae: Renaissance Garden Fountains* (Washington, 1978), p. 97 and figs 6 and 10; Coffin, *Gardens and Gardening in Papal Rome*, pp. 22-24 and plate 15.
210 Bober and Rubinstein, *Renaissance Artists and Antique Sculpture*, p. 475.
211 BL, Althorp MSS, B8, William Kent to Lord Burlington, 12 September 1738, ('When all this work is done [the mason] is to begin upon yr cascade'); Chatsworth, Devonshire Collection, letter 206.3, William Kent to Lady Burlington, 7 October 1738 ('Tell my Ld he shall have an answer to his letter as soon as ye cascade is finished').
212 Coffin, *Gardens and Gardening in Papal Rome*, p. 44; Elisabeth B. MacDougall, 'Introduction', *Fons sapientiae* (1978), p. 10; Oleg Grabar, *The Alhambra* (London, 1978), pp. 68-71.
213 D.R. Coffin, *The Villa D'Este at Tivoli* (Princeton, 1960), p. 21 and plate 15.
214 C. Lazzaro-Bruno, 'The Villa Lante at Bagnaia: An Allegory of Art and Nature', *Art Bulletin*, 59 (1977), pp. 557-58 and fig. 10.
215 Benedetti, *Giacomo del Duca*, pp. 241-82 and figs 218, 219 and 221.
216 Franck, *The Villas of Frascati*, p. 82 and plate 84; Howard Hibbard, *Carlo Maderno and Roman Architecture, 1580-1630* (London, 1971), pp. 210-11.
217 Ronald Martin Steinberg, 'The Iconography of the Teatro dell'Acqua at the Villa Aldobrandini', *Art Bulletin*, 47, December 1965, pp. 453-63, plates 2-5.
218 Elisabeth B. MacDougall and Naomi Miller, *Fons sapientiae* catalogue (1977), pp. 62-63.
219 Thompson, *Chatsworth*, pp. 23, 114.
220 Mark Girouard, 'Dyrham Park, Gloucestershire – II', *Country Life*, 131, 22 February 1962, p. 399.
221 Christopher Hussey, *English Gardens and Landscapes, 1700-1750* (London, 1967), p. 124.
222 Badeslade and Rocque, *Vitruvius Brittanicus*, plate 55.
223 Christopher Hussey, 'Stanway, Gloucestershire – III', *Country Life*, 136, 17 December 1964, pp. 1708-10 and fig. 5.
224 Arthur Oswald, 'A Yorkshire Landscape Garden – I', *Country Life*, 12 June 1958, p. 1296; II, 19 June 1958, pp. 1369-70.
225 Gordon Nares, 'Corby Castle, Cumberland – I', *Country Life*, 115, 7 January 1954, p. 34.
226 Badeslade and Rocque, *Vitruvius Brittanicus*, plates 45-46.

against it and hydraulic engineers failed to make it work.[227] Even if it had worked, it could never have been more than a fountain within an arched recess. Strictly speaking, that makes it a *nymphaeum* or grotto. Of these he was certainly familiar with the *nymphaeum* at the Villa Giulia, Rome,[228] from drawings in his possession.[229] He would have been familiarised by Kent with the grotto at Poggio a Caiano,[230] which Kent described in his journal,[231] with the *nymphaeum* at the Palazzo del Te at Mantua,[232] and with the *Grotta* of Isabella d'Este in the Palazzo Ducale in Mantua.[233] Either or both of them must have known the *Grotte des Pins* at Fontainebleau,[234] whose appearance is reflected in the cascades of Kent's *Venus' Vale* at Rousham Hall, Oxon.[235] Burlington visited Versailles,[236] and therefore probably saw the *Grotte de Thetys* there.[237] He visited Heidelberg,[238] where he may have seen the grottoes in the grounds of the electoral castle.[239] In Rome he may have seen the grottoes framing the *Tigris* and *Cleopatra* statues in the Belvedere Court of the Vatican,[240] the *nymphaeum* in the hippodrome of the Villa Madama,[241] and the grotto in the garden of the Villa d'Este.[242] In Florence, where he spent three days in 1715,[243] he might have seen the Grotto of Moses in the Pitti Palace,[224] the *grottocina* in the Boboli Gardens[245]

227 Defoe, *A Tour*, p. 290; Chatsworth, Devonshire Collection, letter 282.2, Lady Charlotte Boyle to Lord Burlington, 12 Sept. 1743 ('the water come's in to the river very fast but it dry's up in a minute'); Devonshire Collection, 'John Ferrett's Account Currant with the Right Honble the Earl of Burlington 1745', fol. 19, '1746 April 14th Paid Mr John Davis . . . for Aultering and making a new horse Engine at Chiswick – 150.0.0.', fol. 45, 'June 19. Mr John Davis . . . for . . . new horse Engine at Chiswick – 31.2.10.'

228 Heydenreich and Lotz, *Architecture in Italy*, plate 277.

229 London, British Architectural Library, Drawings Collection, Burlington-Devonshire Collection, viii, 1-4.

230 Silvestro Bardazzi and Eugenio Castellani, *La Villa Medicea di Poggio a Caiano* (Prato, 1981), i, plate 35.

231 Wilson, *William Kent*, p. 202.

232 Sicca, 'Kent's Roman Sources', pp. 137-38; Frederick Hartt, *Giulio Romano* (New Haven, 1958), p. 146 and figs 303-4.

233 Clifford M. Brown, 'The *Grotta* of Isabella d'Este', *Gazette des beaux arts*, 6th series, 89 (1977), pp. 155-71; 91 (1978), pp. 72-82.

234 Naomi Miller, 'Domain of Illusion: The Grotto in France', in MacDougall (ed.), *Fons sapientiae* (1978), pp. 177-206, plates 1, 12-14.

235 Christopher Hussey, *English Gardens and Land-*

scapes (1967), plates 205-6.

236 Chatsworth, Devonshire Collection, Lord Burlington's Grand Tour Account Book; Lees-Milne, *The Earls of Creation*, p. 94.

237 MacDougall and Miller, *Fons Sapientiae* (1977), pp. 30-31.

238 Chatsworth, Devonshire Collection, Lord Burlington's Grand Tour Account Book; Lees-Milne, *The Earls of Creation*, p. 90.

239 Roy Strong, *The Renaissance Garden in England* (London, 1979), p. 110; Saloman de Caus, *Hortus Palatinus* (Frankfurt, 1620), passim.

240 Elisabeth B. MacDougall, 'The Sleeping Nymph: Origins of a Humanist Fountain Type', *Art Bulletin*, 57, no. 3, Sept 1975, pp. 359ff.

241 Sicca, 'Kent's Roman Sources', p. 139 and fig. 10.

242 MacDougall, 'The Sleeping Nymph'; MacDougall (ed.) 'L'ingegnoso artifizio', pp. 100-1, fig. 15.

243 Chatsworth, Devonshire Collection, Lord Burlington's Grand Tour Account Book.

244 Naomi Miller, *Heavenly Caves: Reflections on the Garden Grotto* (Boston, 1982), p. 51.

245 D. Heikamp, 'La Grotta Grande del Giardino di Boboli', *Antichità viva*, iv, July-August 1965, pp. 1-18; Detlef Heikamp, 'The Grotta Grande in the Boboli Garden, Florence', *Connoisseur*, 199 (1978), pp. 38-43.

or the Grotto of the Unicorn at Castello.[246] Kent, who spent five months there, is more likely to have seen these.[247] There were other grottoes at the Villas d'Este at Tivoli,[248] Lante at Bagnaia,[249] the Villa del Vescovo at Marlia, near Lucca,[250] the Bastie d'Urfe, near Forez,[251] the Châteaux of Meudon,[252] St-Germain-en-Laye,[253] Ruel,[254] and Vaux-le-Vicomte,[255] Woburn[256] and Wilton Houses,[257] which either of them might have seen.

The Chiswick Cascade combines the grotto type with another type of garden fountain, the artificial mountain, usually a free-standing mound of unhewn rocks. At Chiswick the types are combined by forming a mountain out of earth excavated from the 'river',[258] heaped behind and above the grotto, and using unhewn rocks as part of the grotto masonry. The prototype of the artificial mountain fountain was the ancient *Meta Sudens* in Rome, now reduced to little more than its conical brick core,[259] but clad in unhewn rocks as late as the seventeenth-century,[260] and probably as late as the time of Burlington's visit, when he may well have seen it. The first artificial mountain of the Renaissance was in the garden of Borso d'Este in Ferrara, *c.* 1470;[261] the first artificial mountain to be installed in a pool was in the Château of Gaillon, before 1566.[262] The first artificial mountain which itself dispensed water was that in the garden of Antonio del Bufalo in Rome, described by Aldrovandi in 1558; it was intended to resemble Mount Helicon, with water oozing from Pegasus' hoofprints.[263] Although this long-lost garden was also described by Boissard,[264] a much better-known example of water issuing from an artificial mountain was the *Appenino* at Pratolino, built by Buontalenti in 1568.[265] Burlington had not visited it, but it was well known through an engraving of *c.* 1650 by Stefano della Bella.[266]

246 Liliane Chatelet-Lange, 'The Grotto of the Unicorn in the Garden of the Villa di Castello', *Art Bulletin*, 50 (1968), pp. 51-58.

247 Sicca, 'Kent's Roman Sources', p. 135.

248 Coffin, *Villa d'Este*, figs 16, 17, 18, 19, 30, 31, 38 and 107-10.

249 Lazzaro-Bruno, 'The Villa Lante', pp. 556-57 and fig 7.

250 I.B. Barsali, *Le ville Lucchese* (1964), p. 212, plates 19 and 20; idem, *Catalogo della Mostra delle Villa Lucchesi dal '500* (1975).

251 Miller, *Heavenly Caves*, pp. 53-54 and fig. 41.

252 Ibid., p. 54 and fig. 42.

253 Miller, 'Domain of Illusion', pp. 200, 206 and fig. 21.

254 MacDougall and Miller, *Fons sapientiae*, catalogue (1977), pp. 64-65.

255 Miller, 'Domain of Illusion', p. 206.

256 Strong, *The Renaissance Garden*, pp. 139-41.

257 Ibid., pp. 154-56.

258 Defoe, *A Tour*, p. 290.

259 Ernest Nash, *Pictorial Dictionary of Ancient Rome* (1961), ii, pp. 61-63.

260 G. Lauro, *Antiqua urbis splendor* (Rome, 1612-28), plate 138; reproduced by MacDougall, in 'L'ingegnoso artifizio', fig. 9.

261 MacDougall, 'Ars hortolorum', p. 45.

262 Miller, *Heavenly Caves*, p. 57 and fig. 45.

263 Coffin, *Gardens and Gardening in Papal Rome*, p. 71.

264 J.-J. Boissard, *Antiquae statuae urbis Romae* (Frankfurt, 1597).

265 Webster Smith, 'Pratolino', *Journal of the Society of Architectural Historians*, 20 (1961), p. 162, fig. 12.

266 Ibid.; MacDougall, *Fons sapientiae* (1978), pp. 4-5.

By 1650 it had already been copied, first at St German-en-Laye,[267] and later by Solomon de Caus in the *Parnassus* at Somerset House,[268] the *Appenine* at Richmond Palace,[269] and in the garden of the electoral Castle at Heidelberg, which de Caus published in *Hortus Palatinus* in 1620.[270]

Whatever Burlington may have seen, the available printed material helped him to realise it. Della Bella's view of the *Appenino* may have been in Burlington's mind; it shows the mountain surrounded by cedars, just as Kent's sketches show the Chiswick Cascade.[271] The particular form of the grotto resembles the 'Rustic Fountain' illustrated in *Hortus Palatinus*,[272] three plates in de Caus' slightly later book, *Les raisons des forces mouvantes*,[273] the Fountain of the Muses in Charles le Brun's *Recueil de divers desseins de fontaines at de frises maritimes*,[274] the Neptune Grotto in Jean Le Pautre's *Grottes et vues des jardins inventées et gravees*,[275] and especially Israel Silvestre's views of the grotto at Richelieu's Château de Rueil (Fig. 17b).[276] De Caus' and Silvestre's books, at least, were in Burlington's library.[277]

Finally, the background inspiration is likely to be literary. Scamozzi described ancient grottoes in Campagna and Naples.[278] Alberti did so quite precisely, and his book had been recently translated by James Leoni, an architect whom Burlington had apparently recommended to several of his relations.[279] Alberti (in Leoni's translation) wrote:

The Ancients used to dress the walls of their grottoes with little Chips of Pumice, or soft Tyburtine Stone . . . and some I have known daub them over with green Wax, in imitation of the mossy slime which we always see in moist Grottoes.[280]

Whether Burlington's inspiration was architectural, graphic or literary, it did not come from Palladio.

267 L. de la Tourrasse, 'Le Château-Neuf de Saint-Germain-en-Laye, ses terrasses et ses grottes', *Gazette des beaux arts*, 5th series, 9 (1924), pp. 68-95.
268 Strong, *The Renaissance Garden*, pp. 90-91.
269 Ibid., p. 98.
270 Miller, *Heavenly Caves*, pp. 62-3 and fig. 53; A. Zeller, *Das Heidelberger Schloss: Werden, Zerfall und Zukunft* (1905), pp. 69-71, and fig. 79; De Caus, *Hortus Palatinus*, e.g. fig. 29.
271 Dixon Hunt, *William Kent*, pp. 124-26; Chatsworth, Devonshire Collection, album 26a, nos 15, 18 and 19.
272 Ibid., fig 29.
273 MacDougall, *Fons sapientiae* (1978), pp. 13-15.
274 Ibid., p. 43.
275 Ibid., p. 45.
276 Ibid., p. 65.
277 Chatsworth, Devonshire Collection, Library, MS Catalogue of the Earl of Burlington's Library, 5th unpaginated page, and page 2.
278 Scamozzi, *L'idea dell'architettura universale*, pp. 328, 361, 362.
279 Richard Hewlings, 'James Leoni', in R. Brown (ed.), *The Architectural Outsiders* (London, 1985), pp. 26-27.
280 James Leoni, trans., *The Architecture of Leon Battista Alberti* (London, 1726), p. 192.

Fig. 18a Illustration by Colen Campbell of the Casina, Chiswick

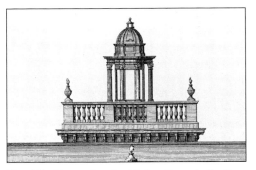

Fig. 18b Illustration by Colen Campbell of the lantern of Wilbury House, Wiltshire

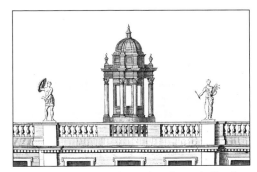

Fig. 18c Illustration by Colen Campbell of the lantern of Thoresby House, Nottinghamshire

Fig. 18d The lantern on the tower of St Michael, Paternoster Royal, London (*RCHME*)

Fig. 18e The lantern of the Royal Hospital, Chelsea (*RCHME*)

The principal components of the façade of the Casina (Fig. 18a), built in 1717,[281] and demolished in 1778,[282] were taken from Jones' and Webb's designs for Whitehall Palace, as interpreted by Campbell, and published in the second volume of *Vitruvius Britannicus*, which came out in that year.[283] But the lantern, as represented by Colen Campbell's engraving, appears to have an octagonal drum with columns at each angle supporting parts of the entablature which break forward, a form which does not occur in Jones' Whitehall designs. If accurately represented thus, it is close to Campbell's own designs for Wanstead and for the earl of Halifax, engraved in an earlier volume of *Vitruvius Britannicus*.[284] It is closer still to William Benson's Wilbury (Fig. 18b), 'Invented and built by himself in the stile of Inigo Jones'.[285] However much Benson and Campbell may have wished this to be the case, Wilbury is not in the style of Inigo Jones. The lantern in particular is unlike any lantern which Jones designed. Its source is Thoresby (Fig. 18c), perhaps designed by Hawksmoor,[286] which in turn belongs within the tradition of lanterns designed by Wren for the City churches. In fact Campbell's slightly ambiguous representation of the Chiswick Casina may show a square drum whose upper stage alone is octagonal: the columns and the broken entablature above them would in these circumstances occur not at the corners, but slightly in from them. This is how Wren detailed the lantern of St Paul's Cathedral,[287] and that of St Mary le Bow,[288] although without breaking the entablature. That detail could have been observed by Burlington on St Michael, Paternoster Royal,[289] (Fig. 18d) or Chelsea Hospital (Fig. 18e).[290] Whichever form the Casina lantern took, its inspiration came from Wren and (perhaps) Hawksmoor, not Jones or Palladio.

Ancient Features

The seventeen features identified above may be compared with a further thirty-three features at Chiswick which are copied from ancient architecture. It appears that one of them may have been taken from a literary, rather

281 Colen Campbell, *Vitruvius Britannicus*, iii (London, 1725), plate 26.
282 Chatsworth, Devonshire Collection, C170, Account Book 1770-83, fo. 115, 27 November 1778.
283 Margaret Whinney, 'John Webb's Drawings for Whitehall Palace', *Walpole Society*, 31 (1942-43), plates ix (for the ground floor), xvib (for the first floor), xxa and xxiie (for the relationship of both floors). Campbell, *Vitruvius Britannicus*, ii, plates 4-7; the necessity of Campbell's mediation is explained by Sicca,

'Lord Burlington at Chiswick', p. 40.
284 Campbell, *Vitruvius Britannicus*, i, plates 25 and 30.
285 Ibid., plate 52.
286 Ibid., plate 91; Howard Colvin, *A Biographical Dictionary of British Architects, 1600-1840* (London, 1978), p. 805.
287 Geoffrey Beard, *The Work of Christopher Wren* (Edinburgh, 1982), plate 76.
288 Ibid., plate 139.
289 Ibid., plate 162.
290 Ibid., plate 71.

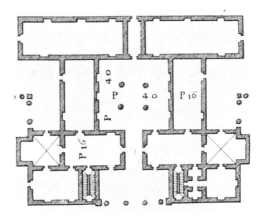

Fig. 19b Illustration by Andrea Palladio of a hypothetical Villa of the Ancients

Fig. 19a The passage leading to the entrance of the first floor of Chiswick House (*English Heritage*)

Fig. 19c Illustration by Andrea Palladio of his design for the Villa Garzadore

than a visual source. Vitruvius, describing the ancient Greek house, wrote that it had 'passageways for people entering from the front, not very wide, . . . shut off by doors at the inner end'.[291] This quite precisely describes a feature of Chiswick, which, in every other way, is inexplicable (Figs 6a, 19a). There is no Italian precedent and no native precedent. The perversity of this feature, which he called 'rather curious than convenient' was the only evidence recorded by Sir John Clerk of Penicuik, visiting on 7 May 1727, in support of his observation that the house was 'in the ancient manner'.[292] The leap, however, from ancient theory to modern practice was undoubtedly aided by Renaissance graphics. Palladio's realisation of Vitruvius' Villa of the Ancients has such a passage (Fig. 19b), but in rather dissimilar circumstances: it leads from the portico to a central kitchen, between the ox stall and the oil press.[293] Palladio illustrates a further eight plans of his own with similar passages, of which the closest to Chiswick is the Villa Almerico.[294] Only one, however, the unbuilt Villa Garzadore, has its outer end open (Fig. 19c).[295] Palladio's book may therefore have aided Burlington's realisation of this curiously ancient feature.

Palladio's book may also have aided him to reproduce ancient features which he had seen, rather than read about. Chiswick's stepped dome, for instance, its most conspicuous component (Fig. 20a), was doubtless suggested by the sight of actual buildings. When in Rome he was bound to have seen the Pantheon,[296] and he probably saw Vignola's S. Andrea in Via Flaminia.[297] However, there were more stepped domes proposed than built. Hawksmoor designed stepped domes for Queen's College, Oxford in 1708-9,[298] All Souls College, Oxford, in 1708-9,[299] Greenwich Hospital in 1711,[300] the Radcliffe Library, Oxford, in 1712-15,[301] and for a Belvedere at Castle Howard in 1723-4:[302] none were built, and Burlington could only have known them from conversation with Hawksmoor. Palladio's book illustrated his proposed Villa Trissino at Meledo (Fig. 6b).[303] Scamozzi's

291 [Marcus] Vitruvius [Pollio], *The Ten Books on Architecture*, translated by Morris Hickey Morgan (Cambridge, MA, 1914), vi, ch. vii, p. 1.

292 John Fleming, *Robert Adam and his Circle* (1962), p. 26.

293 Palladio, *I quattro libri*, ii, plate 51.

294 Ibid., ii, plate 13. The others, all in Bk II, are the Palazzo Valmarana (plate 11), the Palazzo Capra (plate 14), the Villa Pisani at Montagnana (plate 35), the Villa Cornara at Piombino (plate 36), the Villa Emo at Fanzolo (plate 38), and the Villa Trissino at Meledo (plate 43).

295 Ibid., ii, plate 57.

296 Boethius and Ward-Perkins, *Etruscan and Roman Architecture*, pp. 256-60 and fig. 102.

297 Paolo Portoghesi, *Rome of the Renaissance* (London, 1972), plates 241-42; James S. Ackerman and Wolfgang Lotz, 'Vignoliana', in *Essays in Memory of Karl Lehmann*, pp. 12-13 and figs 13-14.

298 Kerry Downes, *Hawksmoor* (London, 1959; 2nd edn, 1979), p. 279 and plates 28b and 50b.

299 Ibid., p. 278 and plate 41a.

300 Ibid., p. 281 and plates 26a and b.

301 Ibid., p. 279 and plates 35a, 38d and 39.

302 Ibid., p. 283 and plate 87a.

303 Palladio, *I quattro libri*, ii, plate 43.

Fig. 20a The dome over the Saloon, Chiswick House (*English Heritage*)

Fig. 20b Illustration by Andrea Palladio of the Pantheon, Rome

book illustrated his Villa Pisani at Lonigo (Fig. 6c)[304] and Villa Bardellini at Asolo (Fig. 6e).[305] Serlio's book illustrated Peruzzi's proposed dome of St Peter's,[306] and eleven different ideal 'temples', all with stepped domes.[307] Illustrated records of ancient Roman domes were also abundant, and probably more appealing than modern ones. Serlio illustrated three, the Pantheon, the Temple of Vesta at Trevi and the Temple of Bacchus.[308] They were surpassed in draughting accuracy by Palladio, who also illustrated three, the Pantheon (Fig. 20b), the Temple of Vesta at Tivoli and the so-called Galluce.[309]

Much of the plan of Chiswick House could also have been suggested by the sight of ancient buildings. For instance, the Lower Tribune and the central part of the Library (Fig. 21a) reproduce the arrangement and relationship of the narthex and exo-narthex of the Baptistery at St John Lateran in Rome, built by Pope Sixtus III as late as 432–40, but in the antique idiom sometimes characterised as the 'Sixtine Renaissance'.[310] Variants of this arrangement are found also in early Christian *mausolea*, such as S. Petronilla and S. Maria delle Fabbre, Rome, and S. Aquilino, Milan.[311] It is, however, not known whether Burlington saw the first or last of these; the two others had been demolished long before his visit to Rome. But he did not have to, because a plan of the Lateran Baptistery was illustrated in Palladio's book (Fig. 21b), which describes it not as Sixtine but as Constantinian;[312] it is this illustration which is followed at Chiswick.

Details at Chiswick were also of ancient type, communicated in the same way. For instance, the octagonal coffered pattern which ceils the dome of the Saloon at Chiswick (Fig. 22a) is based on the pattern of the stucco ornament within the Basilica of Maxentius (Fig. 4b), an ancient building in Rome whose fame and conspicuousness probably ensured his sight of it.[313] There were sixteenth- and seventeenth-century examples of this pattern, which he may equally have seen. For instance, one of the buildings by Alessi which he probably saw in Genoa was the Villa Cambiaso, which is decorated with octagonal coffering.[314] So was Inigo Jones'

304 Scamozzi, *L'idea dell'architettura universale*, p. 273.
305 Ibid., p. 279.
306 Serlio, *Architecture*, iii, 17v.
307 Ibid., v, 2v, 3v, 5v, 6v, 7v, 8, 9, 9v, 12, 12v and 15.
308 Serlio, *Architecture*, iii, 2v and 3 (Pantheon), 8 (Temple of Bacchus), and 11 (Temple of Vesta).
309 Palladio, *I quattro libri*, iv, plates 52-3 (Pantheon), plate 66 (Temple of Vesta at Tivoli) and plate 24 (Galluce).

310 Richard Krautheimer, *Rome: Profile of a City, 312-1308* (Princeton, 1980), pp. 49-50; idem, *Early Christian and Byzantine Architecture* (Harmondsworth, 1965), pp. 64-65 and plate 17a; G.B. Giovenale, *Il Battistero Laterano* (Rome, 1930), passim.
311 Howard Colvin, *Architecture and the After-Life* (New Haven, 1991), pp. 115-117.
312 Palladio, *I quattro libri*, iv, plate 42.
313 Boethius and Ward-Perkins, *Roman and Etruscan Architecture*, pp. 503-6, and plate 265.
314 Lotz et al., *Alessi*, fig. 176.

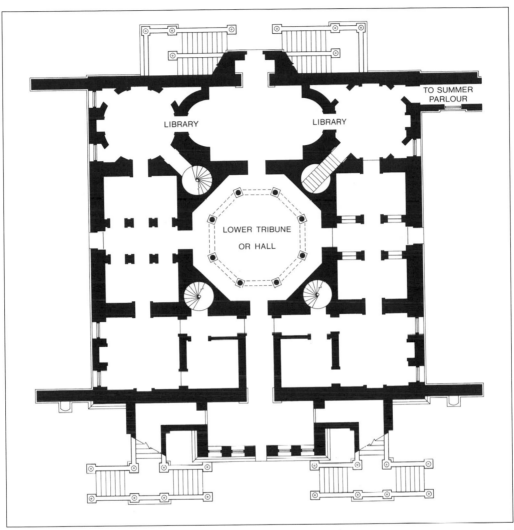

LIBRARY LIBRARY

TO SUMMER
PARLOUR

LOWER TRIBUNE

OR HALL

Fig. 21a Plan of the ground floor of Chiswick
House (*English Heritage*)

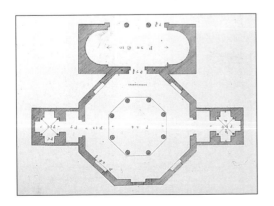

Fig. 21b Illustration by Andrea Palladio of the
plan of the Lateran Baptistry, Rome

chapel at Somerset House.[315] But a note on a sketch for the proposed Chiswick House ceiling (Fig. 22b) indicates that the 'Temple of peace at Room' (as the Basilica was then called) was Burlington's model.[316] In particular this is the name given to it in Palladio's book, which illustrates it in detail sufficient to have made a visit unnecessary.[317]

The lozenge-shaped coffering in the apses of the gallery at Chiswick (Fig. 23a) has another ancient Roman source, the Temple of Venus and Rome, which Burlington may have seen in Rome.[318] Sixteenth-century versions of this ornament are uncommon. Its earliest use since antiquity was by Bramante in the dome of Santa Maria delle Grazie, Milan.[319] Giulio Romano then used it in the Sala del Sole of the Palazzo del Te in Mantua,[320] seen and noted by William Kent.[321] Giulio used it again in the apse of S. Benedetto Po, *c.* 1540,[322] and in the Chapel of the SS. Sacramento in the Duomo of Mantua.[323] Burlington and Kent could have seen it in two places in Genoa, in the apses of the loggia of Alessi's Villa Cambiaso (1548),[324] positions which are very similar to those in which this coffering type is used at Chiswick, or in the apse of Sta Maria in Carignano, begun in 1549.[325] At almost the same time, 1549-50, Philibert de l'Orme had used it to ceil the dome of the chapel in the Châteaux of Anet,[326] which was published by Du Cerceau in 1579.[327] It was used again by Giacomo del Duca in the Capella Mattei of Sta Maria in Aracoeli in 1587,[328] but it presumably reached England by means of Du Cerceau's illustration of Anet, allowing Burlington to have seen it in Wren's St Paul's Cathedral,[329] and the apse of St Clement's Danes.[330] Hawksmoor also used it, in the Buttery of All Soul's College, but as this was built in 1730-3,[331] his inspiration could have been from Chiswick. However inspirational these examples may have been, for the detailed record necessary to recreate its complex geometry, Burlington would have had to turn to the illustrations of the ancient example (then called the Temple of the Sun and the Moon) in Palladio's book (Fig. 23b).[332]

315 Harris and Higgott, *Inigo Jones: Complete Architectural Drawings*, p. 198, fig. 58; Colvin, *King's Works*, iv, pp. 263-6.
316 Chatsworth, Devonshire Collection, album 26a, fo. 34.
317 Palladio, *I quattro libri*, iv, plates 2 and 3.
318 Boethius and Ward-Perkins, *Roman and Etruscan Architecture*, p. 502 and plate 264.
319 Adolfo Venturi, *Storia dell'arte Italiana*, viii, pt 2 (Milan, 1924), pp. 742-43.
320 Hartt, *Giulio Romano*, i, p. 108-9.
321 Sicca, 'Kent's Roman Sources', pp. 137-38.
322 Hartt, *Giulio Romano*, fig. 104.
323 Venturi, *Storia dell'arte Italiana*, xi, pt 1, p. 314,

fig. 282.
324 Ibid., figs 175-76.
325 Lotz et al., *Alessi*, plate 25.
326 Blunt, 90, fig. 60.
327 Ibid., fig. 61; Jacques Androuet du Cerceau, *Les plus excellents bastiments de France*, ii (Paris, 1579-) (unpaginated).
328 Benedetti, *Giacomo del Duca*, p. 351 and plates 290, 293, 297 and 298.
329 Downes, *Wren*, plates 132 and 134.
330 Ibid., plate 68.
331 Downes, *Hawksmoor*, p. 278, plate 50a.
332 Palladio, *I quattro libri*, iv, plate 23.

Fig. 22a Ceiling of the Saloon, Chiswick House (*English Heritage*)

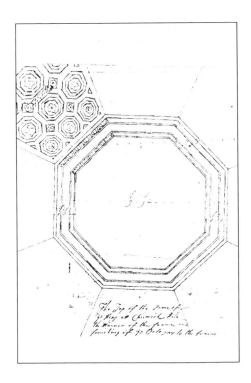

The Top of the Dome of
ye King at Chiswick Hs
ye manner of the frame and
finishing of ye Ceilon to the frame

Fig. 22b Drawing by Samuel Savill for the ceiling
of the Saloon, Chiswick House (*Chatsworth*)

Two of the most distinctive ornaments at Chiswick are the *maeander* (Greek key) (Fig. 24a) and Vitruvian scroll (Fig. 25a) set in raised bands with borders. These ornaments were known to English Mannerist architects, but in this distinctive form their use at Chiswick is the earliest in England. Burlington may have seen it *maeander* among the ruins of the Temple of Mars Ultor in Rome.[333] It is more likely that he saw it in its sixteenth-century form, on the ceiling of Raphael's third Vatican loggia,[334] for instance, or in his Chigi Chapel,[335] on the ceiling of the external *loggia* of Peruzzi's Palazzo Massimo,[336] or on the facade of Antonio da Sangallo's Zecca,[337] these last two both conspicuous Roman buildings. Kent certainly saw it in the Sala dei Cavalli of Giulio Romano's Palazzo del Te in Mantua.[338] They may both have seen it on Alessi's Palazzo Agostino Pallavicini in Genoa,[339] and if they did not, they would have seen it illustrated in Rubens' *Palazzi de Genova*, published in 1622.[340] Burlington could have seen it on Alessi's Palazzo Marini in Milan,[341] or his Palazzo Communale, Bologna.[342] The itineraries of his four visits to France are not known, but in France it was used by the unknown architect of the Château de Cormatin, where it was sketched by Jacques Gentillatre.[343] Serlio illustrated it as typical *all'antica* ornament.[344] Labacco in 1552 recorded its particular appearance at the Temple of Mars Ultor,[345] as did Freart de Chambray in 1650,[346] Desgodetz in 1682[347] and Palladio.[348] Probably it was Palladio's record illustration of this building (Fig. 24b), and of the Maison Carrée in Nîmes (Fig. 24c)[349] which Burlington made use of, although it may be noted that Freart illustrated it in ten different versions.

Burlington may also have seen Vitruvian scroll among the ruins of the Temple of Mars Ultor,[350] or on the Temple of Venus Genutrix,[351] also in

333 Boethius and Ward-Perkins, *Roman and Etruscan Architecture*, pp. 190–92.
334 Christoph Luitpold Frommel, Stefano Ray and Manfredo Tafuri, *Raffaello architetto* (Milan, 1984), p. 376.
335 Ibid., pp. 137–38.
336 Henrich Wurm, *Der Palazzo Massimo alle Colonne* (Berlin, 1965), plate 42a.
337 Portoghesi, *Rome of the Renaissance*, plate 149; Gustavo Giovannoni, *Antonio da Sangallo il Giovane*, i (Rome, 1959), pp. 297–99.
338 Hartt, *Giulio Romano*, ii, plate 179.
339 Poleggi, *Strada Nuova*, fig. 34.
340 Peter Paul Rubens, *Palazzi di Genova* (Antwerp, 1622), ii, fig. 68.
341 Lotz et al., *Alessi*, plate 36.
342 Ibid., fig. 167.

343 Rosalys Coope, *Catalogue of the Drawings Collection of the Royal Institute of British Architects: Jacques Gentilhâtre* (Farnborough, 1972), p. 26 (192v) and fig. 54.
344 Serlio, *Architecture*, pp. 69v, 70v and 71.
345 Antonio Labacco, *Appartenente a l'architettura* (Rome, 1552), p. 12.
346 Roland Fréart, sieur de Chambray, *Parallèle de l'architecture antique et de la moderne* (Paris, 1650), p. 109.
347 Antoine Desgodetz, *Les édifices antiques de Rome* (Paris, 1682), p. 146.
348 Palladio, *I quattro libri*, iv, plate 8.
349 Ibid., iv, plate 85.
350 Boethius and Ward-Perkins, *Roman and Etruscan Architecture*, pp. 190–92.
351 Ibid., 229.

Fig. 23a The apse at the east end of the Gallery, Chiswick House (*English Heritage*)

Fig. 23b Illustration by Andrea Palladio of the interior of the Temple of Venus and Rome, Rome

Rome. He (or Kent) could have seen it in its sixteenth-century form on Raphael's Palazzo Pandolfini in Florence,[352] or the Galerie Henri II at Fontainebleau, known to him from the copy of Pierre Dan, *Merveilles de* la *Maison Royale de Fontainebleau* (Paris, 1642), in his library.[353] Kent would have seen it twice in Mantua, in the Sala dei Cavalli of the Palazzo del Te,[354] and in the *loggetta* of the Palazzo Ducale.[355] They could have seen it on a sketch by Kent's travelling companion, John Talman, for a Trianon at Hampton Court.[356] But if they had not, it is shown in illustrations of the Temple of Mars Ultor published by Labacco,[357] and by Palladio (Fig. 25b).[358] The Temple of Venus Genetrix was published by Palladio (Fig. 25c), although he wrongly identified it as a temple of Neptune.[359] Serlio also published Vitruvian scroll as typical *all'antica* ornament.[360]

The soffits of the ceiling beams at Chiswick are ornamented by *guilloche* (Fig. 26a). Burlington may have seen *guilloche* on the Temple of Venus and Rome,[361] or on the Hadrianeum,[362] both in Rome. He could have seen it in its sixteenth-century form on Raphael's Chigi Chapel in Sta Maria del Popolo.[363] Kent would have seen it in Mantua, in the Sala dei Cavalli of the Palazzo del Te.[364] Burlington certainly saw it on the beam soffits in Inigo Jones' Banqueting House[365] and Queen's House,[366] which he sent Samuel Savill to sketch for him (Fig. 26b).[367] If he then needed dimensioned records, Palladio had published the Temple of Venus and Rome (Fig. 23b),[368] while Desgodetz had published the Hadrianeum (as 'The Basilica of Antoninus').[369] Serlio published *guilloche* too as typical *all'antica* ornament.[370]

As well as building a new house, Burlington also altered the front elevation of the house which he had inherited at Chiswick (Fig. 27a). By *c.* 1729-32 he had added a *serliana* and a Diocletian window (features which the

352 Angelo Calvani, *Raffaello e l'architettura a Firenze* (Florence, 1984), plates 2, 4, 5, 6 and 9.
353 Anthony Blunt, *Philibert de l'Orme* (London, 1958), plate 41. Chatsworth, Devonshire Collection, MS 'Catalogue of the Earl of Burlington's Library', p. 51.
354 Hartt, *Giulio Romano*, i, pp. 112-15; ii, plate 179.
355 Ibid., i, p. 169; ii, plate 356.
356 Harris, *Talman*, plate 40.
357 Labacco, *Libro appartenente a l'architettura*, ii.
358 Palladio, *I quattro libri*, iv, plate 10.
359 Ibid., iv, plate 97.
360 Serlio, *Architecture*, iv, pp. 40 and 71.
361 Boethius and Ward-Perkins, *Roman and Etruscan Architecture*, p. 502.

362 Ibid., p. 267.
363 Frommel, Ray and Tafuri, *Raffaelo architetto*, p. 138.
364 Hartt, *Giulio Romano*, i, pp. 112-15; ii, plate 179.
365 Per Palme, *Triumph of Peace* (Stockholm, 1956), plates iii and vii.
366 George H. Chettle, *The Queen's House, Greenwich*, London Survey Committee Monograph 14 (London, 1937), plates 44, 45, 47, 62, 63 and 64.
367 Chatsworth, Devonshire Collection, Lord Burlington's architectural drawings, Boy 3.
368 Palladio, *I quattro libri*, iv, plate 23.
369 Desgodetz, *Les édifices antiques de Rome*, p. 155.
370 Serlio, *Architecture*, iv, pp. 68 and 71.

Fig. 24a The top of one of the gatepiers to the forecourt of Chiswick House (*English Heritage*)

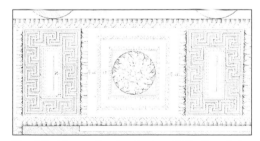

Fig. 24b Illustration by Andrea Palladio of the ceiling of the colonnade of the Temple of Mars Ultor, Rome

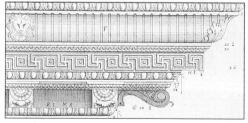

Fig. 24c Illustration by Andrea Palladio of the cornice of the Maison Carrée, Nîmes

Fig. 25a Detail of the north perron of Chiswick House (*English Heritage*)

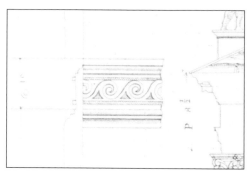

Fig. 25b Illustration by Andrea Palladio of the dado rail of the Temple of Mars Ultor, Rome

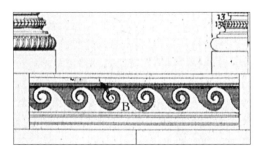

Fig. 25c Illustration by Palladio of the dado rail of the Temple of Venus Genutrix, Rome

Fig. 26a Ceiling of the Red Velvet Room, Chiswick House (*English Heritage*)

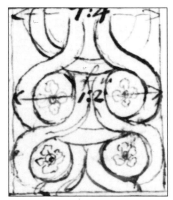

Fig. 26b Detail of drawing by Samuel Savill of the ceiling of the Hall of the Queen's House, Greenwich (*Chatsworth*)

new house also possessed), and had surmounted these with a pediment which was open on its lower side.[371] Between 1727 and *c.* 1733 he also added a porch to the rear of the round (Ionic) temple:[372] this porch also has a pediment which is open on its lower side (Fig. 27b). Open pediments of various types were an ancient Roman invention. Serlio, who did not approve, recorded one grudgingly on the road to Foligno.[373] The type favoured by modern followers was supported on pilasters, columns or occasionally brackets, and usually framed an opening. This type was used by Bramante in Sta Maria presso St. Satiro, Milan, both in the Capella della Pieta, and at the east end.[374] It was used by Giulio on the Palazzo Maccarani, Rome,[375] on the Palazzo del Te[376] and on his own house in Mantua.[377] It was used by Palladio on the Villa Barbaro at Maser.[378] It was used by Antonio de Sangallo the younger on the Palazzo Farnese.[379] It was used by Michelangelo on the Palazzo dei Conservatori, Rome,[380] and on the Medici Chapel in S. Lorenzo, Florence.[381] It was used by Francesco Maria Ricchino on the Collegio Elvetico, Milan,[382] by Giacomo del Duca on Sta Maria di Loreto, Rome,[383] and by Maderno to frame some of the first floor windows on the west front of St Peter's, Rome.[384] It was used by Bernini as a gable pediment at Sta Bibiana, Rome.[385] It was used by Borromini at the Oratorio of S. Filippo Neri,[386] on the altarpiece of SS. Apostoli, Naples,[387] on the façade of the Sapienza,[388] inside the dome of S. Ivo,[389] inside S. Giovanni Laterano,[390] in the Palazzo Pamphili,[391] and on the Collegio di Propaganda Fide.[392] It was used by Inigo Jones at St Paul's Cathedral.[393] It

371 Chatsworth, Devonshire Collection, Inventory of Paintings, no. 333, view of Chiswick House from the south, complementary to those illustrated in Harris, *Artist and Country House*, 182–83, and thus dated *c.* 1729–32; for the dating, see Spence, 'Chiswick House and its Garden, 1726-32', p. 531.
372 William Kent, *The Designs of Inigo Jones* (London, 1727), p. 73, illustrates a plan of this Temple with no rear porch. The rear porch is first illustrated by Rigaud *c.* 1733, Carré, 'Rigaud's Drawings of Chiswick', p. 137, fig. 3.
373 Serlio, *Architecture*, iii, 25v, fig. c.
374 Venturi, *Storia dell'arte Italiana*, viii, pt 2, p. 704, fig. 646; Bruschi, *Bramante*, plate 34.
375 Heydenreich and Lotz, *Architecture in Italy*, plate 229; Christoph Luitpold Frommel, *Der römische Palastbau der Hochrenaissance* (Rome, 1973), ii, pp. 322-26 ; Hartt, *Giulio Romano*, ii, plate 123.
376 Hartt, *Giulio Romano*, ii, plate 156.
377 Ibid., ii, plates 486 and 487; Kurt W. Forster and Richard J. Tuttle, 'The Casa Pippi', *Architectura* (1973), pp. 104-30.
378 Puppi, *Andrea Palladio*, pp. 314-18 and plates

144–47, 150–51 and 411.
379 Heydenreich and Lotz, *Architecture in Italy*, plates 212 and 213.
380 Portoghesi, *Rome of the Renaissance*, plates 394 and 398.
381 Ackerman, *The Architecture of Michelangelo*, plate 31.
382 Rudolph Wittkower, *Art and Architecture in Italy, 1600-1750* (Harmondsworth, 1973), plate 58.
383 Benedetti, *Giacomo del Duca*, plates 89, 106 and 118.
384 Hibbard, *Carlo Maderno*, plates 56, 57b and 57d.
385 Wittkower, *Art and Architecture*, plate 95.
386 Anthony Blunt, *Borromini* (Cambridge, MA, and London, 1979), plate 24.
387 Ibid., plate 78.
388 Ibid., plate 80.
389 Ibid., plates 87 and 90.
390 Ibid., plate 98.
391 Ibid., plate 128.
392 Ibid., plate 139.
393 Harris and Higgott, *Inigo Jones: Complete Architectural Drawings*, p. 247.

was used by Wren at St Michael Bassishaw[394] and at St Swithin,[395] both in the City of London. It was used by Hawksmoor at Christ's Hospital Writing School,[396] at Easton Neston,[397], and in drawings for Greenwich Chapel,[398] All Souls College,[399] St George's Bloomsbury,[400] and a gate for Blenheim.[401] It was used by Talman at Drayton[402] and in the greenhouse at Bretby.[403]

But Burlington's open pediments are more distinctive. They have no supporting members and they do not frame openings. Palladio had designed pediments of this type. Burlington had seen one at the Villa Foscari at Malcontenta,[404] and he owned two of Palladio's drawings illustrating such pediments. One is a proposal for the Villa Valmarana at Vigardolo,[405] and another is the drawing with the three *serlianas*, which also has three such pediments in a row (Fig. 3b).[406] Palladio's Villa Pojana also has this pediment type, and that was illustrated in Palladio's book.[407] It was not unique to Palladio in the sixteenth century. Primaticcio's Grotte des Pins at Fontainebleau has it,[408] and, since that is reflected in Kent's Venus Vale at Rousham,[409] it was evidently known to Kent and Burlington. Wren used it in the design for the west front of St Paul's which was engraved by Simon Gribelin in 1702.[410] Hawksmoor used it more often, at Kensington Orangery in 1704-5,[411] Kensington Charity School in 1711-12,[412] and the Carrmire Gate at Castle Howard;[413] and in drawings for The Queen's College, Oxford,[414] the Radcliffe Library,[415] St Mary Woolnoth,[416] and St Giles in the Fields.[417] The pediment type was used by the Board of Ordnance, possibly following Hawksmoor's designs,[418] for the south entrance to Dial Square, Woolwich in 1717,[419] the frontispiece of the Royal Military Academy,

394　Downes, *Wren*, plate 95.
395　Ibid., plate 93.
396　Downes, *Hawksmoor*, plate 1b.
397　Ibid., plate 6b.
398　Ibid., plates 26a and b.
399　Ibid., plate 42b.
400　Ibid., plate 68a.
401　Ibid., plate 80.
402　Harris, *Talman*, plate 39.
403　Ibid., plate 83.
404　Puppi, *Andrea Palladio*, pp. 328-30 and plates 137-38 and 140-41; Chatsworth, Devonshire Collection, Library, Lord Burlington's annotated copy of Palladio's *I quattro libri*, ii, p. 50, reveals that he had seen the Villa Foscari.
405　London, British Architectural Library, Drawings Collection, Burlington-Devonshire Collection, xvii, 2.
406　Ibid., xvii, 15.
407　Puppi, *Andrea Palladio*, pp. 273-76 and plates 84-87; Palladio, *I quattro libri*, ii, plate 41.

408　Anthony Blunt, *Art and Architecture in France*, plate 65.
409　Margaret Jourdain, *The Work of William Kent* (London, 1948), p. 158, fig. 109.
410　Beard, *The Work of Christopher Wren*, plate 94.
411　Downes, *Hawksmoor*, plate 21b.
412　Downes, *English Baroque Architecture*, plate 504.
413　Ibid., plate 91c.
414　Ibid., plates 28a and 29b.
415　Ibid., plate 38b.
416　Ibid., plate 73b.
417　Ibid., plates 76a and b.
418　Richard Hewlings, 'Hawksmoor's Brave Designs for the Police', in John Bold and Edward Chaney (eds), *English Architecture: Public and Private* (London and Rio Grande, OH, 1993), pp. 226-27.
419　Lawrence Whistler, *The Imagination of Sir John Vanbrugh and his Fellow Artists* (London, 1954), figs 105 and 106.

Fig. 27a Painting by Pieter Andreas Rysbrack of Chiswick House and old Chiswick House from the south (*Chatsworth; photo, English Heritage*)

Fig. 27b The porch added on the south (rear) side of the Ionic Temple at Chiswick (*English Heritage*)

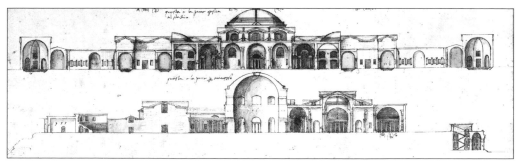

Fig. 27c Drawing by Andrea Palladio of the Baths of Diocletian, Rome (*RIBA*)

Woolwich, in 1718,[420] and the officers' houses at Morice Yard, Plymouth, between 1720 and 1725.[421] Vanbrugh or William Etty used it for the towers of Morpeth Town Hall in 1714.[422]

Palladio's book makes it apparent that this pediment type was not his invention, for it shows it on the Temple of Venus and Rome.[423] Furthermore Burlington's collection of Palladio's record drawings made it clear to him that such pediments, although unusual on temples, were common on at least one type of ancient secular building. These drawings illustrate them on the Baths of Constantine,[424] Titus,[425] Nero,[426] Trajan,[427] Diocletian (Fig. 27c),[428] Caracalla[429] and Agrippa.[430] It is not possible to determine with certainty whether Burlington was more inspired by these seven ancient baths than by Palladio's versions of the same features; but he probably was.

The deerhouse at Chiswick has doors which taper inwards as they rise (Fig. 28a). Burlington could have observed this feature on the windows of Michelangelo's Sforza Chapel in Sta Maria Maggiore, in Rome,[431] or on the windows of his New Sacristy at S. Lorenzo in Florence.[432] Had he penetrated the Vatican Palace, he would have noted the tapered door designed by Antonio da Sangallo the younger in the Sala Regia, leading to the Scala Regia.[433] In Genoa he may have seen the tapering doors in the *salone* and loggia of Alessi's Villa Cambiaso.[434] In Bologna he could have seen a tapering door in the first court of Alessi's Palazzo Communale.[435] A sketch by John Talman reveals that Burlington was not the first Englishman to have observed this feature.[436] It was recorded as ancient in both the Codex Coner[437] and the Codex Corsiniana.[438] Riniero Neruccio da Pisa recorded a

420 Ibid., figs 101, 102 and 103.
421 Jonathan G. Coad, *The Royal Dockyards, 1690-1850* (Aldershot, 1989), plate 198.
422 Downes, *English Baroque Architecture*, plate 494. The building is attributed to Vanbrugh in all published accounts of it, but Vanbrugh's name is not mentioned in the building accounts (Durham, University of Durham, Department of Palaeography and Diplomatic, Howard of Naworth Papers, Northumberland estate, N108/13). William Etty is mentioned, however.
423 Palladio, *I quattro libri*, iv, plate 22.
424 London, British Architectural Library, Drawings Collection, Burlington-Devonshire Collection, i, 3.
425 Ibid., ii, 2 and 6.
426 Ibid., iii, 2, 3, 5, 6, 7 and 8.
427 Ibid., iv, 3 and 4.
428 Ibid., v, 2, 6 and 7.
429 Ibid, vi, 4 and 7.
430 Ibid., vii, 3 and 6.
431 Ackerman, *The Architecture of Michelangelo*, plates 119 and 120.

432 Ibid., fig. 20.
433 Lotz et al., *Alessi*, fig. 160. Antonio also proposed a similar doorway for his own house in Florence; his drawing is illustrated in Gustavo Giovannoni, *Antonio da Sangallo il Giovane*, i, fig. 48. Venturi, *Storia dell'arte Italiana*, viii, pt 1, illustrates two similar doorways in Siena, both attributed to Giacomo Cozzarelli; they are in the Palazzo Petrucci (ibid., p. 888, fig. 677) and the Convento dell'Osservanza (ibid., p. 891, fig. 680). But it is not quite clear from these photographs whether the doors really taper, or whether they appear to do so from the camera angle.
434 Lotz et al., *Alessi*, pp. 161 and 165.
435 Ibid., fig. 164.
436 Harris, *Talman*, fig. 4.
437 T. Ashby, junior, 'Sixteenth-Century Drawings of Roman Buildings Attributed to Andreas Coner', *Papers of the British School at Rome*, ii (1904), pp. 28-29 and plate 32.
438 Hubertus Günther, *Das Studium der Antiken Architektur in den Zeichnungen der Hoch Renaissance* (Tübingen, 1988), fig. 57.

Fig. 28a The deerhouse, Chiswick (*English Heritage*)

Fig. 28b Illustration by Palladio of the door of the Temple of Vesta at Tivoli

door of this type in the Constantinian Basilica of St Peter.[439] Giovanni Battista da Sangallo, author of the Codex Corsiniana, included it in a drawing of a Tuscan temple after Vitruvius. Serlio reproduced it and regarded it as Doric.[440] Palladio recorded it on the Temple of Vesta at Tivoli, which is Corinthian (Fig. 28b).[441] The deerhouse doors at Chiswick follow the illustration in Palladio's book.

Burlington used other architectural books besides Palladio's. Indeed he would have had to if he used any architectural books at all before 1719, because only on 3 November of that year, when in Vicenza, did he buy the first of his twelve copies of Palladio.[442] He also possessed architectural and antiquarian books by Alberti, Labacco, Serlio, Shute, Vignola, De l'Orme, Boissard, Scamozzi, Rusconi, Francini, Bullant, Pirro Ligorio, Fanelli, Rossi, Montano, Desgodetz, Blondel, De Caus, Silvestre, Montfaucon and Villalpando.[443] Serlio and Desgodetz in particular illustrated the same ancient features as Palladio: it is thus difficult to determine which was his particular instructor in these matters. But emphases give an indication. The oak leaf swags in the Bedchamber at Chiswick (Fig. 29a), for instance, have an ancient precedent in the frieze of the Temple of Portumnus, illustrated by both Palladio[444] and Desgodetz (Fig. 43c).[445] They also occur in the 'tombeau vulgairement dit de Bacchus' in the Temple of Bacchus at Rome, which is only illustrated by Desgodetz (Fig. 29b).[446] Perhaps, in these circumstances, it was Desgodetz's mediation which was critical for this feature.

Desgodetz's book may have furnished the critical authority for another feature, the festoons suspended at capital level (not at the less noticeable frieze level) in his design for the Orangery (Fig. 4a).[447] They presumably derive from garlands of actual foliage suspended between temple columns at festivals. Burlington's awareness of its primitive origins is indicated by his possession of a Kent sketch for a rustic shrine garlanded in this way.[448] Garlands of this type in petrified form were recorded on the portico of the Temple of Castor and Pollux at Naples by Francisco d'Olanda in the mid 16th century,[449] and were therefore known in the Renaissance. They were

439   Ibid., fig. 55 and 59.
440   Serlio, *Architecture*, iv, p. 20.
441   Palladio, *I quattro libri*, iv, plate 68.
442   Philip Ayres, 'Burlington's Library at Chiswick', p. 117.
443   Ibid., supplemented by Chatsworth, Devonshire Collection, Library, MS 'Catalogue of the Earl of Burlington's Library'.
444   Palladio, *I quattro libri*, iv, plates 32-33, as the Temple of Fortuna Virilis, as it was then

known.
445   Desgodetz, *Les édifices antiques de Rome*, p. 103.
446   Ibid., p. 73.
447   Chatsworth, Devonshire Collection, Lord Burlington's architectural drawings, Boy 8, p. 39.
448   Dixon Hunt, *William Kent*, p. 132, no 43.
449   Edward Chaney, 'Inigo Jones in Naples', in Bold and Chaney, *English Architecture: Public and Private*, p. 43, fig. 15.

Fig. 29a An overdoor in the Bedchamber, Chiswick House (*English Heritage*)

Fig. 29b Illustration by Antoine Desgodetz of the 'tomb commonly called Bacchus's' in the Temple of Bacchus, Rome

revived by Bramante for the Sacra Casa at Loreto in 1509,[450] of which Burlington owned engravings.[451] They were also used by Raphael in the Chigi Chapel of Sta Maria del Popolo, *c.* 1513,[452] by Giulio Romano in the Sala dei Cavalli of the Palazzo del Te in 1527-35,[453] by Sanmichele on the facade of the Palazzo Bevilacqua, Verona, *c.* 1530,[454] by Guidetto Guidetti on the façade of Sta Caterina dei Funari, Rome in 1560-4,[455] by Michelangelo in Sta Maria degli Angeli, Rome, in 1561,[456] and by Martino Longhi the elder in S. Maria della Consolazione, Rome. Giuseppe Valeriano used them on the façade if S. Ambrogio, the Jesuit church in Genoa, which was illustrated by Rubens in his *Palazzi di Genova*.[457] Burlington may have seen the modern Roman examples and probably (though not certainly) passed through Verona. Kent would have seen those in Mantua. They appealed to Palladio also, who suspended them between the capitals of the Tempietto of the Villa Barbaro, Maser,[458] and those of the Palazzo da Porto-Breganze in Vicenza.[459] Burlington did not see the former, but may have seen the latter, during his fleeting visit to Vicenza in 1719.[460] But he would have had to remember them because neither the Tempietto at Maser nor the Palazzo da Porto-Breganze are illustrated in Palladio's book.

What is more likely to have influenced him is Inigo Jones' Banqueting House, of which he possessed drawings.[461] So would Webb's King Charles Block at Greenwich, for which drawings in his possession proposed festoons between the capitals of internal doors,[462] and Wilton, where similar festoons were placed in the Double Cube Room.[463] The prominence and authority of the Banqueting House would undoubtedly have engaged Burlington's attention, but the authoritative example of Jones was numerically eclipsed by examples designed by Wren. Wren hung festoons between

450 Heydenreich and Lotz, *Architecture in Italy*, p. 163 and plate 166.

451 Chatsworth, Devonshire Collection, Lord Burlington's architectural drawings, Boy 32.5 and 32.6; ibid., album 26a, no. 58.

452 Frommel, Ray and Tafuri, *Raffaelo architetto*, pp. 139-41.

453 Hartt, *Giulio Romano*, i, pp. 112-15; ii, plate 180.

454 Eric Langenskiold, *Michele Sanmichele* (Uppsala, 1938), pp. 61-68 and plate 21.

455 Giovanni Antonio Dosio, *Roma antica e i disegni di architettura agli Uffizi*, ed. Franco Borsi catalogue, (1976), p. 258; Josephine von Henneberg, 'An Early Work by Giacomo della Porta: The Oratorio del Santissimo Crocifisso di San Marcello in Rome', *Art Bulletin*, 52, June 1970, pp. 165-67, and plates 2 and 6; Venturi, *Storia dell'arte Italiana*, xi, pt 2, p. 934,

fig. 859.

456 Ackerman, *The Architecture of Michelangelo*, plate 136.

457 Venturi, *Storia dell'arte Italiana*, xi, pt 2, p. 857, fig. 795. Rubens, *Palazzi di Genova*, i, fig. 65.

458 Puppi, *Andrea Palladio*, pp. 433-35 and plates 257, 258 and 260-64.

459 Ibid., pp. 395-96 and plates 561-62.

460 Narford, Fountaine MSS, Letters, 6 November 1719.

461 Harris and Higgott, *Inigo Jones: Complete Architectural Drawings*, pp. 111, 113, 114, 115, 119, 121 and 123.

462 John Harris, *Catalogue of the Drawings Collection of the Royal Institute of British Architects: Inigo Jones and John Webb* (Farnborough, 1972), p. 24 (no. 150) and fig. 149.

463 John Bold, *Wilton House and English Palladianism* (London, 1988), p. 54, plate 65.

Fig. 30 Illustration by Antoine Desgodetz of the Arco Boario, Rome

Corinthian capitals in four separate parts of St Paul's Cathedral – on the west front, on the transept terminals, on the solid parts of the dome peristyle, and (inside) on the organ screen.[464] He placed them prominently on the east frontispiece of Hampton Court Palace,[465] on the east end of St Lawrence Jewry,[466] and (on paper alone) on his proposed Mausoleum for Charles I.[467] Furthermore he designed two buildings which combined festoons between their capitals with other features of Burlington's Orangery. At Emmanuel College, Cambridge, they are suspended between the capitals of a giant tetrastyle applied portico almost identical to the Orangery and, like the latter, without the high pedestals of Palladio's S. Giorgio.[468] At the Sheldonian Theatre, Oxford, they are part of single-storey tetrastyle applied portico, which is not the same as the Orangery's, but it stands between lower wings which are surmounted by half-pediments,[469] as the Orangery does.

Illustrations were less abundant. The only *aide-memoires* which Palladio offered him were two illustrations of the Palazzo Thiene,[470] a building visited and greatly admired by Burlington,[471] where in fact the festoons, although included in the book, were omitted from the building.[472] Nor did Palladio teach Burlington that it was authentically ancient practice to apply these festoons in this position. Palladio illustrated their ancient use three times in his book, in a hypothetical reconstruction of the Temple of Mars,[473] in an idealised illustration of a Corinthian Hall[474] and in the upper storey of his idealised Egyptian Hall.[475] In all three cases they are internal and the Corinthian columns from which they are suspended are set on high pedestals. In the Chiswick design they are external and the pedestals have been removed. If Burlington thought this authentically ancient, he did so despite Palladio's indications to the contrary. But Palladio's illustrations were all hypotheses.[476] Desgodetz alone illustrated its actual ancient use, on the Arco Boario in Rome,[477] and it is doubtless this illustration which was critical (Fig. 30).

Burlington appears also to have supplemented use of Desgodetz's book with Montfaucon's. One of the avenues of the *patte d'oie* north of the house

464 Downes, *Wren*, plates 80, 81, 138, 141 and 145.
465 Ibid., plate 147.
466 Ibid., plate 33.
467 Ibid., plate 74.
468 Ibid., plates 12 and 18.
469 Ibid., plate 9.
470 Palladio, *I quattro libri*, ii, plates 9 and 10.
471 Chatsworth, Devonshire Collection, Library, Lord Burlington's annotated edition of Palladio's *I quattro libri*, ii, chapter 3, interleaved

page opposite p. 14 ('the most beautiful modern building in the world').
472 Puppi, *Andrea Palladio*, pp. 251-54 and plates 49-50.
473 Palladio, *I quattro libri*, iv, plate 40.
474 Ibid., ii, plate 27.
475 Ibid., ii, plate 28.
476 Ibid.
477 Desgodetz, *Les édifices antiques de Rome*, p. 217.

led to a Doric column carrying a version of the Venus de' Medici (Fig. 31a): its earliest dated illustration falls between 1729 and 1732.[478] Stylite statues are rare but distinctive ancient civic ornament. Burlington would have seen the Columns of Trajan and Marcus Aurelius in Rome. Trajan's Column originally carried a statue of Trajan, but this had been lost by the time Etienne du Perac recorded it in 1575.[479] Sixtus V replaced it with a statue of St Peter, and placed a statue of St Paul on the Column of Marcus Aurelius;[480] so by the time of Burlington's visit both columns would have carried stylite statues again. In Venice Burlington would have seen the two Byzantine columns in the Piazzetta, one carrying St Theodore and the other St Mark's lion.[481] The concept survived the middle ages and can be seen in reduced form as heraldic beasts on posts in, for instance, the Privy Garden at Whitehall Palace.[482] But this was probably unknown to Burlington, as was the early revival of the prototypical form. For example, there was a sixteenth century stylite statue bearing a lion of St Mark outside the church of S. Giovanni in Udine,[483] a place neither Burlington nor Kent are known to have visited. John, Lord Lumley, built a correct Doric column at Nonsuch surmounted by a sphere and a popinjay, his badge, between 1579 and 1592:[484] it was destroyed in the 1650s. The collector Earl of Arundel had a statue on a Corinthian column, also destroyed before Burlington could have seen it.[485] The only modern stylite statue which he may have seen was in the Piazza Ariostea, Ferrara, which he must have passed through *en route* from Bologna to Padua in 1715.[486] Here one column of a proposed triumphal arch in honour of Ercole I d'Este had been erected alone in 1503, then surmounted by a statue of Alexander VII in the seventeenth century.[487] But the idea was in the course of revival in England in Burlington's early lifetime. Wren had proposed a stylite statue for the Monument.[488] It was not built, but an engraved view of Wren's design with a stylite state of Charles II was published by Hawksmoor in 1723.[489] Gibbs, Hawksmoor and Archer designed stylite statues of Queen Anne for the Strand in 1714.[490]

478 Harris, *Artist and the Country House*, pp. 158 and 183, fig. 187h; for dating evidence, see Spence, 'Chiswick House and its Gardens, 1726-32', p. 531.

479 Nash, *Pictorial Dictionary of Ancient Rome*, i, 283-86.

480 Ibid., pp. 276-79.

481 Hugh Honour, *The Companion Guide to Venice* (London, 1990), p. 29.

482 Strong, *The Renaissance Garden*, p. 35 and fig. 13.

483 Venturi, *Storia dell'arte Italiana*, xi, pt. 2, p. 347, fig. 318.

484 Ibid., p. 64, figs 31 and 32.

485 David Howarth, *Lord Arundel and his Circle* (New Haven, 1985), p. 96.

486 Chatsworth, Devonshire Collection, Lord Burlington's Grand Tour Account Book.

487 Venturi, *Storia dell'arte Italiana*, viii, pt 2, pp. 446-47, and fig. 428.

488 *The Wren Society*, 5 (1928), plate xxxvii.

489 Ibid., 18 (1941), plate xviii.

490 Friedman, *James Gibbs*, pp. 307-8.

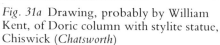

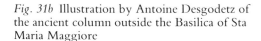

Fig. 31a Drawing, probably by William
Kent, of Doric column with stylite statue,
Chiswick (*Chatsworth*)

Fig. 31c Illustration by Bernard de
Montfaucon of the Columns of Trajan,
Antoninus Pius and Caius Duilius in Rome

Fig. 31b Illustration by Antoine Desgodetz of
the ancient column outside the Basilica of Sta
Maria Maggiore

Fig. 31d Illustration by Bernard de Montfaucon of the Hippodrome in Constantinople, with the
Columns of Theodosius and Arcadius in the middle of it

Fig. 32 The south door on the ground floor of Chiswick House (*English Heritage*)

Hawksmoor proposed a stylite statue of Queen Anne outside St Michael Cornhill in 1714,[491] and another of the duke of Marlborough at Blenheim *c.* 1724:[492] Burlington may have known of these. The exact date of his own Doric column is not known, so it may have been preceded by Prince George's Column at Stowe, which was noted by Lord Perceval in 1724.[493] However, it may have preceded the earliest surviving British example, Lord Pembroke's and Roger Morris' monument to the Duke of Marlborough at Blenheim in 1730,[494] and certainly preceded the next, Gibbs' to William III at Hartwell in 1735.[495] Burlington's inspiration may therefore have been relatively modern. But had he needed graphic authority, as he usually did, he would have found it in his copy of Desgodetz's book, which illustrates the ancient Corinthian column in front of Sta Maria Maggiore, Rome (Fig. 31b).[496] He would have found it more profusely in his copy of Montfaucon's book, which illustrates the stylite statues on the Columns of Trajan and of Antoninus Pius, on the Rostral Column of Caius Duilius,[497] all in Rome (Fig. 31c), and on the Columns of Theodosius and Arcadius in the Hippodrome in Constantinople (Fig. 31d).[498]

Study of the Column of Antoninus in Montfaucon's book would have introduced him to another feature which it is unlikely he saw elsewhere. The exterior of Chiswick House has a plinth distinctive by both its projection (1 foot) and its height (2 feet) (Fig. 32). It is particularly distinctive beneath the portico, since it is surmounted by vermiculated rustic masonry whose functional metaphor (of a rocky foundation) is diminished by the existence of any plinth at all. Attention is directed to the plinth by the entrance door, which abruptly sections it, without the interposition of any framing member. Doors which interrupt plinths usually have an architrave, projecting as far as or further than the plinth, allowing the later to butt against them. The pedestal of Trajan's Column has a door cutting through an equally substantial plinth.[499] The proportional relationship of door and plinth is similar to that at Chiswick and, in general terms, either the sight of Trajan's Column or its illustration by Antonio Labacco[500] might have been the inspiration for the basement door at Chiswick. But the detail differs in one particular; the door into the pedestal

491   Downes, *Hawksmoor*, p. 277 and plate 79b.
492   Ibid., p. 208.
493   M.J. Gibbon, 'The History of Stowe – XI', *The Stoic*, 24, no. 4, 1971, p. 171.
494   David Green, 'Blenheim Column of Victory', *Architectural Review*, 107, April 1950, pp. 271-74.
495   Friedman, *James Gibbs*, p. 292.
496   Desgodetz, *Les édifices antiques de Rome*, p. 107.

497   Bernard de Montfaucon, *Antiquity Explained and Represented in Sculptures*, trans. David Humphreys (London, 1721), iv, plate 38.
498   Ibid., iii, plate 50.
499   Nash, *Pictorial Dictionary of Ancient Rome*, i, pp. 283-86 and fig. 337.
500   Labacco, *Libro appartenente a l'architettura*, plate 7.

Fig. 33a An overdoor in the Blue Velvet Room, Chiswick House (*English Heritage*)

Fig. 33b Drawing by Inigo Jones for a doorway in the Queen's Cabinet Room, Somerset House (*RIBA*)

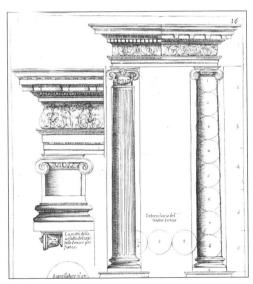

Fig. 33c A doorway in the Bedchamber, Chiswick House (*English Heritage*)

Fig. 33d Illustration by Giovanni–Battista Montano of an ancient frieze of *cyma recta* profile

Fig. 34a Illustration by Giovanni-
Battista Montano of an ancient
mausoleum 'outside the Porta di
San Sebastiano', Rome

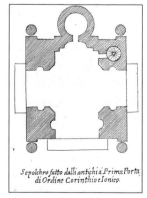

Sepolchro fatto dalli antichi à Prima Porta
di Ordine Corinthio e Ionico.

Fig. 34b Illustration by Giovanni-Battista
Montano of an ancient mausoleum

of Trajan's Column has a moulded architrave. Burlington would have had difficulty in finding any ancient doors interrupting plinths without an architrave, save in Montfaucon's book, where his illustration of the Column of Antoninus, rather than that of Trajan, shows a door at the base of the column which appears to be a model for the ground floor door of Chiswick House.[501]

In addition he used Giovanni-Battista Montano's book of 1684. The internal ornament at Chiswick is the least apparently ancient. For instance, the Blue Velvet Room (Fig. 33a) and Bedchamber doors (Fig. 33c) appear to be early seventeenth century in character. Yet they are ultimately derived from Montano, but at second-hand, altered from Montano's prototype by the mediation of Inigo Jones. They are copied directly from another Jones drawing in Burlington's possession (Fig. 33b) This drawing shows a proposed door for the Queen's Cabinet Room at Somerset House.[502] This room had been altered by Jones in 1628-30, but had retained some of its previous decoration of 1613-14,[503] including (presumably) its former proportions. Doors within a room of such consequence evidently required pediments, but to fit these into a predetermined space Jones apparently had to contract the pediments so that they were no wider overall than the architraved doors which they surmounted. The reduction of width was achieved in the friezes. Instead of being rectangular, the frieze in the drawing has ends of *cyma reversa* profile, so that the top of the frieze, whence springs the pediment, is narrower than the bottom. An ancient precedent for a frieze of *cyma reversa* profile was recorded by Giovanni Battista Montano, although not published until 1684 (Fig. 33d).[504] Jones may have known Montano's sources; but the ancient frieze is not narrower at the top than at the bottom, and that contribution may have been Jones'. Burlington, who had Montano's book,[505] could therefore be confident of the ancient origin of this feature, without needing to know the ancient prototype.

Montano also influenced Burlington directly, without Jones' mediation, in the choice of plans. The Casina (Fig. 18a), built in 1717[506] and demolished in 1778,[507] although a conflation of several sources, owes its plan at least to an ancient building. It was the largest of the garden buildings. It housed four

501 Montfaucon, *Antiquity Explained*, iv, plate 38.
502 Harris and Higgott, *Inigo Jones: Complete Architectural Drawings*, p. 195.
503 Colvin, *King's Works*, iv, 262.
504 Montano, *Architettura con diversi ornamenti*, i, p. 16.
505 Chatsworth, Devonshire Collection, Library,

MS 'Catalogue of the Earl of Burlington's Library', p. 4.
506 Campbell, *Vitruvius Britannicus*, iii (1725), plate 26.
507 Chatsworth, Devonshire Collection, C171, Account Book 1770-83, fo. 115, 27 November 1778.

rooms on the ground floor, two in the centre, and two in one-storey wings; the centre projects on the rear elevation, and in its centre a newel stair projects still further.[508] The first floor could either have had one large banqueting or prospect room, or it could have had two rooms, partitioned as on the floor below. This generous accommodation therefore suggests that it was the building which was described in 1728 as 'used as a room in which Lord Burlington composes drawings – being extremely fond of architecture'.[509] Functionally, therefore, it is in the native tradition of banqueting or prospect houses, and indeed the *serliana* on its south elevation would have given a wide view of the Thames.

Its external ornament, apart from the lantern (which is discussed above), was not individual enough to be recognisable as a version of any particular earlier building: all the details can be found among Jones' Whitehall Palace designs,[510] but on many other buildings also. Its plan, however, is highly individual. Far from resembling that of other prospect towers, it more closely resembles those of the ancient sepulchral buildings illustrated by Giovanni-Battista Montano. The staged diminution towards the rear resembles the mausoleum outside the Porta di San Sebastiano, Rome (Fig. 34a).[511] The newel stair appended to the rear gives it a plan similar to the mausoleum on Montano's succeeding plate (Fig. 34b).[512]

Serlio's book also provided information on features of ancient origin at Chiswick which may otherwise have been inspired by modern versions. Chiswick has, for instance, two obelisks in the garden (Fig. 35a). Palladio did not design any obelisks. Burlington must have seen ancient obelisks, re-erected in sixteenth-century Rome. If these were not sufficient inspiration, he is likely to have seen modern examples in his native county of Yorkshire. The earliest giant isolated obelisk then (as now) standing in England was designed by Hawksmoor for the market place of Ripon.[513] The next was designed by Vanbrugh for Castle Howard.[514] It is possible that Burlington also knew of Hawksmoor's particular interest in obelisks, as conspicuous examples of the ancient ornament which Burlington also was evidently keen to emulate. No doubt he would have been unable to do so without

508   Campbell, *Vitruvius Britannicus*, iii, plate 26.
509   London, Victoria and Albert Museum, MS 86NN2, Pierre-Jacques Fougeroux, 'Voyage d'Angleterre, d'Hollande et de Flandre' (1728).
510   J.A. Gotch, 'The Original Drawings for the Palace at Whitehall, Attributed to Inigo Jones', *Architectural Review*, 31, June 1912, pp. 333-64; Margaret Whinney, 'John Webb's Drawings

for Whitehall Palace', *Walpole Society*, 31, pp. 45-107.
511   Montano, *Architettura con diversi ornamenti*, iii, p. 22.
512   Ibid., p. 23.
513   Richard Hewlings, 'Ripon's Forum Populi', *Architectural History*, 24 (1981), pp. 39-52.
514   Charles Saumarez Smith, *The Building of Castle Howard* (London, 1990), p. 132 and plate 33.

Fig. 35a Obelisk and Ionic Temple in the Orange Tree Garden, Chiswick (*English Heritage*)

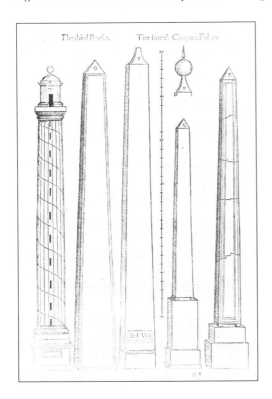

Fig. 35b Illustration by Sebastiano
Serlio of ancient obelisks

graphic assistance. He found this is Serlio's book, where the ancient Roman obelisks were illustrated (Fig. 35b).[515]

Another feature could have been taken from Serlio, or from Leoni's edition of Alberti. It occurs on the 'Volery' illustrated on Rocque's 1736 plan of Chiswick (Fig. 36a).[516] In elevation this was evidently a simple building, consisting mainly of a three-bay arcade supported by caryatids. Rocque's engraving suggests that there was no entablature between the capitals of the columns and the architraves of the arches. This idiosyncracy also appears on the arcade in the hall of Chicheley Hall, Bucks., possibly designed by Burlington in 1722.[517] It appears again on a drawing by Kent 'for a Memorial Temple'.[518] It was apparently an idiosyncracy peculiar, in eighteenth-century England, to Burlington's circle. In *quattrocento* Italy it would not have been an idiosyncracy: both the Tuscan and Venetian arcade traditions habitually omitted the entablature. By the *cinquecento*, however, the period which evidently most interested Burlington, it was perverse to omit it: Palladio always included entablatures, so did Jones, and so did all educated English architects until Burlington. The perverse may have included the unidentified architect of the Palazzo della Cancelleria, in Rome, between 1489 and 1511,[519] and Bramante, Antonio da Sangallo the elder and Antonio da Sangallo the younger, who designed the *rocca* of Civita Castellana.[520] It may have included Andrea Sansovino, to whom the design of the Palazzo Lante, in Rome, of 1513, has been attributed.[521] It included Raphael, who designed the loggia arcade of the Palazzo Pandolfini in Florence without an entablature.[522] It included Peruzzi, whose arcade in the Palazzo Ossoli, Rome, also omits it.[523] It included Giacomo del Duca, who omitted an entablature from the arcade of the *palazzino* at Caprarola.[524] It

515   Serlio, *Architecture*, iii, p. 29.
516   Badeslade and Rocque, *Vitruvius Britannicus*, plates 82-83.
517   Marcus Binney, 'Chicheley Hall, Buckinghamshire – II', *Country Life*, 158, 20 February 1975, p. 437. The payment for the design of this arcade was made to Flitcroft, but it was made very early in the career of a man who had previously only been recorded as a draughtsman, and Binney suggests that he might have been acting on Kent's behalf. In other commissions he acted for Burlington rather than Kent, and the possibility that he did so at Chicheley is increased by the fact that the craftsmen who worked there, Mansfield the plasterer, Lane and Baverstock the joiners, Richards the carver and Fletcher the mason, also worked for Burlington at Burlington House, which was begun before Kent's return to England in 1719. London County Council, *Survey of London*, xxxii (London, 1963), p. 400.

518   Jourdain, *The Work of William Kent*, p. 118, fig. 47.
519   Heydenreich and Lotz, *Architecture in Italy*, p. 69 and plate 63; Armando Schiavo, *Il Palazzo della Cancelleria* (Rome, 1963), pp. 120-24, 133-44 and figs 58-60; Frommel, *Der römische Palastbau*, i, p. 141.
520   Portoghesi, *Rome of the Renaissance*, plate 35.
521   Ibid., plate 61.
522   Frommel, Ray and Tafuri, *Raffaelo architetto*, p. 196; Frommel, *Der römische Palastbau*, ii, pp. 355-65, iii, plate 158a.
523   Dosio, *Roma antica*, p. 150.
524   Benedetti, *Giacomo del Duca*, pp. 252-58 and plates 219, 220, 222-24 and 226; but Loren W. Partridge, 'Vignola and the Villa Farnese at Caprarola – Part I', *Art Bulletin*, 52 (1970), p. 82b, attributes the palazzino to a Maestro Giovannantonio.

Fig. 36a Illustration by John Rocque of the 'Volery' at Chiswick

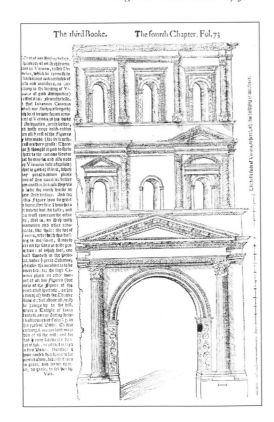

Fig. 36b Illustration by Sebastiano Serlio of the Porta dei Borsari at Verona

Fig. 36c Illustration by Giacomo Leoni of a room with a Doric arcade

included the anonymous designer of the Palazzo della Valle, Rome.[525] In Genoa it included Galeazzo Alessi, who omitted it from the arcade of the Palazzo Doria,[526] the Palazzo Agostino Pallavicino,[527] the Palazzo Nicolo Grimaldi[528] and the Palazzo Luca Grimaldi.[529] At Varallo, Alessi omitted the entablature from the Tribunal of Caiaphus at the Sacro Monte.[530] In Milan it included Domenico Giunti, who designed the Villa Simonetta in 1547,[531] and Martino Bassi, who designed the church of S. Lorenzo in 1573.[532]

Although uncommon, omission of the entablature was therefore not unknown in *cinquecento* Italy. Burlington certainly did not omit it through ignorance: minimal study of arcades would have introduced him to entablatures in that position, while only more extensive study would have introduced him to the fewer instances of their omission. It was omitted by those who chose to do so, doubtless because they knew it was also ancient practice. Burlington certainly must have known. He could have seen Serlio's illustrations of the Porta dei Leoni and the Porta dei Borsari in Verona (Fig. 36b).[533] The former has a first floor arcade without entablatures, and the latter omits them in numerous places. Had he ignored Serlio, he also possessed record drawings of these two arches by an unidentified sixteenth-century draughtsman, not thought to be Palladio.[534] Furthermore, Leoni's edition of Alberti made this point twice, in illustrations of Doric (Fig. 36c) and Ionic arcades.[535] Appearing at an opportune moment, in 1726, this book was probably decisive in the formation of a convincingly ancient appearance for the Volery.

Conspicuous in Burlington's transformation of the garden at Chiswick was the introduction of rectangular spaces with semi-circular terminations. This was the plan of the hippodrome, the ancient race-course; the semicircle alone is known as an *exedra*. A rather squat hippodrome formed the forecourt of the new house at Chiswick from the time of its construction (Fig. 37a);[536] a more usefully proportioned hippodrome was cut through the Grove, north of the house, after 1733[537] but before 1736.[538] Its north

525 Portoghesi, *Rome of the Renaissance*, plate 102.
526 Lotz et al., *Alessi*, fig, 461.
527 Poleggi, *Strada Nuova*, plates 40-41.
528 Ibid., plates 204-07.
529 Ibid., plate 24.
530 Lotz et al., *Alessi*, fig. 422.
531 Heydenreich and Lotz, *Architecture in Italy*, plate 316.
532 Ibid., plate 325.
533 Serlio, *Architecture*, iii, pp. 63, 65 and 65v.
534 Chatsworth, Devonshire Collection, album 36.
535 Leoni, *The Architecture of Leon Battista Alberti*, plates xxxix and xli.
536 Chatsworth, Devonshire Collection, Lord Burlington's architectural drawings, Boy 8, p. 34.
537 Carré, 'Rigaud's Drawings of Chiswick', p. 134, fig 1.
538 Badeslade and Rocque, *Vitruvius Britannicus*, plates 82-83.

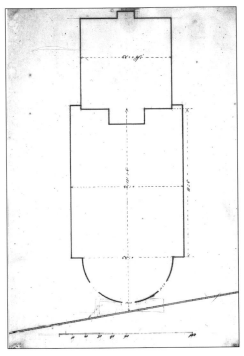

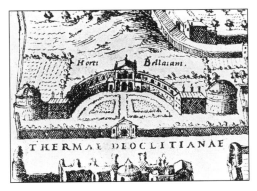

Fig. 37b Illustration by Etienne du Pérac of the Orti Bellaiani, Rome

Fig. 37a Drawing, probably by Lord Burlington, for the layout of Chiswick House and its forecourt (*Chatsworth*)

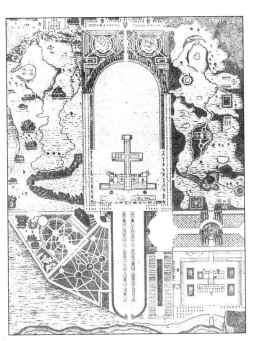

Fig. 37c The *exedra* of the Villa Barbaro, Maser

Fig. 37d Illustration by Robert Castell of an ancient garden plan

end, treated in isolation, is known as The Exedra. Palladio designed a hippodrome-planned garden at the Villa Barbaro, Maser, which was illustrated in his book,[539] but not visited by Burlington. This was, however, one of many in sixteenth-century Italy. Whether or not Burlington visited the early examples in Rome, Bramante's Belvedere Court at the Vatican,[540] or Raphael's Villa Madama,[541] or the most evocative, the Orti Bellaiani (Fig. 37b), which was formed from a curved wall within the Baths of Diocletian,[542] he certainly saw the *exedra* of the Villa Aldobrandini at Frascati.[543] He possessed drawings of the Villa Giulia (Fig. 7)[544] and, even if he had not visited them, he knew of the *exedrae* at the Villas Maffei and Pamphili in Rome from Falda's *Li giardini di Roma*,[545] of which he owned a copy.[546] Although Giulio Romano did not build an *exedra* at the Palazzo del Te, one was added by Nicolo Sebregondi in 1651.[547] When Kent visited Mantua in 1714,[548] he would have seen it, and possibly believed it to have been designed by Giulio. Sebregondi designed another *exedra* at La Favorita, another d'Este villa, near Mantua, *c.* 1620.[549] Burlington also possessed Webb's drawings of his proposed *exedra* at Greenwich.[550] It therefore seems improbable that the single Palladian example (which he never visited) was his particular inspiration. Neither of the Chiswick hippodromes followed the Palladian example in detail; their boundaries are formed by topiary with statues placed in front. Palladio's hippodrome at the Villa Barbaro terminates in a *nymphaeum* with a remarkable pediment its full width and curved in plan (Fig. 37c). There is nothing like this at Chiswick. Its only known English imitation is Leoni's at Carshalton Park.[551] Palladio was uninfluential on Burlington in this particular; both were equally inspired by Roman examples.[552]

539 Palladio, *I quattro libri*, ii, plate 34.

540 Letizia Franchina, 'Il Belvedere Bramantesco', in G. Ragioneri (ed.), *Il giardino storico Italiano* (Florence, 1981).

541 Frommel, Ray and Tafuri, *Raffaelo architetto*, pp. 317, 330 and 337.

542 G. Dickenson, *Du Bellay in Rome* (Leiden, 1960), pp. 51, 102.

543 Steinberg, *The Iconography of the Teatro dell'Aqua'*, plates 3 and 4; Chatsworth, Devonshire Collection, Lord Burlington's Grand Tour Account Book.

544 London, British Architectural Library, Drawings Collection, Burlington-Devonshire Collection, viii, 1r and 3.

545 Giovanni Battista Falda, *Li giardini di Roma* (Rome, 1670).

546 Chatsworth, Devonshire Collection, Library, MS 'Catalogue of the Earl of Burlington's Library', p. 1.

547 Kurt W. Forster and Richard J. Tuttle, 'The Palazzo del Te', *Journal of the Society of Architectural Historians*, 30 (1971), p. 281.

548 Sicca, 'Kent's Roman Sources', pp. 137-38.

549 Forster and Tuttle, 'Palazzo del Te', pp. 281-82.

550 John Bold, 'Greenwich: The Grot & Ascent by Mr Webb', *Burlington Magazine*, 129 (1982), pp. 149-50.

551 John Hassell, *Picturesque Rides and Walks with Excursions by Water*, ii (London, 1818), p. 94; *Estates Gazette*, 6 July 1895, p. 9; Andrew Skelton, 'Project Design for the Grotto of Carshalton', London Borough of Sutton Central Library, SBC 712.

552 Howard Burns, *Andrea Palladio, 1508-1580* (London, 1975), pp. 195-96.

Had all these hippodromes (save those of which he had drawings) been but a hazy memory to him on his return, they would have been brought into sharper focus in 1728 by the publication of a book dedicated to him, Castell's *Villas of the Ancients*, which illustrated hippodromes as the distinctive ancient garden plan (Fig. 37d).[553] Castell's book may have been the critical influence, indicating, if that is so, that antiquity was the ultimate desideratum in Burlington's choice of form.

The information necessary for Burlington to reproduce these features was therefore apparently made available to him by the published record drawings of Palladio, Desgodetz, Montfaucon, Montano, Serlio, Leoni and Castell. In addition he had access to some of Palladio's unpublished record drawings. In 1719 he bought a collection of Palladio's archaeological studies, chiefly of ancient public buildings, especially baths.[54] These beautiful drawings of magnificent buildings evidently inspired him at the very least in a general way. For instance they must surely have inspired the variety of room shapes at Chiswick (Fig. 6a). It must be said that, individually, all the room shapes at Chiswick can be found in Palladio's book, illustrating his own domestic designs, not ancient ones; there are even two of these shapes (cruciform and oval) which Burlington found himself unable to use within Chiswick House.[555] But Palladio's fancy shapes are distributed through a large collection of different designs in which the overwhelmingly predominant room plan is square or rectangular. At Chiswick the fancy shapes are contrived within a single building and compressed into a small compass. Distinctively, along the north side they are connected by open arches. Although the Library at Blenheim consists of discrete spaces connected by open arches, its spaces are rectangles and squares.[556] There were no native models for fancy shapes connected by arches; indeed no modern models of any type were available other than churches. Burlington would have known Bramante's and Peruzzi's plans for St Peter's, the latter from Serlio's book.[557] But Roman baths, not humanistic churches, were the particular prototype: since Burlington had Palladio's records of the former in his own hands, it is these which must have been his inspiration.

Their inspiration was, for some features, more specific. On the opposite side to the entrance of Chiswick House Burlington formed a rectangular

553 Robert Castell, *The Villas of the Ancients Illustrated* (London, 1728), Laurentinum (between pp. 16 and 17), and Tuscum (between pp. 126 and 127).

554 London, British Architectural Library, Drawings Collection, Burlington-Devonshire Collection, i–xv.

555 Palladio, *I quattro libri*, ii, plates 7, 15, 20, 33, 35, 36, 49, 52, 53, 54 and 57, illustrate rooms of oval plan, and plates 30, 33, 34 and 56 illustrate rooms of cruciform plan.

556 Downes, *Hawksmoor*, pp. 79 (fig. 3), 202–3 and plate 82.

557 Serlio, *Architecture*, iii, fol. 16v.

room with apses at each end and a large window occupying most of the outside wall, as if only the English climate prevented the room from being open to the garden beyond. This particular form identifies this space as a *loggia*, of which there were several of this type in sixteenth-century Italy. It had already attracted the attention of at least three Englishmen. John Webb designed the only English example of it to be built before that at Chiswick, in the King Charles Block at Greenwich,[558] and Burlington owned his design drawings.[559] He also owned Webb's drawings for a proposed grotto at Greeenwich,[560] which was not built; and this included a loggia of the same form.[561] William Talman had included it in the plan of his proposed Trianon of *c.* 1699 at Hampton court,[562] and his son John used it in a plan dated 1702.[563] The Italian examples occur in different positions. Some were separated from the main house, in *nymphaea*, as at the Villa Giulia,[564] or *casini*, as at Vignola's Villa Farnese, Caprarola.[565] The loggia proposed for Palladio's Palazzo Thiene, in Vincenza,[566] is comparable to that at Chiswick, as it is formed within the house, opposite the entrance side; but it was intended for the boundary of the property, with no garden to overlook. The *loggia* of Peruzzi's Palazzo Massimo, in Rome,[567] is also comparable, and it has much ornament in common with Chiswick. But what would have made it noticeable also makes it unlike: it is on the street front of the palace and is thus the palace entrance, as Webb's *loggia* is at Greenwich. The *loggia* of Raphael's Villa Madama, in Rome,[568] is in a comparable position to that at Chiswick; but only one end is apsed. But Burlington possessed a plan of the Villa Madama made by Palladio, which erroneously shows apses at both ends.[569] The *loggia* of Giulio's Palazzo del Te, in Mantua is also in a comparable position;[570] but that lacks both apses. The closest is Palladio's plan of the *loggia* of his villa Pisani at Bagnolo;[571] but, like the Palazzo Thiene, it was not built as proposed.[572] These, collectively (and

558 Colvin, *King's Works*, v, pp. 147-50.
559 John Harris, *Catalogue of the Drawings Collection of the Royal Institute of British Architects: Inigo Jones and John Webb* (Farnborough, 1972), p. 24, nos. 122 and 123, and figs 121 and 122.
560 Chatsworth, Devonshire Collection, Lord Burlington's architectural drawings, Boy 18.1 and 18.2.
561 Bold, 'Greenwich: The Grot & Ascent by Mr Webb', fig. 28.
562 Harris, *William Talman*, figs 51, 52 and 57.
563 Ibid., fig. 2.
564 Heydenreich and Lotz, *Architecture in Italy*, p. 269, fig. 87 and plate 277; Land Moore, 'Villa Giulia', fig. 10. There are two *loggie* at the Villa Giulia, but neither have apsidal ends.
565 Georgina Masson, *Italian Gardens* (London, 1961), p. 167, fig. 87.
566 Palladio, *I quattro libri*, ii, plate 8.
567 Heydenreich and Lotz, *Architecture in Italy*, plate 199.
568 Frommel, Ray and Tafuri, *Raffaelo architetto*, 341 and 352.
569 London, Royal Institute of British Architects, Drawings Collection, Burlington-Devonshire Collection, x, 18.
570 Hartt, *Giulio Romano*, i, pp. 91-94, figs a and b; ii, plates 158 and 159.
571 Palladio, *I quattro libri*, ii, plate 30.
572 Puppi, *Andrea Palladio*, pp. 254-56.

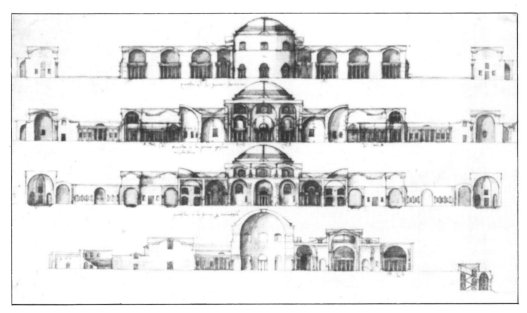

Fig. 38 Drawing by Andrea Palladio of the Baths of Diocletian, Rome (*RIBA*)

Fig. 39 Screens of columns in the room on the first floor of the Link Building, Chiswick House (*English Heritage*)

only collectively), might be regarded as Burlington's sources, were it not that he owned, among Palladio's drawings, surveys of five ancient structures with spaces exactly of this shape.[573] One, in the Baths of Diocletian,[574] is in a similar position relative to the main room of the building as at Chiswick and, like that, it is adjoined by a space of octagonal plan (Fig. 38). It may be concluded either that Burlington wanted a *loggia* of sixteenth-century type, like that in the Villa Pisani, and was encouraged by finding ancient precedent; or, more plausibly, that he wanted a space comparable to that in the Baths of Diocletian, and that sixteenth-century versions of the ancient type helped him to imagine it more fully.

Palladio's record drawings may have also fired Burlington's enthusiasm for sub-dividing rooms by screens of columns with gaps between the entablature and the ceiling. He designed two such screens, with segment-shaped gaps above the entablature, in the Link Room at Chiswick (Fig. 39). That he was enthusiastic about screens in general at the time of his purchase of the drawings can be shown by his observation on the interior of S. Giorgio Maggiore in Venice, made in May 1719, 'behind the great alter, there is an open intercolumn: which discovers the choire, it ends in a semicircle and is one of the most beautiful buildings in the world'.[575] But whether Burlington saw sixteenth-century screens with the particular characteristic of a segmental gap over the entablature is not known. Alberti's S. Pancrazio in Florence has the earliest version since antiquity.[576] Buontalenti designed a rustic version closing the entrance to the *grottocina* in the Boboli Gardens in Florence.[577] Burlington may have seen either during his three days in Florence in 1715.[578] But he need not have done, for screens dividing rooms (as at Chiswick), are illustrated in Palladio's drawings of the Baths of Constantine,[579] Titus,[580] Nero,[581] Trajan,[582] Diocletian,[583] Caracalla[584] and Agrippa.[585] Among these, screens with a segmental gap over the entablature are shown on two drawings of the Baths of Diocletian (Fig. 27c).[586]

573 London, Royal Institute of British Architects, Drawings Collection, Burlington-Devonshire Collection, i, 1 (Baths of Constantine), iv, 1 and 2 (Baths of Trajan), v, 1 and 2 (Baths of Diocletian), vi, 1 and 2 (Baths of Caracalla), vii, 1, 2 and 4 (Baths of Agrippa).

574 Ibid., v, 1 and 2; Ricardo, Conte de Burlington, *Fabbriche antiche* (London, 1730), plate 20.

575 Chatsworth, Devonshire Collection, Library, Lord Burlington's annotated copy of Palladio's *I quattro libri*, interleaved page following the title-page.

576 Venturi, *Storia dell'arte Italiana*, viii, pt 1 (Milan, 1923), p. 205, fig. 131.

577 Heikamp, 'La Grotta Grande', pp. 1-18.

578 Chatsworth, Devonshire Collection, Lord Burlington's Grand Tour Account Book; see below.

579 London, British Architectural Library, Drawings Collection, Burlington-Devonshire Collection, i, 3 and 5.

580 Ibid., ii, 2 and 6.

581 Ibid., iii, 2, 4, 5, 7 and 8.

582 Ibid., iv, 3 and 4.

583 Ibid., v, 2, 4, 5, 6, 7 and 8.

584 Ibid., vi, 4 and 6.

585 Ibid., vii, 3 and 6.

586 Ibid., v, 2 and 4.

Palladio's drawings may have stimulated Burlington's interest in the semi-circular lunette, known as the Diocletian or thermal window because of its prototypical use in the Baths of Diocletian. At Chiswick such lunettes light the drum of the dome (Fig. 20a). He would, however, have been familiar with semi-circular lunettes before he acquired the drawings. They were first introduced to England by Wren at St Benet Fink in 1670,[587] in a variant form at St Stephen Walbrook in 1672,[588] and in unexecuted designs for Trinity College Library, Cambridge in 1676[589] and St Anne, Soho in 1680.[590] Burlington may not have seen these two drawings, but Hawksmoor, whose designs for the Radcliffe Library were the heirs of Wren's Trinity Library proposal,[591] must have done. Hawksmoor included lunettes in proposals for chapels at Greenwich in 1711,[592] The Queen's College, Oxford in 1708-9,[593] and Worcester College, Oxford, in 1717-20;[594] and built a rather more modest one in the Clarendon Building, Oxford in 1712.[595] Christ church, Spitalfields,[596] St Mary Woolnoth,[597] St George Bloomsbury,[598] St Anne Limehouse,[599] and St George in the East[600] all had them, and the first two of these could have been seen by Burlington before he left for Rome in 1714, all of them by 1717.

In Italy he would inevitably have seen several semi-circular lunettes. At Genoa in 1714 and 1719 he would have seen them on the exterior of Galeazzo Alessi's Sta Maria in Carignano,[601] and he also possessed an illustration of this church by Rubens.[602] In Rome he may have seen the earliest modern example, on Raphael's Villa Madama of 1517-23,[603] and later examples by Antonio da Sangallo the younger in the Capella Paolina of the Vatican,[604] and in the chapel of Cardinal Alborense in S. Giacomo degli Spagnoli.[605] He may have seen a semi-circular lunette on the internal elevation of Vignola's S. Andrea Quirinale,[606] or lunettes visible from the

587 Downes, *Wren*, plate 55.
588 Ibid., plate 44.
589 Margaret Whinney, *Wren* (London, 1971), p. 135, fig. 117; *Wren Society*, 5 (1928), pp. 32–34 and plates xx–xxi.
590 Kerry Downes, Whitechapel Art Gallery Catalogue, *Sir Christopher Wren* (London, 1982), p. 69 (no. iv. 31).
591 Downes, *Hawksmoor*, pp. 126–31, 279–80 and plates 37–39.
592 *Ibid.*, pp. 95–96, 281 and plates 26a–b.
593 Ibid., pp. 103–6, 279 and plates 28b, 29a and 30a.
594 Ibid., pp. 147–51, 279 and fig. 28.
595 Ibid., pp. 108–9, 279 and plates 31d, 32–33.
596 Ibid., pp. 179–83, 276 and plate 64b.
597 Ibid., pp. 189–94, 277 and plates 73b, 74a, 74b.
598 Ibid., pp. 184–89, 276 and plates 68b and 70a.

599 Ibid., pp. 171–74, 276 and plate 55a.
600 Ibid., pp. 174–79, 276 and plates 56c and 57c.
601 Lotz et al., *Alessi*, plate 19, figs 170–71.
602 Rubens, *Palazzi de Genova*, i, fig. 63.
603 Frommel, Ray and Tafuri, *Raffaelo architetto*, pp. 341–43, 347 and 350.
604 Gustavo Giovannoni, *Antonio da Sangallo il Giovane*, i, fig. 119; Antonio proposed other semi-circular lunettes in drawings for St Peter's, Rome (ibid., figs 71 and 76), the Sala Regia of the Vatican (ibid., figs 113, 118 and 123), the Capella Medici in Montecassino (ibid., fig. 201), and Sta Maria di Monserrato, Rome (ibid., fig. 226).
605 Venturi, *Storia dell'arte Italiana*, xi, pt 2, p. 597, fig. 548.
606 Ibid., p. 708, fig. 656.

street on Guidetto Guidetti's Sta Maria dell' Orto,[607] and Giacomo della Porta's Trinita dei Monti,[608] beside which he lodged for four months.[609] Travelling from Rome to Venice via Florence in 1715 he would have passed through Ferrara, where he may have seen the semi-circular lunette in the façade of G.-B. Aleotti's S. Carlo.[610] In Venice he could have seen lunettes on all three of Palladio's churches.[611] In Milan he may have seen the lunettes on Alessi's S. Barnabo.[612] In 1719 he drove from Genoa to Vincenza. Depending on what routes he took, he could have seen more lunettes on Vasari's S. Croce at Boscomarengo, near Alessandria,[613] on Alessio Tramelli's Madonna di Campagna at Piacenza,[614] and on the upper part of Sta Maria in Organo in Verona.[615] Kent may also have seen some of these churches on his 1714 tour of northern Italy, which included San Marino, and thus possibly Pesaro, where he could have seen the church of S. Giovanni, attributed to Girolamo Genga.[616]

In Palladio's book Burlington would have seen lunettes ornamenting the Villas Thiene at Quinto,[617] Zeno at Cesalto[618] and Pisani at Bagnolo.[619] In Scamozzi's book he would have seen one ornamenting the Villa Bardellini at Asolo.[620] His particular inspiration is therefore not entirely clear, but since all these other architects may have used them for their antique effect, so may Burlington. He was better placed than most to do so, since he possessed Palladio's drawings of the prototype.[621] It is therefore difficult to believe that this (Fig. 40) was not his particular model.

His decision to use *serlianas* may also have been determined by the sight of Palladio's drawings. *Serlianas* are conspicuous at Chiswick. They first appeared on the Casina, built in 1717 (Fig. 18a).[622] Another appeared on the front elevation of the old house at an unknown date before *c.* 1733 (Fig. 27a).[623]

607 Ibid., p. 764, fig. 707.
608 Ibid., p. 821, fig. 760; Blunt, *Guide to Baroque Rome*, p. 150, points out that although the attribution to della Porta is traditional, there is no supporting evidence.
609 Chatsworth, Devonshire Collection, Lord Burlington's Grand Tour Account Book.
610 Venturi, *Storia dell'arte Italiana* (Milan, 1940), xi, pt 3, p. 933, fig. 876.
611 Puppi, *Andrea Palladio*, pp. 345-49 and plates 470-71; pp. 362-69 and plates 176-78, 181, 185, 188-89 and 193-94; pp. 419-23 and plates 245-46.
612 Lotz et al., *Alessi*, plate 41.
613 Venturi, *Storia dell'arte Italiana*, xi, pt 2, p. 450, fig. 406.
614 Ibid., p. 766-70, figs 712-16.
615 Ibid., xi, pt 3, pp. 272-73, figs 236-37; Langenskiold, *Michele Sanmichele*, pp. 114-15 and plate 52a (only the lower part is by Sanmichele; the upper part dates from 1592).
616 Venturi, *Storia dell'arte Italiana*, xi, pt 1, p. 879, fig. 799.
617 Palladio, *I quattro libri*, ii, plate 47.
618 Ibid., plate 32.
619 Ibid., plate 30.
620 Scamozzi, *L'idea dell'architettura universale*, i, p. 279.
621 London, British Architectural Library, Drawings Collection, Burlington-Devonshire Collection, v, 2 and 6.
622 Campbell, *Vitruvius Britannicus*, iii, plate 26.
623 Carré, 'Rigaud's Drawings of Chiswick', p. 140, fig 8.

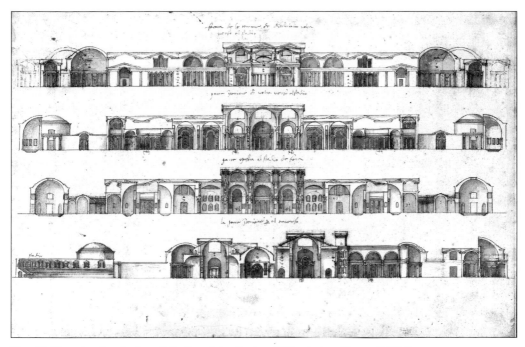

Fig. 40 Drawing by Andrea Palladio of the Baths of Diocletian, Rome (*RIBA*)

The new house has *serlianas* on the side elevations (Fig. 41) and, in the triplicated form discussed above, on the north elevation (Fig. 3a). However, *serlianas*, like semi-circular lunettes, would have been familiar to Burlington before he acquired Palladio's drawings. The earliest use of the feature in England was by Inigo Jones, on the Queen's Chapel at St James' Palace in 1623-5.[624] In an unusual form, with blind side-lights, Jones used it later at Wilton.[625] When he first saw Jones' drawings Burlington would have discovered that Jones had also proposed *serlianas* for the New Exchange in the Strand,[626] the tower of St Paul's Cathedral,[627] and the Queen's House at Greenwich.[628] Before then Burlington would probably have seen Wren's *serlianas* at the east ends of St Dionis Backchurch (1670-4),[629] St Bartholo-mew Exchange (1674-79),[630] St James Piccadilly (1676-84),[631] and St Andrew Holborn (1684-90).[632] It is possible that he saw the *serlianas* on the drawing for Wren's proposed Parliament House.[633] He may have seen the variant form of *serliana*, with a concentric relieving arch and the intervening area glazed, which Wren first used on the south elevation of the Sheldonian Theatre, Oxford (1664-69),[634] and later used at St Bride, Fleet Street (1671-78),[635] and St Stephen Walbrook (1672-79).[636] (But he did not adopt this form; nor did any other English architect until Sir Robert Taylor in 1766.)[637] He may have noticed that Wren designed blind *serlianas*, in shallow relief, on the transept terminals of St Paul's Cathedral,[638] and that the west bay of St Paul's nave arcade is also a form of *serliana*.[639] He may well have seen the Great Model, where the transept terminals are giant *serlianas*,[640] or even one of Wren's proposal drawings for the west end, which combines a *serliana* with a pedimented portico.[641] If he had not seen this drawing, a realised form of it was built by Hawksmoor in 1712-14 on the east end of St Alphege, Greenwich,[642] and a further version of it (without the pediment) was built by Hawksmoor on the west end of Christ Church, Spitalfields, between 1714 and 1729.[643] Nor was this Christ

624 Harris and Higgott, *Inigo Jones: Complete Architectural Drawings*, p. 182.
625 Bold, *Wilton*, p. 39, plates 37 and 38.
626 Harris and Higgott, *Inigo Jones: Complete Architectural Drawings*, p. 37.
627 Ibid., p. 39.
628 Ibid., p. 71.
629 Downes, *Wren*, fig. 31.
630 Ibid., fig. 27.
631 Ibid., fig. 65.
632 Ibid., fig. 105.
633 Kerry Downes, *English Baroque Architecture*, plate 78.
634 Downes, *Wren*, fig. 66.

635 Ibid., figs 36 and 38.
636 Ibid., fig. 43.
637 Marcus Binney, *Sir Robert Taylor* (London, 1984), plate 15.
638 Downes, *Wren*, fig. 79.
639 Kerry Downes, *Sir Christopher Wren: The Design of St Paul's Cathedral* (London, 1988), figs 52 and 53.
640 Downes, *Wren*, fig. 48.
641 Downes, *St Paul's Cathedral*, fig. 133.
642 Downes, *Hawksmoor*, pp. 167-70, 276 and plate 53a.
643 Ibid., pp. 179-83, 276 and plate 65.

Fig. 41 First floor window, west elevation of Chiswick House (*English Heritage*)

Church's only debt to Wren, for it also had a conventional *serliana* as its east window,[644] in the manner Wren had established in the 1670s.

All of these, except for the unusual variant at Wilton, were on churches or public buildings. In Italy Burlington would also have seen *serlianas* on private houses, especially on villas in the suburbs of Rome and Genoa, buildings designed particularly for festivity and informal life. There are at least fifty-five Renaissance buildings with *serlianas* in the towns where Burlington stayed in 1714-15, and more in towns which he may have visited *en route* from Genoa to Vicenza in 1719. This excludes Baroque *serlianas*, which may equally have drawn his attention, and drawings of *serlianas*, which he may have seen in architects' portfolios or collectors' cabinets. The first Italian town where he stayed on his way to Rome in 1714 was Turin: he spent three days there, three more days on his way back in 1715; and he was there again in November 1719. In the heart of the town he could not have failed to be impressed by Ascanio Vitozzi's Piazza Castello of 1612-13, which has arcades in the form of simplified *serlianas*.[645] On the south side of the piazza the church of Sta Cristina was given a façade with a *serliana* window by Juvarra in 1715:[646] he must have seen that on third visit, and perhaps seen it under construction on his second visit. Just off the piazza, he could have seen a similar *serliana* in the facade of Ascanio Vitozzi's church of Corpus Domini of 1603.[647]

From Turin he went to Genoa, where he stayed for six days,[648] revisiting in 1719 in the company of William Kent.[649] There *serlianas* can be seen on the street side of the villa of Andrea Doria,[650] on the garden loggia of Galeazzo Alessi's Villa dei Peschieri,[651] and in the *cortile* of his Villa Sauli.[652] Alessi had also used *serlianas* on a Genoese church, Sta Maria in Carignano of 1549.[653]

In Rome, where he stayed for four months, there are *serlianas* of all types, but they were particularly popular as windows in the houses of the nobility. Burlington could have seen *serlianas* designed by Bramante in the choir of Sta Maria del Popolo of 1509,[654] in the Sala Regia of the Vatican, built some time between 1508 and 1513,[655] by Raphael in the Cortile del Maresciallo of

644 Ibid., pp. 179-83, 276 and plate 67a.
645 Pollak, *Turin, 1564-1680*, pp. 45-49; Carboneri, *Ascanio Vitozzi*, pp. 137-43.
646 Pollak, *Turin, 1564-1680*, p. 130.
647 Carboneri, *Ascanio Vitozzi*, pp. 149-53 and plate 197.
648 Chatsworth, Devonshire Collection, Lord Burlington's Grand Tour Account Book; Lees-Milne, *The Earls of Creation*, p. 90.
649 Lincoln, Lincolnshire Archives Office, 2MM/B19A, Kent to Massingberd, 15 November

1719; Lees-Milne, *The Earls of Creation*, p. 104; Wilson, *William Kent*, pp. 36-37.
650 George L. Gorse, 'The Villa of Andrea Doria in Genoa', *Journal of the Society of Architectural Historians*, 44, March 1985, p. 19, fig. 2.
651 Lotz et al., *Alessi*, plate 28.
652 Ibid., figs 177-78.
653 Ibid., plate xxi.
654 Bruschi, *Bramante*, p. 163 and fig. 172.
655 Portoghesi, *Rome of the Renaissance* plate 361; Blunt, *Guide to Baroque Rome*, p. 203.

the Vatican,[656] by Raphael or Peruzzi in S. Eligio degli Orefici of 1509,[657] by Antonio da Sangallo the younger in the Palazzo Leroy of 1523,[658] by Giulio Romano in the Villa Lante on the Janiculum of *c.* 1523,[659] by Ammanati in the Nymphaeum of the Villa Giulia of 1551-55,[660] in the Palazzo Firenze of 1552-54,[661] and the Villa Medici of *c.* 1580,[662] by Vignola in the *cortile* of Palazzo Borghese of 1561-66,[663] by Michelangelo in the *cortile* of the Palazzo dei Conservatori of 1563,[664] by an unknown architect on the late sixteenth century Palazzo Cenci,[665] by Maderno in the Casino del'Aurora in the garden of the Villa Borghese of 1612[666] and by Flaminio Ponzio and Giovanni Vasanzio on the façade of S. Sebastiano of 1612.[667] How many of these Burlington saw is not known; but he visited the Villa Borghese,[668] and, as mentioned above, he owned drawings of the Villa Giulia.[669]

In Frascati there are *serlianas* designed by Nanni di Bacio Bigio in the Villa Rufina of 1548-55,[670] by Giacomo della Porta on the garden front and the *exedra* of the Villa Aldobrandini of 1598-1603,[671] and by Vasanzio on the *porticus* added to the Villa Mondragone after 1613.[672] Burlington went to Frascati and visited the Villas Mondragone and Aldobrandini.[673]

Serlianas in Florence, where he stayed for three days after leaving Rome in 1715,[674] and where William Kent spent five months,[675] include the earliest modern type of the form, articulating the internal walls of churches and sacristies. These are Brunelleschi's in the *sagrestia vecchia* of S. Lorenzo of *c.* 1429,[676] and the interior of the Pazzi Chapel at SS. Anunziata of 1459,[677]

656 Andres, *The Villa Medici*, i, p. 350.
657 Venturi, *Storia dell'arte Italiana*, xi pt 1, p. 194; Frommel, Ray and Tafuri, *Raffaelo architetto*, pp. 143-56.
658 Portoghesi, *op cit*, plate 362; Venturi, *Storia dell'arte Italiana*, xi, pt 1, p. 577.
659 Hartt, *Giulio Romano*, i, pp. 62-64; ii, plate 118.
660 Heydenreich and Lotz, *Architecture in Italy*, plate 277; Land Moore, 'Villa Giulia', fig. 15.
661 Portoghesi, *op cit*, plate 206; Venturi, *Storia dell'arte Italiana*, xi, pt 2, pp. 247-48.
662 Portoghesi, *Rome of the Renaissance*, plate 243; Coffin, *Villa*, pp. 224-33 and plate 138; F. Boyer, 'La construction de la Villa Medicis', *La revue de l'art ancien et moderne*, 51 (1927), p. 114; Andres, *Villa Medici*, passim.
663 Howard Hibbard, *The Architecture of the Palazzo Borghese* (Rome, 1962), pp. 6, 28-34. Although probably designed by Vignola, the *cortile* was executed by either Martino Longhi the elder or Ottaviano Mascarino.
664 Venturi, *Storia dell'arte Italiana*, xi, pt 2, p. 143.
665 Portoghesi, *Rome of the Renaissance*, plate 262.
666 Hibbard, *Carlo Maderno*, plate 80a.
667 Venturi, *Storia dell'arte Italiana*, xi, pt 2, p. 891.

668 Chatsworth, Devonshire Collection, Lord Burlington's Grand Tour Account Book, Lees-Milne, *The Earls of Creation*, p. 91.
669 London, British Architectural Library, Drawings Collection, Burlington-Devonshire Collection, viii, 1-4.
670 David R. Coffin, *The Villa in the Life of Renaissance Rome* (Princeton, 1979), pp. 42-43 and fig. 19.
671 Venturi, *Storia dell'arte Italiana*, xi, pt 2, pp. 808 and 810; Franck, *The Villas of Frascati*, p. 119 and figs 126, 130 and 134-35.
672 Franck, *The Villas of Frascati*, p. 68 and fig. 60; Coffin, *Gardens and Gardening in Papal Rome*, pp. 191-92 and fig. 162.
673 Chatsworth, Devonshire Collection, Lord Burlington's Grand Tour Account Book.
674 Ibid.
675 Sicca, 'Kent's Roman Sources', p. 135.
676 Heydenreich and Lotz, *Architecture in Italy*, plate 17; Venturi, *Storia dell'arte Italiana*, viii, pt 1, p. 108.
677 Heydenreich and Lotz, *Architecture in Italy*, plate 7; Venturi, *Storia dell'arte Italiana*, viii, pt 1, pp. 123 and 126.

Cronaca's in S. Salvatore of *c.* 1480,[678] and an unknown architect's in the sacristy of Sta Felicita.[679] They also include *serlianas* which form part of colonnades or loggias, as on the exterior of the Pazzi Chapel,[680] on the exterior of Giuliano da Sangallo's Sta Maria Maddalena de'Pazzi of *c.* 1490[681] and in the *cortile* of Cronaca's Palazzo Guadagni of 1504-6.[682] It would have been difficult for Burlington to have missed Vasari's *serlianas* in the river range of the Uffizi.[683] But in Florence (as in Rome) the most frequent designer of *serlianas* was Ammanati: they occur in the entrance arch to his *cortile* at the Palazzo Pitti,[684] in the *cortile* of his Palazzo Grifoni,[685] in the second cloister which he built at S. Spirito,[686] in his Palazzo Giugni[687] and his Palazzo Budini Gattai.[688] Dosio designed a *serliana* in the Palazzo Arcivescovile of 1576-83.[689] Cigoli added two *serliana* loggias conspicuously on the street front of the Palazzo Corsi in the 1590s.[690] Santi de Tito built a house in the Via Cavour with *serliana* windows of *c.* 1600.[691]

In Bologna, where he stayed for two days after leaving Florence in 1715,[692] there are two *serlianas* in churches, a *quattrocento* one in the chapel of Sta Cecilia di Raffaelo in S. Giovanni in Monte,[693] and windows of the 1550s in Pellegrino Tibaldi's Poggi Chapel in S. Giacomo Maggiore.[694] In Padua there is a *serliana* niche below the loggia of Falconetto's Odeo Cornaro of 1524.[695] In Venice, where he stayed for eight days,[696] there are variant forms of *serliana* in two palaces by Sanmichele, the Palazzo Grimani of *c.* 1556[697] and the Palazzo Cornaro of *c.* 1543,[698] and a *serliana* in the *atrium* of the Palazzo Corner-Spinelli of *c.* 1552, also attributed to Sanmichele.[699] Sansovino used the variant form with narrow side openings on the Library of St Mark, begun in 1537,[700] and a conventional *serliana* window on the

678 Venturi, *Storia dell'arte Italiana*, viii, pt 1, p. 427.
679 Ibid., p. 358.
680 Heydenreich and Lotz, *Architecture in Italy*, plate 6.
681 Ibid., plate 141; Venturi, *Storia dell'arte Italiana*, viii, pt 1, p. 451.
682 Venturi, *Storia dell'arte Italiana*, viii, pt 1, p. 429.
683 Ibid., xi, pt 2, pp. 251, 421-23; Nikolaus Pevsner, *A History of Building Types* (London, 1976), plate 2.1.
684 Venturi, *Storia dell'arte Italiana*, xi, pt 2, p. 255; Leon Satkowski, 'The Palazzo Pitti: Planning and Use in the Grand-Ducal Era', *Journal of the Society of Architectural Historians*, 42, December 1983, p. 337, fig. 2.
685 Andres, *The Villa Medici*, i, p. 356.
686 Venturi, *Storia dell'arte Italiana*, xi, pt 2, p. 342.
687 Andres, *The Villa Medici*, i, p. 356.
688 Venturi, *Storia dell'arte Italiana*, xi, pt 2, p. 278.
689 Ibid., p. 361.
690 Ibid., p. 633.
691 Ibid., p. 602.
692 Chatsworth, Devonshire Collection, Lord Burlington's Grand Tour Account Book; Lees-Milne, *The Earls of Creation*, p. 92.
693 Venturi, *Storia dell'arte Italiana*, viii, pt 2, p. 477.
694 Ibid., xi, pt 3, p. 721.
695 Ibid., p. 11.
696 Chatsworth, Devonshire Collection, Lord Burlington's Grand Tour Account Book; Lees-Milne, *The Earls of Creation*, p. 93; see below.
697 Langenskiold, *Michele Sanmichele*, pp. 82-90 and plates 30 and 31a.
698 Ibid., pp. 76-82, fig. 28 and plate 27.
699 Ibid., p. 90 and plate 40.
700 Howard, *Sansovino*, plate 11; Wolfgang Lotz, 'The Roman Legacy in Sansovino's Venetian Buildings', *Journal of the Society of Architectural Historians*, 22 (1963), pp. 3-12.

facade of S. Giuliano.[701] Alessandro Vittoria formed windows by joining up *serlianas* on the Palazzo Balbi in 1582.[702]

In Milan there are early *serlianas* by Dolcebuono in S. Maurizio of 1503[703] and Sta Maria della Passione of *c.* 1530.[704] More arresting are the *serliana* loggias surrounding the entire courtyard of Alessi's Palazzo Marini,[705] and along the street façade of Vincenzo Seregni's Palazzo dei Giureconsulti,[706] both of 1558. Alessi designed *serlianas* on S. Barnaba of 1561-67,[707] and Pellegrino Tibaldi designed them around the chapel of the Lazzaretto in 1564.[708]

It is not known which Lombard route Burlington took between Genoa and Vicenza in 1719 but, whichever he chose, it probably took him past more *serlianas*. In Pavia he could have seen Cristoforo Solari's portal of 1492 to the Certosa[709] or the *cortile* of Pellegrini Tibaldi's Collegio Borromeo of 1564.[710] In Piacenza he could have seen Antonio da Sangallo the younger's S. Bernardino of 1526,[711] or S. Agostino of 1550 by an unknown architect.[712] In Cremona he could have seen the *cortili* of Giulio Campi's Palazzo Pallavicini of *c.* 1560[713] and Palazzo Ugolini Dati of 1561,[714] and the stair loggia of Francesco Dattari's Palazzo Pagliari of *c.* 1580.[715] If he had followed the Via Emilia from Piacenza to Parma he would have seen the *serliana* at the top of G.-B. Magnani's campanile of S. Giovanni Evangelista.[716] He might have seen the garden front of Vignola's Palazzo del Giardino,[717] and the interior of Magnani's S. Allesandro.[718] Nor would he have turned down a chance to see G.-B. Aleotti's famous Teatro Farnesino, ringed by superimposed arcades of *serlianas*.[719] Whatever he missed would have been noticed by Kent, who spent two months in Parma in 1714.[720] The

701 Venturi, *Storia dell'arte Italiana*, xi, pt 3, p. 148; Howard, *Sansovino*, pp. 84-87, and plates 65 and 67.

702 Deborah Howard, *The Architectural History of Venice* (London, 1980), p. 175, fig. 92; Andres, *The Villa Medici*, ii, p. 298.

703 Rudolf Wittkower, 'Pseudo-Palladian Elements in English Neoclassicism', in *Palladio and English Palladianism*, p. 156.

704 Venturi, *Storia dell'arte Italiana*, xi, pt 1, pp. 712 and 717.

705 Heydenreich and Lotz, *Architecture in Italy*, plate 311; Andres, *Villa Medici*, ii, p. 299.

706 Lotz et al., *Alessi*, figs 384, 386, 387 and 390-96; Nancy A. Houghton Brown, *The Milanese Architecture of Galeazzo Alessi* (New York, 1982), i, pp. 377-410; ii, figs 169-73; Costantino Baroni, *Gli edifici di Vincenzo Seregni nella Piazza dei Mercanti a Milano* (Milan, 1934).

707 Lotz et al., *Alessi*, plate 40.

708 Venturi, *Storia dell'arte Italiana*, xi, pt 3, p. 789.

709 Ibid., viii, pt 1, p. 808.

710 Heydenreich and Lotz, *Architecture in Italy*, plate 323.

711 Venturi, *Storia dell'arte Italiana*, xi, pt 1, p. 617.

712 Bruno Adorni, *L'architettura Farnesiana a Piacenza, 1545-1600* (Parma, 1982), pp. 371-80 and 398-406.

713 Venturi, *Storia dell'arte Italiana*, xi, pt 3, p. 566.

714 Ibid., p. 568.

715 Ibid., p. 574.

716 Bruno Adorni, *L'architettura Farnesiana a Parma, 1545-1630* (Parma, 1974), p. 207.

717 Ibid., p. 88.

718 Ibid., p. 209.

719 Venturi, *Storia dell'arte Italiana*, xi, pt 3, p. 929; Adorni, *Parma*, pp. 99-101.

720 Lincoln, Lincolnshire Archives Office, 2MM/ B19A, Kent to Massingberd, 24 November 1714; Wilson, *William Kent*, pp. 27, 31 and 133.

road would then have led Burlington to Reggio Emilia, where he would have seen the *serliana* in the façade of the cathedral, added by Prospero Spani after 1593,[721] and he might have seen the *cortile* of the monastery built by the Pacchioni brothers in 1582.[722] Had he taken that route he would probably turned north at Reggio, to reach Carpi, where there is a *serliana* of *c.* 1515 in S. Niccolo by Peruzzi.[723] This route would have brought him past the abbey of S. Benedetto Po where Giulio Romano had in 1540 formed the nave arcade out of *serlianas*.[724] At Mantua he could have seen *serlianas* conspicuous on the garden front of the Palazzo del Te,[725] on the exterior of the *loggetta* of the *grotto*,[726] and on a painted medallion in the *Sala dei Venti*.[727] He could even have seen another *serliana* in the *loggetta* of the Palazzo Ducale.[728] Even if this was not his route, William Kent had visited Mantua and Parma in 1714, recording the former in some detail.[729] From Mantua Burlington would have gone to Verona, where he would have noticed Sanmichele's Palazzo Canossa of *c.* 1532, with a *serliana* on the street elevation and more in the *cortile*,[730] and the same architect's Palazzo Guastaversa of 1555, with a continuous arcade of *serlianas* in the *cortile*.[731]

Although Burlington spent only a short time in Vicenza[732] he would inevitably have seen Palladio's Basilica of 1546-49, with its two storeys of continuous *serlianas*.[733] Palladio designed *serlianas* for six buildings, all built between 1541 and 1550, in the early part of his career, when he was probably most influenced by Serlio's first two books, published in Venice in 1537 and 1540.[734] These books popularised the feature which eventually took Serlio's name. Apart from the Basilica, Palladio's buildings with *serlianas* are private houses with similar (although not quite the same) social functions as those outside Rome and Genoa. They are the Villa Valmarana at Vigardolo di Monticello of 1541,[735] the Villa Forni at Montecchio Precalcino of 1541-

721 Venturi, *Storia dell'arte Italiana*, xi, pt 3, p. 939.
722 Ibid., p. 937.
723 Wittkower, 'Pseudo-Palladian Elements', p. 215 n.8.
724 Hartt, *Giulio Romano*, i, pp. 241-42; ii, plate 503.
725 Ibid., i, pp. 99-101; ii, plates 158 and 160; but the state of this elevation in the early eighteenth century is described and illustrated by Forster and Tuttle, 'The Palazzo del Te', pp. 275-76 and fig. 8.
726 Hartt, *Giulio Romano*, i, pp. 143-45; ii, plate 302.
727 Ibid., i, pp. 115-22; ii, plate 207.
728 Ibid., i. p. 169; ii, plates 355-56.
729 Sicca, 'Kent's Roman Sources', pp. 137-38.

730 Heydenreich and Lotz, *Architecture in Italy*, plate 225 and fig. 69; Venturi, *Storia dell'arte Italiana*, xi, pt 3, pp. 241 and 243; Langenskiold, *Michele Sanmichele*, pp. 54-61 and plates 15-16.
731 Venturi, *Storia dell'arte Italiana*, xi, pt 3, p. 288; Langenskiold, *Michele Sanmichele*, pp. 68-71 and plate 24a.
732 Narford, Fountaine MSS, letters, 6 November 1719.
733 Puppi, *Andrea Palladio*, pp. 266-70 and figs 55-66.
734 Eileen Harris, *British Architectural Books and Writers, 1556-1785* (Cambridge, 1990), p. 414.
735 Puppi, *Andrea Palladio*, pp. 245-47 and figs 288, 289, 291 and 292.

42,[736] the Villa Pojana at Pojana Maggiore,[737] the Villa Angarano at Angarano, both of 1548,[738] and the alterations to the rear of the Villa Godi at Lonedo in Lugo Vicentino of 1549-50.[739] Burlington is not known to have visited any of the buildings on this list. He would therefore only have known Palladio's executed *serlianas* from the illustrations in Palladio's book, which means effectively from the Basilica,[740] since only two of the others, the Villa Pojana and the Villa Angarano, are illustrated, both at a small scale.[741] Insofar as he was influenced at all by Palladio on this point, it may have been through his collection of Palladio's design drawings, of which four include *serlianas* (Fig. 40).[742]

Burlington was not the only Englishman of his generation to be interested in *serlianas*. Vanbrugh had already built a *serliana* in the west loggia of King's Weston in 1717-18.[743] Within a year of the building of the Casina, Colen Campbell had put them in the end bays of Burlington's own house in Picadilly,[744] and Vanbrugh had built them at Eastbury.[745] In 1720 they appeared at Seaton Delaval.[746] In 1722 they were inserted at Grimsthorpe.[747] At Ledston Hall, Yorkshire, there is a garden pavilion with a *serliana*,[748] almost certainly one of the (undated) works carried out there by William Thornton, who died in 1721.[749] Hawksmoor proposed *serlianas* for Worcester College, Oxford, between 1717 and 1720[750] and for Brasenose College *c.* 1720.[751] The *serliana* which Hawksmoor designed at the east end of the Codrington Library at All Souls College was built *c.* 1718.[752] Hawksmoor's Belvedere proposal at Castle Howard dates from 1724,[753] slightly earlier than the new house at Chiswick and, while the latter was being built, Hawksmoor designed *serlianas* at Ockham in 1729.[754]

For illustrations Burlington possessed Serlio's book, with ten plates of the eponymous feature.[755] Nor could he have been under the illusion that it

736 Ibid., pp. 247-48 and figs 23-24.
737 Ibid., pp. 273-76 and figs 84-88, 90-92, 340 and 344.
738 Ibid., pp. 271-73 and fig. 333.
739 Ibid., pp. 238-40 and figs 21 and 277.
740 Palladio, *I quattro libri*, iii, plates 19 and 20.
741 Ibid., ii, plates 41 (Pojana) and 46 (Angarano).
742 London, British Architectural Library, Burlington-Devonshire Collection, xvii, 1, 2, 15 and 19.
743 Downes, *English Baroque Architecture*, plate 267.
744 London County Council, *Survey of London*, xxxii (London, 1963), p. 399.
745 Kerry Downes, *Vanbrugh* (London, 1977), pp. 114-18 and plates 139-40.

746 Ibid., pp. 102-6 and plate 121.
747 Ibid., pp. 118-21 and plates 151 and 153.
748 'Ledston Hall, Yorkshire', *Country Life*, 21, 29 June 1907, p. 949.
749 Colvin, *Biographical Dictionary of British Architects*, pp. 826-27.
750 Downes, *Hawksmoor*, pp. 147-51 and fig. 28.
751 Ibid., pp. 151-54 and plate 51b.
752 Ibid., p. 141 and plate 49a.
753 Ibid., p. 283 and plate 87a.
754 Lawrence Whistler, 'Ockham Park, Surrey', *Country Life*, 108, 29 December 1950, pp. 2, 218-21, figs 5, 9 and 12.
755 Serlio, *Architecture*, iv, pp. 12, 29, 30, 31, 42; v, pp. 5v, 8, 9, 13v, 15.

was modern, invented by Serlio, for he also owned sketches by Pirro Ligorio of Roman antiquities where it appears,[756] and his collection of Palladio's records of ancient baths includes it repetitively.[757]

It would therefore be extremely difficult to make a case that Burlington was first acquainted with this feature from Palladio's limited use of it, when it was almost the badge of the festive classes of sixteenth-century Italy, and a conspicuous recent innovation on his own home territory. Nor, in detail, did he follow the particular arrangement of continuous *serlianas* used by Palladio at the Basilica. Of all these incentives, we must guess which were likely to be the most influential: probably two were, the knowledge (acquired from Pirro's and Palladio's drawings) that the feature was ancient, and its recent adoption by British architects with objectives similar to his own.

Burlington's collection of archaeological record drawings consisted of many more than those by Palladio. It included drawings by Domenico Ghirlandaio, by the unidentified Raphael associate 'Master C', by Pirro Ligorio, Ammanati, Dosio and Scamozzi. Their subjects included the Heroon of Romulus,[758] the Temple of Vesta,[759] the Mausoleum of Diocletian at Split,[760] S. Stefano Rotondo,[761] the so-called Crypta Balbi,[762] the Temple of Hadrian,[763] the Tomb of Galla Placidia,[764] the Arches of Severus and Janus at Rome[765] and of Trajan at Orange,[766] the Pantheon,[767] and an anonymous ancient villa.[768] One in particular was conscripted directly for use at Chiswick (Fig. 42b). It is almost identical except in the figures which fill its decorative panels to the ceiling of the so-called Link Room at Chiswick (Fig. 42a).[769] The resemblance of drawing to ceiling was unnoticed until 1989.[770] Before then the disimilarity of the ceiling to any known ceiling design, ancient, Renaissance or modern, had caused art historians to consider it in respectful silence.

The Link Room can be dated circumstantially to 1732-33.[771] The drawing can be dated, both from the representation of *putti* shown in some of the

756 Chatsworth, Devonshire Collection, album 37 ('Antiquae urbis praeclarissima aedificia')
757 London, British Architectural Library, Drawings Collection, Burlington-Devonshire Collection, i, 3, ii, 2, iii, 2, 3, 6, 7 and 8, iv, 3, v, 2, 4 and 6, vi, 4 and 7 and vii, 3.
758 London, British Architectural Library, Drawings Collection, Burlington-Devonshire Collection, viii, 1ar.
759 Ibid., viii, 1br.
760 Ibid., viii, 2r and v.
761 Ibid., viii, 3r.
762 Ibid., xi, 3.
763 Ibid., xi, 21r.
764 Ibid., xi, 21v.
765 Ibid., xii, 1.
766 Ibid., xii, 23.
767 Ibid., xiii, 1r and v.
768 Ibid., xiii, 15.
769 Chatsworth, Devonshire Collection, album 35, fo. 57.
770 Hewlings, *Chiswick*, p. 16.
771 Ibid., p. 37.

Fig. 42a The ceiling of the room on the first floor of the Link Building (*English Heritage*)

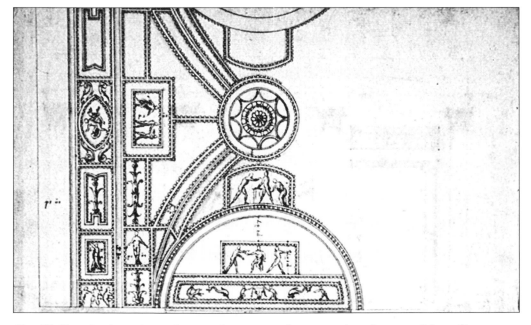

Fig. 42b Drawing by a sixteenth– or early seventeenth–century draughtsman of the ceiling of an ancient mausoleum at Pozzuoli, near Naples (*Chatsworth*)

panels and from the hand which captioned it, to be late sixteenth or early seventeenth century.[772] Its author was north Italian or Roman, as he dimensioned it in *piedi*.[773] He was also methodical enough to note, if not what it represents, the latter's location, which he recorded as 'A Puteolo'. It is therefore not a design, but the model, for the Link Room ceiling.

The ceiling represented in the drawing was evidently in the ancient city of *Puteolum*, north of Naples, and the draughtsman indicated that it was itself antique by giving the location its Latin name, rather than its Italian name, Pozzuoli. The vault form, and its size, together suggest that the ceiling may have ceiled a mausoleum. Whatever it was, it no longer exists;[774] nor did it survive long enough to feature in either the travellers' descriptions,[775] still less the published archaeological accounts of Pozzuoli, Baia or the Phlegrean Fields.[776]

It would of course be interesting to know how Burlington acquired the drawing, whom he believed its author to be, and whether he believed this last to be of any consequence. But without this information, one inference must be that he did not. It suggests that he bought the drawing for the information which it imparted, and that he made use of this information without transforming it. The identification of this drawing clearly raises the possibility that Burlington was indifferent to the creative efforts of Renaissance architects, including Palladio (for Burlington may have believed him to be its author), and perhaps indifferent to all their efforts save as archaeologists.

The circular temple in the Orange Tree Garden, with its attached Ionic portico (Figs 27b, 35a and 43a), could have been suggested by the sight of ancient buildings in Rome. The best preserved of this form was the Pantheon, rebuilt as a temple by Hadrian between 118 and 128 AD (despite the inscription which told the spectator that it was built by Augustus' minister Agrippa in 25 BC), and dedicated as a Christian *martyrium* in 609.[777] Observable as a ruin was the Tor de' Schiavi on the Via Praenestina,

772 This information is based on the advice of Miss Caroline Elam and Dr Arnold Nesselrath.

773 The *palma* was the unit of measurement in southern Italy.

774 Dr R.J. Ling, who has studied the region intensively, advises me that he has found nothing corresponding to the Chatsworth drawing.

775 It is not noted in Ferrante Loffredo, *Antichità di Pozzuoli* (Naples, 1570); Scipione Mazzella, *Sito e antichità della città di Pozzuoli* (Naples, 1594); G.C. Capaccio, *La vera antichità di Pozzuolo* (Naples, 1607); John, Lord Northall,

Travels (London, 1766); Henry Swinburne, *Travels in the Two Sicilies in the Years 1777-1780* (London, 1783-85); R. Freebairn, *A View of the Bay of Naples* (London, 1798); or Katherine C. Walker, 'Vesuvius and Pozzuoli', *Harper's Magazine*, 31 (1865), pp. 756-61.

776 Harald Mielsch, *Römische Stukreliefs* (Heidelberg, 1975), does not record it; nor does Roger Ling, 'Stucco Decorations at Baia', *Papers of the British School at Rome*, 45 (1977), pp. 24-51; nor Roger Ling 'Stanze di Venere', *Archaeologia*, 106 (1979), pp. 36-60.

777 Boethius and Ward-Perkins, *Roman and Etruscan Architecture*, pp. 256-60 and plate 131.

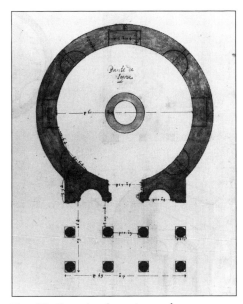

Fig. 43b Drawing by a sixteenth-century draughtsman of the Tor de' Schiavi, Rome (*Chatsworth*)

Fig. 43a Illustration by William Kent of the Ionic Temple, Chiswick

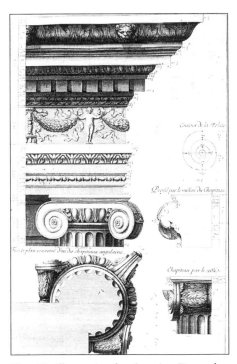

Fig. 43c Illustration by Antoine Desgodetz of the Temple of Portumnus (then called the Temple of Fortuna Virilis), Rome

Fig. 43d Illustration by Giovanni-Battista Montano of the Tor de' Schiavi

dating from *c.* 300, but in Burlington's time believed to have been the *mausoleum* of the Gordian emperors (238-44).[778] Still more ruinous was the Heroon of the Emperor Maxentius' son Romulus (d. 309), built in the grounds of Maxentius' villa on the Via Appia, and intended for Maxentius' own interment.[779] The Chiswick temple could equally have been suggested by the sight of sixteenth-century derivatives of these *mausolea*, Sanmichele's mortuary chapel of the Pellegrini family at S. Bernardino, Verona,[780] or the *tempietto* in the *Sacro Bosco* at Bomarzo, which may also have had a funerary intention.[781] But as it is not known which, if any, of these Burlington saw, the illustrated examples have to be regarded as his sources. Serlio illustrated the Pantheon.[782] Palladio illustrated the Pantheon,[783] and the Heroon of Romulus, which he described as the Temple near S. Sebastiano on the Via Appia.[784] And an anonymous sixteenth-century draughtsman illustrated the Tor de' Schiavi in drawings which Burlington himself owned (Fig. 43b).[785] The Pantheon, with its thick walls and complex internal articulation, least resembles the circular temple at Chiswick. Of the other two, the Heroon of Romulus has alternating large and small niches filling most of the internal wall area, and a deep portico with three rows of columns; these features are not repeated at Chiswick. The Tor de' Schiavi, however, had few niches, of equal size, spaced at generous intervals, and a portico only two intercolumniations deep. The Chiswick temple, simplified still further, most resembles this. It was therefore the Renaissance drawing in his possession, not the illustrations in a book, which Burlington used as his model. But the drawing did not supply information about the ruined monument's ornament; for the Ionic order of its portico Burlington therefore reproduced the unusual diagonally-placed volutes of the corner capitals in the ancient Temple of Portumnus, also published (as the Temple of Fortuna Virilis) by both Palladio[786] and Desgodetz (Fig. 43c).[787]

At Chiswick the broadcasters of myth and moral were led by sphinxes (Fig. 44a). Sphinxes were evidently a particular object of Burlington's interest. By *c.* 1729-32 Chiswick had two on the forecourt gatepiers.[788] By

778 Ibid., 503-4 and fig. 191; Colvin, *Architecture and the After-Life*, pp. 52-53.

779 Boethius and Ward-Perkins, *Roman and Etruscan Architecture*, p. 503; Colvin, *Architecture and the After-Life*, pp. 52-53 and fig. 43.

780 Heydenreich and Lotz, *Architecture in Italy*, p. 222 and fig. 73.

781 Colin Davidson, 'Bomarzo', *Architectural Review*, 106, September 1954, p, 180, fig. 8; Lynette M.F. Bosch, 'Bomarzo: A Study in Personal Imagery', *Garden History*, 10, Autumn 1982, pp. 98, 100 and fig. 1.

782 Serlio, *Architecture*, iii, 2-6v.

783 Palladio, *I quattro libri*, iv, plates 51-55.

784 Ibid., iv, chapter 22 and plate 64.

785 Chatsworth, Devonshire collection, album 36, fos 4r a and b, and 14r a.

786 Palladio, *I quattro libri*, iv, plate 33.

787 Desgodetz, *Les édifices antiques de Rome*, p. 102.

788 Chatsworth, Devonshire Collection, Inventory of Paintings, no. 333, view of the south front of Chiswick House, complementary to those illustrated in Harris, *Artist and Country House*, pp. 182-83, and thus dated *c.* 1729-32; for dating see Spence, 'Chiswick House and Gardens, 1726-32', p. 531.

Fig. 44a Statue of a sphinx at Chiswick (*English Heritage*)

Fig. 44b Drawing by a sixteenth– or seventeenth–century draughtsman of an ancient statue of a sphinx (*Chatsworth*)

Fig. 44c Drawing by a sixteenth– or seventeenth–century draughtsman of an ancient relief of a sphinx (*Chatsworth*)

1742 (probably),[789] and by 1753 (certainly),[790] two more had been added in the Grove. A fifth joined these last two in 1749.[791] Together they outnumbered all other figure types except herms. His collection of drawings also includes more sphinxes than any other figure type.[792] Earlier representations of sphinxes in England are rare. They appear, painted, on two ceilings (those of the Queen's Presence Chamber and Queen's Privy Chamber) at Windsor Castle,[793] and on that of the White Closet at Ham House,[794] all three done in the 1670s by Verrio. Carved sphinxes were supplied for Longleat in 1685.[795] Carved sphinxes appeared on gatepiers at Chatsworth before 1689,[796] and on gatepiers at Bramham Park, Yorkshire, probably *c.* 1719.[797] These appearances, especially the carved versions, are not obviously connected. But from 1724 sphinxes appeared in other decorative schemes connected with Burlington. In that year Kent painted sphinxes on the ceiling of the Presence Chamber at Kensington Palace,[798] apparently under Burlington's patronage.[799] Their next appearance is at Castle Hill, Devon, a house designed by Burlington and Roger Morris in 1729.[800] They can also be seen guarding Carné's Seat at Goodwood, Sussex, a banqueting house probably designed in 1743 by Morris[801] for Burlington's friend (and client), the second duke of Richmond.[802] Their appearance *c.* 1726 at Leeswood Hall, Flintshire,[803] a house not known to have been connected with Burlington, prompts reflection that it may have been.

That the sphinx was a creature of the ancient imagination must obviously have been known to Burlington. But surviving ancient visualisations of it

789 Harris, *Artist and Country House*, p. 261, fig. 276b, illustrates a painting of 1742 by George Lambert which shows the south end of the avenue in which two sphinxes stand now, although in 1742 they were outside the painter's line of vision.

790 Symes, 'John Donowell's Views of Chiswick', pp. 49, fig. 6, and 50, fig. 7.

791 Chatsworth, Devonshire Collection, 'John Ferrett's Account Currant with the Right Honble the Earl of Burlington 1745', fo. 201, 1749, 28 Feb, 'Paid Mr John Cheere . . . for a sphynx in lead . . . 7.7.0.'

792 Chatsworth, Devonshire Collection, album 22, fos 4, 26, 27 and 32; album 35, fos 24b and 38.

793 Edward Croft-Murray, *Decorative Painting in England, 1537-1837*, i (London, 1962), 241a and 241b; Colvin, *King's Works*, pp. 322-23; but neither of these record the sphinxes.

794 Croft-Murray, *Decorative Painting in England*, i, p. 237b.

795 John Harris, 'From Another Point of View', *Country Life*, 185, 14 Nov, 1991, p. 84.

796 Thompson, *Chatsworth*, p. 26 and plate 6.

797 Arthur Oswald, 'Bramham Park, Yorkshire – I', *Country Life*, 123, 20 Feb. 1958, pp. 350 (fig. 1) and 353.

798 Croft-Murray, *Decorative Painting in England*, ii, pp. 28, 234, and plate 41.

799 Colvin, *King's Works*, v, pp. 198-200.

800 Kenneth Woodbridge, 'Landscaping at Castle Hill', *Country Life*, 165, 4 January 1979, pp. 18-19, figs 2, 3 and 4; Colvin, *Biographical Dictionary of British Architects*, p. 131.

801 Christopher Hussey, 'Goodwood House – II, Sussex', *Country Life*, 72, 16 July 1932, p. 68, fig. 5.

802 T.P. Connor, 'Architecture and Planting at Goodwood, 1723-1750', *Sussex Archaeological Collections*, 117 (1979), pp. 187-88, 190.

803 Ifor Edwards, *Davies Brothers Gatesmiths* (Cardiff, 1977), pp. 72-74.

are rare. There is one on a Roman figure of Father Nile in the Vatican Museum,[804] and two of basalt in the Capitoline Museum.[805] A candelabrum base with sphinxes, now in the Musée Condé, Chantilly, was in the Farnesina in the eighteenth century.[806] Van Heemskerck recorded two sphinxes supporting a Roman sarcophagus in the 1530s.[807] Boissard included six plates of ancient sphinxes in his third volume, one each in his fourth and fifth volumes.[808] Montano illustrated two ancient capitals with sphinx ornament.[809] Montfaucon has one plate with six sphinxes illustrated.[810] Three plates in the *Hypnerotomachia Poliphili* feature sphinxes, two associated with fountains.[811] Although Burlington owned these four books,[812] and therefore knew these illustrations, there is no knowing whether he saw any ancient sphinxes at first hand.

Among Renaissance sphinxes in Italy, Donatello's high altar in the Santo in Padua has a sphinx throne.[813] Burlington visited Padua in 1715,[814] and Kent had visited it the previous year.[815] Andrea del Castagno painted a sphinx bench in the *Last Supper* in the former refectory of S. Apollonia in Florence of 1447.[816] There are two sphinxes of *c.* 1470 in the church of SS. Giovanni e Paolo in Venice, flanking the altar.[817] Pintoricchio painted sphinxes in the Room of the Lives of the Saints in the Apartamento Borgia of the Vatican in 1492-94,[818] more on a vault of the Palazzo Colonna in Rome, shortly before 1503,[819] and more again in the Libreria Piccolomini,

804 Nikolaus Pevsner, 'The Egyptian Revival', in *Studies in Art, Architecture and Design*, i (London, 1968), p. 217, fig. 15.

805 Ibid., p. 219 and n. 44.

806 Bober and Rubinstein, *Renaissance Artists and Antique Sculpture*, p. 94.

807 Pevsner, 'The Egyptian Revival', p. 221, fig. 23.

808 Boissard, *Antiquae statuae urbis Romae*, iii, plates 57, 77, 91, 93, 100 and 106 (plates 91 and 106 include vases like those painted on the ceiling of the Summer Parlour at Chiswick, increasing the possibility of these plates being Lord Burlington's inspiration); iv, plate 142; v, plate 81.

809 Montano, *Architettura con diversi ornamenti*, p. 38.

810 Montfaucon, *Antiquity Explained*, ii, plate 42.

811 Francesco Colonna, *Hypnerotomachia Poliphili* (Venice, 1499), fo. 30 (Grand Fountain) and fo. 38 (Banquet Fountain), although in the latter they are described as harpies; the English language version, *Hypnerotomachia Poliphili: The Strife of Love in a Dream* (London, 1592), only includes one sphinx illustration, on p. 47.

812 Chatsworth, Devonshire Collection, Library,

MS 'Catalogue of the Earl of Burlington's Library', pp. 4 and 43.

813 Warren Tresidder, 'A Borrowing from the Antique in Giovanni Bellini's "Continence of Scipio"', *Burlington Magazine*, 134, October 1992, p. 660; John Pope-Hennessy, *Italian Renaissance Sculpture* (London, 1958), pp. 10-12, discusses the altar but not the throne.

814 Chatsworth, Devonshire Collection, Lord Burlington's Grand Tour Account Book; Lees-Milne, *The Earls of Creation*, pp. 92-93.

815 Wilson, *William Kent*, p. 27.

816 Marita Horster, *Andrea del Castagno* (Oxford, 1980), pp. 23-25, 176 and plates 52-53, is the fullest discussion; but there are better illustrations of the sphinxes in Luciano Berti, *Andrea del Castagno* (1966), plates 32 and 43.

817 Franca Zava Boccazzi, *La Basilica di S. Giovanni e Paolo in Venezia* (Venice, 1965), fig. 44.

818 James Stevens Curl, *The Egyptian Revival* (London, 1982), p. 44; Enzo Carli, *Il Pintoricchio* (Milan, 1960), p. 43, dates and describes these paintings, but does not illustrate any sphinxes.

819 Carli, *Il Pintoricchio*, p. 32 and plate 54.

Siena, painted between 1505 and 1509;[820] and there are still more in the Palazzo Saracini, Siena.[821] Burlington passed through Siena on his way to Rome in 1714 and on his way back in 1715.[822] Kent also visited Siena in 1714 and particularly noted the cathedral[823] (to which the Libreria is attached). Other sphinxes feature on the tomb of Angelo Cesi (*c.* 1550) by Vincenzo de Rossi in Sta Maria della Pace, Rome.[824] In the open air Burlington may have seen a carved sphinx on the palazzo Doria in Genoa, dating from 1528,[825] and one which forms a column base in the Piazzo S. Marco in Venice.[826]

They are equally abundant in France. Primaticcio painted sphinxes in the Galerie d'Ulysse at Fontainebleau in 1540,[827] and there are four carved sphinxes in the garden there.[828] Thereafter they occur carved, on the tombs of Guillaume du Bellay at Le Mans in 1557[829] and Diane de Poitiers in 1576.[830] Du Cerceau illustrates them in his *Livre d'architecture*,[831] and in two drawings, one in the Bibliothèque Nationale[832] and another in the Pierpont Morgan Library.[833] There are sphinxes in the Chambre de César de Vendôme in the Château de Chenonceaux,[834] and sphinxes painted on ceilings by Ambroise Le Noble in the Château de Bourdeilles.[835] They are found associated with fountains at the Châteaux of Villesavin[836] and Cormatin (the latter before 1618),[837] Mansart used them at Maisons,[838] and there are more in the gardens at Versailles.[839] It is not known whether Burlington saw any of these but, if he did not, he had a collection of drawings of sphinxes. One drawing is attributed to Perino del Vaga,[840] four more may also be Italian (Fig. 44b, c),[841] and another may be French.[842] One of his drawings of the Villa Giulia also included sphinx ornament (Fig. 14b).

820 Curl, *The Egyptian Revival*, p. 49 and plate 30; Pietro Scarpellini, *Pintoricchio* (Milan, 1968), passim.
821 Curl, *The Egyptian Revival*, p. 49.
822 Chatsworth, Devonshire Collection, Lord Burlington's Grand Tour Account Book; Lees-Milne, *The Earls of Creation*, pp. 90 and 92.
823 Wilson, *William Kent*, p. 26.
824 Pevsner, 'The Egyptian Revival', p. 222, fig. 27.
825 Lotz et al., *Alessi*, p. 351 and fig. 289.
826 Naomi Miller, *French Renaissance Fountains* (New York, 1977), plate 68.
827 Pevsner, 'The Egyptian Revival', p. 224, fig. 31; Jean Guillaume and Sylvie Beguin, *La Galerie d'Ulysse a Fontainebleau* (Paris, 1985), pp. 282-83.
828 Curl, *The Egyptian Revival*, p. 60.
829 Pevsner, 'The Egyptian Revival' p. 224, fig. 29.
830 Ibid., p. 225, fig. 33.
831 Jacques Androuet du Cerceau, *Le second livre d'architecture*, 1561 (reproduced in Miller, *French Renaissance Fountains*, plate 211).
832 Miller, *French Renaissance Fountains*, plate 212.
833 Ibid., plate 127.
834 Curl, *The Egyptian Revival*, p. 60.
835 Ibid., p. 59.
836 Miller, *French Renaissance Fountains*, plate 67.
837 Rosalys Coope, *Catalogue of the Drawings Collection of the Royal Institute of British Architects: Jacques Gentilhatre* (Farnborough, 1972), pp. 20, no. 95r, 26, no. 192v and fig. 54; Rosalys Coope, 'Cormatin, France', *Country Life*, 184, 1 March 1990, p. 98.
838 Rosalys Coope, *Salomon de Brosse*, plate 132.
839 Curl, *The Egyptian Revival*, p. 75.
840 Chatsworth, Devonshire Collection, album 35, fo. 24b.
841 Ibid., album 22, fos 4, 26, 27 and 32.
842 Ibid., album 35, fo. 38.

From at least 1733 the forecourt was flanked by herms (Fig. 45a).[843] In the same year two (of a type which are no longer represented at Chiswick) were shown in the western *patte d'oie*, inside the Burlington Lane Gate.[844] No herms are shown in the views of *c.* 1729-32,[845] and by 1733 they had still not been added to the northern *patte d'oie*.[846] But by 1753 herms, of the first (still surviving) type had been added there also.[847] Herms as male caryatids, supporting a load on their heads, but statically (not with their arms twisted above to take the load, like *atlantes*), were of ancient origin. Whether Burlington saw ancient specimens is unknown; if he had visited the Château de Richelieu on one of his trips to France he would have seen two at either end of a hemi-cycle flanking the gates, placed there by Le Mercier in 1630-40.[848] According to Montfaucon, there was another ancient herm at Versailles,[849] which he visited on 23 April 1715.[850]

But he could have seen numerous sixteenth-century herms in Italy. In Rome they support Michelangelo's Tomb of Julius II,[851] and ornament Pirro Ligorio's Casino of Pius IV.[852] Returning via Milan in 1715,[853] he could have seen them on the fronts of three conspicuous city-centre buildings, Leone Leoni's famous house,[854] Galeazzo's Alessi's Palazzo Marini,[855] and Vincenzo Seregni's Palazzo dei Giureconsulti.[856] At Tivoli, which Kent visited,[857] there are herms in the Room of the Muses, and more flanking the rustic fountain in the Salotto of Pirro Ligorio's Villa d'Este.[858] At Poggio a Caiano herms support the entrance to the Pan grotto,[859] admired by Kent on his visit in 1714.[860] In Mantua Kent saw them in the *cortile* of the *grotta* of Giulio Romano's Palazzo del Te,[861] and he might have

843 Carré, 'Rigaud's Drawings at Chiswick', fig. 8.

844 Ibid., fig. 3.

845 Harris, *Artist and the Country House*, plates xixa, b, and c and figs 187a to h; for the dating, see Spence, 'Chiswick House and its Gardens, 1726-32', p. 531.

846 Carré, 'Rigaud's Drawings at Chiswick', fig. 5.

847 Symes, 'John Donowell's Views of Chiswick', p. 48, fig 5.

848 MacDougall and Miller, *Fons sapientiae*, p. 52.

849 Montfaucon, *Antiquity Explained*, Supplement I, plate 5.

850 Chatsworth, Devonshire Collection, Lord Burlington's Grand Tour Account Book; Lees-Milne, *The Earls of Creation*, p. 94; see also below.

851 De Tolnay, *The Tomb of Julius II*, plates 1-3, 98, 107 and 207.

852 Graham Smith, *The Casino of Pius IV* (Prince-

ton, 1977), plates 7-14 and 41.

853 Chatsworth, Devonshire Collection, Lord Burlington's Grand Tour Account Book.

854 Michael P. Mezzatesta, 'The Façade of Leone Leoni's House in Milan, the Casa degli Omenoni: The Artist and the Public', *Journal of the Society of Architectural Historians*, 44, pt 3, October 1985, figs 1, 3-12.

855 Lotz et al., *Alessi*, plates 35-37, fig. 363.

856 Ibid., figs 384, 391 and 394; Houghton Brown, *Milanese Architecture of Galeazzo Alessi*, i, p. 383, ii, figs 171 and 173; Baroni, *Vincenzo Seregni*.

857 Wilson, *William Kent*, p. 14, fig. 2.

858 Coffin, *The Villa d'Este*, plates 60, 62 and 88.

859 Smith, *The Casino of Pius IV*, plate 36; Bardazzi and Castellani, *La Villa Medicea*, plate 35.

860 Wilson, *William Kent*, p. 202.

861 Hartt, *Giulio Romano*, i, p. 145; ii, plate 297; Sicca, 'Kent's Roman Sources', pp. 137-38.

seen seventeenth-century herms in Antonio-Maria Viani's Palazzo di Gius-
tizia.[862] In Genoa both of them could have seen herms which flank Perino
del Vaga's chimneypiece in the western Sala Grande of the Villa Doria,[863]
herms in the loggia of Alessi's Villa Cambiaso,[664] or herms in the presby-
tery vaults of Alessi's church of S. Matteo.[865] If they managed to miss all
these, Burlington could have still seen them in the drawings which he
owned of the Villa Giulia, where they support the *nymphaeum* (Fig. 45b) and
frame doors (Fig. 45e).[866] He could also have seen three illustrations of
ancient herms in Cartari's *Imagini*.[867] He could have seen illustrations of
ancient herms in his copy of Barbaro's *Vitruvius*, where they represent
Persian prisoners supporting the portico erected by the Spartans.[868] He
could also have seen illustrations of ancient herms in his copy of Montano's
book (Fig. 45c).[869] Montfaucon also illustrates (Fig. 45d) other ancient
variants, a hermaphrodite,[870] and a hermeracles (a composite of Mercury
and Hercules).[871]

These might have supplied the general idea, and even some of the details.
But the Chiswick herms are not male caryatids; they support nothing. They
are derived from ancient boundary stones, terms rather than herms, whose
representation in the sixteenth century is rarer. Pirro Ligorio drew specimens similar to those at Chiswick,[872] but these drawings are not known to
have been seen by Burlington. Sambin published a book exclusively on
terms in 1572,[873] which Burlington owned; but Sambin's inventions are
more complex than those at Chiswick.[874] Two plates in Boissard, however,
illustrate ancient terms, one on the Quirinal,[875] and one near Sta Susanna;[876]
one of these plates was reused by Montfaucon.[877] One of the anonymous
sixteenth-century drawings which he owned also shows an ancient term,
although small and sketchily drawn.[878] Another shows a term with a lion's

862   Lotz et al., *Alessi*, fig. 368.
863   Gorse, 'The Villa of Andrea Doria in Genoa',
      p. 26, fig. 15 and n 49.
864   Lotz et al., *Alessi*, figs 290-93.
865   Ibid., figs 294-95.
866   London, British Architectural Library, Draw-
      ings Collection, Burlington-Devonshire Col-
      lection, viii, 4v; Land Moore, 'Villa Giulia',
      fig. 14.
867   Vincenzo Cartari, *Le imagini de i dei de gli antichi*
      (Venice, 1571), pp. 315, 326 and 332.
868   Mezzatesta, 'The Façade of Leone Leoni's
      House in Milan', fig. 16.
869   Montano, *Architettura con diversi ornamenti*, p.
      41.
870   Montfaucon, *Antiquity Explained*, Supplement

I, plate 31.
871   Ibid., plate 39.
872   Erna Mandowsky and Charles Mitchell, *Pirro
      Ligorio's Roman Antiquities* (London, 1963),
      plates 33, 37b, 38-52 and 55.
873   Hugues Sambin, *Oeuvre de la diversité des termes*
      (Lyon, 1572).
874   Chatsworth, Devonshire Collection, Library,
      MS 'Catalogue of the Earl of Burlington's
      Library', p. 4.
875   Boissard, *Antique statuae urbis Romae*, iv, plate
      177.
876   Ibid., iv, plate 134.
877   Montfaucon, *Antiquity Explained*, i, plate 83.
878   Chatsworth, Devonshire Collection, album
      36, fo. 15c v.

Fig. 45a Statue of a herm at Chiswick (*English Heritage*)

Fig. 45b Detail of a drawing of the *nymphaeum* of the Villa Giulia, Rome (*RIBA*)

Fig. 45c Illustration by Giovanni–Battista Montano of ancient statues of herms

Fig. 45d Illustration by Bernard de Montfaucon of ancient statues of herms

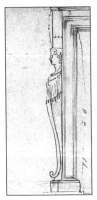

Fig. 45e Drawing of a detail of the Villa Giulia, Rome (*RIBA*)

Fig. 45f Drawing by a sixteenth– or a seventeenth–century draughtsman of an ancient statue of a term (*Chatsworth*)

head and a lion's leg below (Fig. 45f).[879] These last may have furnished him with the term concept, while the herm illustrations filled in the details.

Inside Chiswick House the principal carved ornaments are the female masks in the round and octagonal parts of the gallery (Fig. 46a). They carry baskets with acanthus sprouting from below, illustrating, in telegraphic form, the mythic origin of the Corinthian order, as described by Vitruvius.[880] That Burlington was aware of this myth is made clear beyond doubt by his possession of a drawing which illustrates it more discursively (Fig. 46b).[881] But he did not use this drawing as a model. The need for compression required more allusive expression. A model for this Burlington evidently found in the head of a caryatid supporting a basket. No such model was provided by Palladio. Indeed all but a few of the numerous Renaissance caryatids are without baskets.[882] But there are at least two with baskets which Burlington could have seen. One is in Raphael's Villa Madama;[883] another is in the nymphaeum of Alessi's Villa delle Peschiere, Genoa.[884] Nor did he have to rely on memory alone, for the first of these at least. His friend Thomas Coke owned thirteen drawings of the vault of the Villa Madama, which Kent also saw, for he bought them on Coke's behalf in Rome in 1718.[885]

The avenue from the house to the exedra is lined mainly by urns (Fig. 47a–d). The avenue had not been created in 1733,[886] and was in existence, but without the urns, by 1736.[887] The urns were first illustrated in 1742.[888] Of the fourteen different urn types at (or formerly at) Chiswick, one in the Exedra incorporates ornament which was innovatory in England even by this last date. It has applied panels with fish tail handles, a panel type known as *tabula ansata*. An undated sketch by Kent shows this type of urn with *tabulae ansatae*, alternating with small stone benches which were also ornamented by *tabulae ansatae* set between vertically-symmetrical balusters, linked by festoons.[889] The benches, which have been removed, were not an unrealised whim of Kent's, for they were recorded (Fig. 47d), together with

879 Ibid., album 22, fo. 29.
890 Vitruvius, *The Ten Books on Architecture*, iv, ch. 1, pp. 9-10.
881 Chatsworth, Devonshire Collection, album 35, fo. 50.
882 For instance in the Salle des Cariatides in the Louvre, *Gazette des beaux arts*, i (1906), pp. 185-89; or on Giacomo del Duca's gateway to the Orti Farnesiani in Rome, Benedetti, *Giacomo del Duca*, plates 167 and 170.
883 Frommel, Ray and Tafuri, *Raffaelo architetto*,

catalogue, pp. 316, 352; Sicca, 'Kent's Roman Sources', p. 139.
884 Lotz et al., *Alessi*, fig. 184.
885 Sicca, 'Kent's Roman Sources', p. 139.
886 Carré, 'Rigaud's Drawings of Chiswick', p. 134, fig. 1.
887 Badeslade and Rocque, *Vitruvius Brittanicus*, plates 82-83.
888 Harris, *Artist and the Country Seat*, p. 261.
889 Dixon Hunt, *William Kent*, p. 129, no. 36.

Fig. 46a Carving of a female mask on the
wall of the Round Room of the Gallery,
Chiswick House (*English Heritage*)

Fig. 46b Drawing illustrating the myth of the
origin of the Corinthian capital (*Chatsworth*)

the urns, by a draughtsman working for the third marquess of Bute,[890] tenant of Chiswick House probably from 1879, and certainly from 1881 to 1892.[891] The benches resembled ancient funerary caskets, while the urns resemble ancient funerary urns. Both are variants of ancient prototypes illustrated by Montfaucon.[892]

It is possible that Burlington saw ancient *tabulae ansatae*. *Tabulae ansatae* borne on spears were illustrated among the trophies taken from Jerusalem on the Arch of Titus.[893] Sarcophagi with *tabulae ansatae* survive in Pavia[894] and Ravenna,[895] and another, which became part of the Towneley Collection, was in Rome during Burlington's lifetime,[896] and had been published by Boissard in 1597.[897] Two ancient funerary urns at Castle Howard have *tabulae ansatae*: one was bought from the heirs of Cardinal Gualtiero by the dealer Francesco de Ficoroni in 1738 and sold, probably shortly thereafter, to the fourth earl of Carlisle.[898] One, perhaps both, could therefore have been in England in time for it to have been an inspiration for Burlington. It was easier, however, for Burlington to have seen Renaissance *tabulae ansatae*. Eleven *quattrocento* examples alone could be seen on monuments in

890 London Borough of Hounslow, Library Services, Chiswick Public Library (Reference Branch), Bute Portfolio.
891 Ibid., pencilled note in modern hand 'Earl of Bute leased Chiswick House 1879-92'. Although the Marquess's description as 'Earl' diminishes confidence in this note, it may be right. From 1878 to 1892 the Duke of Devonshire is described as the occupier of Chiswick House in the rate books (London Borough of Hounslow, Library Services, Chiswick Public Library, Reference Branch, Chiswick Parish Poor Rate Books). In November 1892 'Duke of Devonshire' has been struck out and 'Thomas Seymour Tuke and Charles Molesworth Tuke', the subsequent tenants, have been pencilled in (ibid.). This must represent a *terminus ante quem* of the Bute tenancy, which evidently did not include the obligation to pay rates. Nonetheless the Marquess was certainly the occupant between 1881 and 1890: he and the Marchioness were resident at the time of the 1881 Census (PRO, RG11/1350), and he is included at 'Chiswick house' in *Kelly's Directory of Middlesex* in 1882 (p. 800), 1887-88 (p. 182) and 1890 (p. 1,001). In 1878 *Kelly's Directory* named no resident of Chiswick House; so

it may have been empty, and available for letting, the following year.
892 Montfaucon, *Antiquity Explained*, v, plates 6 and 7 (urns), plates 8-20, 22 and 30 (caskets).
893 Bober and Rubenstein, *Renaissance Artists and Antique Sculpture*, p. 203 and plate 173.
894 Gaetano Panazza, *Lapidi e scultore paleocristiane e pre-romaniche di Pavia* (1950).
895 Fernando Rebecchi, 'Sarcofagi cispadani di età imperiale Romana', *Mitteilungen des Deutschen Archaeologischen Instituts, Römische Abteilung*, 84 (1977), pp. 107-58, plates 60 and 63.
896 A.H. Smith, *A Catalogue of Sculpture in the Department of Greek and Roman Antiquities, British Museum*, iii (London, 1904), pp. 289-90, no. 2,275. Another sarcophagus with a *tabula ansata* in the British Museum (ibid., p. 366, no. 2,404) was in the Towneley Collection, but its location in Burlington's life is not established.
897 Boissard, *Antiquae statuae urbis Romae*, iii, plate 137.
898 Hansgeorg Oehler, *Foto & Skulptur*, Catalogue of an exhibition of classical sculpture in English private collections, University of Cologne (Cologne, 1978), pp. 27 and 28. I am indebted to Dr Elizabeth Angellicousis for drawing my attention to these urns.

Fig. 47a-c Carved urns at Chiswick
(*English Heritage*)

Fig. 47d Drawing of carved urns and benches
in the Exedra at Chiswick (*Richard Hewlings,
after drawing in Chiswick Public Library*)

Roman churches.[899] The door of S.Lorenzo in Damaso has *tabula ansata* ornament.[900] And, although otherwise largely confined to Rome, *tabulae ansatae* had reached northern Europe in the fifteenth century by means of the Italophile Count René of Anjou: *tabula ansata* ornament appears on Francesco Laurana's tomb of Count Charles IV of Anjou in Le Mans Cathedral.[901] Whether or not Burlington saw these, it may be regarded as certain that he saw the *tabulae ansatae* borne by soldiers on spears in the first two canvasses of Mantegna's *Triumphs of Caesar*, since it was displayed in the Queen's Gallery at Hampton Court,[902] where, as Captain of the Band of Gentlemen-Pensioners,[903] and husband of a Lady of the Bedchamber,[904] he had to be a frequent visitor. Whatever his initial inspiration, he did not have to remember it, because it also appears in Renaissance books. The *Hypnerotomachia Poliphili* includes three *tabulae ansatae*,[905] Boissard illustrated eleven ancient *tabulae ansatae* on sarcophagi,[906] and Montfaucon illustrated *tabulae ansatae* both on grotesque ceilings and on funerary urns,[907] and the panel from the Arch of Titus where the *tabulae ansatae* are displayed.[908] Burlington even possessed a drawing of an ancient *tabula ansata*.[909] An architectural *capriccio* drawn by Juvarra in 1729, and given to Burlington in 1730, also includes *tabulae ansatae*.[910] His particular source may therefore have been his own collection.

Around the *patte d'oie* east of the Exedra a set of stone benches were placed: they are first shown in a view of 1753.[911] Burlington modelled them on an

899 Gerald Davies, *Renaissance Tombs in Rome* (London, 1910), illustrates *tabulae ansatae* on the tombs of Pope Martin V (d. 1431) in S. Giovanni Laterano (pp. 227-29, fig. 17); Cardinal Jacopo Tebaldi (d. 1466) in Sta Maria sopra Minerva (p. 270, fig. 56); Constantia Ammanati (d. 1471) in the cloister of S. Agostino (p. 194, fig. 42); Cardinal Alanus Cetivus (d. 1474) in Sta Prassede (pp. 353-54, fig. 27); Cardinal Cristofor della Rovere (d. 1477) in Sta Maria del Popolo (pp. 306-8, fig. 36); Cardinal Pietro Ferrici (d. 1478) in the cloister of Sta Maria sopra Minerva (p. 283, fig. 76); Meria Duce Cicada (d. 1481) in S. Giovanni dei Genovese (pp. 222-23, fig. 64); Bishop Pietro Guglielmo Rocca (d. 1482) in Sta Maria del Popolo (p. 295, fig. 37); Giovanni della Rovere (d. 1483) in Sta Maria del Popolo (pp. 296-97, fig. 44); Cardinal Bernardino Lonate (d. 1497) in Sta Maria del Popolo (p. 300, fig. 52); and Cardinal Giorgio Costa (d. 1508) in Sta Maria del Popolo (pp. 292-93, fig. 77).
900 Venturi, *Storia dell'arte Italiana*, xi, pt 2, p. 769, fig. 710.
901 Ibid., viii, pt 1, p. 563, fig. 414.
902 Andrew Martindale, *The Triumphs of Caesar by Andrea Mantegna* (London, 1979), p. 112, describes the location; canvas I is illustrated opposite p. 20, canvas II opposite p. 56.
903 Henry Brackenbury, *The Nearest Guard* (London, 1892), pp. 207, 155.
904 George Edward Cockayne, *The Complete Peerage*, ii (London, 1912), p. 433.
905 Colonna, *Hypnerotomachia Poliphili*.
906 Boissard, *Antiquae statuae urbis Romae*, iii, plates 137, 145 and 146; iv (1598), plate 68; v (1600), plates 19, 29, 39, 56, 85, 98 and 127.
907 Montfaucon, *Antiquity Explained*, v, plates 2, 4 and 7; supplement ii, plate 118.
908 Ibid., iv, plate 32.
909 Chatsworth, Devonshire Collection, album 36, fol. 30.
910 Wittkower, *Studies in the Italian Baroque*, fig. 254; Chatsworth, Devonshire Collection, album 30, fol. 10.
911 Symes, 'John Donowell's Views of Chiswick', p. 48, fig. 5.

ancient source, not apparently an ancient bench but an ancient sarcophagus. The wide consoles which form the legs are those which, in the ancient type, lifted the chest of the sarcophagus off the ground. Burlington probably saw sarcophagi of this type in Rome: a tomb in the portico of the Pantheon has one and, if Burlington missed it, it was illustrated by Desgodetz.[912] Palladio made a record drawing of an ancient sarcophagus, but there is no reason to believe that Burlington saw this drawing.[913] The type was used as a model for numcrous Renaissance tombs, of which the best known was Michelangelo's tomb of Julius II in St Peter's.[914] But he did not have to remember examples, ancient or modern, for he possessed a design by Giulio Romano for a casket which similarly used ancient sarcophagi as a source for its legs.[915] It may have been this drawing which inspired him to use sarcophagus legs as a model for bench legs.

There is one feature at Chiswick of ancient origin, which Burlington seems to have reproduced in a manncr transmitted to him by Inigo Jones. This is the vermiculated masonry of the gatepiers (Fig. 24a), of the ground floor of the portico of the house (Fig. 32), and of the Rustic House. It was illustrated in all thrcc locations in paintings of *c.* 1729-32.[916] Vermiculated masonry was no novelty in England in the 1720s, but it occured almost exclusively on gatcs, screens or portals. Jones' drawings illustrate it ornamenting gates to Arundcl House[917] and Hatton House,[918] both in London, Bcaufort House, Chelsea,[919] and Oatlands Palace.[920] It was used to ornament the Water Gate to York Housc, London,[921] the screen of Castle Ashby, Northants,[922] the 'Front Portall att' Hampstead Marshall, Berkshire,[923] the garden gate at Kirby Hall, Northamptonshire,[924] the portal of the Haberdashers' Hall, London,[925] the portal of the Queen's College, Oxford,[926] the gate piers of Easton Neston Hall, Northamptonshire,[927] the

912 Desgodetz, *Les édifices antiques de Rome*, p. 19.
913 Anthony Blunt, *Philibert de l'Orme*, plate 456.
914 Charles de Tolnay, *The Tomb of Julius II*, plate 56.
915 Hartt, *Giulio Romano*, ii, plate 139.
916 Chatsworth, Devonshire Collection, Inventory of Paintings, no. 333, illustrates the gatepiers and the portico, and is complementary to the paintings illustrated in Harris, *Artist and the Country House*, pp. 182-83, dated *c.* 1729-32; the Rustic House is illustrated at fig. 187h of the latter; for the dating, see Spence, 'Chiswick House and its Gardens, 1726-32', p. 531.
917 Harris and Higgott, *Inigo Jones: Complete Architectural Drawings*, p. 127.
918 Ibid., p. 135.
919 Ibid., p. 129.
920 Ibid., p. 77.

921 London County Council, *Survey of London*, xviii, plates 31-33.
922 Gervase Jackson Stops, 'Castle Ashby, Northamptonshire – I', *Country Life*, 179, 30 January 1986, p. 251, fig. 6.
923 Oliver Hill and John Cornforth, *English Country Houses: Caroline, 1625-1685* (London, 1966), p. 142, fig. 226.
924 Ibid., 15, fig. 7.
925 John Summerson, *Architecture in Britain, 1530 to 1830* (Harmondsworth, 1953), plate 78b, where it is incorrectly attributed to Edward Jerman.
926 Howard Colvin, *Unbuilt Oxford* (New Haven, 1983), p. 51, fig. 45.
927 James Lees-Milne, *English Country Houses: Baroque, 1685-1715* (London, 1970), p. 140, fig. 224.

piers of the perron of Castle Howard, Yorkshire,[928] the Hensington Gates of Blenheim Palace, Oxfordshire,[929] the gatepiers and ornamental piers in the garden of Bramham Hall, Yorkshire,[930] and the doorway of Emral Hall, Flintshire.[931] Its rarer but alternative use was on ornamental garden buildings: Jones designed vermiculation for a stable (perhaps for the earl of Salisbury),[932] and it was subsequently used on the Orangery at Dyrham Park, Gloucesterhire,[933] and the Cascade House at Chatsworth, Derbyshire.[934] In this context its use on the Rustic House at Chiswick, a garden ornament styled as a portal, is unexceptional.

Ornamenting the entire ground floor of the main portico at Chiswick, however, it was without English precedent. Its extent, and the deepness of its undercutting, contrive to make it one of the most striking features of the house today; it was doubtless even more striking in 1727. It must surely have been intended less to resemble English garden gates of the seventeenth century than the massive walls of vermiculated masonry of the early Imperial (especially Claudian) period of ancient Rome. When in Rome Burlington may have seen the back wall of the Forum of Augustus, the podium of the Temple of Claudius on the Celian Hill, the Forum Pacis, the Porta Maggiore and the arches of the Aqua Virgo.[935] In Verona he may have seen the Amphitheatre.[936] This type of vermiculation, fused with the Ghibelline and Tuscan traditions of rusticated masonry, was extensively copied in sixteenth-century Rome, beginning with Bramante's Palazzo dei Tribunali in 1508-11.[937] Burlington could hardly have avoided seeing it somewhere, but to refresh his memory, he owned drawings of one of the buildings on which it occurs, the Villa Giulia.[938] It was also exemplified by both Serlio[939] and Palladio.[940] It is therefore arguable that Burlington used it to create an impression of sixteenth century, rather than ancient Rome. It is also true hat Palladio's use of it, on the Palazzo Thiene,[941] especially

928 H. Avray Tipping, 'Castle Howard, York-shire', *Country Life*, 61, 4 June 1927, pp. 884-85, figs 1 and 2.

929 David Green, *Blenheim Palace* (London, 1951), p. 112., fig. 51.

930 Oswald, 'A Yorkshire Landscape Garden', pp. 350, fig. 1, and 353, fig 7.

931 Lees-Milne, *English Country Houses: Baroque*, p. 271, fig. 437.

932 Harris and Higgott, *Inigo Jones: Complete Architectural Drawings*, p. 49.

933 Lees-Milne, *English Country Houses: Baroque*, p. 88, fig. 142.

934 Kerry Downes, *English Baroque Architecture*, plate 154.

935 James S. Ackerman, 'The Tuscan/Rustic Order: A Study in the Metaphorical Language of Architecture', *Journal of the Society of Architectural Historians*, 42, March 1983, pp. 31-32.

936 Ibid., p. 28.

937 Bruschi, pp. 169-173 and plate 177.

938 London, British Architectural Library, Drawings Collection, Burlington-Devonshire Collection, viii, 1-4.

939 Serlio, *Architecture*, ii, p. 19; iii, frontispiece; iv, 8v, 9, 14v, 15, 24 and 40.

940 Palladio, *I quattro libri*, i, p. 9; ii, plates 9 and 10; iii, plates 9 and 10.

941 Puppi, *Andrea Palladio*, pp. 251-54 and plates 49-54.

Fig. 48a Drawing by Inigo Jones for the Queen's House, Greenwich (*RIBA*)

Fig. 48b Drawing, probably by Henry Flitcroft, after Inigo Jones' drawing for the Queen's House, Greenwich (*RIBA*)

Fig. 49a Painted Corinthian capital on the south side of the ceiling of the Blue Velvet Room, Chiswick House (*English Heritage*)

Fig. 49b Painted Corinthian capital on the north side of the ceiling of the Blue Velvet Room, Chiswick House (*English Heritage*)

Fig. 49c Painted Corinthian capital on the east side of the ceiling of the Blue Velvet Room, Chiswick House (*English Heritage*)

Fig. 49d Painted Corinthian capital on the west side of the ceiling of the Blue Velvet Room, Chiswick House (*English Heritage*)

Fig. 49e Drawing by John Webb of a Corinthian capital (*RIBA*)

Fig. 49f Drawing by John Webb of a Corinthian capital (*RIBA*)

Fig. 49g Drawing by John Webb of a Corinthian capital (*RIBA*)

Fig. 49h Drawing by John Webb of a Corinthian capital (*RIBA*)

impressed him. He noted in his copy of Palladio's book that the Palazzo Thiene was 'the best school that ever was for rusticks'.[942] But Palladio's book also makes it clear that vermiculation is masonry of an ancient type. On an earlier page a note on ancient masonry techniques illustrates vermiculated masonry specifically described as being visible on the back wall of the Forum of Augustus.[943] Even if Burlington did not follow up that lead, he cannot have been unaware that it was a technique of ancient provenance.

Nevertheless, Burlington's unaided memory (for he did not sketch) of Italian masonry, both ancient and modern, together with the books and drawings in his possession, cannot have been enough to realise the vermiculation at Chiswick. The illustrations in Palladio's book show vermiculated masonry as wavy-edged stones, each with one or two squiggles, suggesting merely an unfinished surface. Jones followed Palladio's graphic technique.[944] The drawings of the Villa Giulia show the rough edges, but without the squiggles on the surfaces. Serlio used irregular hatching instead of squiggles, but omitted the wavy edges. None illustrates the deep holes of travertine or tufa so effectively imitated at Chiswick. To achieve this Burlington would have to have followed the built examples, and thus inevitably the English ones, at least in technique if not in overall design. One of these, the gate to Beaufort House, Chelsea, actually came into his possession in 1738,[945] although he had doubtless seen it earlier. As it happens, there is some evidence that English examples were critical in the evolution of the vermiculation at Chiswick, despite Burlington's enthusiasm for Palladio's school of rustics and the far more numerous examples he had seen abroad. One English building for which vermiculation was proposed, but not executed, was the Queen's House at Greenwich.[946] Jones' drawing, which Burlington owned,[947] illustrates what must be proposed vermiculation (Fig. 48a), using the graphic technique employed by Palladio to illustrate the vermiculated Palazzo Thiene, and by Jones himself to illustrate the vermiculated Beaufort House gate.[948] Burlington had this drawing copied by Flitcroft,[949] showing the vermiculation more clearly, complete with individual holes (Fig. 48b). Jones' drawing of the Queen's House is unique among all seventeenth-century English uses of vermiculated masonry in showing it applied to more than a gate or a garden

942 Chatsworth, Devonshire Collection, Library, Lord Burlington's annotated copy of Palladio's *I quattro libri*, ii, ch. 3, interleaved page opposite p. 14.
943 Palladio, *Andrea Palladio*, i, p. 9.
944 Harris and Higgott, *Inigo Jones: Complete Architectural Drawings*, passim.
945 Hewlings, 'The Inigo Jones Gate'.
946 Colvin, *King's Works*, pp. 114-15, 119-22.
947 Harris and Higgott, *Inigo Jones: Complete Architectural Drawings*, p. 69.
948 Ibid., p. 129.
949 London, British Architectural Library, Drawings Collection, Burlington-Devonshire Collection, vi, 15; Harris and Higgott, *Inigo Jones: Complete Architectural Drawings*, p. 68, fig. 18.

building: it covers the whole of the ground floor. Although Burlington must have been aware that vermiculation was an ancient feature, and probably copied it for that reason, it was evidently Jones' proposed treatment of the Queen's House which helped him to realise it. Palladio's school was, in the end, of little use to him.

Burlington also owned drawings by John Webb, some of which he may have believed were the work of Inigo Jones. One Composite and three Corinthian capitals painted on the ceiling of the Blue Velvet Room (Fig. 49a–d) are copied from some of these drawings (Fig. 49e–h).[950] Both models and their copies are vigorous and lively exercises, conflicting with the representation of Burlington's allegedly sober and inflexible taste which is usually propagated. The capital on the south side has inturned volutes (Fig. 49a), a favourite device of Borromini's which Burlington is usually held to have deplored. No doubt Burlington would have believed, like Borromini, that these lively forms were of ancient provenance.[951] The capital on the north side is certainly a derivative of those on the Maison Carrée at Nîmes (Fig. 49),[952] although Burlington's version is not taken from the prototype, nor from Palladio's record of it,[953] but from the Webb drawing (Fig. 49).

Modern Architecture

Nothing which Burlington wrote on the work of his contemporaries has been identified. But he was evidently not indifferent to it. He owned drawings by Filippo Juvarra (1678–1736)[954] and Francesco Muttoni (1669–1747),[955] possibly because politeness compelled him to accept them as gifts, or otherwise because he was interested in their work. The Juvarra drawings were given to him in 1730, and the sphinxes and *tabulae ansatae* included in them may therefore have contributed to his realisation of these features among the ornament lining the avenue leading to the *exedra*, begun after *c.* 1733. In addition eight features at Chiswick of ancient origin had previously been employed by Burlington's English contemporaries. Six of them had

950 Harris, *Catalogue: Inigo Jones and John Webb*, p. 27, nos 207/1, 208/2 and 212/6: the capital on the west side of the room is copied from the top left sketch on sheet 207/1, that on the south side is copied from the top right sketch on sheet 208/2, that on the east side is copied from the bottom left sketch on sheet 212/6, and that on the north side is copied from the central sketch on sheet 212/6.

951 Blunt, *Borromini*, pp. 34–46.

952 Boethius and Ward-Perkins, *Roman and Etruscan Architecture*, p. 348, and plate 184.

953 Palladio, *I quattro libri*, iv, plate 84.

954 Chatsworth, Devonshire Collection, album 30; Wittkower, *Studies in the Italian Baroque*, passim.

955 Franco Barbieri, 'I disegni di Francesco Muttoni a Chatsworth', *Arte Lombarda*, 55–57, pp. 219–35.

been used by Hawksmoor: he had designed obelisks from 1702, unsupported open pediments from 1704-5, stepped domes from 1708, semi-circular lunettes from 1711, stylite statues from 1714, and *serlianas* from *c.* 1717. Five had been used byWren: he had designed *serlianas* from *c.* 1664, stylite statues perhaps from *c.* 1671, semi-circular lunettes from 1672, lozenge-shaped coffering from *c.* 1680, and unsupported open pediments from *c.* 1702. One had been used by the Talmans: William Talman had designed an apsed loggia *c.* 1699; and John Talman designed another in 1702. One had been used by Vanbrugh and Campbell; both had designed *serlianas* from *c.* 1717. These contemporaries must therefore also be regarded as transmitters to Burlington of the architecture of the ancients. It may not be strictly accurate to call him their follower, since he had sources of information independent of them. But it is evident that he shared their purpose, and thus that the long-established distinction made by historians between those English architects whose style was Baroque, and those whose style was 'Palladian' cannot be drawn.[956]

The Sources of Chiswick's Design: Conclusion

Burlington's categorisation as a 'Palladian' architect evidently requires revision, at least in respect of Chiswick House. On what can it be based? He used Palladio as a source of information on antique architecture, although content to use other sources as well. He used three features of Palladio's own invention, four used by Palladio in common with his contemporaries, and ten more used by Palladio's contemporaries, but not by Palladio. This indicates little dependance on Palladio but somewhat more on Palladio's contemporaries. It also raises a further question. Why did he use these seventeen features of sixteenth-century provenance at all if ancient architecture was his objective?

The answer may reside in the eighteenth-century critic's perception of the sixteenth-century. The eighteenth-century critic believed that sixteenth-century architecture furnished a vision of the ancient. Pirro Ligorio's Casino of Pius IV, for instance, enjoys a high twentieth-century reputation, but not for being a scholarly reconstruction of a Roman villa. Pirro is admired today as an inventive genius. He was not, however, by Burlington's contemporary, Agostino Taja, who admired the Casino instead as a convincing replication of ancient architecture.[957] Palladio, as antiquary

---

956 Richard Hewlings, 'Jones the Baroque', *Spectator*, 264, 1 February 1990, pp. 35-37, makes a similar point by different means.

957 Agostino Taja, *Descrizione del Palazzo Apostolico Vaticano* (Rome, 1750), p. 500.

rather than as architect, was used by Burlington more than other sixteenth-century antiquaries, presumably because he was widely believed to be the best. Goethe subscribed to this belief. Visiting Padua, he wrote

> Many striking portrait busts evoked the glorious days of antiquity. I feel myself, alas, far behind in my knowledge of this period, but . . . Palladio has opened it to me, and the way to all art and life as well.[958]

Palladio evidently stood between Goethe and antiquity as Chapman did between Keats and Homer.

Goethe was too observant and thoughtful to belittle Palladio's own creativity,[959] but when he attended a debate at the Accademia Olimpica in Vincenza he found that 'Palladio's name came up wherever the speakers were in favour of Imitation.'[960] Palladio the Imitator? Should 'Palladian' architecture be known as Mimetic architecture instead? If it is no more than a good imitation of something else, presumably it does not exist.

958 J.W. Goethe, *Italian Journey, 1786-1788*, trans W.H. Auden and Elizabeth Mayer (Harmondsworth, 1970), p. 95. I am indebted to my wife, Patricia Hewlings, for drawing this and the following quotation to my attention.
959 Ibid., pp. 64 and 103.
960 Ibid., p. 67.

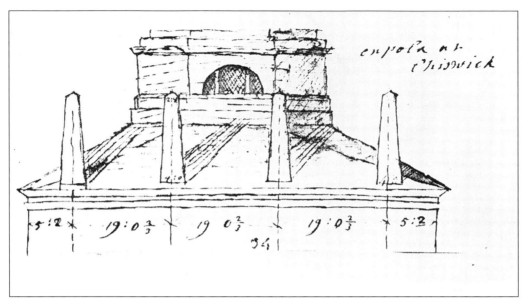

Fig. 50a Drawing by Lord Burlington for the chimney stacks at Chiswick House (*Chatsworth*)

Fig. 50b Drawing by Samuel Savill of the balcony in the hall of the Queen's House, Greenwich (*Chatsworth*)

Part II

Meaning

Why did Burlington choose ancient architecture as his model? One explanation is suggested by his working method. It is illustrated by the design of the obelisk-shaped chimneys. The only surviving drawing for them (Fig. 50a) does not indicate where smoke would have emerged.[961] They were illustrated with smoke emerging from the top in views of *c.* 1729–32.[962] By 1733 they were shown slightly taller, with chimneypots added to some.[963] By 1742 they were shown rebuilt in the conventional straight form.[964] (The present ones are dummies of 1956-57.) Presumably they did not work. Presumably they do work in Venice. It is possible that they might have worked had they been built on the Venetian model, with smoke vents lower. Scamozzi's illustrations are not detailed enough to show this, which suggests that it was these which Burlington used as a source of information. He was therefore either too hurried or too dignified to sketch the original models.

His dependence upon graphic sources is confirmed by an absence of record drawings in his own hand. No sketched details made in Italy or France survive among his papers. Kent reported his movements in Italy in November 1719: 'he was going towards Vicenza and Venice to get Architects to draw all ye fine buildings of Palladio . . . '.[965] Kent went on to describe how Burlington had visited palaces in Genoa 'which he had order'd to be drawn'.[966] In England Samuel Savill was sent off to sketch details of the Queen's House, which Burlington wished to reproduce (Fig. 50b).[967] On another occasion he sent Isaac Ware to Coleshill to make 'very correct

961 Chatsworth, Devonshire Collection, album 26a, fol. 35.

962 Harris, *Artist and the Country House*, p. 182; for the dating, see Spence, 'Chiswick House and its Gardens, 1726-32', p. 531.

963 Carré, 'Rigaud's Drawings of Chiswick', p. 140, figs 7 and 8.

964 Harris, *Artist and the Country House*, p. 261.

965 Lincoln, Lincolnshire Record Office, 2MM, B19A, William Kent to Burrell Massingberd, 15 November 1719; Lees-Milne, *Earls of Creation*, p. 104; Wilson, *William Kent*, p. 36.

966 Ibid., p. 36.

967 Chatsworth, Devonshire Collection, Lord Burlington's Architectural drawings, Boy 3; album 26a, fos 27r and 27v.

drawings' of the ceilings 'for his own study'.[968] The numerous record drawings which Burlington collected are matched by those in his collection which he had made – by Kent or Flitcroft, not by him.[969] Evidently he no more measured buildings than he sketched them. But how could he? Men whose pretensions to gentility were far more inferior to those of Lord Burlington threatened them by measuring. Michelangelo was disgusted by a present of a measuring rod. Robert Adam concealed his drawing expeditions in Rome in order to maintain 'the footing of a gentleman'. Burlington had some cause to de diffident. Chesterfield advised his son:

> You may soon be acquainted with the considerable parts of civil architecture; and for the minute and mechanical parts of it, leave that to masons, bricklayers and Lord Burlington; who has to a certain degree, lessened himself, by knowing them too well.[970]

The practice of architecture therefore presented Burlington with a social problem. He answered it by distancing himself as far as he was able. He bought, rather than made, records. He did not supervise the execution of his designs. He maintained a succession of clerks and executant architects, Savill, Garrett, Flitcroft, Kent and Wright.[971] The publications he sponsored or encouraged came out under other names.[972] However, one did not. It was a volume of record drawings made, of course, by Palladio, Burlington's creature for the purpose; and its subject, far removed from modern architectural politics, was ancient buildings.[973] His propagation of antique culture may therefore have been in part an answer to a social problem: the need to distance himself from the present, or, borrowing a phrase from contemporary political speech, to rise above faction.

Politics may offer another explanation. In this volume Jane Clerk and Eveline Cruickshanks show that Burlington was a critic of the political order. His critique was shared by Pope (his friend), Hoare (his banker) and Cobham (who resigned simultaneously). Pope's verse and the others'

968 H. Avray Tipping, 'Coleshill House – II, Berkshire', *Country Life*, 46, 2 August 1919, p. 138.

969 Chatsworth, Devonshire Collection, Lord Burlington's architectural drawings, Boy 2, 4, 5, 7, 9, 10, 13, 14, 15 and 16.

970 B. Dobrée (ed.), *The Letters of Lord Chesterfield* (London, 1932), iv, p. 1331.

971 Colvin, *Biographical Dictionary of British Architects*, pp. 128-29; Chatsworth, Devonshire Collection, 'An Account Current with the Rt Honble the Earl of Burlington or Receipts & Disbursements commencing April 11th 1750 by John Ferrett', records annual payments to Wright ' for Measuring and Making out all the Artificers Bills' from Christmas 1748 to Christmas 1753.

972 Timothy Connor, 'Burlingtonian Publications', in *Lord Burlington and his Circle*, Georgian Group Symposium (1982), pp. 52-59.

973 Riccardo, conte di Burlington, *Fabbriche antiche*.

gardens were targetted, by allegorical means of varying opaqueness, at the moral shortcomings of modern public life.[974] The ideal with which they contrasted their object of scorn was Ancient Virtue. The allegories by which these contrasts were expressed were drawn from ancient myth. In both ways, ancient architecture was the beneficiary, organically by association with the virtue of the ancients, semantically as the only clear architectural expression of ancient myth. Burlington's partisanship of ancient architecture was, in these circumstances, not an arbitrary and restricted change of taste, but part of a wider ethical critique. The interest in ancient art which, as Burlington's designs demonstrate, developed earlier than the *late* eighteenth century, cannot just be explained, as art historians so often have explained it, in terms only of the dynamics of patronage and visualisation.

This puts art history at the service of political historians. Historiographically the eighteenth century is changing its appearance. Until recently it was the century when nothing happened. Historians condescended to identify its stability (political) and growth (economic).[975] In this period of respite between periods when struggles of consequence were fought and resolved, only the inconsequential luxuriated – art, music, philosophy. Even art historians suspected that the art of the eighteenth century was a holiday, the evolving spirit's day off between Renaissance and Romanticism, free of content, formally derivative, and untroubled by any lien on the psyche.

Recently, however, the Victorians' contempt of the eighteenth century has ceased to seem merely quaint. From historians of the Left has come the hypothesis that all was not well, that too many were hanged, social constraints were unreasonably ferocious, rioting was not purposeless, and that the Revolution Settlement did not introduce the salad days of bourgeois liberalism.[976] From historians of the Right has come the hypothesis that Thought occured, that religious debate was both vivid and consequential, that politics previously thought to be moribund were creatively reactionary.[977]

974 Howard Erskine-Hill, 'Alexander Pope: The Political Poet in his Time', *Eighteenth-Century Studies*, 15, (1981-82), pp. 123-49; Malcolm Kelsall, 'The Iconography of Stourhead', *Journal of the Warburg and Coutauld Institutes*, 46 (1983), pp. 133-43.

975 J.H. Plumb, *The Growth of Political Stability in England 1675-1725* (London, 1967), and Neil McKendrick, *The Birth of a Consumer Society: The Commercialisation of Eighteenth Century England* (London, 1982), may represent the first and second of these well-founded points of view.

976 E.P. Thompson, *Whigs and Hunters* (London, 1975); D. Hay, P. Linebaugh and E.P. Thompson (eds), *Albion's Fatal Tree: Crime and Society in Eighteenth-Century England* (London, 1975).

977 J.C.D. Clark, 'Eighteenth-Century Social History', *Historical Journal*, 27 (1984), pp. 773-88; idem, *English Society, 1688-1832: Ideology, Social Structure and Political Practice during the Ancien Regime* (Cambridge, 1985); idem, *Revolution and Rebellion: State and Society in the Seventeenth and Eighteenth Centuries* (Cambridge, 1986).

If the foregoing explanation of Burlington's aesthetic preference is correct, could it therefore be that the architectural evidence offers a similar hypothesis; that architecture, long thought to be flourishing in the absence of graver issues, was actually vehicle for the *expression* of grave issues; that an architecture once thought to be so accessible because of its blithe freedom from meaning, pleased its contemporary spectators, on the contrary, because it was meaningful?

In the foregoing analysis of the sources of the different features at Chiswick the large number of novelties may have been apparent. No fewer than twenty-two were actually without precedent in England: these were the group of three *serlianas*, the type of ball crenellation, the obelisk chimneys, the asymetrical link, the Blue Velvet Room ceiling, the grotto type, the entrance passage, the stepped dome, the Greek Key and Vitruvian scroll in raised bands, the tapering doors of the Deerhouse, the unframed door cut through the plinth, the Casina plan, the hippodrome plan, the conjunction of fancy room plans, the screens of columns, the ceiling of the Link Room, the circular temple, the terms, the *tabulae ansatae*, the benches and possibly the perron type. Burlington would have been aware of the Renaissance theory of *mimesis*: it advised copying and making minor adjustments, not introducing novelties.[978] Burlington would have excused himself by arguing that his introductions were not novelties: they all had ancient precedents. But he would still have known how conspicuous they were in England, and he can only have desired that in order to draw attention to them, individually. Visitors would be bound to ask why he had introduced them – what did they mean?

The first rare objects to which the visitors' attention would have been drawn were the sphinxes on the gatepiers. Familiarity with Sophocles' *Oedipus* would have ensured that visitors knew the sphinx guarded Thebes.[979] Thebes had been built by the musician Amphion, who had received a present of a lyre from Hermes: when he played his lyre, the stones moved into place of their own accord. Hermes was patron of Free Masonry.[980] So was Burlington.[981] In the case of Amphion, Hermes was also the patron of a musician, as Burlington was many times over.[982] In political allegory musicians were the bringers of harmony, particularly after

978   Rensselaer W. Lee, 'Ut Pictura Poesis: The Humanistic Theory of Painting', *Art Bulletin*, 22 (1940), pp. 203–10.
979   Robert Graves, *The Greek Myths* (London, 1960), ii, p. 10.
980   F.A. Yates, *Giordano Bruno and the Hermetic Tradition* (London, 1964), pp. 1–19, 273–74;

David Stevenson, *The Origins of Freemasonry* (Cambridge, 1988), p. 85.
981   Clark, 'For Kings and Senates Fit', p. 56.
982   Stanley Boorman, 'Lord Burlington and Music', in John Wilton-Ely (ed.), *Apollo of the Arts: Lord Burlington and his Circle* (Nottingham, 1973), pp. 16–18.

Fig. 51 The garden of Chiswick House, looking northwards from the house towards the Exedra (*English Heritage*)

strife – concord following discord. So far as Thebes was concerned, Amphion was also its architect, inasmuch as architects are the only participants in the building process who do not move the stones themselves. Architecture also had the political meaning of order imposed on inchoate form, and beauty resulting from harmony imposed on base matter. Visitors would have known that Burlington was the architect of this Thebes. The sphinx posed riddles and strangled unsuccessful candidates for admission, at least until Oedipus, the rightful but excluded king, solved the riddle. Burlington supported another rightful but excluded king, James III,[983] and perhaps intended the sphinxes to be seen as guarding his patrimony until his return.

Past the sphinx, the visitor stood in a forecourt lined with herms (Fig. 45a), whose rarity would also have ensured attention. Generally herms represented Hermes, and would thus have been welcoming to Free Masons. Their presence at Athens guaranteed its ancient constitution. In 415 BC Alcibiades, leader of an expedition to Sicily, just as Charles I led an expedition to Scotland, was wrongly accused of mutilating them. Popular fear interpreted this as an attempt to overthrow the constitution and Alcibiades, like James II, was banished. In exile he won notable victories for Athens, and in 407 he was recalled with enthusiasm.[984] James III had yet to fulfil that programme, but had he done so, the herms would have been there, unmutilated, to demonstrate the calumny.

Beyond the house the visitor was drawn up an avenue of dangerous beasts. First he passed a wolf and a boar. His memory of the wolf's participation in the foundation of Rome, always an analogue of good government, would have needed no refreshment. But in conjunction with the boar this might not have been its purpose. At the Villa Aldobrandini Burlington would have seen, at the centre of the *teatro d'acqua*, an allegory of the triumph of virtue over vice, a representation of a terrible fight between a lion and a boar.[985] Here the lion represented fortitude of soul, reflective action and intellect; the boar represented fortitude of body, instinctive action and bestiality. At Chiswick, led up an avenue of urns (Fig. 51), and avoiding strangulation by two more sphinxes, the visitor came to a lion and a lioness (Fig. 52a, b). He had progressed from a world of vulpine and bestial responses to a zone of far-sighted and thoughtfully planned action.

983 Jane Clark, 'The Mysterious Mr Buck', *Apollo*, 129, May 1989, pp. 317-22.
984 E.H. Blakeney (ed.), *A Smaller Classical Dic-*
tionary (London, 1910), p. 29.
985 Steinberg, 'The Iconography of the Teatro dell'Acqua', pp. 459-60.

Fig. 52a Statue of a lion at Chiswick
(*English Heritage*)

Fig. 52b Statue of a lioness at Chiswick
(*English Heritage*)

To one side was a statue of Samson and the Philistine,[986] which, together with Hercules and Cacus or Hercules and Antaeus, was a well-known representation of the triumph of truth over falsehood. Ahead of him was the Exedra. Its central position is occupied by three Roman statues, whose costume indicates membership of the ruling elite,[987] and whose pose is one of calm authority. They are flanked by named busts. Only one of these names, Socrates, is now visible, but two more are supposed to represent Lycurgus and Lucius Verus.[988] Verus was co-emperor with Marcus Aurelius, and together they represented benevolent government. In addition, their partnership represented strict observance of constitutional delicacy, and the rejection of the absolute power which was within the grasp of either of them.[989] Lycurgus was yet another absentee ruler, who refused the throne of Sparta in favour of the rightful king, his nephew; undertook long

986 Harris, *Artist and the Country House*, p. 183, fig. 187f; London Borough of Hounslow, Library Services, Chiswick Public Library (Reference Branch), Bute Portfolio, fol. 18.

987 Hans Rupprecht Goette, 'Mulceus-Embas-Calceus: Ikonografische Studien zu römischem Schuhwerk', *Jahrbuch des Deutschen Archaeologischen Instituts*, 103 (1988), pp. 401-64.

988 Thomas Faulkner, *The History and Antiquities of Brentford, Ealing and Chiswick* (London, 1845), p. 428.

989 Michael Mezzatesta, 'Marcus Aurelius, Fray Antonio de Guevara and the Ideal of the Perfect Prince in the Sixteenth Century', *Art Bulletin*, 66 (1984), pp. 620-33.

and celebrated travels to Crete, Ionia, Egypt and even India; returned, at his country's request, to remodel its constitution; and, when that job was done, retired to a life of stoical contemplation.[990] He could be apostrophised as a model for another exiled and travelling king.

Beyond the Exedra stood Venus on a column (Fig. 31a).[991] To ensure that she passed tests of taste as well as of ideology the particular Venus chosen was that in the *tribuna* in the Uffizi. An illustration of this figure in his copy of Montfaucon's book would have enabled an English statuary to copy it.[992] It was, among Burlington's contemporaries, the cynosure of contemporary pulchritude. Joseph Spence, connoisseur of ancient sculpture as well as of Burlington's gardens, paid her 'perhaps a hundred visits' in the Uffizi. He was troubled by her fingers, but fond of her breasts. Charles Greville was denied 'a proper enthusiasm' by her ankles, but was told to overcome this by repeated visits. Four days later he liked her better. Smollett also had reservations but they did not extend to her 'back parts'.[993] Burlington kept the connoisseurs in order by sticking Venus on top of a column, and, lest there be any mistake, made the column Doric. Had Venus' presence been intended to signal amatory dedication of the *topos*, her order would have been the coquettish Corinthian.[994] Burlington knew this. He possessed a drawing of a garden with ornamental buildings which included a Doric column surmounted by a female figure carrying a spear and a shield,[995] the attributes of Minerva, for whom Doric would be perfectly appropriate. Aware of the drawing, his substitution of Venus for Minerva must have been calculated. The association of Venus with Doric would be bound to provoke reflection. Such reflection might include remembrance that Venus was the mother of Aeneas, and thus the ancestress not only of Romulus and Remus, founders of the ideal republic, but of Caesar, and especially of Augustus, who restored benevolent order following political chaos. Julius Caesar made the association explicit. He established the cult of his ancestress in Rome, as Venus Genetrix, and built a temple in her honour,[996] rebuilt by Trajan in AD 113.[997] The connection with the imperial house was reinforced by Hadrian, who in AD 135 built the gigantic Temple of Venus and Rome,[998] and by Maxentius, who rebuilt it *c.* 306-12.[999]

990 Blakeney, *A Smaller Classical Dictionary*, pp. 316-17.
991 Harris, *Artist and the Country House*, p. 183, fig. 187h; Dixon Hunt, *William Kent*, p, 127, nos 32 and 33.
992 Montfaucon, *Antiquity Explained*, i, plate 52.
993 Francis Haskell and Nicholas Penny, *Taste and the Antique* (1981), pp. 325-26.
994 Vitruvius, *De architectura*, i, ch. 2, p. 5.
995 Chatsworth, Devonshire Collection, album 21, 'Pictura antiqua'.
996 Ward-Perkins, *Roman Architecture*, p. 44, fig. 67; Boethius and Ward-Perkins, *Roman and Etruscan Architecture*, p. 190.
997 Boethius and Ward-Perkins, *Roman and Etruscan Architecture*, p. 229.
998 Ibid., pp. 265-66.
999 Ibid., p. 502.

Although the association is less explicit at Chiswick, visitors might recall that there is a bust of Augustus over the front door (Fig. 53). Admitted to the Blue Velvet Room or to the Bedchamber, they would notice more emblems of Augustus' ancestress, the shell on which she had been born, and tritons, inhabitants of the foam from which she had emerged (Figs 29a, 33a). Another illustration in Montfaucon's book shows Venus sitting on her shell supported by tritons, 'as represented in a fine Marble belonging to the Palace Matthei in Rome',[1000] and for this reason, wrote Montfaucon, she was sometimes called Tritonia (Fig. 54). Venus and Augustus were favoured patrons of rulers who believed their historical mission was to restore good government after their own exile and their country's anarchy: Cosimo I of Tuscany installed Botticelli's *Birth of Venus* in his villa at Castello to illustrate the rebirth of government and peace.[1001] Venus on a Doric column is less easily associated with love than with the grave and purposeful Roman state which she begot and protected.

This area of the garden was known as the Grove, a somewhat foppish name presumably intended to stimulate speculation about its origin. It translates the Italian *bosco*, and thus aligns itself with the *Sacro Bosco* of Bomarzo,[1002] and the *Bosco* of the Vatican in which Pius IV's Casino was set,[1003] rather than with more regular *orti* of Renaissance Rome.[1004] Such *boschi* were settings for Poggio Bracciolini's and Pomponio Leto's *Accademie*, themselves modelled on the glade where Aristotle tutored Alexander, on Plato's garden academy, and on Socrates' grove.[1005] An allusion to the garden where a wise adviser inducted a victorious monarch must have been appealing to Burlington.

An alternative association was with Arcadia. Rysbrack's painting (Fig. 55) shows that the Grove was stocked with deer,[1006] an unusual feature of a

1000 Montfaucon, *Antiquity Explained*, i, p. 101 and plate 50.
1001 D.R. Edward Wright, 'The Iconography of the Medici Garden at Castello', *Journal of the Society of Architectural Historians*, 34 (1975), p. 314.
1002 S. Lang, 'Bomarzo 2', *Architectural Review*, 121 (1957), p. 427; S. Settis, 'Contributo a Bomarzo', *Bolletino d'arte*, 5th series, 51 (1966), p. 17; J. von Hennenberg, 'Bomarzo: The Extravagent Garden of Pier Franceso Orsini', *Italian Quarterly*, 11 (1967), pp. 3-19; J. von Henneberg, 'Bomarzo: nuovi dati e un interpretazione', *Storia dell'arte*, 13 (1972), pp. 43-45; J. Oleson, 'A Reproduction of an Etruscan Tomb in the Parco dei Mostri at Bomarzo', *Art Bulletin*, 57 (1975), pp. 410-17; L. Quartermaine, 'Vicino Orsini's Garden of Conceits', *Italian Studies*, 32 (1977), pp. 68-85; Bosch, *op cit*, p. 97.
1003 Smith, *The Casino of Pius IV*, pp. 5, 9 and 10.
1004 For *boschi*, see Elisabeth MacDougall, 'Ars hortulorum: Sixteenth-Century Garden Iconography and Literary Theory in Italy', in David R. Coffin, *The Italian Garden* (Dumbarton Oaks, Washington, DC, 1972), pp. 41-44; for *orti*, see Coffin, *Villa*, *op cit*, viii.
1005 Elisabeth B. MacDougall, 'The Sleeping Nymph: Origins of a Humanist Fountain Type', *Art Bulletin*, 57, September 1975, p. 362; MacDougall, 'Ars hortulorum', p. 56.
1006 Harris, *Artist and the Country House*, p. 183, fig. 187e.

garden rather than a park. Arcadia was a woodland area, inhabited by pre-agricultural hunting people of Pelasgian origin. Deer would thus be an effective attribute. Mythologically, Arcadia was the preserve of Pan and nymphs, specifically dryads in trees, oreads in rocks and naiads in springs. There is no apparent representation of dryads, and Pan, whose musical patronage would have been interesting to Burlington, is represented only by the deer, and by pine trees, which Kent's sketches reveal were at least intended.[1007] But oreads and naiads are suggested by the Cascade and artificial water. The rocks of the Cascade would have been associated with the Cave of the Nymphs from the Odyssey, the *domus nympharum* from the Aeneid, perhaps with the abandoned Ariadne,[1008] or (at the Villa Aldobrandini) with Parnassus.[1009] The Parnassian analogy was made by the consideration of Muses as a form of nymph. The Corcyrian cave on Mount Parnassus, for instance, was the haunt of the Muses, but sacred to Pan and nymphs.[1010] Pliny's Home of the Muses (*Musaeum*) was a grotto, hollowed rocks.[1011]

Muses might seem appropriate symbols for Burlington, as the friend of Pope, patron of Gay and Handel, and as a director of the Opera of the Nobility;[1012] and, as the Cascade was presumably visualised as a spring, it would have suggested the Hippocrene spring on Mount Helicon or the Castalian spring at Delphi, both of which were guarded by the Muses. As inspirers of song, the Muses were usually associated with Apollo, and other Apollonian imagery could also be found at Chiswick. Principally it was conveyed by a cast of the Apollo Belvedere placed in an unidentified location within the house.[1013] But it could also be recognised by the palm branches ornamenting the Bedchamber, and by the sunflowers in the Octagonal and Round Rooms of the Gallery. The association of Apollo with dolphins had been expressed by Ammanati in the fountain in the Palazzo Vecchio, Florence.[1014] Apollo was represented by palms because his mother had given birth to him while clinging to a palm

1007 Dixon Hunt, *William Kent*, pp. 123, nos 23 and 24, 124, no. 25, 125, nos 27 and 28, 126, nos 29 and 30, 127, nos 32 and 33, 128, no 34, 130, nos 38 and 39, 132, nos 33 and 35. The associ-ation of Pan with pine trees is discussed by Naomi Miller, 'Domain of Illusion: The Grotto in France', in MacDougall, *Fons sapien-tiae*, pp. 191–92.

1008 MacDougall, 'Sleeping Nymph', p. 361.
1009 Steinberg, 'The Iconography of the Teatro dell'Acqua', p. 461.
1010 Miller, 'Domain of Illusion', p. 194.
1011 Ibid., p. 187.

1012 Boorman, *op cit*, p. 18.
1013 John Soane, *Description of the House and Museum on the North Side of Lincoln's Inn Fields* (London, 1835), p. 42; the cast is now in Sir John Soane's Museum, and is illustrated in Peter Thornton and Helen Dorey, *A Miscel-lany of Objects from Sir John Soane's Museum* (London, 1992), fig. 74.

1014 Detlef Heikamp, 'Bartolomeo Ammanati's Marble Fountain for the *Sala Grande* of the Palazzo Vecchio in Florence', MacDougall, *Fons sapientiae* (1978), pp. 124 and 127.

Fig. 53 Bust of Augustus over the first floor entrance door at Chiswick House (*English Heritage*)

Fig. 54 Illustration by Bernard de Montfaucon of an ancient relief carving of the birth of Venus supported by tritons

tree.[1015] And his presence was implied by sunflowers, by virtue of his personification of the Sun. Burlington's contemporaries would have regarded Apollo principally as the patron of music and poetry, like Burlington himself. But both in ancient Rome and in the sixteenth century this had frequently been given a political meaning, with music and poetry representing order and calm imposed on discordant peoples. Augustus, who claimed descent from Apollo, emphasised his possession of these hereditary powers by building the Temple of Palatine Apollo, and by enlarging the Temple of Apollo at Actium.[1016] Cosimo I of Tuscany, by the use of Apollonian imagery (including the Apollo/dolphin *impresa* of Augustus), drew attention to his achievement as the bringer of concord.[1017] Burlington associated Chiswick with at least the first of these rulers by placing his bust over the front door,[1018] and possibly with both of them by purchasing a statue of a goat from Michael Rysbrack in 1749:[1019] Capricorn was both Augustus' and Cosimo's horoscope.[1020]

There were, however, other concepts suggested by springs or, more precisely, by water. At the Villa Aldobrandini, it represented Divine Wisdom, poured in generous quantities over Atlas and Hercules.[1021] Usually it represented good government; its copious supply in Rome was practical evidence of the benevolence of the ruler. In Ammanati's fountain in the Palazzo Vecchio in Florence, for instance, water represented the benevolent government of God, in cycle and perpetually renewing itself.[1022]

Lest the Grove as an analogy of good government appears to stretch the imagery beyond its power of effective representation, the history of the site should be recalled.[1023] The Grove was described (by Sir John Clerk),[1024] and depicted (by Peter Andreas Rysbrack),[1025] as mature in 1727–32. Only in 1728 did Burlington acquire Sutton Court to the west,[1026] and ownership of

1015 David Watkin, 'The Migration of the Palm', *Apollo*, 131, February 1990, p. 79.
1016 Heikamp, 'Bartolomeo Ammanati's Marble Fountain', p. 128.
1017 Ibid., p. 127.
1018 Dodsley, *London and its Environs*, ii, p. 116.
1019 Chatsworth, Devonshire Collection, 'John Ferrett's Account Currant with the Right Honble the Earl of Burlington 1745', fo. 235, 1749, May 24 'Paid Mr Michael Rysbrack Statuary . . . for the figure of a Goat in Portland Stone: + for a Box to Send it to Chiswick . . . 37.16.6.'
1020 Wright, *op cit*, p. 314.

1021 Steinberg, 'The Iconography of the Teatro dell'Acqua', p. 460.
1022 Heikamp, 'Bartolomeo Ammanati's Marble Fountain', p. 124.
1023 Hewlings, *Chiswick*, pp. 40-49, is a summary account.
1024 Fleming, *Robert Adam*, p. 26.
1025 Harris, *Artist and the Country House*, p. 182, figs 187a, 183, 187e; for the dating, see Spence, 'Chiswick House and its Gardens, 1726-32', p. 531.
1026 Victoria History of the Counties of England, *Middlesex*, vii (Oxford, 1982), p. 71; Chatsworth, Devonshire Collection, L/21/30-32.

Fig. 55 Painting by Pieter Andreas Rysbrack of the Grove at Chiswick (*English Heritage*)

Fig. 56 Painting by Pieter Andreas Rysbrack of the Orange Tree Garden and Ionic Temple at Chiswick (*English Heritage*)

the Bollo Brook, which had hitherto only been his boundary. At the time he laid out the Grove, presumably some years earlier, he owned no water and therefore had no better means of expressing the accepted analogy of good government than by creating (in the Grove) a likely habitat for water nymphs. Lest this somewhat tortuous analogy be overlooked, he decorated the Bedchamber, evidently the state bedchamber of the house, with Tritons (Fig. 29a), denizens of Ocean, to indicate that this room, where a king might lie, was a reservoir of benevolent actions.

Beyond the Grove lay the Orange Tree Garden (Fig. 56). Castiglione compared the orange trees in the Statue Court of the Belvedere in the Vatican to the Garden of the Hesperides.[1027] The comparison was well established, as oranges were regarded as the most similar fruit to the golden apples given by Earth to Juno, and guarded by the Hesperides on the bank of the River Oceanus in the far west.[1028] Burlington evidently envisaged his oranges too as the golden apples of the Hesperides, on the bank of a river which, at the time when the garden was laid out, was the western boundary of his estate. The Garden of the Hesperides was often used as a representation of the Golden Age, when the earth was in a state of uncorrupted perfection. Thus the orange trees at Chiswick are laid out in concentric circles around a circular pond, fronting a temple of circular plan, for the circle was the perfect figure. At Stowe a circular temple represents Ancient Virtue.[1029] At Chiswick the temple has an Ionic portico, an order suitable for scholars,[1030] who alone would be learned enough to realise the perfect world. The Orange Tree Garden was to the Grove as the Golden Age was to Arcadia – more perfect, more spiritual, representative of intellectual effort – less natural, less material, less innocent. Progress from the Grove to the Orange Tree Garden was comparable to progress from the wolf and boar to the lion and lioness. And perhaps this progress had a political moral also – progress from the disorder resulting from instinctive and selfish responses, to the order gained by thoughtful design and spiritual goals.

Taken together, the meaning of the ornament at Chiswick is political. It is possible that the meaning is quite specific. Sunflowers, whose heads follow their sun and therefore represent courtiers or lovers,[1031] are carved in the

1027 Coffin, *Gardens and Gardening in Papal Rome*, p. 203.
1028 Blakeney, *A Smaller Classical Dictionary*, p. 262.
1029 M.J. Gibbon, 'The History of Stowe – XI', *The Stoic*, 24, no. 4, pp. 175–78 and plate 3.
1030 John Onians, *Bearers of Meaning* (Cambridge, 1988), pp. 273 and 277.

1031 Dr Elizabeth McGrath introduced me to this symbol. It also occurs in the chimneypiece of Sir Robert Walpole's Levée Room at No. 10 Downing Street, designed by Kent in 1732–35 as the principal room in the residence of the king's chief minister, facing directly across St James' Park to St James's Palace.

round and octagonal rooms of the Gallery. Here (as at Wilton, where they occur in the Single Cube Room)[1032] they must represent courtiers, indicating either that Chiswick was a courtier's house, or that courtiers waited in the gallery, in attendance upon a king. There is more regal imagery. The ball finials (Fig. 8a) may be meaningless ornament, or they may represent celestial orbs. They were not meaningless in other places. In Spain *bolas*, almost identical to those at Chiswick, were 'virtually confined to royal buildings' during the entire period between the death of Charles V and that of Philip IV.[1033] On the Porta Pia in Rome, built by the Medici Pope Pius IV, they were Medicean *palle*.[1034] Cloths of estate carved in the window recesses of the Bedchamber at Chiswick (Fig. 57) indicate that it is made ready for a king. Palm fronds carved over its doors indicate that he is also a victor.[1035] An exiled king is alluded to by images connected with Oedipus, Alcibiades and Lycurgus. A particular exiled king, the Stuart Prince of Wales, is alluded to by oak leaf festoons over the Bedchamber doors (Fig. 29a), and by Prince of Wales' feathers ornamenting the overmantel (Fig. 58). His cause is represented by roses and thistles, Jacobite badges,[1036] carved at minute scale in the much larger fruit festoons of the friezes of the Red Velvet Room chimneypieces (Fig. 59). It would only be noticeable to someone leaning on the chimneypiece waiting the favour of admission to the Blue Velvet Room. No visitor would notice the rats and mice painted among the acanthus fronds in the higher cornice of the Blue Velvet Room, unless they were pointed out to him; but rats and mice ate the body of Hiram Abif, architect of Solomon's Temple,[1037] and that information would be intelligible to a Mason.

If, on the other hand, such precision was unintelligible or unintended, the ornament is still, in unspecific terms, of a political nature. Its lowest common denominator is an allegory of good government. The Roman statues in their senatorial costumes represent government. Samson and the lion and lioness indicate that it is virtuous. The herms guarantee that it is constitutional. Water, actually present on the Cascade, alluded to by tritons in the Bedchamber and by a habitat suitable for water nymphs in the Grove,

1032 Bold, *Wilton*, p. 53, figs 61 and 62.
1033 Catherine Wilkinson Zerner, *Juan de Hererra* (New Haven and London, 1993), p. 153.
1034 Ackerman, *The Architecture of Michelangelo*, p. 257.
1035 Smith, *The Casino of Pius IV*, p. 38.
1036 Great Francis, *The Romance of the White Rose* (London, 1933); idem, 'Jacobite Drinking Glasses and their Relation to the Jacobite Medals', *British Numismatic Journal*, 16 (1921-

22); Paul Kleber Monod, *Jacobitism and the English People, 1688-1788* (Cambridge, 1989), pp. 70-95, discusses Jacobite imagery in a wider context.
1037 Dr Paul Monod brought this story to my attention. But it does not occur in the accounts of Solomon's Temple in I Kings, 5-7, II Chronicles, 2-4, nor in Flavius Josephus, *Antiquitates Judaici*, trans. H.St J. Thackeray (1934), viii, pp. 50-129.

Fig. 57 Carved cloth of estate in a window recess of the Bedchamber, Chiswick House (*English Heritage*)

Fig. 58 Detail of the Bedchamber overmantel, Chiswick House (*English Heritage*)

Fig. 59 Detail of the festoon in the frieze of the Red Velvet Room chimneypiece (*English Heritage*)

Fig. 60 Bust, possibly representing Vitellius, in a niche on the north side of the Summer Parlour, Chiswick House (*English Heritage*)

Fig. 61 Drawing by Lord Burlington for a door at Chiswick (*Chatsworth*)

represent the benevolent actions of the ruler. Strong leaders (Oedipus and Alcibiades) are alluded to. Philosophers (Socrates) and lawgivers (Lycurgus) are represented. So are the emperors who were then understood to be good – Augustus over the front door, Vitellius outside the Summer Parlour (Fig. 60)[1038], and Trajan, whose bust Burlington proposed to place over an internal door (Fig. 61).[1039] Ancient Rome is represented as the cynosure, established by Venus, nurtured by the she-wolf and saved by Augustus.

House and garden were framed as a miniature city state. It has gates. The terrace is its rampart. It has a temple facing an amphitheatre. The Casina, sometimes called the Bagnio,[1040] is its bathhouse. The Exedra is its basilica. The house is its palatine, or its acropolis. Sphinxes exclude the vicious. Architects, the framers and interpreters of arcane mysteries, guide the elect. That is what Palladio and Jones are doing there.

Acknowledgements   I am indebted to the owners of archives for permission to consult them, in particular the British Architectural Library (especially the Drawings Collection), the Board of the British Library, the Trustees of the Chatsworth Settlement, the University of Durham, the Society of Genealogists and Lincolnshire Archives, the London Borough of Hounslow (Chiswick Public Library), the London Borough of Sutton (Central Library), the Corporation of London (Guildhall Library), and the Trustees of the Victoria and Albert Museum.

I am most grateful to those who have answered my questions, namely Elizabeth Angellicoussis (Roman sculpture and Roman costume), John Bold (Greenwich), Jane Clark (Lord Burlington), Glyn Coppack (Thornton Abbey), Rosalys Coope (Fontainebleau), Hugh Cullum (Borgonio), Peter Day (Lord Burlington's library and papers), Caroline Elam (Renaissance draughtmanship and calligraphy), Andrea Fabbri (Daniel Defoe), Lynda Fairbairn (Palladio's drawings), Peter Goodchild (the demolition of the garden buildings at Chiswick), Todd Gowan (Stanway), John Harris (Visentini; Pedro Machuca), Caroline Hammond (Chiswick rate books), David Jacques (Leeswood), Jeremy Knight (Montgomery), Roger Ling (Pozzuoli), the late Hugh MacAndrew (Talman's collection), Grace McCombie (Shotley), Elizabeth McGrath (sunflowers), Oliver Moore (sarcophagi), Arnold Nesselrath, Johannes Röll and Ruth Rubinstein (Renaissance drawings after the antique), Margaret Richardson (the Apollo statue formerly at Chiswick), Peter Ryder (Shotley), Andrew Saint (Ludgate), Alison Shell (Hugues Sambin), Andrew Skelton (Carshalton), and Alan Thacker (Chester).

I am particularly grateful to Ian Campbell, Howard Colvin, Patricia Hewlings and Paul Monod, whose suggestions I have adopted.

1038 Faulkner, *The History and Antiquities of Brentford, Ealing and Chiswick*, p. 433, identifies the two busts in niches on this side of the house as Augustus and Vespasian; but Dr Elizabeth Angellicousis advises me that one of them may be Vitellius.

1039 Chatsworth, Devonshire Collection, Lord Burlington's architectural drawings, Boy 8.23, illustrates this proposed bust, with the inscription 'TRAIANUS'.

1040 Campbell, *Vitruvius Britannicus*, iii, calls it 'the Casina' in the description on p. 8, but 'The New Bagnio' in the caption to plate 26.

2

Edward Lovett Pearce and the New Junta for Architecture

Edward McParland

It is reasonable to claim that only two architects resident in Ireland in the eighteenth century were of the first rank internationally.[1] One was James Gandon, the late eighteenth-century architect of the Custom House and Four Courts in Dublin. The other was the early eighteenth-century architect Edward Lovett Pearce.

Pearce died young in 1733 after an architectural career of no longer than six years. But in that time he designed and supervised the erection of the Parliament House in Dublin, though he did not live to see it completed (Fig. 62). It is perfectly reasonable to assert that this building alone established Pearce as one of the most interesting architects practising in Europe in the late 1720s. This is a large claim, but it is made after bearing contemporary London, Paris and Rome in mind.

It is not known where Pearce was born, nor even exactly when. He was Irish, at least in the sense that his mother's family was settled in Dublin by the mid seventeenth century; and his father (who held an estate in Norfolk and was a soldier) had made his career in Ireland. Pearce's father's brother, another soldier, was a member of the Irish House of Commons. Pearce's own career was almost exclusively Irish.

It takes some effort of historical imagination to place Pearce's Parliament House critically in contemporary Irish architecture. The earliest exercise of monumental classical architecture in the country was William Robinson's Royal Hospital, Kilmainham, of the 1680s. Although this was a most important building for Ireland, it would be wrong to portray it, or any other seventeenth-century Irish building, as more than provincial. Before Pearce came to prominence, the only resident Irish architect of note in the early eighteenth century was Thomas Burgh. His library in Trinity College Dublin, his finest building, is large, sober, correct and – for Ireland – of

---

1 This essay is a revised version of a paper read at the Sesquicentennial Swift and Irish Studies Conference, University of Notre Dame, 18 October 1991.

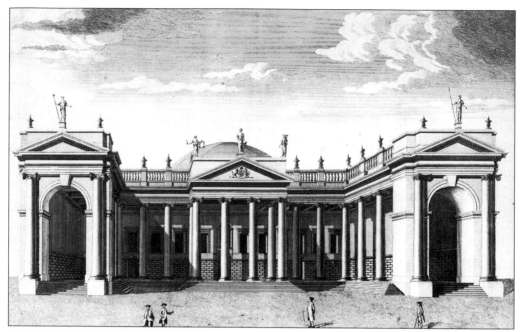

Fig. 62 Parliament House, Dublin, engraved perspective from the south (1767), after Rowland Omer

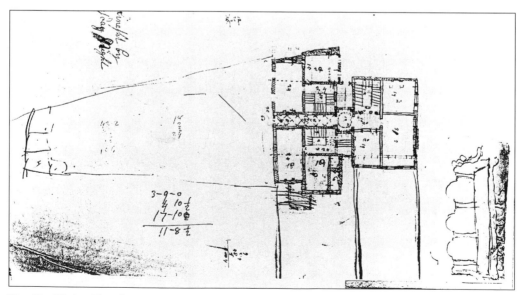

Fig. 63a Christ Church Deanery, Dublin, plan by Edward Lovett Pearce (*Victoria and Albert Museum*)

Fig. 63b Christ Church Deanery, Dublin, now demolished, from *The Georgian Society Records of Eighteenth–Century Domestic Architecture and Decoration in Dublin*, iv (Dublin, 1912), plate cxxi

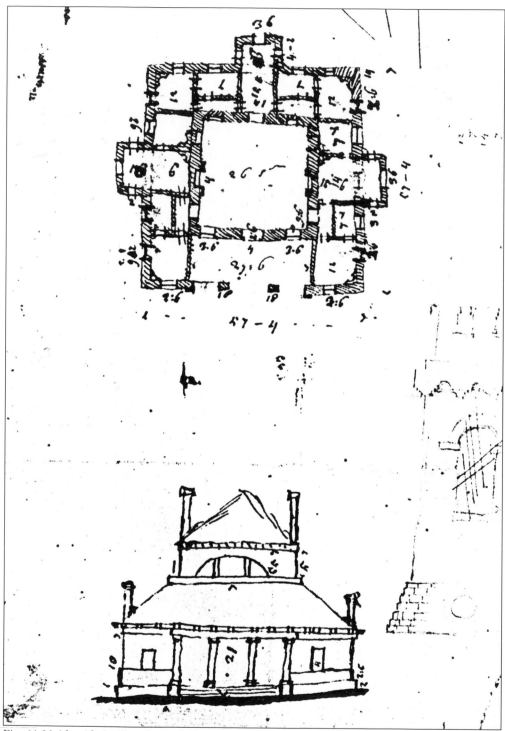

Fig. 64 Unidentified villa, plan and elevation here attributed to Edward Lovett Pearce
(*Victoria and Albert Museum*)

immense importance, but it cannot compete on the international stage with the best buildings of Burgh's British and European contemporaries.

Suddenly in the late 1720s Dublin was endowed with Pearce's work of unprecedented genius. The scale, monumentality and complexity of the Parliament House, and its total command of the repertoire of European architectural classicism, were revolutionary. Furthermore, it is becoming clear that Pearce's revolution was not merely stylistic, with neo-Palladianism replacing Dutch-inspired classicism, but extended to structural systems so that the world of late medieval masonry yielded to the greater urbanities of more daring masonry, brick and wooden systems.[2] This building, and the emergence of its architect, must tell us something about the Dublin of the 1720s.

In one way, the Parliament House can be 'placed' easily enough: as an exercise in neo-Palladian public building, it is as significant as the nearly contemporary (slightly later) Assembly Rooms in York. Yet Pearce's cubes and double cubes in the Parliament House, and his wholly Campbellian façade of the Deanery of Christ Church in Dublin (Fig. 63b), go hand in hand with an affection for the work of Vanbrugh, to whom the (unidentified) plan of the Deanery was once attributed (Fig. 63a).[3]

What did Pearce learn from Vanbrugh? His drawing style is somewhat similar, as is his fondness for breaking the cube (Fig. 64). There is nothing particularly unclassical in this, Vanbrughian though it is. And Pearce never follows Vanbrugh's fractured, mannered, or baroque handling of the classical orders. Pearce is almost Greek in his strictly trabeated treatment of the orders. It is not the baroque side of Vanbrugh which appealed to Pearce; instead, he liked the particular geometrical approach of Vanbrugh's planning and massing.

We do not know how this learning from Vanbrugh took place. We know of course, thanks to Colvin and Craig, that Pearce's father was a first cousin of Vanbrugh. We know that the large collection of Vanbrugh drawings once in Elton Hall and now in the Victoria and Albert Museum must have passed, on Vanbrugh's death in 1726, to his kinsman Pearce, thence (with

---

2 This matter is being studied at the moment by Arthur Gibney in the Department of the History of Art, Trinity College, Dublin.

3 The identification of a 'Vanbrugh' drawing from Elton Hall as a plan for Pearce's Deanery of Christ Church in Dublin, allows the reattribution of the drawing to Pearce, and illustrates a similarity of approach between the two architects; see H.M. Colvin and M.J. Craig, *Architectural Drawings in the Library of Elton Hall by Sir John Vanbrugh and Sir Edward Lovett Pearce* (Oxford, 1964), p. 6. The Elton Hall drawings are now in the Victoria and Albert Museum. See Edward McParland, 'Edward Lovett Pearce and the Deanery of Christ Church, Dublin', in Agnes Bernelle (ed.), *Decantations: A Tribute to Maurice Craig* (Dublin, 1992), pp. 130-33.

Pearce's own drawings) to Pearce's patron Lord Allen, and thence to Elton Hall. But why Vanbrugh's drawings passed to Pearce rather than to another relative or colleague is unclear, since we have no record of any communication between Pearce and Vanbrugh. Pearce was not mentioned in Vanburgh's will.

It is probable that Pearce was not trained by Vanbrugh. He seems to have been raised to be a professional soldier, like his father and his uncle, both of whom were generals. His father secured a commission for Pearce as captain in 1707 but, since he is listed as cornet nine years later, this 1707 commission must have been secured for him when he was still a child: such child commissions were rare, but not unknown.[4] He seems, however, not to have had a military constitution: in 1725 he was 'brought to Convulsions and even to Deaths Door' with an 'Inveterate Cholick'; three years later a milk diet had restored him to health from being 'very infirm'. And five years after that, he died (aged about thirty-four) of a violent cholick in the stomach according to the *Dublin Evening Post*. It begins to look as if Pearce abandoned, through ill health, the military career wished upon him by his father. It may even be that he was introduced to architecture in the army: Irish architecture at this time had a distinctly military aspect, with major early Irish architects, Robinson and Burgh, both soldiers.

By the time Pearce went on the Grand Tour in 1723 and 1724 the focus of his attention was architectural. He drew his classical antiquities, and looked at modern architecture; he toured the Veneto and annotated his *Quattro libri*; he corresponded with, and no doubt met, the Florentine architect Alessandro Galilei; and he seems to have acted as agent for Speaker William Conolly of Castletown for whom he negotiated the purchase of statuary.

On Vanbrugh's death in 1726, perhaps in the role of architecturally-minded relative, he closed up Vanbrugh's office and, perhaps, took on some of Vanbrugh's office staff (is this how he came in contact with Richard Castle?). He began to make a name for himself professionally in the late 1720s. John Buxton wrote in 1728 that 'Mr Pearce . . . begins to be taken notice of as an architect & I believe will soon make a figure in that profession & he follows it *Con studio con dilligenza & con amore* . . . '[5] Six years later he was dead.

4 The date of Pearce's commission as captain in Neville's Dragoons, 13 December 1707, is given in 'List of Officers with the Dates of their Commissions . . .', PRO, WO 64.6, p. 13, and confirmed in Charles Dalton, *English Army Lists and Commission Registers, 1661-1714*, 6 vols (London, 1892-1904), vi, p. 263;

Charles Dalton, *George the First's Army, 1714-1727*, 2 vols (London, 1910-12), ii, p. 133, dates Pearce's commission as cornet to 16 February 1715/16.

5 University Library, Cambridge, John Buxton to Robert Buxton, 21 July 1728 (Buxton MSS, box 35).

The architectural historian trying to place Pearce, this neo-Palladian disciple of Vanbrugh, when frustrated by the absence of any documented links (other than those of kinship) between Pearce and Vanbrugh, turns to the neo-Palladian world presided over by Lord Burlington. What documented links were there between the two? Only one, and that indirect. In 1726 Pearce surveyed the ruins of Jigginstown House, County Kildare, for Lord Burlington, in the mistaken belief that Jigginstown was the work of Inigo Jones.[6] The contact, however, between the two men was indirect, for Pearce sent the survey not to Burlington himself but to an intermediary. Rudolf Wittkower made an extensive study of Burlington, much of it unpublished. Maurice Craig and others have spent many hours studying Pearce. Yet none of this work has produced a direct, documented link between the two men. Pearce's Parliament House is certainly the earliest Burlingtonian public building to be erected in the British Isles. Burlington was patron of at least four Irish boroughs sending members to sit in Pearce's House of Commons; as earl of Cork, he had a seat in Pearce's House of Lords (which he never took, as he never went to Ireland). It was at Burlington's instigation that designs for new Houses of Parliament in Westminster were drawn up in the 1730s. Yet a single direct documented link between Burlington and Pearce is still to be established. Ironically, when Burlington sent to Ireland a copy of Fréart's treatise, inscribed to the chief architect of Ireland, he directed his gift to Jonathan Swift.[7] Failure to establish firm links between Pearce and Burlington is of course frustrating. But there comes a stage when these negative results have their own force. Perhaps Pearce was not Lord Burlington's man in Ireland?

If exploring the Burlingtonian context for Pearce is fruitless, there are other approaches which, at least at first sight, seem to hold out promise. Some of these turn out to be equally fruitless, but it is worth noting them if only in passing, as they may some day, with further research, be found to illuminate proto-Palladian Ireland.

One initially promising herald of the Pearcean revolution is George Berkeley. Before the researches of Edward Chaney, Berkeley's architectural activities were little acknowledged.[8] Yet Berkeley was one of the most informed architectural connoisseurs of the early eighteenth century in Ireland. He held profoundly radical views, based on his direct observation

6 M.J. Craig, 'New Light on Jigginstown', *Ulster Journal of Archaeology*, 33 (1970), pp 107-10.

7 Information from Hermann Real and Heinz Veinken in 'Notes and News', *Bulletin of the John Rylands Library*, 62 (1980), pp 262-44.

8 E.g. E. Chaney, 'George Berkeley in the Veneto', *Bolletino del centro interuniversitario di richerche sul viaggio in Italia*, 1 (1980), pp 82-88.

of the Greek temples in Sicily, on the superiority of Greek to Roman architecture. His respect for the baroque architecture of Apulia found no echo until the twentieth century. Edward Chaney has discovered that he was in Padua in 1719, when it seems inconceivable that he did not inspect Palladio's buildings *in situ*. The Speaker of the Irish House of Commons, William Conolly, consulted him on the design of Castletown, County Kildare. He collaborated with William Kent in the design of a tomb in Chester Cathedral. He was Burlington's nominee as chaplain to the lord lieutenant, the duke of Grafton. Writing from the fastness and seclusion of Cloyne in 1750 he spoke wistfully of being 'haunted with a taste for good company and the fine arts that I got at Burlington House'.[9] When one hears him, in 1721, echoing Shaftesbury's call of some years earlier for the erection of a royal palace, and a new Parliament House, as fillips to national (admittedly British rather than Irish) sentiment, one wonders if there is a serious role for Berkeley as an Irish proto Palladian. There the trail goes cold. He was, for instance, away from Ireland for the full course of Pearce's active career as architect.

Another initially promising herald of the Pearcean, and neo-Palladian, revolution was the dean of Down, Charles Fairfax. Fairfax, while dean, was in charge of the erection of a school and almshouse in Downpatrick for the Southwells. It is architecturally notable only in an Irish context. It is probably the finest public building erected at the time outside Dublin and, more for this reason than for any other, is commonly attributed to Pearce. The datestone of 1733 seems to fit, though this turns out to commemorate the completion of the building, long after its initiation.

The patronage of Edward Southwell alone justifies our interest in this building. He commissioned Pearce's cousin Vanbrugh to design his house, King's Weston, in Gloucestershire; he was a connoisseur of the drawings of Inigo Jones; in *Vitruvius Britannicus* he was hailed as the Angarano of the age. Further, as an intimate of Marmaduke Coghill he was in touch with one of Pearce's patrons. Downpatrick, therefore, begins to emerge as a potential centre of early Irish neo-Palladianism, particularly when we learn that Charles Fairfax had published in 1709 an edition of Palladio's *L'antichità di Roma*.

Again the trail to a coherent body of early neo-Palladian activity goes cold. Fairfax was dean of Down for little more than a year before his death;

9 Chatsworth, Devonshire Papers, first series, 364/0, George Berkeley to Lady Burlington, 2 April 1750; see also G.N. Cantor, 'Two Letters Relating to Berkeley's Social Circle', *Berkeley Newsletter*, 4 (1980).

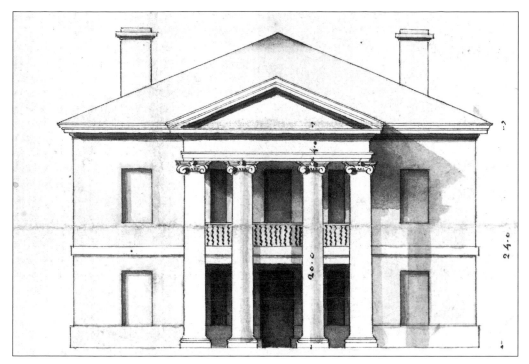

Fig. 65 Unidentified villa, elevation by Edward Lovett Pearce (*Victoria and Albert Museum*)

the Southwell papers show that the school was designed before Pearce had taken up architecture,[10] and so we are left without an architect for it. Downpatrick in 1722, with its Angarano patronage and its editions of Palladio was a meteorite, rather than a comet, in Irish neo-Palladian skies.

Architectural historians will regret this. As well as Southwell gossip, and Palladio gossip, Fairfax must also have talked of his friend Henry Aldrich, dean of Christ Church, Oxford. On Aldrich's death, Fairfax had been the one to see his *Plato* through the press, and it was at Aldrich's suggestion that Fairfax undertook his own translation of Palladio. But there we must leave it. However interesting the dinner table conversation of Charles Fairfax was, it seems to have borne no architectural fruit other than its modest Downpatrick almshouse.

If Vanbrugh, Burlington, George Berkeley and Edward Southwell and his circle all fail to provide the key to early neo-Palladianism in Ireland, we can

10 The school is inscribed with the date 1733 which must record completion of the building which 'was done in Dean Fairfax's time . . . when Dean Fairfax dyed . . . the Workmen remained unpaid . . . until 1732 . . . ', BL, Add. MS 21131, 'Ireland, Downe Estate Papers', fos 110-11.

make slightly more progress by considering the New Junta for Architecture. The cast of the New Junta was assembled in a letter of October 1717 from Robert Molesworth to Lord Stanhope, first lord of the treasury, in which he says 'Mr Hewett My eldest son Signr Galilei & I, & (if you can engage him) Sr George Markham . . . are of the new Junta for Architecture'.[11] This, I believe, is the clique that provides the best context in which to set the emergence of Edward Lovett Pearce as architect.

Robert, first Viscount Molesworth, is familiar. He was the property speculator who laid out much of the land immediately to the south of Trinity College in Dublin. His son, the third viscount, nearly managed to get the new Parliament House erected on this land. Robert Molesworth laid out spectacular gardens and waterworks on his Yorkshire estate at Edlington, and on his Irish estate at Breckdenstown, near Swords, County Dublin. He was the committee man involved in the building of St Werburgh's church in Dublin, who struggled to get Alessandro Galilei appointed as architect. Almost as interesting for us is that he was the 'oracle and confident' of the third earl of Shaftesbury.

Molesworth's eldest son John, another member of this New Junta, became not just an hereditary friend of Shaftesbury's but one in his own right, when both men were in Italy: Shaftesbury an invalid and dying in Naples; Molesworth envoy to the Tuscan court. In Florence, Molesworth came across the architect Alessandro Galilei, then in his mid twenties, and invited him to England in 1714, where he stayed – apart from a six-month trip to Ireland in 1718 – for four years. It is probable that Galilei recommended himself to John Molesworth by his skill in hydraulics, and the design of fountains. This had been a preoccupation of John's father Robert. It is possible that this interest, which veered in one direction towards garden design, veered in another into the more scientific concerns of the Royal Society, of which Robert Molesworth and Sir George Markham, his colleague on the New Junta, were members. Galilei's papers in Florence include drawings for scientific instruments and records of an experiment conducted in London in 1715, on driving a fountain by steam.[12]

In the early 1720s John Molesworth was appointed envoy to Turin. Here again he can be seen to be architecturally involved. His dealings with Galilei – who by now had returned to Florence from Ireland – will be described later. In Turin he was obviously dealing with the royal architect

11 Kent Archives Office, U1590/C9/35, Lord
    Molesworth to Lord Stanhope, 5 October
    1717.

12 Archivio di Stato, Florence, 'Diversi disegni
    d'architetta del Sig. Alessandro Galilei', no.
    314 (Carte Galilei, filza N, no. 2).

Filippo Juvarra, soliciting fresco designs from other parts of Italy for Juvarra's approval. He was also host to Edward Lovett Pearce in 1724.

The other members of the New Junta may be introduced briefly. Sir George Markham, Bt, seems to have been in Shaftesbury's circle;[13] he had Irish relatives (whom he detested); and he had architectural responsibilities as a Whig appointee to the commission for building fifty new churches in London, for which commission Galilei made designs. As we have seen, Markham was (like Robert Molesworth) a fellow of the Royal Society.

The two professional architects named by Molesworth as belonging to this New Junta were Alessandro Galilei and Sir Thomas Hewett. Like all other members of this clique, Hewett had Irish connections though not, to my knowledge, an Irish practice. Hewett as surveyor general retained, and reciprocated, the animosity of Nicholas Hawksmoor, whom he refused to reinstate at the Office of Works after Benson's fall. He seems also not to have been well-disposed to Colen Campbell, who was closely identified with the disgraced Benson. Hewett left his estate to the Irish painter Hugh Howard, whose papers in the National Library of Ireland contain many references to Hewett and to Irish links with connoisseurs in London. Thanks probably to Hewett's influence, Howard succeeded Charles Dartiquenave as paymaster of the works.

Hewett built little, but it is worth noting that he displayed distinctly neo-classical tastes, or at least distinctly neo-classical pretensions. In this he voiced what seems to have been the ambition of the New Junta: to reinvigorate the late baroque tradition with inspiration derived directly from an archaeologically based study of classical antiquity. At a time when few architects were citing Greek, rather than Roman, models Hewett showed marked interest in Greek architecture. While it is difficult to know exactly what 'Greek' meant to him, he spoke of his work at Kensington Palace as being 'of the fine Grecian taste', and George Vertue described the 'Greek Tempietto' in Hewett's own gardens in Nottinghamshire. To anticipate my argument somewhat, these Greek interests of Hewett are one of his links with Pearce, who justified his own designs for the Dublin Parliament House in terms of what he called Grecian peristyles and Grecian exedrae. Hewett's complaint that English architecture of the 1720s was no longer mathematically based, found a sympathetic echo in Pearce's uncommon and explicit arithmetical and geometrical principles of design.

The final member of Molesworth's New Junta, Alessandro Galilei, was a mathematician turned architect. With few or no architectural achievements

---

13 I am indebted to David Hayton for this suggestion.

behind him, he was brought by the Molesworths to London in 1714. He made designs, unexecuted, for the commission for the building of fifty new churches on which Sir George Markham sat. Though many of them have undeniably baroque flourishes, one of his church designs fits into the neo-classical milieu of the New Junta. It is a vast peripteral temple, wholly unlike any baroque church ever built, and indeed more thoroughgoing in its neo-classicism than most buildings erected before the early nineteenth century.[14] The order of the columns was, admittedly, a Roman and not a Greek Doric order. Otherwise the form of the temple is explicitly Greek. While the Romans perched their colonnades above a substructure which was approached only in the front by a flight of steps, we can see Galilei here carrying his steps right around the entire temple in a uniquely Greek fashion. Hewett and Pearce would have been impressed, as would George Berkeley.

Galilei was little employed in England or Ireland. He made designs for Speaker Conolly's house at Castletown, County Kildare but, though the design of the main block is commonly attributed to him, we may wonder about just how much Galilei had to do with the house. Conolly did not begin to build Castletown until three years after Galilei had returned to Florence. John Molesworth wrote to Galilei in Florence saying that now Mr Conolly was building, he would welcome Galilei's advice now and then if Galilei were back in Ireland. This is hardly the kind of involvement one would expect if Conolly was proceeding on Galilei's plans. All we can be sure of is, that Conolly was certainly employing Pearce after Pearce's return from Italy in 1724.

This, then, was the cast of Robert Molesworth's New Junta for Architecture. Piecing together the fragments of evidence, we can see them, about 1715, seeking an alternative to current architectural fashion, interested in reanimating design with fresh inspiration derived directly from classical antiquity, and particularly from what Hewett described to Galilei in 1720 as antiquity of the 'Grecian & best taste'. Each one of them has Irish connections. They had Palladian connections (Galilei in England went into partnership with the translator of Leoni's edition of Palladio's *I quattro libri*), but seem to remain suspicious of neo-Palladians like Colen Campbell. Their movement was short-lived, at least in England, where the baton of reform was snatched from them by Lord Burlington. With the exception of

14 Archivio di Stato, Florence, 'Diversi disegni', no. 328 (Carte Galilei, filza N, no. 2), elevation and section reproduced in Ilaria Toesca, 'Alessandro Galilei in Inghilterra', in Mario Praz (ed.), *English Miscellany*, iii (Rome, 1952), figs 7, 8.

Markham, they were all dead (or in Italy) by 1726. Politically, as one would guess even from the name of their clique, they were Whig, and (with members such as Robert Molesworth and George Markham, and associates such as Shaftesbury), radically inclined Whigs.

I have, speculatively, smuggled Shaftesbury into the New Junta. This is partly because of his known links with Markham and the Molesworths, but also because of his ideas expressed in his letter *Concerning the Art of Design* of 1712 which was addressed, we may note, to Lord Somers of the Whig Junta. In this, Shaftesbury attacks the architecture of Wren, and calls for the formation of a national style which will find worthy expression in the building of new Houses of Parliament in Westminster, and a new royal palace. He is unspecific as to what these buildings should look like, but Shaftesbury was distinguished for his classical, specifically Greek, attainments. Now it is a cliché of architectural history to present Shaftesbury, on this evidence, as prophet of Burlingtonian neo-Palladianism. If this is true, it is because the Burlingtonians appropriated him from the New Junta, with whom Shaftesbury had the closer personal ties. Shaftesbury's call for a new Parliament House in a newly revived national style may have eventually led to William Kent's designs for Westminster in the 1730s.

It had already been picked up by Berkeley and physically embodied in Pearce's building in College Green, which Pearce himself saw as an assertion of Irishness: he called for the use in his building of Kilkenny marble which, he wrote, 'is equal in goodness and Beauty to any foreign Marble and [is in addition] the Produce of the Kingdom'.[15] William Kent rose to Shaftesbury's call for designs for a royal palace, but only after Galilei had made his designs, which are now lost; and after Pearce had produced his unexecuted designs, which survive, for a palace at Richmond. Robert Molesworth was Shaftesbury's 'oracle and confident'.

What did the Molesworths, and the New Junta, achieve by bringing their architect Galilei to Ireland? Very little. They failed to get him the job of designing St Werburgh's thanks to Archbishop King, who was suspicious that they were trying to offload on Dublin a second-rate foreigner. King secured the job instead for that dull Tory, Thomas Burgh. Just as Molesworth urged Speaker Conolly to employ the landscape gardener Stephen Switzer, so it may have been Molesworth who urged Conolly to commission designs for Castletown from Galilei. To Galilei is attributed a garden

15 Quoted in Edward McParland, 'Edward Lovett Pearce and the Parliament House in Dublin', *Burlington Magazine*, 131 (1989), p. 100.

temple erected in Drumcondra in Dublin on the estate of Marmaduke Coghill. But Galilei's career in Ireland, as in England, fizzled out. He returned to Italy in 1718, where John Molesworth, as envoy in Turin, continued to make efforts to attract him back to Ireland.

By this time Pearce was of this group and shared their interests. Correspondence between Galilei, the Molesworths, Thomas Hewett and Pearce is found together in both Galilei's own papers in the Archivio di Stato in Florence, and in the Molesworth letters among the Clements papers, which are now untraceable but are on microfilm in the National Library of Ireland. From these we see Galilei in Florence in the 1720s keeping up some Irish contacts, as for instance when he sold some bogus Correggios to Robert Clayton. Hewett, Galilei and Pearce exchanged letters concerning, and designs for, a palace which some historians have assumed to mean Castletown, but which is more probably the New Junta's scheme (derived from Shaftesbury) for a royal palace for London. John Molesworth instructed Galilei to study Palladio, now – that is, in 1726 – all the rage in London. Presumably he gave the same advice to his kinsman Pearce (they shared an uncle by marriage) who of course went to the Veneto, conned his *I quattro libri* and annotated it, and visited Molesworth in Turin. Looking at Pearce's later designs for a royal palace at Richmond, it seems inconceivable that his cousin John Molesworth had not brought him, while in Turin, to see and wonder at the architecture, and particularly the staircases, of Molesworth's fellow courtier Filippo Juvarra.

Quite suddenly, there were big changes. Robert Molesworth died in 1725, his son John and Sir Thomas Hewett in the following year. Galilei soon headed from Florence to Rome where he pursued the attempt to introduce in the Italian late baroque the neo-classical lessons he had learnt in England. And in 1726, when Vanbrugh too died, his cousin Pearce closed up Vanbrugh's practice, collected Vanbrugh's drawings, and began to make a name for himself in architecture. Among his earliest patrons were Speaker Conolly at Castletown and Marmaduke Coghill at Drumcondra, who earlier had been patrons of Galilei.

He entered into his own practice after absorbing the New Junta's precocious neo-classical tastes. He could quote Vitruvius at his Irish patrons and was, as far as I know, the first Irish architect to be documented as having done so. He had looked at Palladio's buildings *in situ* and, in his Parliament House and royal palace, he went through his modish Burlington paces. But he was no strict Burlingtonian. Schooled in a different post-Wren world, he was at the same time even more neo-classical and also less doctrinaire than this. He was for instance more neo-classical in this unprepossessing and gloomy little villa from the Elton Hall collection (Plate 65). It is certainly Palladian, but it is not Burlingtonian. It is too gloomily neo-antique for that. Had this been built in France, say by Ledoux in the 1780s, and if it survived, it would be a textbook monument for neo-classical architecture *à la Grecque*. In another unexpected villa design from Elton Hall, there appears a basically Palladian villa with an antique reference of the greatest rarity: a canvas awning to be stretched across the rooftop terrace, to act as *velarium* as in the Colosseum. While he learnt from Palladio and from antiquity, he was learning too from Vanbrugh and was breaking the cube by pulling out bays and projections to enhance the liveliness of plan and chiaroscuro and silhouette of his block.

Thomas Hewett's circle and that of the Molesworths, and Pearce's own examination at first hand of Roman antiquities, had left him with his antique taste and with a taste for Palladio, but also with a suspicion of Burlington and of the modern school. His cousinship with Vanbrugh had opened him to formal excitements denied to strict followers of Lord Burlington, while his contact with Galilei, and perhaps Juvarra, opened him to what was in effect a whole range of European late baroque classicism. Perhaps it was part of his Irishness that he could slip the leash of doctrinaire Burlingtonianism to enrich his architecture with a wider eclecticism which was, of course, at the heart of the excitement in his buildings.

3

Land and the Limits of Loyalty:
The Second Earl of Cork and First Earl of Burlington
(1612-98)

T.C. Barnard

The second earl of Cork and first earl of Burlington lived long and owned much.[1] Neither longevity nor riches entitle their possessors to historical attention, and indeed Lord Cork and Burlington plodded dutifully through his inherited tasks. In life, a foil to his dazzling siblings, the earl of Orrery, Robert Boyle, Lady Ranelagh and Lady Warwick; after death he transmitted his titles to his more celebrated great grandson, the architect earl, having husbanded the resources that the latter so spectacularly dissipated. Three themes thread through the earl's career: land, family and loyalty. In dramatically changing scenes – at the ritualised court of Charles I in the 1630s; in Ireland during bouts with the insurgent Catholics, in one of which

Throughout this essay the following abbreviations are used: BL (British Library, London); NLI (National Library of Ireland, Dublin); PRO (Public Record Office); TCD (Trinity College, Dublin). I am grateful to the Duke of Devonshire and the Trustees of the Chatsworth Settled Estates for permission to read and cite manuscripts which they own. I also thank Peter Day at Chatsworth and the Very Rev. A. Bowder and Mrs Bowder at Lismore for their help. Finally, for urging me to complete a scheme first conceived in 1970, I owe much to Jane Clark and Anthony O'Connor.

1 In the matter of names, since Burlington during his life had three (until 1643, Viscount Dungarvan; from 1643 to 1665 earl of Cork; and then earl of Cork and Burlington), when writing generally of him I call him Burlington, but when referring to precise occasions, shall use the name that he then bore. The same principle is applied to his wife, and to his brother Roger, until 1660 Lord Broghill and thereafter earl of Orrery.

a brother was killed beside him;[2] in the cramped royal bunker at Oxford during the Civil War; then, in penury in France, followed by a discreet retirement to Ireland throughout the Interregnum; and finally, close to the powerful in England and Ireland after Charles II's restoration – he struggled to reconcile the contrary claims of dynasty, religion, honour, loyalty and fortune. What he lacked in guile and subtlety, he made up in unremitting application. This transparency ('I am a very plain and punctual dealer and cannot forbear telling truth, let it offend whom it will')[3] may explain why the earl, notwithstanding his wealth, industry and extensive connections, never won the highest offices. A mediocrity he may have been, but never a nullity. By studying his lives on both sides of the Irish Sea, we can see something of how the prosperous and active Anglo-Irish helped to unite the several provinces ruled by the Stuart monarchs.

After 1660, Burlington was among the wealthiest peers. Most of his income was derived from Ireland: from lands, mainly in the southerly province of Munster, accumulated in the early seventeenth century by his ruthless father, the first ('great') earl of Cork, whose long shadow chilled his heir.[4] Although segments of the apanage had been peeled away to feed his four younger brothers, Burlington's share supplied him with an income which, in the 1670s, probably approached £30,000.[5] Back in the 1630s, with such riches in the offing, Burlington's father had bought him an English heiress as his bride, Elizabeth Clifford, only surviving child of the fifth earl of

---

2 I have skimmed over the formative years at court since they are covered admirably by P.J.S. Little in 'Family and Faction: The Irish Nobility and the English Court, 1632-42' (unpublished M.Litt. dissertation, Trinity College Dublin, 1992). This work offers a more satisfying account than that in N.P. Canny, *The Upstart Earl: A Study of the Social and Mental World of Richard Boyle, First Earl of Cork*, (Cambridge, 1982). Dungarvan's activities during the Irish rebellion can be glimpsed in BL, Sloane MS 1008, fo. 41; Chatsworth, Londesborough MSS, box I (i), 99; W.H. Coates, ed., *The Journal of Sir Symonds D'Ewes* (New Haven, 1942), pp. 127, 165, 189, 353; W.H. Coates, A.S. Young and V.F. Snow, eds, *The Private Journals of the Long Parliament 3 January to 5 March 1642* (New Haven and London, 1982), pp. 100, 148, 149, 156, 429; James Hogan, ed., *Letters and Papers Relating to the Irish Rebellion between 1642-46* (Dublin, 1936), pp. 14, 156-58; J.A. Murphy, 'The Politics of the Munster Protestants, 1641-1649',

Journal of the Cork Historical and Archaeological Society, 75 (1971), pp. 1-19; *A true relation of the miserable estate that Ireland now standeth in . . . in a letter of Lord Dungarvan to Sir Arthur Magennis* (London, 1642).

3 Chatsworth, Lismore MS 34/48.

4 The essential background is in M. MacCarthy-Morrogh, *The Munster Plantation* (Oxford, 1986); idem, 'The English Presence in Early Seventeenth-Century Munster', in C. Brady and R. Gillespie, eds, *Natives and Newcomers* (Dublin, 1986); T.O. Ranger, 'The Career of Richard Boyle, First Earl of Cork in Ireland, 1588-1643' (unpublished D.Phil. thesis, University of Oxford, 1958); idem, 'Richard Boyle and the Making of an Irish Fortune', *Irish Historical Studies*, 10 (1957), pp. 257-97.

5 NLI, MSS 6302, 6303, 6307. The deaths of Lewis (Kinalmeaky) in 1642 and of Robert in 1691 brought back some of the lands to their eldest brother.

Cumberland. Eventually she endowed Burlington with large (if not particularly remunerative) tracts of Yorkshire, including their future seat there, Londesborough in the East Riding.[6] In 1661 his elder son, on marriage, received lands in Ireland worth an annual £8,000, English estates with a yearly rental of £2,700, and an annual £1,500 to maintain the couple.[7] Each daughter was dowered with £10,000.[8] At his death, Burlington was rumoured to have bequeathed to his heir, Lord Clifford, £22,000, with a further £4,000 *p.a.* to Clifford's younger brother.[9] By then war and its aftermath, together with Burlington's own absence from Ireland since 1686, diminished the Irish receipts. By way of comparison with Burlington's income in its heyday, estimated at £30,000, we know that, in the 1690s, the duke of Newcastle's rents yielded £25,000 p.a., and that, a few years earlier, the earls of Rutland and Devonshire enjoyed £15,000 and £17,000 respectively from their estates. In Ireland, its only duke, Ormonde, alone matched Burlington's riches.[10]

Burlington, whether from temperament or from habits dinned into him by an overbearing father, was more bowed by the duties than elated by the opportunities of his patrimony. An Irish neighbour approvingly reported that Burlington had confided to him, 'that he was ten years in studying his father's deeds, and perhaps no lord in England is half so much master of his titles and lands as that rich man'.[11] As age forced the earl to haunt his chamber more than his stables, he ruled his satraps with obsessional attentiveness. Paper books of accounts and rentals shuttled across the Irish Sea, and followed the earl on his English progresses. Endless, pernickety queries resulted, to be dreaded and parried by careless underlings. Gardeners were instructed how to plant; agents were lectured on their lack of

6 Chatsworth, Londesborough MSS, box I (i), 74, 79; Canny, *The Upstart Earl*, pp. 54-56; B. English, *The Great Landowners of East Yorkshire, 1530-1910* (Hemel Hempstead, 1990), p. 105; L. Stone, *The Crisis of the Aristocracy, 1558-1641* (Oxford, 1965), p. 761 note c; R.T. Spence, 'The Cliffords, Earls of Cumberland, 1579-1646' (unpublished Ph.D. thesis, University of London, 1959), p. 170. In the 1650s the Bolton Abbey estates were yielding an average of £3,000 annually, a figure which suggests that earlier the income from the estate had been considerably underestimated: Chatsworth, Bolton Abbey MSS 274-278.

7 Chatsworth, Lord Burlington's diary, 11 Feb. 1660[1], 7 May 1661, 25 June 1662; Lady Burlington's journal, 6 May 1661; *HMC, Finch MSS*, i, p. 119.

8 The exception was Frances, married in Ireland in 1656, who received only £3,000. Chatsworth, Burlington's diary, 2, 12 June 1662; 9, 11 April 1664; 1, 18, 23 Feb. 1664[5]; 13 Feb. 1668[9]; Lismore MSS 28/47-49.

9 *CSPD, 1698*, p. 36. Cf. Brynmor Jones Library, Hull, DD BM 32/1, A. Bosville to G. Bosville, [1698].

10 TCD, MS 847; Bowood House, Wiltshire, Petty Papers, F. 53; McGill University Library, Montreal, Osler MS 7612, letter of 26 Oct. 1666; Bodl., Carte MSS 33, fo. 657; 34, fo. 318; J.V. Beckett, *The Aristocracy in England, 1660-1914* (Oxford, 1986), pp. 288-89; Stone, *Crisis of the Aristocracy*, p. 761.

11 BL., Add. MS 46961, fo. 154v, printed in *HMC, Egmont MSS*, ii, p. 142.

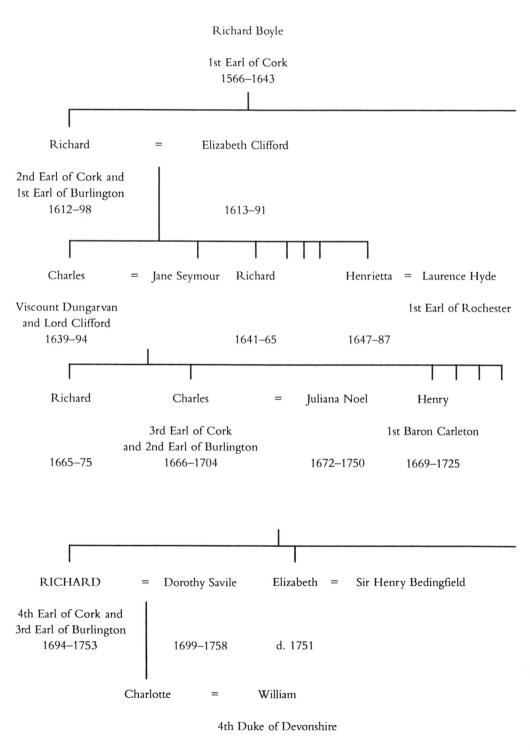

Richard Boyle

1st Earl of Cork
1566–1643

Richard   =   Elizabeth Clifford

2nd Earl of Cork and
1st Earl of Burlington
1612–98   1613–91

Charles   =   Jane Seymour   Richard   Henrietta = Laurence Hyde

Viscount Dungarvan
and Lord Clifford   1st Earl of Rochester
1639–94   1641–65   1647–87

Richard   Charles   =   Juliana Noel   Henry

                 3rd Earl of Cork
          and 2nd Earl of Burlington   1st Baron Carleton
1665–75   1666–1704   1672–1750   1669–1725

RICHARD   =   Dorothy Savile   Elizabeth = Sir Henry Bedingfield

4th Earl of Cork and
3rd Earl of Burlington
1694–1753   1699–1758   d. 1751

Charlotte   =   William

4th Duke of Devonshire

1731–54

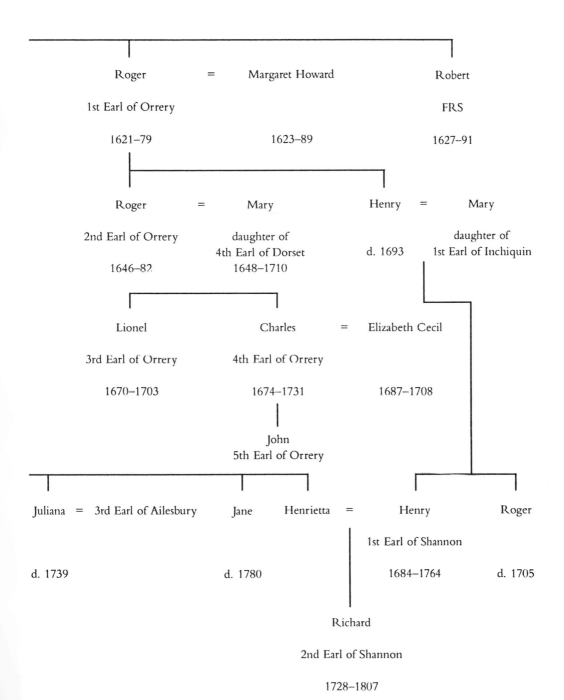

Fig. 66 Burlington family tree

Roger = Margaret Howard   Robert

1st Earl of Orrery   FRS

1621–79   1623–89   1627–91

Roger = Mary   Henry = Mary

2nd Earl of Orrery   daughter of 4th Earl of Dorset   d. 1693   daughter of 1st Earl of Inchiquin

1646–82   1648–1710

Lionel   Charles = Elizabeth Cecil

3rd Earl of Orrery   4th Earl of Orrery

1670–1703   1674–1731   1687–1708

John
5th Earl of Orrery

Juliana = 3rd Earl of Ailesbury   Jane   Henrietta = Henry   Roger

1st Earl of Shannon

d. 1739   d. 1780   1684–1764   d. 1705

Richard

2nd Earl of Shannon

1728–1807

system. He fussed constantly, not only over rent arrears, but about putting down cakes of rat poison in his Youghal house or reclaiming broken chairs and worn pewter dishes borrowed by poorer relations.[12] In 1691 a secretary feelingly added to one of the earl's letters, 'my lord is as ill-humoured as ever'; and, in 1697, a grandson had to apologise to an Irish bishop for an imperious letter, explaining that it had been written only at Burlington's dictation.[13] A fine example of the earl's vigilance arose from an item in the Irish accounts for 1689. The earl, despite his frequent absences from his principal Irish seat, Lismore Castle, allowed grand guests, such as the viceroy on tour or the judges on assize, to be accommodated there. The judges, luxuriating in this berth, lengthened their stay from one to two nights, and enlarged their entourage.[14] But in March 1689 a more illustrious visitor put up at the castle: the fugitive James II, hopeful of using Ireland as the base from which to recover his other two kingdoms. Burlington, vetting the 1689 account in July 1691, by which time James had fled to France, expostulated, 'for one supper and a breakfast, and in Lent, when there were very few but papists there, and neither the king nor any of them did eat a bit of flesh, yet for the expenses, I say, of two meals, there was disbursed of my money, £171 8s. 6d.'[15]

Over the decades Burlington had laboriously acquired, and from the 1670s now displayed, a grasp of the solvency and foibles of individual tenants and farms which none of his agents could rival. Irksome such close scrutiny might be to the subordinates, who, careless or crooked, hoped to slip items through. But what could happen when the rein slackened was demonstrated by all too many of his contemporaries, including his more relaxed relations in Munster, and even on Burlington's own holdings in the 1690s. Immediately after his death in 1698, one Irish account was almost £8,000 in the red;[16] by 1737, arrears were estimated at £80,000, and the

12 BL, Althorp MS B.7, Burlington's letters of 10 Jan. 1681[2] and 28 Feb. 1681[2]; Chatsworth, Lismore MS 34/91; NLI, MS 13226, Burlington's letters of 30 July 1691, 10 Oct. 1691, 9 Feb. 1691[2], 3 Sept. 1692, 8 Dec. 1692, 11 Sept. 1694, 30 July 1695, 10 April 1697, 24 July 1697.

13 BL, Althorp MS, B.7, Burlington's letter, 28 Nov. 1691; TCD, MSS 1995-2008/557.

14 Chatsworth, Lismore MS 34/59; NLI, MSS. 6300, 18 Oct. 1686; 13226, Burlington's letters of 10 May 1694, 8 June 1697, 15 June 1697; 13227, 2nd Lord Burlington's letter of 12 Jan. 1700[1]; P. Melvin, ed., 'Sir Paul Rycaut's Memoranda and Letters from Ireland, 1686-

1687', *Analecta Hibernica*, 27 (1972), p. 132; S.W. Singer, ed., *The Correspondence of Henry Hyde, Earl of Clarendon* (London, 1828), i, p. 584.

15 NLI, MSS 6300; 13226, Burlington's letters of 7, 21 and 30 July 1691.

16 Borthwick Institute, York, will of second earl of Burlington, 1704; Chatsworth, Lismore MSS, Miscellaneous MS labelled '6', rental for 1699; Londesborough MSS, box I (v), 15, Burlington's letter of 9 Oct. 1694; NLI, MSS 13226, Burlington's letter of 3 Oct. 1691 and 10 Sep. 1695; 13227, 2nd Lord Burlington's letters of 30 April 1698 and 12 Nov. 1698.

dismemberment of the Irish estates had begun in earnest.[17] Now they had become capital to be raided to finance the architect earl's projects.

Estates of this extent and value had not only to be managed but defended. Their being in two kingdoms necessitated different, if linked, strategies. Twice – after 1641 and in 1689 – war wasted the Irish lands, and jeopardised the Boyles' ownership. Each upheaval wrenched land-owning into new patterns.[18] Only by lobbying, intrigue and bribery at the highest levels – at the viceregal court in Dublin and the royal court in England, and in the English and Irish privy councils and parliaments – could Burlington preserve and, sometimes, add to his empire. Defence of the lands engendered a wiliness towards neighbours, lest they compete; a wariness towards those Irish Catholics whom he and his father had supplanted; and, most seriously, it limited and in the end overmastered his devotion to the later Stuarts. In England, the Yorkshire estates were menaced by different threats: in the 1640s and 1650s they had to be saved from the consequences of Burlington's attachment to Charles I. In the event, his wife recovered and protected these lands: appropriately, since they had constituted her portion.[19]

Burlington, conscious that so long as the dispossessed Irish Catholics were welcomed at court his Irish titles were endangered, seemed to share with many Irish Protestants 'a perfect and universal hatred to the whole Irish nation'.[20] He, like many of his kind, fretted lest the Irish Catholic claimants trump his own royalist cards with their aces of diehard allegiance to and exile with the Stuarts. These Catholic rivals alternated between pressing the Stuarts legally to uproot johnny-come-latelies, such as the Boyles, and taking matters into their own hands, as they did after 1641 and in 1689. His lands drew Burlington into, and financed, a public career dedicated to maintaining a Protestant owned Ireland. Yet, although he sat in

---

17 Hampshire County Record Office, Winchester, Heathcote MSS, 63M84/210, 211; PRO, Northern Ireland, Shannon MS, D 2707/B9/2, 3, 5, 6, 10; D. Dickson, 'An Economic History of the Cork Region in the Eighteenth Century' (unpublished Ph.D. thesis, Trinity College, Dublin, 1977), pp. 73-79; E. Hewitt, ed., *Lord Shannon's Letters to his Son* (Belfast, 1982), pp. xxix-xx. The new attitude is captured well in the 1724 inventory for Londesborough, which mentioned scattered through the garrets there 'several old and late books of accounts, writings, vouchers and other papers relating to the estate'; Chatsworth, Londesborough MSS, box G, 22.

18 L.J. Arnold, 'The Irish Court of Claims in 1663', *Irish Historical Studies*, 24 (1985), pp.

417-30; T.C. Barnard, 'Planters and Policies in Cromwellian Ireland', *Past and Present*, 61 (1973), pp. 31-69; K.S. Bottigheimer, *English Money and Irish Land* (Oxford, 1971); idem, 'The Restoration Land Settlement in Ireland: A Structural View', *Irish Historical Studies*, 18 (1972), pp. 1-21; J.G. Simms, *The Williamite Confiscation in Ireland, 1690-1703* (London, 1956).

19 Chatsworth, Bolton Abbey MS 278, pp. 20-22; Lismore MS 28/17; Londesborough MSS, box I (i), 47; J.W. Clay, ed., *Yorkshire Royalist Composition Papers*, ii, Yorkshire Archaeological Society, 18 (1895), pp. 122-24.

20 Bodleian Library, Oxford, Clarendon State Papers, 79, fo. 90v.

the Westminster and Dublin parliaments throughout much of his life (he was elected to the Short and Long Parliaments in 1640)[21] and, after 1660, periodically graced the Irish council board as a privy councillor and hereditary Lord High Treasurer, he hovered on the edges of power. In London, for example, he was regularly consulted about Irish matters as one of a knot of resident Anglo-Irish grandees, but was never sworn of the English council.[22] Unlike others in the group – Ormonde, Ossory, Anglesey and Conway – he never rose above the lord lieutenancy of a county. This is surprising when we recall that he had known the court and its habitués since the golden 1630s, through kinship and marriage was 'allied with many of the best families in England',[23] and in Munster, where most prosperous landowners were his tenants or relations, headed a powerful affinity. These assets could not lift him into public prominence. Either lack of appetite or aptitude stunted his career. In Ireland, his supple brother Roger, Lord Broghill and, after 1660, earl of Orrery, an adept of intrigue and cajolery, proved the superlative political fixer. Broghill it was who defended the family home at Lismore against the Irish rebels in 1642, mobilised the Boyles' tenants and dependants in the neighbourhood to contain the insurgents and, after 1649, steered them towards the English parliament and Cromwell.[24] Broghill's talents and charm won Ireton's and Cromwell's admiration, and launched him into English and Scottish politics. He valued his local base and, in default of any activity by (though evidently with the approval of) his eldest brother, Broghill aligned the family connections behind the Cromwellian usurpers.[25] Thanks to Broghill, the political potential of the Boyle interest, latent under his father and brother, was realised, and would soon serve new turns in the Dublin

21 In the Clifford interest, for Appleby, M.F. Keeler, *The Long Parliament, 1640-1641* (Philadelphia, 1954), pp. 113-14.

22 Nor was the suggestion that he be appointed lord president of Munster in 1645 acted upon. Chatsworth, Burlington's diary, 9, 11, 12, 13, 14 May 1665, 19 Dec. 1667, 20 Feb. 1667[8], 17, 25 March 1668[9]; Victoria and Albert Museum, London, Orrery MSS, iii, account of a journey in 1675; *CSPD, 1680*, p. 76; *CSPI, 1669-1670*, p. 121; T. Carte, *The Life of James, Duke of Ormonde* (Oxford, 1851), vi, pp. 211, 221; *HMC, Finch MSS*, iv, pp. 68, 216; *House of Lords, 1678-88*, pp. 168-69, 219; *Ormonde MSS*, new series, v, pp. 474.

23 F.R. Harris, *The Life of Edward Montagu, K.G., First Earl of Sandwich* (London, 1912), ii, p. 178.

24 For Broghill's activities in the 1640s: BL, Add. MS 25287; NLI, MS 6900; Bottigheimer, *English Money and Irish Land*, pp. 76-114; K.M. Lynch, *Roger Boyle, First Earl of Orrery* (Knoxville, TEN, 1965), chapter 2; *A manifestation directed to the honourable Houses of Parliament in England sent from the Lord Inchequin, the Lord Brohill . . .* (London, 1644); Murphy, 'The Politics of the Munster Protestants'; J.A. Murphy, 'Inchiquin's Change of Religion', *Journal of the Cork Historical and Archaeological Society*, 72 (1967), pp. 59-67.

25 On Broghill in the 1650s: Barnard, 'Planters and Policies', pp. 55-60; idem, 'The Political, Material and Mental Culture of the Cork Settlers, *c.* 1650-1700', in P. O'Flanagan, (ed.), *Cork: History and Society* (Dublin, 1993), and the works cited there.

Convention of 1660 and Irish Parliament of 1661.[26] By 1665 Orrery, as Broghill now was, could boast how he had engaged to his and the government's side twenty-five Munster members of parliament.[27]

In all this, Burlington acted the compliant auxiliary. Whatever reservations he may have felt about Orrery's chameleon qualities, Burlington ordered the family's electoral influence to be swung behind his brother's candidates.[28] For Burlington, the success of these nominees who in 1661 included his second son, Richard, had as much to do with dynastic prestige as with politics. Nevertheless, from this material, Orrery was fashioning a buckler with which to defend Protestant Ireland, prove his own and his family's usefulness and, when necessary, thwart competitors. Without Orrery's management, the Irish parliament might well have broken up in disorder; as it was, English and Irish politicians, taken aback by its peevishness, let it hibernate after 1666. No longer were Burlington and Orrery obliged to include Dublin on their annual itineraries; the former also cut back on the splendour with which he had stunned Restoration Dublin (in 1662 a provincial goggled, 'there is not in Ireland such state and attendance, and all the dishes plate, with the foreign varieties of wine to complete his cheer'), and let his town residence there, henceforward lodging with his son-in-law, Lord Roscommon.[29] This was part of a dangerous process by which the Anglo-Irish magnates, not needed in Dublin for regular parliaments, detached themselves from Ireland.

Only in 1692 was the Irish parliament roused from its slumber. By then Orrery was long dead and the Boyle interest wanted a local impresario. From England, Burlington deputed his grandson, Harry Boyle, to assume the vacant role. This he did, at first to his grandfather's plaudits, being elected for the Burlington borough of Youghal. But, all too soon, this stripling threw up the tedium of estate supervision in Munster and the prospects of a bad-tempered session in Dublin for an English parliamentary seat proffered by his maternal and ducal relations. Burlington's acute family pride was outraged but all he could do was to quibble over the cost (£40) of

26 In the Convention Broghill sat for the prestigious seat of Dublin University. *An account of the chief occurrences of Ireland . . . 12-19 March* [1660] (Dublin, 1660), p. 37. For his electoral management: Victoria and Albert Museum, Orrery MSS, i, fo. 1; T.C. Barnard, 'Lord Broghill, Vincent Gookin and the Cork Elections of 1659', *English Historical Review*, 88 (1973), pp. 352-65.

27 Bodleian Library, Clarendon State Papers, 79, fo. 184v; Barnard, 'The Cork Settlers', p. 319.

28 BL, Stowe MS 744, fo. 140; Chatsworth, Lismore MS 32/3-5.

29 Chatsworth, Burlington's diary, 11 Oct. 1661, 22 April 1663, 15 Nov. 1663; Lismore MSS, miscellaneous, rental for 1693, p. 2; Cork University Library, U.55, letters of R. Southwell, senior, 18 Nov. 1662 and 20 Dec. 1662.

entertaining the Youghal electors.[30] Next, his grandson and heir, Lord Clifford, was persuaded to interest himself in Irish affairs. He took his seat as Viscount Dungarvan in the Irish House of Lords in 1695, and immediately excited hopes that he would champion the Irish Protestant interest.[31] Instead he fell into the more familiar family habit of quarrelling with neighbours, notably with the local bishop,[32] who resented the Boyles' rewarding raids into the church's endowments. Clifford involved himself in Ireland only briefly, his successors hardly at all. The Boyles' electoral machine, powered by the deference, self-interest and prickly independence of the electors in Bandon, Clonakilty, Dungarvan, Lismore, Tallow and Youghal, required constant lubrication.[33] It was left to the grandson of the first earl of Orrery, Henry Boyle, the future earl of Shannon, to perfect what Orrery had pioneered in the 1650s and to ground his political supremacy in the eighteenth-century Irish parliament in part on his ability to mollify and manipulate the Munster squirearchy.[34]

Burlington might loftily disdain grubby politicking. Nevertheless, for all that he distanced himself from, and often disagreed with, Orrery, the latter could damage him with guilt by association. Throughout the tricky 1650s and 1660s, the two brothers regularly met or corresponded. As Orrery himself later stressed, they had diverged over several important matters, starting with the truce made with the Irish insurgents in 1643 and continuing with the religious settlement after 1660.[35] Detractors thought Burlington was putty in others' hands. Once Orrery had died, in 1679, his sister Katherine, Lady Ranelagh, an opinionated blue-stocking and an unrepentant religious and political radical, was credited with an unwholesome

30 NLI, MSS 6903, 14 Sept. 1692; 13226, Burlington's letters of 16, 23 and 27 Aug. 1692, 1 Sept. 1692, 18 Oct. 1692, 17, 19 Nov. 1692; D.B. Henning, ed., *The History of Parliament: The House of Commons, 1660-1690* (London, 1983), i, pp. 390, 701. £251 had been spent at Appleby in 1690 in electing his elder brother, Charles: Chatsworth, Londesborough MSS, box I (iv), 6.

31 Nottingham University Library, Portland MS, Pw A 251; TCD, MSS 750/1, pp. 132-34, 138-39; 1995-2008/484, 547; R. Caulfield, ed., *Council Book of the Corporation of Youghal* (Guildford, 1878), p. 394; *Lords' Journal, Ireland*, i, pp. 501, 533.

32 St Carthage's Cathedral, Lismore, chapter book 1663-1829, fos 5-5v, 30; NLI, MS 13226, Burlington's letter, 18 June 1696; Nottingham

University Library, Pw A 258a-b; cf. Ranger, 'Earl of Cork', pp. 71-73, 175-79, 322-33.

33 NLI, MSS 13243, 13247; Dickson, 'Cork Economy', pp. 127-28.

34 D. Hayton, 'The Beginnings of the "Undertaker System" ', in T. Bartlett and D. Hayton, eds., *Penal Era and Golden Age* (Belfast, 1979), pp. 52-54; A.P.W. Malcomson, 'Introduction', in Hewitt, *Shannon's Letters*, pp. xxiii-lxxix; Malcomson, ' "The Parliamentary Traffic of this Country" ', in Bartlett and Hayton, *Penal Era*, pp. 146, 152-53.

35 Bodleian Library, Carte MSS 147, fo. 197; R. Cox, *Hibernia anglicana* (London, 1689-90), part ii, p, 133; *A manifestation . . . sent from the Lord Inchequin, the Lord Brohill.*

influence over Burlington.[36] Certainly since the 1650s she had kept him informed, interlarding the London news with her own sententious observations. When in London, he would sometimes join Lady Ranelagh, his philosopher brother, Robert, and his unhappily married and intensely devout sister, Mary, countess of Warwick, for the evening. Their edifying conversation probably centred more on religion, for all possessed an unforced piety, than on metaphysics or politics. As late as 1690, Lady Ranelagh in Dublin could report at first hand on the fighting through which William III delivered Protestant Ireland from Catholic slavery.[37] More revealing, perhaps, of her relationship with her eldest brother (he was desolated by her death which occurred in the same year as his wife's and in the same week as Robert Boyle's)[38] were the lectures she read him on the perils of a rich French diet 'of mixed meats and high taste': yet another instance of how the uncritical francophilia of Charles II's court was corrupting the fashionable.[39]

Close though Burlington remained to his siblings, the jibes about their malign influence on his behaviour missed the mark. Attitudes within the family ranged across the spectrum, from the frank royalism of his younger brother, Viscount Shannon,[40] through the agile collusion of Broghill, to the principled republicanism of Lady Ranelagh. As nephews and cousins multiplied, though they might touch Burlington for subs, they seldom took their politics from him. In 1666, for example, Lady Ranelagh's son, Arthur Jones, scandalised the family when, in the Irish parliament, he attacked not only the land settlement but specifically its generosity towards his uncles, Burlington and Orrery.[41] Even Burlington's heir, Charles, Lord Clifford, by the 1670s had rejected his father's deferential courtliness, and was feted as

36 BL, Althorp MS, B. 4, letter of Lord Clifford, 1 June [1667]; *HMC, Ormonde MSS*, new series, vi, p. 138.

37 BL, Add. MSS 17017, fo. 76; 27351, fos 41, 62v, 63v; Althorp MS B.4, Lady Ranelagh's letters, 2 Sept. [1665], 11 Jan. [1666], 19 Jan. [1666], 20 April [1667], 25 May 1667; Chatsworth, Lismore MSS 30/95, 96, 98, 99; 31/11, 15, 15*, 17, 18, 46, 47, 50; Scottish Record Office, Edinburgh, Panmure MSS, GD 45/14/237/3; R. Spalding, ed., *Contemporaries of Bulstrode Whitelocke, 1605-1675* (Oxford, 1990), p. 231.

38 PRO, Northern Ireland, De Ros MSS, D 638/6/1; NLI, MS 13226, letter of Burlington, 5 Jan. 1691 [2].

39 BL, Althorp MS B. 4, letter of Lady Ranelagh, 31 Jan.[1666]; Chatsworth, Bolton Abbey MS 279, p. 47; Burlington's diary, 8 Feb. 1668[9].

40 Bodleian Library, Clarendon State Papers, 59, fos 23-26; 61, fos 19-20. For coolness between the brothers: Chatsworth, Burlington's diary, 23 Oct. 1652; PRO, PROB 11/448/259; Francis Boyle, Viscount Shannon, *Moral Essays and Discourses upon Several Subjects* (London, 1690), pp. 59-69; Barnard, 'Cork Settlers'. pp. 316, 231.

41 BL, Althorp MS B. 4, letter of Lord Roscommon, 23 Jan. 1665[6]; Kent Archives Office, Maidstone, Sackville MSS, U 269; C 18/2; *CSPI, 1663-65*, pp. 682-83.

'an excellent patriot' by the English parliamentary opposition.[42] The numerous individual interpretations of honour and interest within the Boyle dynasty confute any notion of a rigid family tradition.

Burlington's inclination by the later 1660s to treat Ireland chiefly as a source of money, good sport and congenial company was encouraged by his appointment to office in England. Briefly in 1667, and then again from 1679 to 1688, he served as the king's lord lieutenant for the West Riding of Yorkshire: a post which flustered the earl and which obliged longer (and grander) residence at Londesborough.[43] In Munster no one could dispute, though some disliked, the earl's primacy. In Yorkshire, competitors were numerous and formidable. The Clifford interest there, divided now between Burlington's wife and her cousin, the dowager countess of Pembroke,[44] when activated, still commanded respect, and secured Lord Clifford's election as knight of the shire in 1679, 1681 and 1685. The earl himself had been readily admitted as an honorary Yorkshireman to the northern lobby which, in the 1660s, met to push the region's special interests.[45] But equally, once the Earl was installed in the lieutenancy, rivals cavilled and caballed. These local animosities, particularly on the parts of Buckingham and Danby, affected Burlington's standing with, and his own regard for, the court between 1667 and 1679. Office, as well as exposing these feuds, oppressed Burlington. More at home in the East than in the West Riding, where he was required to govern, he fussed lest he blunder. As on his estates, so in the county's administration, he badgered hapless subordinates over minutiae.[46]

These cares loosened Burlington's Irish ties but enmeshed him in new networks. The Clifford connection benefited both its members and Burlington: the former gained a further arena for activity, so that, for example,

---

42 BL, Add. MS 17017, fo. 14; A. Browning, *Thomas Osborne, Earl of Danby* (Glasgow, 1951), iii, pp. 43, 154, 162; A. Gooder, *The Parliamentary Representation of the County of York, 1258-1832*, ii, *Yorkshire Archaeological Society Transactions*, 96 (1938), p. 172; Henning, *House of Commons, 1660-1690*, i, pp. 468-69, 700-1.

43 BL, Add. MS 18979, fos 288-96, 299, 303; West Yorkshire Record Office, Leeds, Reresby MSS, MX 2/14-24; 33/2-11; 39/42; *CSPD, July-September 1683*, pp. 29, 66, 87, 96, 123, 134, 251, 270, 374-75.

44 Chatsworth, Londesborough MSS, box G, 28; D.J.H. Clifford, *The Diaries of Lady Anne Clifford* (Stroud, 1990), p. 108; Henning, *House of Commons, 1660-1690*, i, pp. 434-36.

45 Chatsworth, Burlington's diary, 15, 26 Feb. 1661[2], 3, 6 March 1664[5]; P. Seaward, *The Cavalier Parliament and the Reconstruction of the Old Regime* (Cambridge, 1989), pp. 134-35.

46 Bodleian Library, Rawlinson MS D. 204, fo. 43; Brynmor Jones Library, Hull, DD FA/39/ 30; West Yorkshire Record Office, MX 14/16, 50, 73a, 102, 107, 126, 129; 15/11; 29/12, 14, 23; 31/42; Gooder, *Parliamentary Representation of Yorkshire*, pp. 91, 94, 137-39, 172-74; D. Parsons, eds., *The Diary of Sir Henry Slingsby* (London, 1836), pp. 369-71; Reresby, *Memoirs*, pp. 65, 312, 361. In the East Riding, there were only three resident peers, of whom the other two, Dunbar and Langdale, were Catholics: BL, Add. MS 40132, fo. 109.

the Appleyards, the Congreves and Musgraves were all employed in the Boyles' Munster bailiwick;[47] for Burlington, that baffled owl, the mob of lesser birds that surrounded him enhanced his importance. Through those who served the Burlingtons in Yorkshire there ran a strong strain of ultra-royalism, incubated by fighting, intrigue and exile. Yet it would be rash to assume that Burlington used the Grahams, Musgraves, Sir John Reresby,[48] and Sir Allen Apsley simply because he liked their opinions. The drunken Apsley, who played the major-domo at Londesborough in 1665, probably owed his intimacy to Irish links: he was a kinsman of the first wife of Burlington's father.[49] 'Honest' Richard Graham, for long the family's indispensable man of business and a trustee of Lady Burlington's 1685 will, was appointed principal of Clifford's Inn in London (itself part of Lady Burlington's inheritance) and advanced into James II's service thanks to the Burlingtons' high regard.[50] This later Jacobite, Graham, was yoked as a trustee to the Burlingtons' near neighbour in the rolling wolds, James Moyser, first intruded and then removed by James II as recorder of Beverley.[51] The personable Moyser shared with the earl a love of the turf, gardening and building. His friendship and frequent forays to Londesborough hint already at a cultivated local circle around Burlington which

47 PRO, PROB 11/404/48; Henning, *House of Commons, 1660-1690*, iii, pp. 116-19. Sir Matthew Appleyard served as governor of Youghal. For Musgraves employed by the Burlingtons in Ireland: Brynmor Jones Library Hull, DD LO/11/27; NLI, MS 13253.

48 In 1660 Reresby returned from the Continent with Burlington's two sons: Reresby, *Memoirs*, p. 32.

49 BL, Althorp, MS B.5, Lady Henrietta Hyde's letter of 30 Aug.[1665]; Henning, *House of Commons, 1660-1690*, i, pp. 941-42; *HMC, Bathurst MSS*, p. 2; Seaward, *The Cavalier Parliament*, pp. 81, 84; D. Townshend, *The Life and Letters of the Great Earl of Cork* (London, 1904), pp. 54, 110, 119.

50 Graham may well have been the countess's servant who accompanied her two boys to France in 1659. Bodleian Library, Rawlinson MS A. 492, fos 1-12; BL, Add. MS 15892, fos 140-41; Althorp MS B. 4, Graham's letter of 9 May 1667; Chatsworth, Lady Burlington's journal, 8 March 1658[9], 6 May 1661, 22 Feb. 1665[6], 27 June 1667; Lismore MSS 30/43; 33/64, 67, 70, 84-86; Londesborough MSS, box I (i), 42, 82; PRO, PROB 11/404/48; *CSPI, 1663-65*, p. 166; Henning, *House of Commons, 1660-1690*, ii, p. 427; E. MacLysaght, ed., *Calendar of the Orrery Papers* (Dublin, 1941),

pp. 6, 46, 59, 180, 218, 227, 281, 283, 360. Notwithstanding his father's political disgrace, the younger Richard Graham was entrusted with delicate tasks by the second earl of Burlington: Borthwick Institute, York, will of Charles, earl of Burlington, 1704.

51 Moyser was Reresby's step-father, though not so financially straitened as Reresby implied. See the heraldry and family tree in the Eastoft chapel of Lockington church, East Yorkshire; Borthwick Institute, York, will of James Moyser, proved 1695; Brynmor Jones Library, Hull, DD MM 29/62 (ag); Humberside (*recte* East Riding) County Record Office, Beverley, DD BE/23/54, 60, 62; PRO, E 179/205/504; J.W. Clay, ed., *Dugdale's Visitation of Yorkshire* (Exeter, 1894-1917), iii, p. 89; J. Dennett, ed., *Beverley Borough Records, Yorkshire Archaeological Society Transactions*, 84 (1933), pp. 107, 110, 143; G.C.F. Forster *The East Riding Justices of the Peace in the Seventeenth Century* (York, 1973), p. 28; J. Foster, *The Register of Admissions to Gray's Inn, 1521-1889* (London, 1889), p. 234; G. Oliver, *The History and Antiquities of the Town and Minister of Beverley* (Beverley, 1829), pp. 236-37; Reresby, *Memoirs*, pp. 3, 22, 26, 53, 350 n. 1, 520 n. 2, 523; J. and J.A. Venn, *Alumni Cantabrigienses*, part i (Cambridge, 1924), iii, p. 225.

prefigures, both in membership and interests, that which gathered around the architect earl in Yorkshire.[52] The earlier group, we must conclude until we have evidence otherwise, though fervently royalist, was unencumbered with any sinister political programme.

By looking harder at two periods – the 1650s and 1680s – we can see better the tension between Burlington's position in England, where he could play the courtier, and his financial dependence on Ireland, where his fortune was repeatedly endangered by the Stuarts' actions. In addition, his principal patrons tell something of his personal and political affiliations. Most illuminating in this respect are Charles I's queen, Henrietta Maria; her younger son, James, duke of York and future James II; the father of James's first duchess, Edward Hyde, earl of Clarendon; and the first duke of Ormonde, the king's lieutenant in Ireland throughout the 1640s and again after 1660. These four were united by an unflinching loyalism which had doomed them to continental exile during the 1650s: bonds which might exclude Burlington, a quisling – no matter how reluctantly – under the Cromwellians. The friendships forged in court and camp before 1645, and in dingy Norman lodgings in the late 1640s, were renewed after 1660 and assisted Burlington back to social eminence. There remains the suspicion that he had been compromised by his cooperation in the 1650s so that his later reputation was stained by his unsteadiness.

During Burlington's own continental sojourn, his wife (like others) paid off the fines and regained the Yorkshire lands. Already, in berating the parliamentarian steward intruded at Londesborough for denying her children freedom to walk in the park, she blazed with Clifford fire.[53] Courageously she had voyaged to Youghal in 1648, and there set about patching the damaged estates. She discreetly interrupted the work of granting new leases when the conquering Cromwell wintered at the Corks' Youghal

52 The intimacy is suggested in 1700 when a principal room at Londesborough was known as 'Mr Moyser's room': Chatsworth, Londesborough MSS, box G, 19, p. 8; Burlington's diary, 15, 17 Oct. 1672; BL, Althorp MS B.7, Burlington's letters, 15 Nov. 1681, 24 Dec. 1681, 23 Dec. 1682, 1 Oct, 1689; Borthwick Institute, York, James Moyser's will; Brynmor Jones Library, Hull, DD CV/38/30; DD SY/39/7; H.M. Colvin, *A Biographical Dictionary of British Architects, 1600-1848* (London, 1978), pp. 565-66; J. Fairfax-Blakeborough, *Northern Turf History*, ii, ([?London], 1950), p.

143; P. Rogers, 'The Burlington Circle in the Provinces: Alexander Pope's Yorkshire Friends', *Durham University Journal*, 57 (1974-75), pp. 219-25; Victoria County History, *A History of the County of York: East Riding*, ed., K.J. Allison, vi (Oxford, 1989), pp. 109, 184, 186.

53 BL, Althorp MS B.7, Lady Cork's letter of 4 July [1646]; Add. MS 46931C, fo. 109; Chatsworth, Bolton Abbey MS 274, p. 19; J. Nickolls, *Original Letters and Papers of State Addressed to Oliver Cromwell* (London, 1743), pp. 84-85.

house later in 1649.[54] In 1651, the earl, weary of his double life in Caen as Mr Richardson, journeyed, via Yorkshire, to Ireland.[55] Thankful to see again what the rebels had wasted and threatened to keep, he began modest repairs.[56] From this decade, no doubt, dated that unrivalled grasp of the estate on which its later wealth rested. In Ireland, in contrast with Yorkshire, the consequences of his royalism were less quickly shaken off. Competitors within the Protestant community, especially the newly disembarked English soldiers and administrators, salivated at the prospect of feasting on the juicy portions of his vast inheritance. Predictably enough, rumours were spread that Cork was plotting against the Cromwellian regime, and even that he planned to marry a daughter to Charles II. Inventions these stories were; but they possessed an inherent plausibility given the unconcealed views of his brother Shannon and others within his circle.[57] Such rumours, as they were intended, impeded the delicate business of freeing his own, his relations' and his clients' lands from the threat of permanent confiscation. A complex campaign was conducted. While Cork caressed the local commissars, naively noting their civility and promises of favour,[58] Broghill and his henchmen laboured in London to prevail with the protectoral council and successive parliaments to uphold the established, as well as to promote a new, Protestant interest in Ireland.[59] The local activity resulted in temporary enjoyment of rents and lands; eventually, the English endeavours provided a legal basis for permanent repossession.[60]

Cork circumspectly picked his way through the mined landscape of Cromwellian Ireland. He lived retiredly and did the minimum to solicit the necessary favours. Yet once or twice the mask slipped. In the matter of religion – of the greatest importance to Cork, as we shall see – it was hinted that he clung still to the old, but now forbidden, forms of the Church of

54 Chatsworth, Lismore MS 28/9, 10; NLI, MSS 6143, 6254; T.C. Barnard, 'Irish Images of Cromwell', in R.C. Richardson, ed., *Images of Oliver Cromwell* (Manchester, 1993), p. 190; *CSPD, 1649-50*, p. 537.
55 He had also visited Middleburgh. BL, Add. MS 46931B, fo. 191; Althorp MS B.6, letters to 'Mr Richardson' at Caen, 27 Dec, 1649, 14 Jan, 1650?; Chatsworth, Burlington's diary, 4 Aug. 1653; *CSPD, 1650*, p. 278.
56 Chatsworth, Burlington's diary, 17 Aug. 1652; NLI, MS 6256, 28 Sept. 1657, 23 Oct. 1657, 28 Oct. 1657.
57 Bodleian Library, Clarendon State Papers, 59, fos 23-26; 61, fos 19-20, 87-88; Chatsworth, Burlington's diary, 5, 7 May 1653, 10 Aug. 1655; W. Gorstelow, *Charls* [sic] *Stuart and*

Oliver Cromwell United (London, 1655), pp. 3-125; T. Birch, *A Collection of the State Papers of John Thurloe* (London, 1742), v, pp. 672-75.
58 Chatsworth, Burlington's diary, 28 May 1651, 28 Aug. 1651, 1 Nov. 1651, 5 Jan. 1651[2], 15 Sept. 1652, 25 March 1653, 14 Aug. 1654, 17 Oct. 1654, 17 Feb. 1654[5], 30 May 1655, 4 June 1655; Barnard, 'Planters and Policies', pp. 34-39.
59 Chatsworth, Lismore MS 28/22, 25-27, 31, 36, 39; R.T. Dunlop, ed., *Ireland under the Commonwealth* (Manchester, 1913), i, pp. 116, 125.
60 C.H. Firth and R.S. Rait, eds, *Acts and Ordinances of the Interregnum* (London, 1911), ii, pp. 933-37, 1015-16, 1132.

England. Lismore Castle sheltered, as earlier the parish of Londesborough had, a clergyman, Peter du Moulin, outspoken as a supporter of episcopacy and the Stuart monarchy.[61] In public, the earl followed what the law enjoined. Thus, in 1656, a daughter was married according to the novel civil, as well as the religious, ceremony.[62] However, once the English ordinance to flush banned Anglicans from secluded country retreats stimulated Irish enquiries, Cork forestalled trouble and sent away the embarrassing du Moulin. But the chaplain, far from being dismissed, accompanied the countess and her two sons, whom du Moulin had been tutoring, to the greater anonymity of England, there to continue their spiritual improvement.[63]

In his dealings with Henry Cromwell who, from 1655, headed the Dublin government, Cork moved beyond cool correctness to liking. Henry Cromwell's progress through Munster in 1658, a political mission as well as a holiday, enabled Cork to parade his provincial might, for he rode out (as he would to meet another lord lieutenant in 1666)[64] with a semi-feudal array of 300 horsemen (many his tenants and kinsmen) to greet the impressionable Cromwell, whom he then conducted to the luxury of Lismore and thrilled with horse races run on the strand at Youghal.[65] This jaunt deepened a friendship organised around hunting and talks in Dublin.[66] Bit by bit Cork was being lured back into public life. In 1658, for example, he started to officiate as a justice of the peace in counties Cork and Waterford.[67] For Henry Cromwell and for his confidant, Broghill, Cork's capitulation was important both in itself and as a sign that the usurping regime, through

61 Chatsworth, Burlington's diary, 31 Jan. 1655[6], 14 June 1656; Londesborough MSS, boxes G, 12b; I (i), 36; A.G. Matthews, *Walker Revised* (Oxford, 1948), p. 392.

62 Chatsworth, Burlington's diary, 2 June 1656.

63 BL, Althorp MS B.6, H. Hughes to Lady Cork, 28 Sept. 1657; Chatsworth, Bolton Abbey MSS 278, 24 Sept. 1656; 279, p. 13; 280, 22 Dec. 1660; Lady Burlington's journal, Sept. 1656, 9 April 1675; Lismore MS, 30/42 T. Birch, ed., *The Works of the Honourable Robert Boyle* (London, 1745), v, pp. 595-96; P. du Moulin, *Défence de la religion reforme et de la monarchie et l'église anglicane contre l'impiété & tryannie de la ligue rebelle d'Angleterre* (n.p., 1650); idem, preface to F. Perreaud, *The devil of Mascon* (2nd edn, Oxford, 1658); idem, *Of peace and contentment of mind* (London, 1657), sig. A3-A3v; idem, *A week of soliloquies and prayers with a preparation for the holy communion* (London, 1657), sig. *10.

64 Bodleian Library, Clarendon State Papers, 84, fos 284-286; Chatsworth, Burlington's diary, 1 Sept. 1666; *CSPI, 1666-69*, p. 205.

65 Chatsworth, Burlington's diary, 2, 3 Aug. 1658; Lismore MS 30/12; NLI, MS 6256, 7 Aug. 1658; T. Stanley to Lord Cork, 29 July 1658, now forming the binding of NLI, MS 6259.

66 Chatsworth, Burlington's diary, 23, 25 Sept, 1656, 11, 15 Nov. 1656, 2 Dec. 1656, 16 April 1657, 26 Jan. 1657[8], 31 Jan. 1657[8], 8 Feb. 1657[8], 21 Nov. 1658; Barnard, 'Planters and Policies', pp. 58-59.

67 Chatsworth, Burlington's diary, 24, 27, 28, 30 April 1657, 10 Feb. 1657[8], 9 March 1657[8]; NLI, MS 6256, 9 March 1657[8]. Symbolic of this greater public prominence was Cork's instruction to have his arms set again above the gate to Lismore: NLI, MS 6256, 28 Sept. 1657.

transformations effected by Henry Cromwell and Broghill, was winning over quondam royalists. Cork was not alone in succumbing to these blandishments; even the wife of the Stuarts' upright viceroy, Lady Ormonde, compromised with the usurpers in order to protect the ancestral acres.[68] But, as will become clear, the cases of Cork and the Ormondes differed, because, while Lady Ormonde amused Henry Cromwell in her grand houses, her husband endured the privations of continuing exile, varied only by a foray as a secret agent, with badly dyed hair, into Cromwellian London to plot a royalist rising.[69] It was this contrast between Ormonde's steadfastness, and Cork, whose icy reserve towards the interlopers had thawed in the warmth of Henry Cromwell's company, that would dog Cork.

Cork and Orrery dextrously extricated themselves from the wreckage of the collapsed Cromwellian Protectorate. After 1660, they had every reason to minimise their compliance with the usurpers, and to push back the date at which they had acted to bring home Charles II. Little that was later said about Broghill's role can be believed;[70] with Cork, the contemporary clues are sparse and ambiguous. First the reinstatement of the Rump Parliament in May 1659, and then its suspension by the army in October, which was paralleled in Ireland by the reappearance of an aggressive administration, again threatened Cork's estates. Throughout the summer of 1659 Lady Ranelagh reported English events (which she generally approved) and Cork periodically met Broghill.[71] But, by the beginning of December 1659, Cork had decided to station himself in London.[72] Earlier in the same year, his sons, after various delays, had been sent to tour the Continent.[73] Meanwhile, his openly royalist brother, Shannon, kept in touch with the exiles scheming to restore the king, and in April 1660 was in Holland.[74] Broghill,

68 Chatsworth, Burlington's diary, 17 Oct. 1654, 29 April 1658, 17 Nov. 1658; NLI, MSS 2500, fo. 62; 6256, 22 July 1658, 2 Aug. 1658.

69 D. Underdown, *Royalist Conspiracy in England, 1649-60* (New Haven, 1960), pp. 216-17.

70 PRO, Dublin, M.2449; T. Morris, 'Life', prefaced to T. Milward *State Letters of Roger Boyle, First Earl of Orrery* (London, 1742), i, of which there are fuller versions in BL, Sloane MS 4227, and PRO, Dublin M. 473. One piece of contemporary evidence is in Bodleian Library, Clarendon State Papers, 61, fos 87-88. N.K. Maguire, 'Regicide and Reparation: The Autobiographical Drama of Roger Boyle, Earl of Orrery', *English Literary Renaissance*, 21 (1991), pp. 257-82, sensitively discusses his dilemma.

71 Chatsworth, Burlington's diary, 1, 10, 27

Aug. 1659, 14 Sept, 1659, 22 Oct. 1659, 28 Jan. 1659[60], 11 Feb. 1659[60], 17 & 21 March 1659[60]; NLI, MS 6256, 20 Jan. 1658[9], 29 Jan. 1658[9]; 9 May 1659, 8 Aug. 1659; Spalding, *Contemporaries of Whitelocke*, p. 231.

72 Chatsworth, Burlington's diary, 2 Dec. 1659; Birch, *Works of Robert Boyle*, v, p. 557.

73 Chatsworth, Burlington's diary, 1, 19 March 1659[60]; NLI, MS 13228, Sir Maurice Fenton to Cork, 12 April 1659; Birch, *Works of Robert Boyle*, v, p. 631; *CSPD, 1658-9*, pp. 295, 581, 582.

74 Bodleian Library, Clarendon State Papers, 59, fos 23-26; 61, fos 19-20, 87-88; Chatsworth, Burlington's diary, 12 April 1660, 18 May 1660; Lady Burlington's journal, 21 April 1659; Lynch, *Orrery*, p. 102.

however, stayed on in Ireland, where he would guide the Convention summoned to meet in Dublin and organise his Munster following.[75] These family dispositions facilitated the speedy passage of news between the Continent, England and Ireland, and so we may reasonably assume that they had been arranged for this purpose. Without more evidence we can only speculate whether Cork had deliberately positioned himself in London so that he could act as well as spectate. In public he still did little to commit himself before the king's return became inevitable. Only in April 1660 did he contact exiled courtiers. On 14 May, he ordered his sons home from Paris, and on the 23rd was among the loyalists and turncoats who flocked to meet the king at Dover. By June a familiar world was being reshaped, and Cork found his proper place within it: on the 8th he took his seat in the Lords (as Baron Clifford), on the 28th he was confirmed in his father's post as Lord High Treasurer of Ireland, and the following day kissed the king's hand on appointment; on the same day, he was reunited with his two boys, who, two days later, thanks to Ormonde, were introduced into the monarch's presence.[76] On 28 August he received the surest indication that the accommodations of the 1650s were understood and excused, when the king supped with him and Orrery.[77] But in that evening we can detect an augury of the troubles to come. Among the company were Taaffe and O'Neill: prominent members of the exile community of Irish Catholics who were already intriguing for the return of their confiscated estates.[78] Such claims inevitably conflicted with those of incumbents like Cork. The willingness of the king (and others) to listen to the aggrieved Irish disquieted Cork and Orrery.

At the Restoration Cork, regardless of what he had done to engineer it, permanently forsook his reclusive life in Ireland for the expansive routines of an Anglo-Irish magnate, moving regularly between London, Yorkshire, Dublin and Munster. His good standing with the returned Stuarts was signalled most conspicuously in 1665 when he was advanced to an earldom in the English peerage. Henrietta Maria, now as queen mother a troublesome and uncertain influence at court, assisted him to this honour; and he

75 Lynch, *Orrery*, pp. 101-2; *Thurloe State Papers*, vii, pp. 817-20.
76 Chatsworth, Burlington's diary, 14, 23, 29 May 1660, 8, 28, 29, 31 June 1660; Bodleian Library, Carte MS 30, fo. 563.
77 Chatsworth, Burlington's diary, 28 Aug. 1660.
78 For Taaffe's success in recovering lands, and for later conflict with Burlington: BL, Stowe MS 211, fos 9v, 208; *CSPD, 1676-77*, p. 469; H. O'Sullivan, 'Land-Ownership Changes

in the County of Louth in the Seventeenth Century' (unpublished Ph.D. thesis, Trinity College, Dublin, 1991). Generally for the favour enjoyed by Taaffe: T. Crist, *Charles II to Lord Taaffe: Letters in Exile* (Cambridge, 1974). The threat from O'Neill was removed when he died in 1664: D.F. Cregan, 'An Irish Cavalier: Daniel O'Neill', *Studia Hibernica*, 3 (1963), pp. 60-100; 4 (1964), pp. 104-33; 5 (1965), pp. 42-77.

reciprocated with deft courtliness when he chose the title of Burlington.[79] This commemorated not only the port near his Londesborough estate, but the landing there in 1643 of his broker, Henrietta Maria, with reinforcements for her husband.[80] The Burlingtons' social success had already been advertised in 1664 when first the king and queen, and then the queen mother and the Yorks, dined at their London house. These were occasions for display. The chimneys were swept, the best as well as ordinary claret laid in, plate hired from a city goldsmith and musicians engaged. Although Burlington employed his own French chef, he borrowed cooks from Lady Newport, Lord Berkeley, the marquess of Worcester and Sir Thomas Ingram. Other neighbours, such as Lords Devonshire, Dorset, Fauconberge, Manchester and Paget, all lent their butlers. The Burlingtons themselves served their monarch and his consort on bended knees. Entertaining the king cost £107 more than the usual weekly budget for diet; the second party, for the Yorks, a mere £60. Shortly afterwards, the frugal earl ordered housekeeping economies, by reducing the number of dishes of meat to be served at supper and urging his family to accept more invitations to eat out.[81]

Henrietta Maria's regard for the Burlingtons probably dated back to the pre-war court and to the royal headquarters in wartime Oxford.[82] But, since she was an unstable power by the 1660s, to depend too much on her could be unwise. More, useful, at least in the 1660s, was the backing of the duke of York. Burlington's links with the king's brother did not obviously pre-date the Restoration. After 1660, however, Burlington, like other Anglo-Irish magnates, earned gratitude by facilitating the grant to York of Irish lands worth £8,000 *p.a.*[83] By the autumn of 1665 the Yorks were on visiting terms with the Burlingtons, not only in London but also at Londesborough. Lady Burlington, the anxious chatelaine, protested that the guests would find only 'a woeful house and a woeful dinner'. The Yorks instead esteemed Londesborough 'a paradise on earth', and were captivated by the sport there.[84] Zest for the chase, coupled with autocratic instincts,

79 Chatsworth, Burlington's diary, 16 March 1664[5]; Lady Burlington's journal, 13 March 1664[5].

80 M.A.E. Green, ed., *Letters of Queen Henrietta Maria* (London, 1857), pp. 166-68.

81 Chatsworth, Bolton Abbey MS 283, 12-19 Feb. 1663[4], 8-15 April 1664, note appended to week 3-10 June 1664; Burlington's diary, 14, 21 April 1664; Lady Burlington's journal, 14, 21 April 1664.

82 Canny, *The Upstart Earl*, p. 57; Ranger, 'Cork', p. 368; M. Toynbee and P. Young,

Strangers in Oxford (London and Chichester, 1973), pp. 206-7. Their youngest daughter, born at Londesborough on 20 August 1647, was christened Henrietta: Chatsworth, Lady Burlington's journal.

83 Bodleian Library, Clarendon State Papers, 83, fos 148-49, 156-57; Guildford Muniment Room, Midleton MSS, 1248/1, fos 111-13, 124.

84 BL, Althorp MSS B.4, letters of Lady Burlington, 29 Aug. [1665], 8 Sept. [1665]; B.5, letter of Lady Henrietta Hyde, 30 Aug. [1665].

might unite York and Burlington, but soon marriage bound them more solidly. The duchess of York, Anne Hyde, was the daughter of the king's chief minister, Clarendon. In 1665 the duchess's talented and amusing brother, Lawrence, married Burlington's daughter, Henrietta. Both Charles II and York promoted the match, and promised to underwrite the modestly estated bridegroom.[85] At least at the social level, the Burlingtons remained on good terms with the Yorks: in 1681, for example, the new duchess, Mary of Modena, was confiding in Lady Burlington.[86]

If the Hyde marriage in 1665 registered a new link with the Stuarts, it also revealed Burlington's closeness to Lord Chancellor Clarendon. Both had sat in the Long Parliament in 1640 and had gravitated to the king at Oxford; each valued hierarchy and order, whether in church or state.[87] For a time after 1660 they both had apartments in Berkshire House. Burlington's affection for Clarendon is suggested when he bought the unfurnished carcase of Sir John Denham's Piccadilly house next door to Clarendon's spanking new mansion. Indeed, while Burlington House was being completed, the Burlingtons were for ever in and out of Clarendon House, worshipping in its chapel and filching ideas for their own decor. They even considered moving into Clarendon House, only to be warned by their daughter, who was living there, of the inconveniences of sharing a kitchen.[88]

Given this intimacy, Clarendon's fall in 1667 disordered Burlington's political universe. It opened the way for Clarendon's enemy, Buckingham, to be reconciled with the king; and Buckingham's return to favour humiliatingly ended Burlington's own short reign as lord lieutenant in the West Riding.[89] Burlington recorded at length his private interview with Charles II, at which he was asked to resign so that Buckingham could be reinstated; it is clear that his own sense of his worth was severely jolted.[90] This proved

85 BL, Althorp MS B.6, letter of duke of York, 17 April [1665]; Chatsworth, Burlington's diary, 24 April 1665, 8 May 1665; Lady Burlington's journal, 5, 18, 26 March 1665, 7 April 1665.

86 BL, Althorp MS B.6, letters of Mary of Modena, 24 March [1681], 4 May 1681, 2 March 1681[2].

87 P. Seaward, *The Cavalier Parliament*, pp. 15-22; H.R. Trevor-Roper, *Edward Hyde, Earl of Clarendon* (Oxford, 1975).

88 Bodleian Library, Carte MS 47, fos 128v, 134; BL, Althorp MSS B. 4, letter of Lady Ranelagh, 27 Aug. [1667]; B.5, letter of Clarendon, 18 July 1665, letter of L. Hyde, 16 April [1667]; Chatsworth, Burlington's diary, 20 April 1666, 2 Feb. 1666[7], 4 April 1667, 4 Nov.

1667, 30 Jan. 1667[8], 4 Feb. 1667[8], 4, 9 March 1667[8], 27 March 1668, 18 April 1668, 15 Jan. 1668[9]; G. Burnet, *History of My Own Time*, ed. O Airy (Oxford, 1897), i, p. 457; Reresby, *Memoirs*, p. 67; F.H.W. Sheppard, ed., *Survey of London*, xxxii. *The Parish of St James, Westminster*, pt 2, *North of Piccadilly* (London, 1963), pp. 390-94.

89 Seaward, *The Cavalier Parliament*, pp. 300-3, 311-18; B. Yardley, 'The Political Career of George Villiers, 2nd Duke of Buckingham (1628-1687)' (unpublished, D.Phil. thesis, University of Oxford, 1989), pp. 99, 120-29, 139.

90 Chatsworth, Burlington's diary, 20 Oct. 1667; West Yorks Record Office, MX 3/24.

to be merely one in a series of slights which may have weakened his infatuation for the returned Stuarts. The dismissal of Clarendon also showed Burlington's punctilious code of honour. In the company of York and Lords Bridgewater and Peterborough, he preferred to withdraw from the Lords rather than vote on the motion that the king should not again employ Clarendon. Again, in December, he absented himself when the Lords discussed the bill to banish the disgraced minister.[91]

Burlington had scarcely acclimatised himself to the new world of the 1660s when the reassuring landmarks vanished. He was disoriented by more than the fall of old friends; policies, too, were in flux, as the king veered towards France, as York disclosed his Catholicism, and as ways were explored to help English and Irish Catholics. Burlington was so alarmed at the danger from these proposals to his own family's position in Ireland that he distanced himself from the court and from Danby's ministry in the 1670s.[92] Nothing better shows his disillusionment than the entries in his diary before it breaks off abruptly in May 1673. Asked his opinions about schemes to allow Catholics more power within Irish towns (a proposal already vigorously opposed by Orrery), he denounced the idea as 'in many particulars extraordinary and in my opinion illegal'. The next day he was distracted by the novelty of an Italian play starring Scaramouche. But he was soon remonstrating with the king against these measures that so unsettled Protestant Ireland.[93]

Political patterns dissolved and reformed after 1678 when Danby, a Yorkshire no less than national adversary, was toppled. Once more the Hyde alliance served Burlington well, for soon his son-in-law, Lawrence Hyde, ennobled as earl of Rochester, moved into government.[94] In 1679 Burlington was reappointed lord lieutenant of the West Riding[95]. He was said to have opposed the attempt to exclude York from the succession but, with a canniness that would recur over the next decade, kept away from controversial debates.[96] Doubts about him persisted and denied him those Irish offices vacated by Orrery when the latter died in 1679. Instead they adorned the needy and less compromised Shannon: tardy recompense for

91 BL, Althorp MS B.4, letter of Lady Ranelagh, 27 Aug, [1667]; Chatsworth, Burlington's diary, 15 Oct. 1667, 19 Dec. 1667; C. Roberts, 'The Impeachment of the Earl of Clarendon', *Cambridge Historical Journal*, 12 (1957), pp. 1-18; Seaward, *The Cavalier Parliament*, pp. 312-22.
92 Browning, *Danby*, iii, pp. 124, 143, 146, 148 n.6; A.C. Swatland, 'The House of Lords in the Reign of Charles II, 1660-1681' (unpub-

lished Ph.D. thesis, University of Birmingham, 1985), pp. 249, 351, 384, 386, 391.
93 Chatsworth, Burlington's diary, 7, 8, 9 May 1673.
94 R. Hutton, *Charles II* (Oxford, 1989), pp. 404-5.
95 *CSPD, 1679-80*, p. 133.
96 Kent Archives Office, U 1713, Dering MS, C 2/35; Browning, *Danby*, iii, pp. 126 n. 2, 127.

having been cuckolded by the king early in the 1650s.[97] Burlington's estrangement in the 1680s belonged to the larger process in which the bulk of the aristocracy coyly embraced William of Orange. Old loyalties and friendships, powerfully seconded by his son-in-law Rochester, made Burlington reluctant to ditch James, even after he had again been dropped as lord lieutenant in 1688.[98] But, as before, the Irish rentals governed his responses. In Ireland, public favour to the Catholic majority emboldened Burlington's local rivals, such as the Villiers of Dromana and Lord Tyrone, more brazenly to encroach on his holdings.[99] Ominous rumours circulated that Burlington would be forced to disgorge his church lands. In 1686 he had conveyed over to England as much as he could of his stock and wealth.[100] No doubt he exaggerated when, in March 1688, he complained that he had received no rents from Ireland, and characteristically proposed to economise by parting with his pack of beagles and one of his two falconers (an annual saving of £8).[101] Soon uneasiness about the future of his Irish estates turned to panic. Refugees chilled the earl with their stories of losses and atrocities. His mind reverted irresistibly to the 1640s and he accepted that Ireland needed a new Cromwell to roll back the Catholic advance.[102] This calculation, born of his awareness that his grandeur was still sustained by Irish remittances, aligned him behind William III. By now advanced years and uncertain health excused his opportune absences from difficult debates.[103] Nevertheless, once the revolution was accomplished, he returned to his favourite trade, seeking advantages for himself, his kinsmen and clients. Since he was too powerful to antagonise lightly, the new order generally agreed to his requests.[104] In return, he rallied to it with mounting

97 *HMC, Ormonde MSS*, new series, v, pp. 225, 229-30, 236, 264; Barnard, 'Cork Settlers', p. 321.

98 Dr Williams's Library, London, Roger Morice Ent'ring book, ii, Morice MS Q, p. 59; *CSPD, June 1687–February 1689*, p. 161; *HMC, Ormonde MSS*, new series, vi, p. 405; H. Horwitz, *Revolution Politicks: The Career of Daniel Finch, Second Earl of Nottingham* (Cambridge, 1968), p. 55; J.P. Kenyon, *The Nobility and the Revolution of 1688* (Hull, 1963); Reresby, *Memoirs*, p. 551.

99 BL, Stowe MS 210, fos 292, 300; Chatsworth, Lismore MS 34/48; NLI, MS 6300, 26 Aug. 1684, 27 March 1685, 27 Feb. 1685[6]; *CSPD, 1683*, p. 174; ibid., *June 1687–February 1689*, p. 360.

100 Dr Williams's library, Morice MS Q, p. 71; MacLysaght, *Orrery Papers*, p. 318.

101 BL, Althorp MS B.7, letter of Burlington, 26 March 1688; NLI, MS 6300, 7 Aug. 1686; codicil to Lady Burlington's will, PRO,

PROB 11/404/48.

102 R. Caulfield, ed., *Journal of the Very Rev. Rowland Davies* (London, 1857), pp. 3, 59; *HMC, Finch MSS*, ii, pp. 218-19; *House of Lords MSS, 1689-90*, pp. 138, 181-82; Singer, *Clarendon Correspondence*, ii, p. 239. For a further explicit comparison of 1649 and 1689, see Chatsworth, Lismore MSS, miscellaneous volume labelled '1688-9'.

103 *HMC, House of Lords MSS, 1692-93*, pp. 297-98; Singer, *Clarendon Correspondence*, ii, p. 261. Lady Burlington tersely noted on 22 December 1688, 'the king absented himself the second time and went into France': Journal (Chatsworth).

104 Abbey Leix, Co. Laois, de Vesci MS H/2, letter of 14 Feb. 1692[3]; NLI, MS 13226, Burlington's letters of 20 Oct. 1691 and 10 May 1692; PRO, Northern Ireland, D 638/6/2, 638/6/8; TCD, MSS 1995-2008/104; *CSPD, 1690-91*, p. 272.

enthusiasm, and, though an octogenarian, made a point of attending the Lords when the Jacobite conspirator, Fenwick, was attainted.[105]

The tension between material calculation and courtly deference accounted for much of the hesitancy and opacity in Burlington's conduct; it also affected his relationship with the fourth of his great patrons, James Butler, the first duke of Ormonde. On the surface affability characterised their dealings. After all, they had shared digs and a meagre diet of mushrooms in Caen in the late 1640s.[106] In much they resembled one another: in age, abiding Protestantism, the value of their Irish estates, and service of Charles I in the 1640s. Only in the 1650s had their paths diverged. It is true that in Ireland during the Interregnum, Cork assisted Ormonde's wife to save the estate.[107] But behind the elaborate courtesies lurked envy and suspicion. Not only had Ormonde remained steady when Cork wavered, and as a result harvested the richer rewards after 1660, but a hereditary rivalry seemed entailed on the heads of the two houses. Cork's apanage in Munster had been carved from what, in the 1580s, the Desmond Fitzgeralds had forfeited.[108]

Traditionally, the Fitzgeralds had disputed with the Butlers, Ormonde's ancestors, for predominance within Ireland. In some measure the Boyles slipped into the Fitzgeralds' role as the Butlers' main rivals. Indeed, in 1697, an Irish politician would beg Clifford to balance the overmighty Butlers.[109] Furthermore, the Boyles had connected themselves by marriage with the Fitzgeralds and other Old English families at odds with the Butlers.[110] These long-standing dynastic and regional animosities spiced Burlington's relationship with Ormonde. They were separated, too, by important differences of outlook. Ormonde, correctly Protestant himself, headed an affinity many of whose members remained Catholic, which he ruthlessly protected. Temperamentally indolent, Ormonde neglected his estates and drifted ever deeper into debt. Yet, apparently easy-going and amiable, he could humble those who forgot his dignity. No more intelligent than

105 Chatsworth, Lismore MS 34/125, 127; NLI, MS 13226, letters of Burlington, 2 May 1695, 25 Feb. 1695[6], 29 Feb. 1695[6]; *Lords' Journal*, xv, pp. 620, 712, 716, 721; xvi, pp. 25, 33, 39, 41, 42, 43, 45, 48, 50. When the plot to kill William III was uncovered, Burlington noted that at least thirteen of the intending assassins were Irish.
106 *HMC, Ormonde MSS*, new series, iv, p. 144.
107 Chatsworth, Burlington's diary, 16, 17 Oct. 1654, 29 April 1658, 17 Nov. 1658, 26 June 1662; NLI, MS 2500, fo. 62.
108 MacCarthy-Morrogh, *Munster Plantation*, pp. 1-19.
109 BL, Add. MS 38150, fo. 127; TCD, MSS 750/1, pp. 138-39.
110 In 1656 Cork surprised his brother-in-law, Kildare, with a whore. Later he leased Cork House in Dublin to the Kildares and sold the earl his smart French coronation suit. By the 1680s a Fitzgerald was Burlington's favourite nephew. Chatsworth, Burlington's diary, 3 Aug. 1655, 4 Dec. 1656, 12 April 1663; *HMC, Ormonde MSS*, new series, vi, pp. 187, 189, 193-94, 200.

Burlington, and much lazier, he effortlessly landed what Burlington missed: a dukedom, the Garter, two long tours of duty as lord lieutenant, and an intimacy with Charles II which was formalised with his appointment as lord high steward.[111] The bonhomie wore thin after 1662, when Orrery, mortified that he had been pushed into provincial obscurity while Ormonde ruled Ireland, criticised and schemed to replace Ormonde.[112] For all that Burlington dissociated himself from his brother's wilder accusations, he had his own reasons for disliking Ormonde. The latter upset Burlington by routinely undervaluing him. They had squabbled first over who, whether Ormonde as lord lieutenant or Cork as lord treasurer, had the right to grant lucrative offices in the customs.[113] Next, notwithstanding letters patent and royal instructions, Burlington's daily allowance as lord treasurer of 20 shillings was withheld.[114] Then, Ormonde omitted him from a committee to inspect the Irish revenues, laughing it off as simple forgetfulness.[115] Most galling of all, Burlington, despite promises which dated back to 1644, was repeatedly passed over for the command of a troop of horse.[116] Burlington's resentment so disrupted the earlier amity that in 1668 intermediaries had, with difficulty, formally to reconcile the two.[117] Thereafter, the old cordiality returned, but we may suspect that suspicions lingered, and that Ormonde helped block Burlington's way to the positions which he coveted.[118] The martial and heroic values of the first duke, together with a fixation with ceremony and precedence, were inherited by his grandson, the second duke, who, after two spells as lord lieutenant in Dublin, elected to follow the Old Pretender into exile. This ultimate loyalty to the Stuarts added political to the financial ruin of the family. Ormonde's enforced

111 Carte, *Life of Ormonde*; J.C. Beckett, *The Cavalier Duke: A Life of James Butler, 1st Duke of Ormond* (Belfast, 1990).
112 BL, Add. MS 21484, fo. 42v; Bodleian Library, Carte MSS 37, fos 155; 50, fos 62v, 68v; 70, fo. 529; NLI, MS 2485, fo. 294; Barnard, 'Cork Settlers', pp. 319-21; *HMC, Ormonde MSS*, new series, iv, pp. 247, 279-80, 286-87, 299-300, 548; J.I. McGuire, 'Why Was Ormond Dismissed in 1669?', *Irish Historical Studies*, 18 (1973), pp. 295-312.
113 Chatsworth, Burlington's diary, 21-29 Nov. 1660, 1 Dec. 1660, 4, 15, 21 Jan. 1660[1], 20 Feb. 1660[1], 30 March 1661, 10 July 1661, 22 Aug. 1661, 1, 3 Oct. 1661, 10, 11 Dec. 1662, 23 Jan. 1662[3]; Lismore MS 32/113-15; *CSPI, 1660-62*, pp. 28, 200-1, 214, 289.
114 Chatsworth, Burlington's diary, 4, 11 May 1665; Lismore MS 33/35; PRO, Northern Ireland, D 638/6/15; *CSPD, 1671*, pp. 141, 154,

262-6; *CSPI, 1660-62*, p. 506; ibid., *1663-65*, pp. 39, 77, 397; ibid., *1666-69*, pp. 77, 193.
115 Chatsworth, Burlington's diary, 2 July 1668.
116 BL, Althorp MS B.4, letters of Lady Ranelagh, 25 May [1667], 22 June [1667]; Chatsworth, Burlington's diary, 6 July 1662, 29 April 1663, 8, 9 July 1663, 2 July 1667; *Orrery State Letters*, ii, pp. 53-54.
117 Chatsworth, Burlington's diary, 3, 30 June 1668, 1, 2, 3 July 1668.
118 The marriage of Ormond's grandson, Ossory, to Burlington's grand-daughter, Lady Anne Hyde, was expected to improve relations, but the bride died soon afterwards. BL, Add. MS 15892, fo. 141v; Chatsworth, Lady Burlington's journal, 20 July 1682; NLI, MS 2482, fo. 95; *CSPD, October 1683-April 1684*, p. 262; *HMC, Ormonde MSS*, new series, vi, p. 405.

absence from Ireland cleared the way for the supremacy of the Boyles, in the person of Henry, earl of Shannon, and their connections, within Augustan Ireland.[119]

Little of the earl's personality enlivens the usually laconic entries in his diary. Contemporaries, in so far as they remarked on the man, singled out his wealth rather than any individual attributes. This emptiness contrasts with the more endearing impressions left by his wife. Pepys caught her well when he noted, 'a very fine speaking lady – and a good woman, but old and not handsome [this in 1668 when she was fifty-five] – but a brave woman in her parts'.[120] Yet, in unbuttoned ease, relishing, for example, at Christmas 1696, 'the joy of the season, and the crowd of company that have been eating brawn, plum porridge and mince pies', we glimpse an essentially simple man.[121] Cards, horses, music and the theatre refreshed him when he left the oversight of his great estates. The earl, always au fait with the latest hit, in 1693 was congratulating his Irish agent, Congreve, on the London success of his son's play.[122]

Burlington, stiff towards strangers and inferiors, had the fear of the rich of being cheated and, as we have seen, might arbitrarily impose footling economies. Overcharged once at the George Inn at Stamford, where he halted his caravan as it lumbered north towards Londesborough, he vowed never again to patronise it, and thereafter stayed at the rival Bull.[123] Just as his own youthful profligacy had angered his father, so in turn his heir's fecklessness soured their relationship.[124] Poorer kinsfolk (and all his relations were poorer) might be helped, but woe betide them if they overstepped the mark.[125] Presumptuous nephews who hunted across his precious deerpark without permission would be banned.[126] A great nephew, the earl of Barrymore (one of those dubious Old English families into which his father had been keen to marry his children) had borrowed

119 For something of the Tory following behind Ormonde in Queen Anne's reign: BL, Egerton MS 917, fos 234, 236, 244; D.W. Hayton, 'Ireland and the English Ministers, 1707-16' (unpublished D.Phil. thesis, University of Oxford, 1975), pp. 135, 166-67.
120 R. Latham and W.R. Matthews, eds, *The Diary of Samuel Pepys* (London, 1970-83), ix, p. 322.
121 Chatsworth, Lismore MS. 34/129.
122 Chatsworth, Bolton Abbey MS 279, 5 Dec. 1661, 8-17 Jan. 1662[3], 10-17 April 1664; Burlington's diary, 30 June 1666, 8 Dec. 1668; Londesborough MSS, box I (v), 4, and

account of 1664, entry for 22 Nov. 1664; NLI, MS 13226, Burlington to Congreve, 11 March 1692[3]. The play, *The Old Bachelor* (Congreve's first) was dedicated to Charles Boyle, the future second earl of Burlington.
123 Chatsworth, Burlington's diary, 19 Nov. 1661, 23 March 1661[2].
124 Bodleian Library, Rawlinson MS. A. 492, fos 1-12; Borthwick Institute, York, 2nd earl of Burlington's will; NLI, MS 13226, letters of Burlington, 21 Sept. 1695, 25 Jan. 1695[6].
125 NLI, MS 13226, letters of Burlington, 16 July 1695, 24 Aug. 1695, 12, 22 Oct. 1695.
126 NLI, MS 7177, 20 July 1672, 5 Sept. 1677.

Burlington's parliamentary robes, but the latter, when he requested their return, was asked to pay to redeem them from pawn.[127] In Sir William Petty, probably the richest commoner in Restoration Ireland, Burlington met his match, for Petty, asked to repay a small debt when staying at Lismore as a guest, pleaded poverty.[128]

Like all within the landed orders, Burlington cared whom his children married. In contrast to his father – at least as portrayed by Professor Canny – Burlington engaged in conventional calculations. So far from exhibiting the neurotic insecurity of a despised member of a colonial elite, he behaved as any other grandee might.[129] For his heir he secured the daughter of an English duke, with royal connections, and may have scaled down his financial demands in return for this prestigious alliance, since Lady Jane Seymour brought with her only £8,000 as dowry.[130] The daughter married from Lismore in the straitened 1650s had to be content with a County Limerick baronet, but even she, as a widow after the Restoration, nabbed an Irish earl.[131] Burlington's other three surviving daughters married the sons and (in two cases) the heirs of English earls. The girls were allowed some choice. Thus, when the earl of Bedford's heir was suggested, his daughter decided (against). He absolutely vetoed only two proposed bridegrooms: Lord Digby and Dick Talbot, both Catholics.[132] His closeness to at least one child pulses strongly through the letters of his youngest daughter, in which she excitedly recounts the form of their horses at Kipplingcotes races near Londesborough. Equally, the shock of loss broke through when Burlington complained of the manner in which he was told 'very abruptly' of the death in a naval battle of 'my dear son Richard', and he gratefully recorded those relations and neighbours who hurried to Lismore to console him.[133]

127 For tensions with the Barrymores: Chats-
     worth, Burlington's diary, 8 Aug. 1671; Kent
     Archives Office, U 269, C 18/25, 26; NLI, MS
     13226, letters of Burlington, 5, 10 May 1692,
     29 June 1692; Canny, *The Upstart Earl*, p. 47.
128 Chatsworth, Burlington's diary, 6 June 1669;
     T.C. Barnard, 'Sir William Petty, Irish Land-
     owner', in H. Lloyd-Jones, V. Pearl and B.
     Worden, eds, *History and Imagination* (London,
     1981), pp. 201-17.
129 Canny, *Upstart Earl*, ch. 4; A.P.W. Malcom-
     son, *In Pursuit of an Heiress* (Antrim, 1982);
     Stone, *Crisis of the Aristocracy*, pp. 633-49,
     790-91.
130 Chatsworth, Burlington's diary, 29 Jan.
     1660[1], 11 Feb. 1660[1], 1 April 1661, 7, 16
     May 1661.
131 Chatsworth, Burlington's diary, 2 June 1656,
     19 April 1661, 18 May 1661; Lismore MS 28/

     47-49, 67, 70.
132 Chatsworth, Burlington's diary, 27 May 1661,
     2 Dec. 1661, 14 July 1662, 22 Nov. 1663; Lady
     Burlington's journal, 24 April 1665. A
     widowed sister married Dick Talbot's brother,
     Gilbert, 'a half-witted fellow', interested
     chiefly in showy clothes and gambling. Burl-
     ington's diary, 3 June 1665; *The Life of Edward,
     Earl of Clarendon* (Oxford, 1760), ii, p. 270.
     The Burlingtons maintained intermittent
     social dealings with Dick Talbot, as Tyrcon-
     nell James II's Irish generalissimo: Burl-
     ington's diary, 1 March 1668 [9], 2 May 1672.
133 BL, Althorp MS B.5, letters of Lady Henrietta
     Boyle, 6 April [?], and undated; Chatsworth,
     Burlington's diary, 20-27 June 1665; P. du
     Moulin, Παρεργα: *poematum libelli tres* (Cam-
     bridge, 1670); *HMC, Bathurst MSS*, p. 2.

Similarly the death of his heir in 1694 distracted the earl when he might reasonably have been composing himself for his own end. He took refuge in nagging his daughter-in-law over the funeral arrangements, remonstrating with her for lingering in 'that solitary place' Londesborough, and criticising the settlement made by Clifford for his heir.[134]

Burlington never ceased to rejoice in the happiness of his arranged marriage with Elizabeth Clifford. Each partner moved beyond formulae to note the length and affection of the union. Lady Burlington, as we have seen, travelled and toiled to regain their estates after the Civil Wars, and often thereafter, during her husband's inevitable absences, oversaw vital business. It was she who, initially, handled negotiations for the Hyde marriage.[135] Later, conscious of her destiny as the head of the Cliffords, she asked – in vain – for the Cumberland title to be revived in the family, worried lest, with the death of Prince Rupert, the last holder, it might now be conferred on a stranger. Her acumen was exemplified when she advised the equally wily duchess of Ormonde how to remit money from Ireland to England most cheaply.[136] The earl's tender uxoriousness is demonstrated clearly in 1667: while sleeping together, the countess suffered a convulsive fit; the earl, unsure what to do, at first thought to summon a servant from the closet nearby; instead he stayed with his wife and, by propping her on pillows, congratulated himself that he had saved her life. His thankfulness that she had not died animates the diary entry.[137]

The countess shared, may indeed have dictated, the earl's fondness for splendour. Back in London after 1660, advanced within the English peerage allied now with the finest families and apparently secure in ample wealth, they lived up to their station. At first they titivated the countess's old city house at Whitefriars, tricking it out with seven Mortlake tapestries of Abraham and Isaac for £216.[138] In regard to building, at Lismore in the 1650s Cork confined himself to essential repairs, and to improving the sport.[139] At Londesborough, the countess bewailed the lack of a setting appropriate to receiving royalty. For the moment, however, improvements

134 Chatsworth, Londesborough MSS, box I (v), 15, letters of Burlington, 15, 16, 18 Oct. 1694.
135 Chatsworth, Lady Burlington's journal, 5, 18, 26 March 1665, 7 April 1665.
136 BL, Add. MS 15892, fo. 192; NLI, MS 2503/71; *CSPD, 1683*, p. 556.
137 BL, Add. MS 15892, fo. 152; Althorp MS. B.4, letter of 2 July 1667, Lady Ranelagh's letter of 10 Aug. 1667; Chatsworth, Burlington's diary, 18 April 1667, 3 July 1672; Lady Burlington's journal, 18 April 1667.
138 Chatsworth, Burlington's diary, 28 Jan. 1660[1]; Londesborough MSS, box I (v), 15 Nov. 1664.
139 Chatsworth, Burlington's diary, 17 Aug. 1652; T.C. Barnard, 'Gardening, Diet and "Improvement" in Late Seventeenth-Century Ireland', *Journal of Garden History*, 10 (1990), pp. 73, 74, 77-78.

were modest and executed by local craftsmen.[140] The purchase of Burlington House in 1667 marked the Burlingtons' entry into the competitive world of aristocratic building. Even so, the house, designed by Hugh May, was self-effacing when compared with its Piccadilly neighbours, Clarendon and Berkeley Houses, and cost less money than Orrery had lavished on his County Cork mansion.[141] Both in England and Ireland, the Burlingtons mingled with peers, like the duchess of Ormonde, the Conways and Orrery, interested and even expert in architecture. Once Burlington House was finished – the chapel, replete with silver-gilt candlesticks and altar plate, was consecrated in 1674 – Burlington turned his attention to Londesborough. In 1672 Burlington had joined with his talented neighbour, Moyser, and John Etty, 'architect' of York, to design a new building. Etty was also engaged to build for the earl at nearby Goodmanham.[142] Soon a more gifted amateur, Robert Hooke, a scientific crony of his brother, Robert, and much employed by his close friend Conway, advised on further work at Londesborough: suitable to his enhanced public role as lord lieutenant.[143] A visitor in 1701 belittled these additions when he wrote, 'the old Lord Burlington left here a small brick seat . . . which is neither beautiful on the outside, nor in, having no gardens nor furniture'.[144] This comment, from a Munster rival eager to lance the Boyles, spoke more of envy than accuracy. Knyff's engraving of the same period contradicts the jaundiced tourist, as do the accounts and inventories of Londesborough. This 'small brick seat' boasted seventy rooms. Extensive plantations and formal gardens with a canal and bowling green abut the house, in which the central block of sixteenth-century workmanship is flanked by wings with hipped roofs pierced by dormer windows which date from the first Lord Burlington's building

---

140 Burlington used the 'surveyor' Cateline: Chatsworth, Burlington's diary, 8, 11, 15 June 1661, 30 Oct. 1661, 10, Oct. 1664. The brick-layer, John Catyln, contracted to rebuild the town hall in Hull in 1633: E. Gillett and K.A. MacMahon, *A History of Hull* (Oxford, 1980), p. 108.

141 Barnard, 'Cork Settlers', pp. 321, 356.

142 BL, Althorp MS B.7, letter of Burlington, 28 Nov. 1682; Chatsworth, Burlington's diary, 3, 15, 17, 18 Oct. 1672; Lady Burlington's Journal, 16 April 1668, 21 Dec. 1674; Londesborough MSS, box I (iv), 3 (contract with Etty for Goodmanham, 21 Sept. 1683); PRO, PROB 11/448/259. For Etty, see G. Beard,

Craftsmen and Interior Decoration in England, 1660-1820 (London, 1981), p. 259; Colvin, *Biographical Dictionary*, pp. 300-1.

143 Chatsworth, Burlington's diary, 13 Oct. 1663, 20 June 1666, 1 July 1666; Colvin, *Biographical Dictionary*, pp. 428-31; D. Neave, *Londesborough* (Londesborough, 1977), pp. 13, 30; H.W. Robinson and W. Adams, eds, *The Diary of Robert Hooke* (London, 1968), pp. 247, 248, 252, 254, 258, 260, 268.

144 M.R. Wenger, ed., *The English Travels of Sir John Percival and William Byrd II: The Percival Diary of 1701* (Columbia, 1989), pp. 106-7. Cf. C. Morris, ed., *The Journeys of Celia Fiennes* (London, 1947), p. 86.

campaign.[145] Not content with his London and Yorkshire homes, in 1684 he removed his family to the recently acquired suburban retreat of Chiswick. For some time, he had been seeking a place convenient to London and suited to summer recreation. The abandonment and demolition of Clarendon House in 1683 perhaps precipitated the removal from Piccadilly with its reminders of vanished glories.[146] At Chiswick, so far as we can judge, little was done to the old mansion in the first earl's time. But, scarcely had he been buried, than his heir was clamouring for cash from Ireland, because he was 'at a great charge in altering my house, which must be done with ready money'. Where the work was to be done is not specified.[147]

Burlington housed his family in what he and his wife took to be a fittingly modish style. In this, as in all he undertook, he was measured and methodical: ruin, he knew, awaited the compulsive builder. Educating their children was another matter which exercised the earl and countess. In Burlington's own and his brothers' cases, short spells at university had been supplemented by study in the Calvinist redoubts of Saumur and Geneva: indoctrination which cemented the family's fierce anti-Catholicism.[148] The same regimen was planned for Cork's two sons. First educated at home by the Huguenot exile, du Moulin, the boys went in 1656 to England. John Evelyn, consulted about future plans, tactlessly recommended a Catholic as tutor.[149] Instead Lady Cork quizzed the educational experts within the family. In consequence, her sons entered Christ Church at Oxford: their father's old college.[150] There they were taught by the young John

145 Humberside Record Office, Beverley, DDX 31/173 (1739 survey of Londesborough by Pattison); Chatsworth, Londesborough MSS, box G, 17, 19-22; D. Neave, 'Lord Burlington's Park and Gardens at Londesborough', *Garden History*, 8 (1980), pp. 69-90; Neave, *Londesborough*, pp. 29-31; D. Neave and E. Waterson, *Lost Houses of East Yorkshire* (Bridlington, 1988), pp. 42-49.

146 BL, Add. MS 15892, fo. 152; Chatsworth, Burlington's diary, 4, 23 March 1671[2]; Lady Burlington's journal, 7 June 1684, 1 Oct. 1685; West Yorks Record Office, MX 21/2; E.S. de Beer, ed., *Diary of John Evelyn* (Oxford, 1955), iv, pp. 320-21, 338-39; D. Lysons, *The Environs of London* (London, 1795), p. 194; Victoria County History, *A History of Middlesex*, vii, ed. T.F.T. Baker (Oxford, 1982), pp. 74-75. For an earlier social contact between Burlington and the previous owner of Chiswick, Sir Edward Seymour, Victoria and Albert Museum, Orrery MSS, i, fo. 23.

147 NLI, MS 13227, letter of 2nd Lord Burlington, 25 July 1699.

148 BL, Althorp MS B.4, Dungarvan's letter from Saumur, 1 June 1633; T.C. Barnard, 'Crises of Identity among Irish Protestants, 1641-1685', *Past and Present*, 127 (1990), pp. 72-74; R.E.W. Maddison, *The Life of the Honourable Robert Boyle, F.R.S.* (London, 1969), pp. 24-45; J. Stoye, *English Travellers Abroad, 1604-1667* (2nd edn, New Haven and London, 1989), p. 293.

149 Evelyn, *Diary*, iii, p. 379; Stoye, *English Travellers*, pp. 216, 222.

150 Chatsworth, Bolton Abbey MS 278, p. 12; Burlington's diary, 16 June 1656; J. Foster, *Alumni Oxonienses*, early series, i (Oxford, 1891), p. 163; A.R. Hall and M.B. Hall, eds, *The Correspondence of Henry Oldenburg*, i, *1641-1662* (Madison and Milwaukee, WI, 1965), pp. 82, 83, 85, 107-8.

Locke, with whom they read geography, astronomy and logic.[151] They also profited from the benign oversight of their brilliant uncle, Robert. Despite the profusion of royalists in and around Oxford, the Corks chose a governor carefully. Even so, the suspicion arises that the boys in France during 1659 were repairing their parents' friendship with the royalist exiles.[152]

Foreign travel helped to form the Boyles, as it did others of the Anglo-Irish aristocracy. In Burlington's own youth, the itineraries had been plotted to avoid those torrid zones where Catholicism and pederasty thrived. In consequence, the family's links with the centres of international Calvinism were unusually close, and fostered the sense that they in Munster, as much as their continental co-religionists, were members of an elect minority environed by predatory Catholics. Destinations changed, as war closed hitherto popular routes, and as educational theory, perceptions of popery and the fashionable accomplishments of the young milord all evolved. Burlington himself never saw Rome, though his younger brother, Robert, and his son-in-law, Lord Thanet, had, with some misgivings, been allowed there.[153] In 1661, the precocious son of another Munster dynasty visited Rome, interrogating cardinals and noting the table talk of the republican Algernon Sidney.[154] By the 1680s, Burlington relaxed his ban, so that a great nephew, to whom he was guardian, could visit the Vatican and an aristocratic kinsman who happened to be a cardinal.[155]

A life passed intermittently in Ireland, served by and among the Catholic Irish, preserved an anti-Catholicism which, in the court circles frequented by Burlington, grated. The security of his inheritance obliged him to uphold as axioms the untrustworthiness of the Irish Catholics and their unfitness for power. More than brutal self-interest sustained this animosity. Catholics were attributed with failings destructive of civil society and inimical to agriculture and trade. Wherever possible he intended to grant

151 Chatsworth, Lismore MS 30/32, John Downes to Lord Cork, 18 Oct. 1658. For Locke at this time, E.S. de Beer, ed., *The Correspondence of John Locke*, i (Oxford, 1976), p. xviii; John Locke, *Two Tracts on Government*, ed. P. Laslett (Cambridge, 1967), introduction.

152 Chatsworth, Burlington's diary, 1, 19 March 1659[60]; Lismore MS 30/21; A.B. Dugan, 'Walter Pope 1628-1714: A Study of his Life and Work' (unpublished B.Litt. thesis, University of Oxford, undated, but library stamp for 1954), pp. 16-17, 21-22, 26-29, 32-

36; W. Pope, *The Life of the Right Reverend Father in God, Seth, Lord Bishop of Salisbury* (London, 1697), pp. 96, 115; Reresby, *Memoirs*, p. 32.

153 BL, Althorp MS B.4, Orrery's letter of 1666; Clifford, *Diaries of Lady Anne Clifford*, p. 108; Maddison, *Robert Boyle*, pp. 39-41; Stoye, *English Travellers*, p. 159.

154 BL, Egerton MS 1632.

155 Petworth House, West Sussex, Orrery MSS, general series, 30, letter of J. Hall, 5 Nov. 1687; MacLysaght, *Orrery Papers*, pp. 344, 346.

tenancies to those of English descent and Protestant faith.[156] In practice, though, such paragons were too few, and needed to be concentrated in his boroughs, leaving farms and lands to the Irish Catholics. Indeed, even in Lismore, under the walls of his precious castle, Burlington would tolerate Catholic labourers, so long as they were 'able and honest', and wanted only the beggarly cabin-dwellers to be expelled. Thus, among the Irish, as much as among his Protestant tenants and relations, he distinguished between the meritorious and the undeserving.[157] At moments of danger, it is true, his intolerance, at least in rhetorical terms, hardened. By the 1690s, it expressed both the testiness of age and the weary sense of *déjà vu*, as seemingly prosperous and stable settlements were overrun: the 1640s had returned and called for (and soon found) a new Cromwell.[158]

Religious observances ordered Burlington's routines. Often he closeted himself to fast and prepare to receive the sacrament.[159] We sense behind these rituals strong religious instincts. As patron of livings in Ireland and England, he necessarily interested himself in promoting his clients, and to this end frequently bothered bishops. Yet his regular meals in the 1660s with the archbishop of Canterbury and bishop of Winchester (a protégé of Clarendon) speak of more than lobbying. Similarly, he appreciated how 'the good bishop of Cork' had comforted him after his younger son's death.[160] In Ireland, where his first concern was to see that livings were served, he did not enquire too minutely into a candidate's theology. He did, however, prefer those who would reside and officiate regularly rather than

156 Chatsworth, Lismore MSS 34/106, 114; Londesborough MSS, box I (v), 15, Burlington's letters of 13, 23 Sept. 1694; NLI, MS 13226, Burlington's letters of 23 Feb. 1691[2], 14 April 1692, 8 May 1694, 1, 2, 9 April 1695, 25 May 1695, 19 Nov. 1695, 12 Dec. 1695, 23 March 1696[7], 17 April 1697.

157 Chatsworth, Lismore MSS 34/57, 91; Burlington's diary, 22 Sept. 1662, 7 Oct. 1662; NLI, MS 13226, Burlington's letters of 27 June 1691, 6 Oct. 1691, 24 March 1691[2], 25 Feb. 1696[7], 4 March 1696[7], 18 May 1697, 17 June 1697, 8 July 1697. Cf. Ranger, 'Cork', pp. 265-67.

158 Barnard, 'Cork Settlers', p. 349-50; *HMC, Finch MSS*, ii, pp. 218-19.

159 Chatsworth, Burlington's diary, 6 April 1656, 25 May 1656, 30 Sept. 1664; NLI, MS 13226, Burlington's letter of 24 Dec. 1695. The library catalogue of Chiswick in 1742 (now at Chatsworth) contains much late seventeenth-century theology, more to the taste, I suspect,

of the first rather than the third earl of Burlington. There is no clue to the subjects of the 206 books recorded at Londesborough in 1724, other than that there were eight prayer books and one sermon: Chatsworth, Londesborough MSS, box G, 22.

160 BL, Althorp MS B.6, letters of Archbishop Sancroft, 14 Dec. 1665, and of Bishop Morley of Winchester, 10 Jan. 1665[6]; Bodleian Library, Add. MS C.306, fo. 172; Chatsworth, Burlington's diary, 28 Dec. 1663, 11, 18, 25 Jan. 1663[4], 7 March 1663[4], 30 Oct. 1664, 7 Nov. 1664, 21 Nov. 1664, 17 May 1665, 21-23 June 1665, 11 Dec. 1665, 31 March 1666, 16 Oct. 1666, 30 June 1668, 3 Dec. 1668, 28 May 1670, 3 May 1672. Morley was connected with both the Cliffords and the Hydes: Burnet, *History*, i, p. 457; J.W. Clay, 'The Clifford Family', *Yorks Archaeological Journal Transactions*, 72 (1905), p. 406; G. Morley, *Several Treatises* (London, 1683), pp. vi-viii, xv.

potential pluralists and absentees.[161] In England, where the choice was wider and needs different, he advanced men who had suffered in the 1650s for their adherence to the proscribed Church of England.[162] It is likely that these orthodox beliefs matched Burlington's. If this were so, then, in religion, as in politics, he differed from Lady Ranelagh and Orrery who continued to long for Protestant comprehension.[163]

Burlington decreed that he should be buried in the Clifford vault at Londesborough, in a 'decent but not splendid manner'.[164] There his body was borne deep in the winter of 1698, ferried directly across the Humber rather than paraded through York. In his modest interment, as in much of his life, he showed how far he had departed from the values and conduct of his father. The latter had raised in Ireland two swaggering monuments, one of which blocked the east end of St Patrick's Cathedral in Dublin; at Londesborough only a brass coffin plate commemorates his son. This burial in Yorkshire, also, emphasised how Burlington had loosened his ties with Ireland and now lived as a grandee in England. So long as he survived, the head of the Boyles, expert and vigilant, knew how heavily the dynasty's fortunes depended on the proper care of the Irish holdings. As late as 1692, he was planning to revisit Lismore and, as we have seen, sent his grandsons in his stead. But soon the accidents of minorities and the quirks of heredity doomed Lismore, though spring-cleaned to await its owners' intended visits, to house only stewards, bailiffs and the occasional traveller. As the Burlington' absences lengthened, rats – two, as well as four-legged – desported themselves there, care deteriorated and arrears accumulated, until, in the late 1720s, the estates were looted for capital and the process of divestment started. In Ireland, the disengagement by the Burlingtons

161 NLI, MS 13226, Burlington's letters of 8 Aug. 1691, 3 Sept. 1691, 3 Oct. 1691; PRO, PROB 11/448/249. Nevertheless he winked at local pluralism, to enable incumbents to enjoy an adequate stipend. Petworth, Orrery MSS, general series, 30, letter of H. Boyle, 23 April 1686; BL, Stowe MS 206, fo. 288.

162 J. Hawket, *An account of the late reverend and worthy Dr George Seignior* (London, 1681), pp. 10-11, 15; G. Seignior, *God, the King, and the Church . . . being the subject of eight sermons* (London, 1670), sigs A2-A3v.

163 Here I differ from the view offered in Swatland, 'The House of Lords in the Reign of Charles II', pp. 186, 364. For Orrery and Lady

Ranelagh, T.C. Barnard, *Cromwellian Ireland* (Oxford, 1975), p. 134 n. 207; R. Spalding, *The Diary of Bulstrode Whitelocke, 1605-1675* (Oxford, 1990), pp. 749-53; C. Webster, *The Great Instauration: Science, Medicine and Reform, 1626-1660* (London, 1975), pp. 62-63, 102-3, 501; C. Webster, 'New Light on the Invisible College', *Transactions of the Royal Historical Society*, 5th series, 24 (1974), pp. 27-31.

164 Borthwick Institute, York, PR LON 2, fo. 18v; PRO, PROB 11/448/259. The decencies extend to sides of beef and veal, three sheep, a turkey, numerous chickens, rolls of brawn and sturgeon, together with wine and ale. Chatsworth, Londesborough MSS, box G, 18.

created opportunities from which cadets of the Boyles and former dependants profited.[165] Also, the less the Londesborough Boyles knew Ireland, or
relied on it for their regular income, the more their attitudes towards the
Irish, Catholics and even the Stuarts could be modified.

165 D. Dickson, 'Property and Social Structure in
     Eighteenth-Century South Munster', in L.M.
     Cullen and F. Furet, eds, *Irlande et France,*
     xviie-xxe siècles: pour une histoire rurale comparée
     (Paris, 1980), pp. 129-30.

4

The Political Career of the Third Earl of Burlington

Eveline Cruickshanks

It has been a general assumption that a man as versatile and as accomplished in the arts as Lord Burlington could have found little time for or shown little interest in politics. This was not the case. The *Lords' Journals* enable us to trace every particular day on which Burlington attended parliament (a useful way of tracking down the movements of this elusive man), as well as to see which matters and issues interested him. Parliament in the eighteenth century has been called the best club in England, but the House of Lords at that time was an uncomfortable place – stiflingly hot in the summer and bitterly cold in the winter – so that he would not have been there had he not had a special reason to be. No speeches of his have been recorded, not surprisingly as only a minority of peers are reported as speaking regularly. There was no official record of debates; furthermore, it was technically forbidden for the press to publish them and reports of few debates have survived.

After his return from the Grand Tour, Lord Burlington took his seat in the Lords on 26 April 1715, the day after his coming of age.[1] Like most newcomers he attended more assiduously at first than he was to do later in his life. In July 1715 he was present at every sitting when the articles of impeachment against Robert Harley, earl of Oxford, were read. In August and September he was there every day on the attainders of Henry St John, Viscount Bolingbroke and the duke of Ormonde, the great Tory Anglo-Irish magnate, and on the impeachment of the earl of Strafford, one of the principal negotiators of the peace of Utrecht and a large landowner in Yorkshire. During the rebellion of 1715 he did not attend at all. This was because as lord lieutenant of the West Riding and the city of York, he was expected, after the suspension of the Habeas Corpus Act, to carry out the

---

1 A. Boyer, *The Political State of Great Britain*, 60 vols (London, 1711–40), ix, p. 300. Unless otherwise stated all references to the House of Lords are from the *Lords Journals*, vols xx–xxviii.

instructions of the secretary of state for the arrest of disaffected persons, Nonjurors and Roman Catholics. At the great sessions in Leeds in October the lord lieutenant gave a handsome dinner to his deputy lieutenants and the justices at the Swan, as a contemporary reported:

> He began several healths, and amongst the rest he began 'A confusion to the Pretender, and all his adherents and to all his open and secrett friends'.

The actions of his deputy lieutenants belied these words, for Sir Walter Hawksworth, the lord mayor of York, and one of Burlington's deputies, prevented the arrest of Sir William Blackett, M.P., a suspected Jacobite, by hiding him in his own house, while all the other Jacobite prisoners were set free on bail. In a letter to his lieutenancy on 31 January 1716, Burlington wrote:

Gentlemen,

   To use your own words I own I am not a little surprised at the letter I received last night signed by the Lord Mayor of York, Sir Walter Hawksworth & Sir William Robinson, in which I expected an excuse rather than a justification for so unlawful & unwarrantable proceedings. I cannot imagine what those gentlemen mean by saying they were ignorant of my sentiments, after you all have heard me explain myself so fully upon this point at all the meetings where I was present. And if you would give yourselves the trouble of recollecting you'll find I even told you that the Deputy Lieutenants & Justices of the Peace had no power of bailing without my orders: & the letter I sent about a week before my leaving the country (which you are pleased to say you never saw) was positively to command you not to admit of bail for anyone till I acquainted you with the King's further pleasure. It is a great grief to me to be so unhappily situated, & to be forced to trouble the King so often as I am, & I believe I can safely say that I am the only Lord Lieutenant in his Dominions that has never been obeyed by the Deputies in any one particular; but it is with the highest concern that I find gentlemen who profess themselves friends to the King & his government acting in a manner that would much better become those whom you have set at liberty & at a time when the Pretender to his Crown is at large in his Kingdom. I have not yet received His Majesty's Commands but as soon as I have you shall hear further from

Your humble servant

Burlington

It can be remarked on that these were the deputies he had himself chosen. Burlington dismissed Hawksworth and Sir Walter Calverley, another of the chief culprits, but later reinstated them.[2]

Parliament reassembled in February 1716 and Burlington attended all but one of the sittings on the trial of the earl of Derwentwater, who had led the rebellion with Thomas Forster, M.P. for Northumberland, and on the attainder of the earl of Mar, who had started the '15 in Scotland. In March he attended every day but one of the trial of Lord Winton, another rebel lord. He was in the House on 10 April when a bill from the Commons was sent up to enable him to take the oaths as lord treasurer of Ireland in England. This place, which Swift says was 'hereditary in his family', had not the importance or the profits of that office in England, being worth about £1000 p.a.[3] The bill passed on 17 April.

Burlington was at this time a leading Whig peer, but one who took an independent line. The Septennial Bill was brought in in April to continue the life of the present parliament without holding an election in order to consolidate the Whig oligarchy but, on the second reading, Burlington 'left the Court' along with the duke of Somerset and the duke of Rutland and joined the Tories in voting against it.[4] In May he attended eight out of twelve of the sittings on the attainder of the earl Marischal, the hereditary earl marshal of Scotland and a leader of the '15. In the eighteenth century, unlike today, all lords took part in legal cases, not only the law lords, so that on 12 May he was appointed to his first committee on the case of James Mynde, an attorney at law. He attended on the first day of the new session on 20 January 1717, when he was named to the committee of privileges and he was reappointed to it several times in subsequent years. This was one of the principal standing committees of the Lords, which examined breaches of privilege committed against peers. Parliamentary privilege had gradually been extended to cover servants, animals and every piece of property of peers, but it was enforced only when parliament was sitting.

On the Whig split of 1717 Burlington adhered to Walpole and Townshend against Sunderland and Stanhope. The split gave the opportunity to the friends of Robert Harley, earl of Oxford, to have him released from the Tower where he had been since 1715. On a forecast of his probable supporters Oxford at first put the earl as 'doubtful', then as 'pro': correctly

2 *Yorkshire Diaries*, Surtees Society, 77 (1883), pp. 139, 141–42. The original of Burlington's letter of 31 January 1716 is in the Brotherton Library in Leeds University (I am grateful to Jane Clark for providing me with a copy). It is printed in part in *HMC, Various*, ii, p. 410; BL, Add. MS 27411, Calverley MSS (unfoliated).

3 Jonathan Swift, *Prose Writings*, ed. Irvin Ehrenpreis, ix, p.58.

4 *HMC, Stuart*, ii, p. 42.

since Burlington voted for Oxford's acquittal in June 1717. He voted with Henry Boyle, Lord Carleton, his uncle and an old friend of Oxford's since the days of Queen Anne.[5] On 8 May 1717 he was appointed to the committee on a private bill (necessary to break the entail) to sell the estates of Sir Thomas Heath, a former M.P., for the payment of his debts. He naturally took an interest when Irish matters came before the House and on 8 May he was appointed to the committee on a bill to allow the sale of part of the estate of the earl of Kildare. He attended on the first day of the session in November 1718, when he joined Lord Carleton in signing his first Lords' protest against deleting an amendment to the address to congratulate the king on the success of his navy rather than on the success of his army, a favourite 'Country' point.

In December 1718 the bill was introduced to repeal the Occasional Conformity and Schism Acts, passed in 1711 and 1714 respectively, to preserve the Church of England monopoly of office by preventing Dissenters qualifying themselves by taking the Anglican sacrament and to cut down on the number of nonconformist schools and academies. This was a move on the part of Sunderland to reward the Dissenters for their steady support of the Whig party. On 23 December Burlington acted as teller (the more important of the only two occasions he did so), in favour of an amendment to the bill to repeal these acts to enforce more strictly the exclusion of non-Trinitarian Dissenters from the Toleration Act of 1689 by making all persons taking office swear faith 'in God the Father; and in Jesus Christ, His Eternal Son, the true God; and in the Holy Spirit, one God blessed for evermore'. This amendment was defeated by thirty-nine votes in an unusually full House. He voted against the repeal of these two acts.[6]

On 9 January 1719 he was appointed to the committee on an Irish legal case involving Maurice Annesley. He attended regularly in February–March, particularly when the peerage bill was before the House, an attempt to restrict future creations of peers. He was there on only three days out of fifteen in April. His absence abroad thereafter coincided with the recess, though he did not return in time for the opening of parliament on 23 November. He was back in the House on 7 December, when he was appointed to the committee to go the Tower to inspect public records,

5 C. Jones, 'The Impeachment of the Earl of Oxford and the Whig Schism of 1717: Four New Lists', *Bulletin of Institute of Historical Research*, 55 (1982), pp. 66-87.

6 Sir John Sainty, *Division Lists in the House of Lords* (1976), microfiche. I am indebted to David Johnson of the House of Lords Record Office for a search of the Lords records on this division. *A List of the Lords Spiritual and Temporal, who voted for or against the Repeal of the Several Acts made for the Security of Church of England* [1718-19].

which were then in such a poor state that maggots were crawling out of them. On the 18 December he was named to a committee on a bill to supply defects in the will of Edmund Dunch, a former MP and a Junto Whig. When parliament reassembled in January 1720, Burlington was present virtually every day. On the 13 January he was named to the committee on a legal appeal from the commissioners of forfeited estates against Colonel Alexander Mackenzie. He was absent from Westminster for the whole of February. In March he was appointed to committees on a bill to enable the duke of Kingston to contest the duke of Newcastle's will; on a petition from the belt-makers of Scotland against a decision of the Lords of Session; and on a bill to enable Cambridge University to enlarge its library. These were motley topics, but a vital part of the work of parliament and he would have been picked because he was in the House on that particular day rather than because of any special knowledge of the matters involved. Nor does this mean that he took an active part in the work of these committees. He attended but half the sittings in April, but was there on the 29th when he was appointed to a committee on a naturalisation bill. He was in the Lords infrequently from April to June, but he was there on 6 June when he was appointed to a committee on an appeal against a decree of the court of Chancery in Ireland. When parliament reassembled in December he attended but little except on the 11th, when he was named to a committee on a bill concerning the corporation of Galway. On the 13 December he was named to the committee to prevent disorders in the House when the king was present on his throne.

In January and February 1721 he attended on only five days when the South Sea Bubble was being debated and on the bill to confiscate the estates of the South Sea directors, events which rocked the country; he was there on only two days in March when Walpole's engraftment scheme, to make South Sea stock part of the national debt, was considered. He was present on 17 March and 18 April on the case of Francis Atterbury, dean of Westminster, against the attorney general, which turned on whether the college garden was the proper place to build the dormitory of Westminster school. This subject would have interested him as Atterbury had appointed him as the architect of the new dormitory. He attended twice in May, and in June he was named to a committee on a bill concerning the manor of Latham in Lancashire but, surprisingly, was absent from the division on the Westminster dormitory on 16 May.[7] He was absent for the rest of the

7   BL, Harl. MS 7190, fo. 310. For this case, see C. Jones, 'Jacobites under the Beds: The Earl of Sunderland, Bishop Atterbury and the New Dormitory for Westminster School, 1721', *British Library Journal* (1995, forthcoming).

session but returned to Westminster in November and December, when he attended a few times.

The victory of the Walpole-Townshend section of the Whigs over Sunderland's was expected to bring rewards to those who had adhered to them during the Whig split of 1717-21. Burlington was in this category and there was a rumour in January 1722 that he would be made 'King of Ireland', i.e. viceroy or lord lieutenant, while William Pulteney would be secretary of state, neither of which offices materialised.[8] He was in parliament only once in January and once in February, when he was appointed to a committee on 12 February to prevent abuses in the packing of butter in the city of York. The death of Sunderland in April threw the political world in turmoil and Burlington was busy behind the scenes. Acting with his brother-in-law Lord Bruce, the son of the Jacobite earl of Ailesbury and a Tory peer, he was active in pressing for Lord Carleton to succeed Sunderland. As lord president of the council Carleton had direct access to the king and, it was hoped, would make the most of his chances. However, Robert Bruce, MP, wrote to Lord Bruce his nephew on 13 May:

We came to town on Friday night last to meet my Lord Carleton at supper at Burlington House as we did last night at his, and I could not discern, either at those times or Sunday when he was all day at Chiswick, anything in him to enable me so much as to give a guess how his affair stands at Court, but am in great fears that he has let slip his opportunity and through want of resolution or something will fail of what everybody thought at my Lord Sunderland's death he could not fail of, but by his own fault.[9]

These expectations were, in my view, unrealistic. Although Carleton had been chancellor of the exchequer and secretary of state in Queen Anne's reign, he had not enough following to get large sums of money out of parliament, as Walpole could, and this was what George I was mainly concerned with. When parliament reassembled in October, Burlington attended on only two occasions: he was there three days in November and was absent for the whole of December.

The beginning of 1723 saw the trials following the discovery of the Atterbury Plot to restore the Stuarts. Lord Burlington acted as bail for his kinsman, Lord Orrery, one of the leaders of the conspiracy, who had been imprisoned in the Tower, while Carleton was said to have undertaken to prevent any proceedings for high treason against Orrery in the House of

8 HMC, *Various*, viii, pp. 330-31.　　9 *HMC, Fifteenth Rep, app. vii*, pp. 226-27.

Lords.[10] He attended two days of the trial of Christopher Layer, one of the lesser conspirators, in January. He was appointed to the committee on a bill to confirm the articles of marriage between a daughter of the duke of Montagu and the son of the duke of Manchester on the 14 February and he attended the call of the House on 21 March. He was absent for the whole of April but attended on six occasions in May, once when Atterbury was heard at the bar and twice when the bill against him was discussed, then was absent till the prorogation in December. Burlington remained on terms of friendship with William Pulteney, who stayed at Londesborough in the East Riding while nursing his pocket borough of Hedon.[11]

While Pulteney, who had been disappointed of office by Walpole and Townshend, remained in opposition, Burlington went over to the court, appearing on 14 March 1723, for the first time, on a list of lords summoned to the ministry's pre-sessional meeting to hear the heads of the king's speech and to concert measures for the forthcoming session.[12] Summoned to the pre-sessional meeting of court lords on 8 January 1724, Burlington was absent in March, but in April he was appointed to the committee on the bill for the better manufacture of cloth in the West Riding on the 15th and heard debates on the bill on the 20th and the 22nd. In May he attended all but four of the sittings on the impeachment of the earl of Macclesfield, the lord chancellor, who was accused of selling offices in Chancery; and on the pardon for Bolingbroke, who had made his peace with the government through the duchess of Kendal, George I's mistress. He did not attend for the rest of the year nor in 1725, except for one day on 28 February on an enclosure bill concerning Yorkshire manors.

Invited by Townshend to attend the pre-sessional meeting on 19 January 1726, he probably did not attend, as he was away from parliament for the whole of that year and for the whole of 1727, except for being appointed to a committee on a private bill dealing with the Southcott estates (a Roman Catholic family) and to take the oaths to George II on his accession on 27 June. He was absent from the House for the whole of 1728 and for 1729, except for the opening of the session on 21 January.

Lord Townshend summoned Burlington to the meeting of court lords on 12 January 1730 and he was classed as for the government in January-March.

10 E. Cruickshanks 'Lord North, Christopher Layer and the Atterbury Plot 1720-3', in *The Jacobite Challenge*, ed. Eveline Cruickshanks and Jeremy Black (Edinburgh, 1988), p. 102.
11 Chatsworth, Devonshire MSS, MS 1690, William Pulteney to Lord Burlington, 11 March 1722. I am obliged to Peter Day and Jane Clark for providing me with photocopies of Burl-ington's correspondence at Chatsworth.
12 For this and subsequent Lords lists, see C. Jones, ' "That Busy Senseless Place": An Analysis of Government and Opposition Lords in Walpole's House of Lords, 1721-42', *Parliamentary History* (forthcoming). I am grateful to Clyve Jones for comments and suggestions on the contents of this essay.

He was present on the first day of the session on 23 January. When the treaty of Seville was considered on the 27th, Burlington was in the House but did not vote in the division on the treaty that day. In March he attended on four occasions, twice on Irish legal cases, on the bill to exclude placemen and pensioners from parliament and he was appointed to the committee on a bill to repair the road from Buxton to Manchester. In April he was named to a committee on a bill to export salt from England to New York, but he did not attend again before the prorogation. Summoned to the meeting of court lords on 20 January 1731, he was absent from the opening of parliament. In February he attended on the 8th on the bill to enable the duke of Chandos to make a settlement on the marriage of his son, Henry Brydges, to a daughter of Lord Bruce and on the 27th on an estate bill concerning the Yorkshire estates of John Aislabie, the chancellor of the exchequer at the time of the South Sea Bubble. Although classed as for the government in the forecast of the division on the pension bill, which would have made public the list of secret service pensions, he duly voted against it on 2 March. On 10 April he was named to the committee on the bill to break the duke of Grafton's marriage settlement with his late wife in order to provide for their younger children. Lord and Lady Burlington were on close terms with Grafton (frequently staying at Euston) and he took an interest in any matter affecting that duke in parliament. He was involved in the Irish lobby to try and get better terms for Irish trade in the face of opposition from English merchants and on 6 May he voted for a clause in the woollen bill removing the duty on Irish yarn.[13]

At this time the Charitable Corporation affair broke, one of the scandals which rocked Walpole's administration. The corporation had been founded in Queen Anne's day to provide loans for the industrious poor, but it had been turned into a bubble by leading government supporters in parliament. Denis Bond, one of the directors principally responsible, was pilloried by Burlington's friend Alexander Pope: 'Bond damns the poor and hates them in his heart.' The affair was of more than general interest to the earl, for the Charitable Corporation had swallowed up the York Buildings Company, a water company set up to supply water to the Piccadilly area, in which so many of his building projects were situated. The company had been turned into a bubble too by an attorney called Chase Billingsley, who used York Buildings Company stock to buy forfeited estates in Scotland, unsaleable to private individuals because of the hostility of the local population. Principally involved was Sir Alexander Grant, MP, a director of the Charitable

---

13 *HMC, Egmont Diary,* i, pp. 189-90.

Corporation, who ruined the York Buildings Company by using nearly £500,000 of its stock to guarantee the non-existent pledges or securities of the corporation.[14]

After the prorogation, Burlington went to court on 11 June when the duke of Devonshire kissed hands for the important post of Privy Seal. This duke, whose family eventually inherited Burlington's estates, was regarded as being particularly dim: the first earl of Egmont commented that it was like watching Caligula making his horse a consul. Immediately afterwards, Burlington kissed hands for the place of captain of the Band of Gentlemen Pensioners.[15] Traditionally, holders of this post used to lead the army in battle but, as a letter from the duke of Montagu in Walpole's correspondence explains: 'the captain of the band of gentlemen pensioners is also undoubtedly a military post though I believe not generally regarded so of late.'[16]

He was summoned to the pre-sessional meeting of court lords on 12 January 1732, attended the opening of Parliament the next day, voted with the government on the pension bill on 17 February, and was more often in the House. In March he was appointed to the committees on the bills to rebuild Woolwich church and to consider the state of the sugar colonies. He was also on the committee on the bill to reward Sir Thomas Lombe for introducing Italian engines for the weaving of silk, which brought a substantial advance in upholstery and would have been of special interest to the earl. In April and May he attended every single day when the fraudulent sale of the Derwentwater estates was considered. These estates, some of the most valuable in the north of England, worth £200,000, had been forfeited after the '15 and sold for £1,060 to one Smith, a jobber in Aldgate, popularly known as 'Smith of the other gate – meaning Newgate', for the benefit of prominent court supporters in Parliament.[17] In May he attended regularly on further hearings of the Charitable Corporation affair. On the 19th he acted as teller in favour of a motion that Wainwright, a witness against Sir Robert Sutton, should be heard at the bar. Sutton, an MP and one of the directors principally responsible for the fraud, was governor of Hull and popularly known as 'Sutton, governor of Hell'. Walpole threw Sutton and Sir Archibald Grant to the wolves but saved Sir John Eyles, one of the other

14 David Murray, *The York Buildings Co.: A Chapter in Scottish History*, (Glasgow, 1883); *The House of Commons, 1715-54*, ed. Romney Sedgwick, 2 vols (London, 1970), i, pp. 470-71; ii, pp. 21, 77-78, 456-58.

15 *HMC, Egmont Diary*, i, pp. 182, 192; BL, Add. MS 47081, fo. 22.

16 Cambridge University Library, Cholmondeley Houghton MS 2008, duke of Montagu to ?, 5 July 1733.

17 Eveline Cruickshanks, 'The Political Management of Sir Robert Walpole', *Britain in the Age of Walpole*, ed. Jeremy Black (London, 1984), pp. 36-37.

guilty directors, as he managed the City of London elections for the government.[18] On the 26 May he managed a conference with the House of Commons (the only occasion in his career when he did so) to prevent frauds by bankrupts. He attended regularly on the bill for the relief of West Riding clothiers. Invited to the pre-sessional meeting on 15 January 1733, he attended the opening of parliament on the 16th. In March he attended regularly on an appeal by the earl of Thomond to reverse a decree of the court of Chancery in Ireland.

May 1733 was a watershed in Burlington's political career. On 3 May he wrote to George II resigning all his posts, not only the gentlemen pensioners but the lord treasureship of Ireland and the lord lieutenancy of the West Riding. The letter ran:

> I shall not presume to trouble your Majesty with the reasons that oblige me to desire your leave to resign those employments in which I have the honour to serve you. I will only beg leave to assure your Majesty that nothing but absolute necessity could have forced me to it. No one can have a more grateful sense than I have of the many marks of your royal goodness and I will only add that your Majesty will never find my zeal for your service be lessened by my ceasing to be in it.[19]

Queen Caroline asked Lady Burlington if her lord had meant to resign his lord lieutenancy, to which she replied he had 'quitted all'. The duke of Newcastle, who had succeeded Townshend in the management of the House of Lords, made strenuous efforts to get Burlington to reconsider. Sir Thomas Robinson, a Yorkshire MP and one of Newcastle's closest associates, went to see Burlington three times at Chiswick but found him adamant. Robinson reported that when the earl accepted the Band of Gentlemen Pensioners 'he was promised the first employment which fell vacant that might entitle him to be a Cabinet Councillor' and which was worth £3,000 a year.[20] Lord Hervey reported that 'Burlington's sole objection was to the King, who had told him a lie and broke his word, having promised him the first white staff that should be vacant'. What had happened is that when the duke of Devonshire was made lord steward, the privy seal was given not to Burlington but to Lord Lonsdale, an opposition peer who was thus brought over to the court.[21] Though some historians

---

18 Sedgwick, ed., *The House of Commons, 1715-54*, ii, pp. 77-78, 456-58.
19 BL, MS Althorp B8.
20 *HMC, Carlisle*, p. 115.

21 John, Lord Hervey, *Some Materials towards Memoirs of the Reign of George II*, ed. Romney Sedgwick, 3 vols (London, 1931), pp. 188-97.

believe Burlington resigned because he disapproved of the excise bill, this was not the case.[22] The excise bill was dropped by Walpole before it came to the Lords, but he was not one of the peers, like Chesterfield or Cobham, who were dismissed for joining in the campaign against the scheme.

Though Burlington ceased to attend parliament at this time, he went into opposition at once, voting by proxy against Newcastle's motion to examine a witness in the South Sea Company's affairs and in favour of a motion on 1 June in favour of censuring the directors of the South Sea Company; he was classed as an opponent to the ministry. Listed as against the ministry in the pre-sessional forecast of January 1734, he attended the upper House more regularly. On 13 February he voted for the duke of Marlborough's bill to prevent army officers being deprived of their commissions except by court martial or an address from parliament, a move to prevent their dismissal for political reasons as had happened to those who voted against the excise. He was in the House on the 18 February when a bill to enable him to grant leases on ground at the back of Burlington House was brought in. In March he attended on the bill to enable Walter Calverley to take the additional name of Blackett; and on the bill for the better manufacture of cloth in the West Riding. On the 29 March he signed a Lords' protest against an augmentation of the land forces without specifying numbers.

Burlington left for Londesborough to attend to his parliamentary interest in Yorkshire well ahead of the 1734 general election. As lord of the honour of Knaresborough he had an interest for one seat, sharing the representation with the Slingsbys of Scriven, a Tory family who owned most of the burgages.[23] He also had considerable influence at Beverley, which lay near Londesborough.[24] The city of York was too large a constituency to be controlled, but Burlington had a good deal of influence there and this had been strengthened by his designing the Assembly Rooms, the most notable public building in the town.[25] The greatest source of his electoral strength, however, was in the county of Yorkshire, the largest and most populous constituency in the country and seen, like London, Westminster and Middlesex, as a barometer of public opinion. The earl of Burlington's interest was regarded as 'the greatest in Yorkshire'.[26]

As late as December 1733, the government hoped the earl would not align himself with the opposition in the Yorkshire election of 1734, one of the

22 James Lees-Milne, *The Earls of Creation* (London, 1962), p. 87.
23 Materials on Knaresborough in possession of History of Parliament Trust.
24 VCH, *Yorkshire: The East Riding*, vi, p. 186.
25 VCH, *Yorkshire: York*, p. 544.
26 C. Collyer, 'The Yorkshire Election of 1734', *Proceedings of the Leeds Philosophical and Literary Society*, 7 (1952), pp. 53–82.

most bitterly contested in the eighteenth century. Sir Thomas Robinson went to see him at Chiswick and had 'a good deal of talk with Lord Burlington about our county contest. He says he is not engaged any way and is still entirely master of his interest'.[27] Sir John Lister Kaye, a Tory MP, thought that Burlington would not support Sir Rowland Wynn, one of the government candidates who had been hearty for the excise scheme (the other being Edward Wortley Montagu, the unpopular husband of Lady Mary Wortley Montagu), and that he might allow his tenants to vote for Sir Miles Stapylton, a Tory whose family had been strong Jacobites. The general opinion was that if Lord Burlington 'stands fast . . . it will be easy to carry two against Sir Rowland and Wortley'.[28] Charles Bruce, his brother-in-law, who had succeeded as earl of Ailesbury, urged Burlington to back Stapylton and Chomley Turner, an independent Whig who had voted against the excise, stressing that 'the safety and happiness of the nation plainly depends as to York co. in particular tho' tis but two Members, the credit of having two chosen in opposition to the minister would be of considerable service to the opposition'. Ailesbury's influence prevailed and Burlington came down firmly on the side of the opposition, acting with Lords Cardigan, Exeter, Strafford and Thanet, all Tory lords, and with the dukes of Bolton and Somerset, two opposition Whigs.[29] Stapylton was returned at the top of the poll, defeating Wynn, while Turner was next and Wortley last. Wynn insisted on a scrutiny, but the sheriff declared Stapylton and Turner had been returned. Lords Carlisle, Irwin and Malton, government supporters, sent round a circular letter to raise a county subscription in support of Wynn's petition against Stapylton's return.[30] Burlington attended the meeting at Sir Miles Stapylton lodgings in London in support of Stapylton's election, in company with William Pulteney, Lord Ailesbury, Kaye and Slingsby, two High Tory MPs. Between £5,000 and £8,000 were raised in subscriptions to support Stapylton. This was an expensive exercise, as numerous witnesses had to be brought to and lodged in London until January 1735 when the petition was heard. Although 1,600 of Stapylton's votes were disallowed by the Walpole-dominated House of Commons, Stapylton kept his seat.[31]

Burlington was present at the opening of the session on 14 January 1735, but did not attend parliament otherwise that year. Thereafter he attended

27 *HMC, Carlisle*, P. 137.
28 *The Wentworth Papers, 1705-1739*, ed. J.J. Cartwright (London, 1883), pp. 488, 492.
29 BL, Althorp MS B8, earl of Ailesbury to Lord Burlington, 4 August 1733.
30 Chatsworth, Devonshire MSS, 218.0, circular letter (1734) signed by Lords Carlisle, Irwin and Malton; 219.0, York 21 May 1734 list of freeholders who subscribed to Wynn's petition; 219.0 Edward Finch to Lady Burlington, 10 June 1734.
31 Collyer, 'The Yorkshire Election of 1734', pp. 53-82.

only intermittently, hearing the debate on the army on 13 March 1736 and the debate on an increased allowance for the Prince of Wales on 27 February 1737. He made sure he was in the House on 16 March 1737, when the bill to sell the estates of the Jacobite Lord Preston and other Grahme (or Graham) estates for the payment of debts was before the House. The bill concerned his secretary Richard Graham, the son of Richard Graham, MP, James II's regulator of corporations.[32] From March to May he attended every single day on the Porteous Case, the *cause célèbre* of the time, immortalised by Sir Walter Scott in *Heart of the Midlothian*. Smuggling was then the Scottish national pastime and there was bitter resentment when Captain Porteous of the Edinburgh militia ordered his men to fire on the crowd at the execution of Andrew Wilson, a popular Edinburgh merchant who had been caught smuggling. Sentenced to death but reprieved by the authorities, Porteous had been summarily executed by persons said to have been highly placed but never identified. As a result parliament passed a bill to penalise the provost and other civic dignitaries of Edinburgh. In April he was appointed to a committee on a bill to enable the proprietors of Red Lion Square to clean and pave it. He was naturally in the Lords on 11 May when his successful claim to the barony of Clifford was heard.

In March 1738 Burlington attended the hearing of his petition for leave to bring in a private bill to sell some of his estates in counties Cork and Waterford for the payment of his debts. Surprisingly, he was appointed to the committee on this bill, which was quickly engrossed. Sir William Heathcote, a wealthy Whig merchant and an MP, who bought £3,000 a year worth of Burlington's estates in Ireland, thought that Burlington's debts amounting to £169,000 had been paid with an overplus of £10,000, leaving him with £8,000 p.a. in Ireland and £4,000 p.a. in England, but with arrears of £80,000 owed by his tenants.[33]

Burlington attended parliament regularly in February–March 1739 on the debates on the Spanish Convention and the merchants' complaints against Spanish depredations on English trade. He voted with the opposition on 1 March against the address on the Spanish Convention. He was there in April for the hearing of legal cases involving the earl of Inchiquin and the earl of Westmeath, two Irish peers. In March 1740 he attended on the bill relating to the duke of Grafton's pension out of the hereditary excise and on a bill to make the River Dun in Yorkshire navigable, but did not go to the House again. He was absent from parliament during the whole of 1741 and

32 *Survey of London*, xxxii, *St James's Westminster*, p. 392.

33 *HMC, Egmont Diary*, ii, p. 252; 11 Geo. II, cap. 4.

was, therefore, away from the vote on the motion for the removal of Walpole on 13 February. This did not mean that he was politically inactive out of doors, for he supported Sir John Lister Kaye, a Jacobite, and Godfrey Wentworth, another Tory, in the hotly contested York election of 1741. He was the patron of Dr Drake, the Jacobite historian of York, whom he used as his electoral agent in the course of the election, defraying the cost of treats for the freemen there.[34] On the other hand, he continued to return his life-long friend Richard Arundel at Knaresborough, though Arundel remained a government supporter. He was present in the Lords on 19 January 1742 on the motion to appoint a committee of the whole House on the state of the nation, but abstained from the vote on it. In March he attended on the bill to sell the earl of Carlingford's (an Irish peer) estate and on the petition of the duke of Grafton to sell lands in the parish of St James's, Westminster, and to settle other lands in lieu thereof. Absent from parliament for the rest of the year, he was away for the whole of 1743, 1744 and 1745.

Burlington's name was sent to the French as one of the opposition lords who were expected to declare for a restoration of the Stuarts in the event of a successful landing led by Prince Charles Edward in 1744.[35] Burlington was at Londesborough during the '45. In a letter dated 6 September, William Kent sent him details of those joining 'the Pretender', adding that 6,000 Dutch troops had been sent for.[36] The earl did not attend the county meeting to organise measures in defence of the Hanoverian succession called by the archbishop of York. The archbishop reported to lord chancellor Hardwicke: 'I enclose Lord Burlington's letter, which I am not quite pleased with. For tho' Mr Arundel was with him when he received mine, there is a coldness of indolence or incredulity in it.' The lord chancellor was of the opinion that 'the coldness and dryness' of Burlington's letter to the archbishop stemmed 'from the indolence of his temper, rather than from any other motive'. Lady Burlington's letters to her lord at this time are sybilline, as she preferred not to comment on the situation in letters sent through the post office and which could have been opened by it. Burlington, however, eventually sent his subscription to the archbishop of York, who concluded from this that he was 'certainly a warm friend' after all.[37] The majority of people subscribed to or took the Association in

34 VCH, *Yorkshire: York*, p. 544; *HMC, Various*, ii, p. 418.
35 Cruickshanks, *Political Untouchables*: pp. 320–22.
36 Chatsworth, Devonshire MS 206.9.
37 R. Garnett, 'Correspondence of Archbishop Herring and Lord Hardwicke during the Rebellion of 1745', pp. 537, 542, 544.

defence of the Protestant Succession at this time, including prominent Jacobites lest they be suspected. Lord Nottingham sent the earl the latest news on the progress of the Jacobite army, including details of Lord Kilmarnock's orders to the bailiff of Kelso, in a letter written from York on 6 November.[38]

Burlington attended the House of Lords regularly in July-August 1746 for the trial of rebel Lords Balmerino, Kilmarnock and Cromartie; and he sat every day in Parliament during the trial of Lord Lovat in 1747. Thereafter, he ceased to attend the House of Lords. Though he was something of a recluse in the years before his death in 1753, his correspondence gives some indication of matters which still interested him. He was sent the best extant account of the Jacobite demonstrations at the Lichfield races in 1747 when Tory MPs and country gentlemen appeared wearing plaid waistcoats (which the Jacobites had taken as their badge since the '45) and some white roses, an older symbol of the Stuarts.[39] In a letter sent through Waters jnr, the Jacobite banker in Paris in June 1749, the earl was sent an account of the arrest of 'him they call Prince Edward' at the Paris opera, of the hostile reaction of the people of Paris for whom Prince Charles Edward had become a popular hero and of the many lampoons and verses written against the French ministers as a result, though it was deemed unsafe to send samples of these satires.[40]

This survey of Lord Burlington's political career enables us to conclude that the third earl of Burlington was indeed interested in politics and had high expectations of office, adhering to Walpole from 1717 to 1733 and going into opposition after George II broke his word to him. This talented man was not above attending faithfully when matters concerning Yorkshire, Irish affairs, or affecting his friends or dependants, came before parliament. The particular interest he took in the trials and forfeitures of Jacobites may be a clue to the hidden sympathies of a man who was also intensively secretive.

38 Chatsworth, Devonshire MS 328.0.
39 Chatsworth, Devonshire MS 343.1.
40 Chatsworth, Devonshire MS 206.15.

5

'Avowed Friend and Patron': The Third Earl of Burlington and Alexander Pope

Howard Erskine-Hill

'The key to Pope's career', Ian Jack has observed, 'is that he was a Court poet born at a time when the Court was ceasing to be the cultural centre of England'.[1] Jack's remark is supported by the contrast between an early poem of Pope, *Windsor Forest* (1713), which certainly is courtly, and all the mock-panegyric and mock-compliment to be found in Pope's later work, ironically celebrating the Hanoverian court and government. Yet this is to endorse Pope's own view of Hanoverian England, and it is right to remember that another major poet of the time, Edward Young, held a positive view of the court and administrations in the time of Sir Robert Walpole.

All this is relevant to Burlington because Pope's vision of the court obliged him to look elsewhere for powerful protection and encouragement. If the monarch on the throne did not seem to represent the political and cultural qualities required in a good ruler, this threw particular importance on such powerful and perceptive figures as English society could provide, men whom James Lees-Milne has called 'Earls of Creation'.[2] Several noblemen of this kind can be found among Pope's closer friends: Charles Mordaunt, third earl of Peterborough (1658-1735), Allen, Earl Bathurst (1684-1755) and Edward Harley, second earl of Oxford (1689-1741) are prominent examples. They were men of wealth and influence though usually, one notices, in opposition or retirement. They were men of taste and sometimes learning, often with a consuming interest in architecture and landscape gardening. They were affable and friendly, willing to honour talent with their friendship. This indeed is one of the positive aspects of

1 Ian Jack, *The Poet and his Audience* (Cambridge, 1984), p. 32.
2 James Lees-Milne, *Earls of Creation: Five Great Patrons of Eighteenth-Century Art* (London, 1962).

what constituted the Augustan Idea in the earlier eighteenth century: a relation between ruler and artist in which patron and client became friends on a familiar footing.[3] This Pope was to sum up when, late in his life and long after he had ensured his own financial independence, he wrote to the countess of Burlington of her husband's being 'his avowed Friend & Patron' (*c.* 8 Sept. 1738).[4]

Among those powerful and discerning friends to whom, in Pope's eyes, the Augustan ideal had been displaced, the earl of Burlington was of exceptional importance. This was because he was himself both patron and artist, a great landed magnate who not only supported poets, painters and architects but was a brilliant architect himself. Suetonius, in an often-quoted remark, said that Augustus had found Rome brick and left it marble;[5] the one architectural treatise to come down to us from classical antiquity is Vitruvius's *De architectura*, dedicated to Augustus. For Pope as for Vitruvius architecture was a mark and a metaphor of civilisation. In his epistle *To Burlington* (1731) he urged him to 'be what e'er Vitruvius was before'.[6] For Pope Burlington was a truly Augustan figure.

Pope's friendship with Burlington, like that with John, second Baron Caryll (in the Jacobite peerage), seems to spring fully grown from nowhere. No letters survive to trace its early development. But in a poem of probably May 1715, *A Farewell to London*, Pope says how much he is going to miss Burlington's hospitality:

> Luxurious Lobster-nights, farewell!
>   For sober, studious Days;
> And *Burlington's* delicious Meal,
>   For Sallads, Tarts, and Pease![7]

Eleven months later, when in the wake of the 1715 Jacobite rebellion the laws against Roman Catholics were being applied in their full severity, Pope and his family had to abandon their house at Binfield in Windsor Forest and came to live in Chiswick 'under the wing of my Lord Burlington'. That was how Pope put it to his fellow Catholic, Caryll, on 20 April 1716.[8] Burlington not only gave dinners: he was willing to protect a vulnerable family

3   Howard Erskine-Hill, *The Augustan Idea in English Literature* (London, 1983), pp. 16–20, 234–49.
4   George Sherburn, ed., *The Correspondence of Alexander Pope* (Oxford, 1956), iv, p. 124. This edition is henceforth referred to as Pope, *Correspondence*.

5   Erskine-Hill, *The Augustan Idea*, p. 15.
6   *The Poems of Alexander Pope*, general ed. John Butt (London, 1939–1964), iii, pt 2, ed. F.W. Bateson (1951), p. 150, (line 193). This edition is henceforth referred to as *TE*.
7   *TE*, vi, p. 130, lines 45–48.
8   Pope, *Correspondence*, i, p. 339.

during a severe political crisis. This was an important moment in Pope's life, and one wonders how he had become acquainted with Burlington. There are perhaps two answers. They may have met through Charles Jervas the painter, whom Pope had known at least since 1713.[9] This would attest to their common interest in the arts. On the other hand Pope may have come to know Burlington through the Roman Catholic Bedingfield family, into which Burlington was to marry his sister Elizabeth in 1719.[10] This suggests that Burlington knew the effect of the disabilities suffered by Catholics at this time and sympathised with them in their difficulties. Indeed it must be accounted unusual that a Protestant nobleman, traditionally considered to have been a Whig, should at this of all times have contracted a marriage alliance with an old Catholic family.[11]

It is interesting to survey Pope's correspondence with Burlington over its period of some twenty-eight years. It opens with a carefully crafted comic letter recounting Pope's journey on horseback to Oxford in company with the bookseller Bernard Lintot.[12] Dated November 1716, it first appeared in Pope's printed correspondence and does not, like almost all the rest of his letters to the earl, survive in his own hand. It was probably much revised, and reads as a satirical travelogue, somewhat after the manner of Horace's journey to Brundisium (*Satires*, i, 5) but in prose. It is a decided effort to entertain and gives a brilliant sketch of the literary scene in that year. If we look to the end of the correspondence we find another comic set piece, the petition of Dorothy, countess of Burlington, Pope and others on behalf of 'a certain Tree' threatened by a terrace of the architect William Kent, who has plotted 'the Destruction, Abolition, Overthrow and Total Subversion of This Your Honour's Tree the said Tree to cut down, or saw down, or root & grub up, and ruin for ever . . . '.[13] These two letters, twenty-five years apart, exemplify what seems to have been a constant *motif* in the relation of the two men: Pope's eagerness to entertain and the earl's warm appreciation of the poet's company. The greater number of their letters, however, are brief and hasty practical suggestions about meeting, or hurried apologies

9 Ibid., i, pp. 174, 347.
10 Ibid., i, pp. 91, 141–42; ii, p. 392.
11 Family history and political calculation may help to explain this marriage. The title of earl of Burlington came to the family at the recommendation of Charles I's Roman Catholic queen, Henrietta Maria, in reward for services to the royal cause during the Civil War. If Burlington thought it possible that the Stuarts would be restored, an alliance with a family such as the Bedingfields might prove an advantage in the future. See Jane Clark, 'For Kings and Senates Fit', *Georgian Group Journal* (1989), pp. 55–56, 63. For Jervas as the link between Pope and Burlington, see Maynard Mack, *Alexander Pope: A Life* (London, 1985), pp. 286–89.
12 Pope, *Correspondence*, i, pp. 371–75.
13 ? 1741; ibid., iv, p. 323.

when the suggested meeting proves impossible. This may be illustrated by a
letter I was lucky enough to come upon recently, here printed for the first
time:

> My Lord   saturday morning
> What has kept my natural impatience of seeing you, from rapping every
> morning at your door, was a sad & severe Illness, that has confined me to keep
> Garret these four days at Jervas's. I am just able to stir abroad; & if you dine to
> day En Famille, would fain Invite myself to your table, and Treat you with
> laughing at me, when the Ladies are remov'd.
> Hei mihi quod Amor nullis est medicabilis herbis.
> I am, My Lord,
>
> Y^r L^{d}ships most obed^t &
> most obliged ser^t
>
> A. Pope[14]

This is one of Pope's numerous undated notes to Burlington. We see Pope's
unfeigned familiarity in inviting himself to a family supper at Burlington's;
we also notice the bait of slightly improper amusement at the poet's own
expense. There is a sense of the licensed jester about this; the relationship
seems not quite equal, but the concluding quotation from Ovid (*Metamorphoses*, i, line 523) with *medicabilis* replacing the more usual *sanabilis*, is
drawn from a well-known passage claiming a divine origin for poets, who
sing of what is past, or passing or to come (i, lines 517–18). The poet as *vates*
lurks behind the witty entertainer, and uses an Augustan poetic text to
insinuate as much.

Burlington's own tone, in his few surviving letters to Pope, is unaffect-
edly kind and appreciative. Here is his first letter to Pope as printed by
Sherburn:

> My dear Pope, I was agreably surprised last post with your letter, I need not tell
> you that it is always the greatest pleasure in the world to me to hear from one
> that I love so well and whose Epistles are something more entertaining than
> those, that one receives from the rest of mankind. You can expect no return, to
> your news paper from this remote quarter, but however to let you see that we
> are not quite void of curiosity I send you a weekly paper from Yorke I am my
> dear Pope your most affectionate humble servant, Burlington.[15]

This fairly represents his style of writing to Pope for the duration of their
correspondence.

---

14 The Greater London Record Office (Middle-
    sex Records), Acc. 1128/185/27. I am grateful
    for permission to publish this item.
15 Pope, *Correspondence*, i, p. 491.

On Pope's side there are some exceptional matters which alter the regular character of his letters. There is a preliminary point worth making, namely the surprising absence of letters for the period February 1719 to December 1728, nearly ten years. Now it may be that the nine undated notes printed by Sherburn fill this gap,[16] but even if they were all to belong to this period they would not seem to be sufficient. There are nine letters between 1729 and 1731. Again, Burlington was sometimes abroad during those ten years, but only briefly. It seems more probable that some letters were destroyed, perhaps after having been returned to Pope. On 29 October 1729 Pope mentions in passing that he has not recently written to Burlington partly 'because your Ldship lately chanc'd to tell me that you kept some of my silly Letters'.[17] Pope had various motives for wanting several of his friends to return his letters. He asked Caryll to return 'the whole cargoe' to him as early as 1712, ostensibly because he wanted to use them in a literary project, probably writing periodical essays.[18] In 1726 Edmund Curll acquired and published his early letters to Henry Cromwell; December of that year saw Pope again asking Caryll to return his letters, this time so that he might review them 'and return whatever can do no hurt to either of us, or our memories'.[19] What troubled Pope here is that something embarrassing to him might fall into the wrong hands, perhaps something political, since the Carylls were steadfast Jacobites. When, later, Pope asked Swift to return his letters, Swift reviewed them and found 'nothing in any of them to be left out: None of them having any thing to do with Party' but, worryingly, he notes and cannot explain 'a chasm of six years' (1717-22) in the correspondence.[20] The 'chasm' of ten years in the Pope-Burlington correspondence suggests that letters were destroyed, either because they were *risqué*, or because they were risky. There is some evidence that Burlington was a dark horse politically.[21] Apart from the letter on his journey to Oxford and the letter on the reception of the epistle *To Burlington*, no letter of Pope to Burlington ever appears in the poet's printed correspondence during his lifetime.

Among the matters which modify the stream of Pope's social notes to Burlington, three of the most interesting fall within the years 1730-32. The

16 Ibid., iii, pp. 515-18.
17 Ibid., iii, p. 61.
18 Ibid., i, p. 156.
19 Ibid., ii, p. 419.
20 Ibid., iv, p. 72.
21 This rests chiefly on an interpretation of Burlington's activities abroad, which may not have been entirely devoted to art, architecture and music. It is also possible that in 1715 Burlington used his influence in East Yorkshire to protect suspect persons from arrest. This may have been on a par with his assistance to the Pope family a year later. For the view that Burlington was, despite being a Whig office-holder, periodically active in the Jacobite movement, see Jane Clark, 'The Mysterious Mr Buck', *Apollo*, 129, May 1989, p. 327, pp. 317-22.

first of these is Burlington's acceptance of the Order of the Garter from
George II in May 1730. Pope does not sound pleased:

> I have try'd to wait upon you, unsuccessfully; It was to Condole with you for
> being made Knight of the Garter, having known you to be so many Better
> Things before. Some of them, I think, will be remembered, longer than that you
> had this Honour; if either marble or Virtue can long remain – However, Princes
> are honourd for having plac'd Honors justly, & it will be said that King George
> the Second made the Earl of Burlington Knight of the Garter, &c. I need not say
> I am too good a subject to Envy Him this; or too sincerely Your Lordships
> Friend & Honourer not to be Pleasd he has done it . . .

Pope's *risqué* amusing style breaks out in the postscript:

> Pray, if you dare, tell my Lady B. I know you are Embrac'd by something better
> than a Garter.[22]

The poet's reaction could be most directly explained by Jane Clark's
hypothesis that both Burlington and his father, the second earl, had already
received the Garter from the hands of Stuart kings in exile.[23] Such a
proposition is by no means so implausible as it might once have seemed.
However that may be, Pope's evident disapproval also has much to do with
his own contempt for the Hanoverian court. The Variorum *Dunciad* with all
its anti-Hanoverian innuendo had been published only the year previously.
Now, this satirically displaced Augustus, George II, showed himself capable of conferring honour by the highest Augustan standards.

The second important matter of 1730-32 was Pope's composition of his
epistle *To Burlington*, and to this I shall return. The third matter was
Burlington's own architectural work, especially the Assembly Rooms at
York and the famous 'villa' at Chiswick. Having reported the view of a
mutual friend on the Assembly Rooms ('the finest thing he ever beheld,
inspite of Italy') Pope returns to Chiswick: 'You have no Flatterer here in
me, & I assure you Chiswick has been to me the finest thing this glorious
sun has shin'd upon.'[24] At the end of this letter Pope speaks of his own
architectural improvements at Twickenham, and asks for Burlington's
practical advice. These letters, concerning kings, honour, the achievement
and practice of architecture, form a context for the epistle *To Burlington* and

22 Pope, *Correspondence*, iii, p. 111.
23 Edward T. Corp, ed. *La cour des Stuarts a Saint-
    Germain-en-Laye au temps de Louis XIV* (Paris,

1992), programme note by Jane Clark on
Kneller's portrait of Burlington, pp. 195-97.
24 Pope, *Correspondence*, iii, p. 313.

are to some extent the materials from which it grew. Indeed it is possible that the king's bestowal of the Garter on Burlington prompted Pope to consider how *he* would wish to honour the earl.

The celebrated Epistle evolved through a series of manuscripts and printed stages to more or less its final form in Pope's *Works* (1735). It seems to have been shown to Burlington in an early state, perhaps shortly before 4 April 1731, when there was some discussion whether it might preface a folio of Palladio's designs which the architect then planned to bring out. Pope's letter of 4 April perhaps implies that this had been Pope's suggestion (he may have considered his epistle *To Mr Addison* [1721] a useful precedent) and as a first response Burlington seems to have agreed to it. Pope then made some additions with this in mind, including 'Some lines . . . added towards the End on the Common Enemy, the Bad Imitators & Pretenders' (in architecture). With these modifications made, he sent his poem off to Burlington as 'some Testimony of my Esteem for your Lordship among my Writings'. The idea, he said, had been 'on my conscience' for over ten years. Pope was, however, clear that the poem was so far in provisional form only: 'I beg your Lordship will not show the thing in manuscript, till the proper time: It may yet receive Improvement, & will, to the last day it's in my power'.[25] On receiving the poem Burlington had it copied and, it is to be presumed, returned the manuscript to Pope together with a letter of thanks. This manuscript does not appear among the other surviving manuscripts. More surprisingly, no letter of thanks (such as that sent by Lord Oxford in acknowledgement of Pope's Epistle to him) has been preserved. One wonders why not.

It is not my intention to recapitulate the critical discussion of *To Burlington* which has appeared during the last thirty or forty years. It is sufficient to say that the poem, in its 1735 form, opens in the shared atmosphere of *cognoscenti* but then steadily widens its range so as to encompass the whole of society and develop a glowingly affirmative vision of the future. Approximately half way though comes the satirical narrative of the visit to 'Timon's Villa', after which the poet's positive perceptions and descriptions sweep 'grandly towards the Vergilian dream of the poem's close.[26] More

---

25 Ibid., iii, pp. 187–88.
26 Maynard Mack, *The Last and Greatest Art: Some Unpublished Poetical Manuscripts of Alexander Pope* (London, 1984), p. 157. For earlier discussion of *To Burlington*, see R.A. Brower, *Alexander Pope: The Poetry of Allusion* (Oxford, 1959), pp. 243–49; Howard Erskine-Hill, *The Social Milieu of Alexander Pope: Lives, Example and the Poetic Response* (London, 1975), pp. 294–304, 318–25.

relevant, I believe, to an account of the relation between Pope and Burlington, is a discussion of the draft which the latter had copied, and its
differences from the various printed states of the poem.

Maynard Mack has edited all the manuscripts of *To Burlington* in facsimile. In his introduction to these he rightly concentrates on the one really
crucial, structural, change Pope made between the manuscripts and early
printed versions on one hand, and the later printed versions on the other.
This change was the repositioning of the lines:

> Let the Golden Ear
> Inbrown thy slope: and nod on thy Parterre
> Deep Harvests bury all thy Pride has Plann'd . . .

In Burlington's draft (known as the Chatsworth Draft) and the other MSS.,
versions of these lines occur relatively early in the poem. In the Chatsworth
Draft, as Pope had indicated in his letter of 4 April 1731, lines on 'Bad
Imitators' appear towards the end. Pope's great creative revision was to
exchange these two passages and their associated lines, so that the satire on
false imitation joined other similar satire in the earlier part of the poem,
while the passage in which 'Let the Golden Ear . . . ' appears now
negotiated the transition from Timon's Villa to the peroration in praise of
Burlington at the end. Pope thus not only avoided anti–climax, but sustained and enriched the ideal vision of the end: he brought, in a way entirely
consistent with the precepts of the poem, nature to support architecture in
his idealisation of Burlington's work.

This revision has ramifications not discussed by Mack. Lines immediately
preceding the 'Golden Ear' passage, and repositioned with it, run as follows
in the Chatsworth Draft:

> Yet hence the Poor are Clothd. the hungry Fed
> Health to himself: And to his Infants Bread
> The Lab'rer bears: What thy hard heart Denies
> Thy Charitable Vanity Supplies –
> Wouldest thou Do better: Let the Golden Ear . . .

It can be seen that what after 1735 refers back to Timon, that lord of vanity
and bad taste, in the version sent to Burlington refers to Burlington himself:
'his hard Heart' (1735) 'thy hard heart' (1731).[27] This is a fascinating moment in

---

27 Mack, *The Last and Greatest Art*, p. 165. The
    use of 'thy . . . /Thy' in the Chatsworth Draft
    is also found in the Autograph MS and in
    Mack's transcript of this, though in his intro-
    duction the passage is quoted with 'the' replac-
    ing 'thy' (p. 156).

Pope, both morally and personally. The large moral stretch in the later version between Pope's condemnation of Timon and his recognition that even tasteless and selfish expenditure can benefit the needy is less precarious in the Chatsworth Draft. At the same time the Draft confronts us with a paradox about Pope's view of Burlington. Can Pope really have thought him interchangeable, in any respect, with the composite satiric portrait, Timon? Even if there were not so much biographical evidence for Pope's admiration of Burlington, the Chatsworth text itself praises the earl, both before and after this passage (e.g. lines 21-26, 146-50). Almost certainly what we have here is a moral judgement expressed, not without a measure of raillery, within the mutual awareness of an intimate and confident friendship. Pope knew he dared take a liberty, could exaggerate without being misunderstood, and so make the point that all those who lavish money on building, including Burlington, must have hard hearts, for they could give to the poor and unemployed directly. As it is, the medley of human nature at least produced the paradox of 'Charitable Vanity' from which real benefits flow. Even here, however, it is clear that the moralist in Pope holds to higher standards: 'Wouldest thou do better . . . ' We should notice that here and at the beginning of the peroration in the Chatsworth Draft Pope uses the intimate second person singular (lines 69, 70, 73; 163-67). Previously he has used 'You' to denote both Burlington (line 21) and Burlington together with other readers (line 46). Here 'thou' and 'thy' invoke a specially needed intimacy to guard against wit being taken the wrong way. Elsewhere Pope never seems to fear he will offend Burlington; he can call Bolingbroke 'the Greatest Man I know, ever knew, or shall know' in a context precluding raillery, without expecting to hurt Burlington's feelings. One might think the latter the greater man. Nothing could better exemplify the Augustan notion of a genuine friendship between patron and client, in which criticism can be voiced without offence being taken. This is the more remarkable in that 'thy hard heart', which might seem understandable within coterie manuscript circulation, survived into the first printings of 1731.[28]

As we have seen, the second person singular is used again in the Chatsworth Draft. 'Yet thou Proceed . . . ' (line 161) seems to echo the Second Ode of Horace's Fourth Book, line 49: 'tuque dum procedis, io Triumphe . . . ', in which Antonius, son of Mark Antony, is urged to take the lead in celebrating the return of a victorious Augustus. The second person singular is a little closer to Horace's words than the 'You too proceed!' Pope eventually chose. There are differences more striking than

---

28 *TE*, iii, pt 2, p. 149.

this in the Chatsworth Draft's peroration. We notice the difference between 'While' and 'Till' in the Draft's 'While Kings Call forth th' Ideas of thy mind'.[29] This may be a general allusion to Burlington's creation of Chiswick, which seems to have been a kind of Palladian shrine to the earlier Stuarts, with a copy of one of Van Dyck's paintings of the royal family of Charles I and Henrietta Maria prominently displayed: more than one regal figure are there.[30] But if the line is to be taken literally we have to ask who were the kings currently calling forth Burlington's ideas? If George II was one, by virtue of his recent bestowal of the Garter, who was the other Augustus?

The couplet which begins: 'Bid the broad Arch the dang'rous Flood contain' concludes in the Draft: 'Far chearing Beacons light their Subject main' which, while it speaks of public works such as harbours and bridges, the purpose of the beacon being to clarify the sea–routes and warn of dangerous coasts, also has a celebratory feeling absent from the line Pope replaced it with: 'The Mole projected break the roaring Main.' 'Th' incroaching Surge' in the Draft, and the 'subject Sea' in the printed versions make it clear that this catalogue of public works forms one of the those emblematic landscapes designed to express a political harmony of different elements, such as is found among other places in Sir John Denham's *Cooper's Hill*.[31] In both versions of Pope's poem the line: 'And roll obedient Rivers thro' the Land' clinches the idea of a loyal polity.

The final difference of the Draft from the printed versions is the relegation of the couplet which immediately followed:

> Till Tyber Stoop to Thames and his White hall
> Rise With the fortune of Romes Capitol

and which made the epistle at once more Stuart and more Roman. It reminds of the theme of emulating Roman achievement in *To Mr Addison*, but more of *Windsor Forest* where a personified Thames recalls '*Tyber's* Streams' but can declare:

> I see, I see where two fair Cities bend
> Their ample Bow, a new *White-Hall* ascend![32]

The allusion to Whitehall is highly appropriate in an Epistle *To Burlington* with its earlier homage to 'Jones and Palladio' (line 193) since the one part of

29 Mack, *Last and Greatest Art*, p. 166, line 167,; cf. line 195, *TE*, iii, pt 2, p. 150.

30 Jane Clark, 'For Kings and Senates Fit', p. 55.

31 *TE*, lines 159-92; T.H. Banks, ed., *The Poetical Works of Sir John Denham* (New Haven, 1928),

pp. 73-77. See also, J.P. Kenyon, ed., *The Stuart Constitution, 1603-1688* (Cambridge, 1966), p. 21.

32 *TE*, lines 356-57, 379-80; ibid., i, pp. 185, 187-88.

the palace to survive the fire of 1698 was the Banqueting House designed by Inigo Jones, whom Burlington so admired. Like the 'villa' at Chiswick the couplet recalls the Stuart origin of English Palladianism. It is probable that this couplet remained private to Pope and Burlington because it was too much in the idiom of *Windsor Forest*, politically compromised since the accession of the House of Brunswick.[33]

Pope's revisions from the Draft are largely improvements in the interest of clarity and consistency, but sometimes made out of political prudence. The exact tone of 'thy hard heart' was hard to catch; the change from 'While' to 'Till' introduced the acceptable implication that Burlington had not yet received proper royal encouragement; the slightly volatile image of the 'Beacons' was reduced to the architectural 'Mole projected'; but the couplet about Whitehall, which would in my view have lent a more local and historical flavour to the starkly architectural conclusion, was arguably a loss.[34]

There are of course many other moments in Pope's correspondence with Burlington when matters more serious than their next meeting arise. The reception of the Epistle *To Burlington* is one of these, after hostile commentators had attempted to identify Timon's villa with Lord Chandos's Cannons.[35] This was the occasion of the second letter of Pope to Burlington to appear in print.[36] Another such moment is when we find Pope advising the countess of Burlington on the publication of some of the political writings of her great-uncle, Henry Savile.[37] But it will be right to conclude this essay with the last surviving letter of Pope to Burlington, written some three months before the poet's death in May 1744.

> If my Lord Burlington goes to Chiswick on Saturday or Sunday, & cares to be troubled with me, I will, upon his sending a warm Chariot (for I dare not go in a Chaise) put my self into his power, like a small Bird half starved, in this miserable weather.
>
>   A. Pope.[38]

---

33 For a brief account of the literary consequences for Pope of the events of 1715-16, see Howard Erskine-Hill, 'Alexander Pope: The Political Poet in his Time', *Eighteenth-Century Studies* (1981-82), pp. 129-35.

34 I am grateful to Julian Ferraro for several discussions of the manuscripts of *To Burlington* upon which he is himself working.

35 See Maynard Mack's discussion of this point in *The Garden and the City: Retirement and Politics in the Later Poetry of Pope, 1731-43* (Oxford, 1969), pp. 122-26.

36 Pope, *Correspondence*, iii, pp. 265-66.

37 Ibid., pp. 303, 322-23.

38 Ibid., iv, p. 490.

Appendix

Unrecorded References to Pope in

Letters of Burlington's Circle

The bulk of the Pope–Burlington correspondence is preserved at Chatsworth. The Greater London Record Office possesses one letter (see n. 14 above). The Althrop Papers, now in the British Library, contain letters of William Kent to Burlington which cast a most amusing and interesting light on Pope, the best of this material appearing in Sherburn's edition of Pope's *Correspondence* (iv, pp. 149-50, 162-63, 125n.). However, in Althrop, B8, there is a scatter of further and possible references to Pope which, though of minor interest, are worth recording.[39] They are in letters not yet individually classified, where the person addressed is rarely obvious.

1   Robert, seventh Baron Fairfax to [?] Burlington, 10 Oct. [?] 1727:

'The 4th Occasional Writer is much cried up & father'd upon Ld Bolingbroak & Mr Pope, it is beyond the common stile but not equal I think to what He coud say upon such occasion.'

2   Juliana Noel, Dowager Countess of Burlington (1672-1750), letter of 'Jan 2' 1730/31:

'my Service to Mr Fairfax & to the little Signor'. The latter term does not refer to William Kent who is referred to in the same letter as 'the Signor'. It seems possible that it refers to Pope who also appears in these letters under his own name.

3   Juliana Noel, letter of [?] 1733:

'I had a visit this Evening from the small Signor who intends to go to this: by 6 in ye morning.'

---

39 I am grateful to Dr Eveline Cruickshanks for   Althrop B8.
    drawing my attention to the Pope references in

'I have not yet deliver'd Pope's message to Cherub: not having had a proper opportunity, but I intend to do it, if possible to put him to shame before a good deal of Company.'

4 Juliana Noel, letter of 1733:

'pray let me know when you will meet me at Popes.'

5 Thomas Coke, Lord Lovell, later first earl of Leicester, to Burlington, 20 Oct. 1736:

'but to think of those damned dull walks at Jo: Windhams, Those unpictoresk, those cold & inspid strait walks wch w^d make the signor sick, to that they, wch even Mr Pope himself c^d not by description enliven, s^d be scenes of such a romantick passion, makes me mad.'

6 William Kent to [?] Burlington, 10 Nov. 1738:

'in my way to windsor about a fortnight agoe, I call'd on Pope, he had write me word twice he had great besness with me, but when I came I found it was for some drawings to send to ye bath for Vases secunda il suo solito – & something he say'd he had mention'd to me about ye Prince – & that he wanted to know if my Ld Bruce is serund [his servant?] y^t had the great livcing was dead or dying, and if my Lady Burlington had it not in her Guift to all these I was Ignorant . . . '
'I wonder what P will say I here yt his Friend yt was marry'd lately to L^d B will come to court . . . '

6

The *Aeneid* in the Age of Burlington: A Jacobite Text?

Murray G.H. Pittock

The *Aeneid* was evidently a party piece, as much as *Absalom and Achitophel*.
Virgil was as slavish a writer as any of the gazeteers.

Alexander Pope

To be sure we may say with Virgilius Maro, *Fuimus Troes*.

The Baron of Bradwardine[1]

As the first monarchs of both England and Scotland, the Stuarts found themselves inheritors of the foundation myths of both their kingdoms. Geoffrey of Monmouth had been instrumental in creating a genesis of the British from Brutus, the great-grandson of Aeneas, and from this story 'the English appropriated themselves the heroic exploits of a British race whose Welsh descendants they were rather less inclined to honour'. The Brut myth, in fact, developed in the direction of an English hegemony in the British Isles: Brutus's eldest son, Locrinus, was supposed to have inherited England, and to be overlord of Wales and Scotland by virtue of the feudal rule of primogeniture. By the sixteenth century, a legend of spiritual authority had sprung up alongside that of political power: 'England was an Elect Nation'. This was a self-assessment which directly influenced both the claims of nascent Anglicanism, and the image-building of the reign of Elizabeth.[2]

Within the Brut myth, particular emphasis had been laid on King Arthur by Henry VII and his successors. Henry wanted to emphasise his role as a reconciler, a fulfiller of Cadwallader's vision of a restored British monarchy:

---

1 Cited in Stephen Zwicker, *Politics and Language in Dryden's Poetry: The Arts of Disguise* (Princeton, 1984), p. 233 n.; Sir Walter Scott, *Waverley*, ed. Claire Lamont (Oxford, 1981), p. 303. Scott as a boy heard stories of 'the old Trojans of 1745 nay 1715' (ibid., p. xviii).

2 Roger A. Mason, 'Scotching the Brut: Politics, History and National Myth in Sixteenth-Century Britain', in Roger A. Mason, ed., *Scotland and England, 1286-1815* (Edinburgh, 1987), pp. 60-84, especially 61, 62. This is a very full discussion of its subject.

the Welsh (and thus British, Celtic and Arthurian) king who had brought peace to England and self-respect to Wales. In pursuit of this image he named his eldest son Arthur, who like that Prince Arthur from an earlier age of enthusiasm for the myth (murdered on King John's orders) came to an early end. When James VI and I came to the throne of England in 1603, he inherited the Arthurian bias of Tudor renderings of the Brut story. 'James was not only *like* Arthur: he was also considered to *be* Arthur returned', the 'glorious stem' of the 'Great Monarch of the West': 'our Second Brute (Royall King James)', as Anthony Munday put it.[3]

James also inherited, albeit as a most unsuitable candidate, the propaganda imagery of Astraea, the virgin of the golden age, which had grown up in the reign of Elizabeth, rendering the queen a kind of Protestant substitute for the Blessed Virgin in the elect Anglican state which she had ordered and stabilised. John Dowland's substitution of '*Vivat Eliza!* for an *Ave Mari*' was symptomatic of a cult which could place Elizabeth as 'In earth the first, in heaven the second Maid', one who had 'brought againe the golden dayes,/And all the world amended'. Like Mary too, Elizabeth was 'termed "the lactating mother of the church" ', a role still being attached to Britannia in the 1740s.[4] The Astraea myth was linked to Virgil's Fourth Eclogue, with its famous promise of the return of a virgin bringing a new golden age: 'Redit et virgo, redeunt Saturnia regna' (this virgin was variously held to be Astraea or Mary, depending on the interpretation of Virgil's prophecy adopted). James seems to have rather played down his role as Astraea in favour of the less iconic feminine representations of Britannia and Minerva (the latter perhaps a regendering of his role as the British Solomon), since 'Astraea went into retreat as less suitable for a king, and also associated with "tendencies towards witchcraft and political partisanship" '. It was notable, though, that the feminization of the monarchy which had been so developed under Elizabeth still continued under these forms, and thereafter was never lost by the Stuarts. The Astraea myth was later to be used as a code of hope for their return; and after 1688 it was linked to Virgil's more famous *Aeneid*, which, in its turn, was the root text for the Brut myth. The myths of Astraea and that of the messianic hero Aeneas (in effect the same story of Augustan accession and renewal) were used by

3 Roberta Florence Brinkley, *Arthurian Legend in the Seventeenth Century*, John Hopkins Monographs in Literary History, 3 (Baltimore, 1932), pp. 9, 12, 21.
4 Frances Yates, *Astraea* (London, 1985), pp. 30-31, 41, 42, 59, 60, 62, 66, 67, 78; Madge Dresser, 'Britannia', in Raphael Samuel, ed., *Patriotism: The Making and Unmaking of British National Identity*, 3 vols (London, 1989), iii, pp. 26-49 (32). Astraea as *virgo spicifera* was associated with fertility (Yates, *Astraea*, pp. 30-31): we can see her presence in this context in Pope's prophecy of Ceres' return in the *Epistle to Burlington*.

supporters of the Stuarts in exile as one great metaphor of departure and return, a classical language they strove to control as being crucial to their concept of monarchical authority, and indeed the sacramental status of that monarchy. Those are the grounds for the argument presented in this essay.[5]

In Dryden the Stuarts found the laureate Pope later never fully consented to be.[6] In 'Astraea Redux', Dryden had distanced himself from his Cromwellian poetic past by seeking to herald a new age, and to assume the mantle of Virgil to Charles's Augustus. The poem was headed by the quotation from the Fourth Eclogue, lest there be any mistaking. Just as in this poem Dryden seized a central metaphor for the Restoration, so thirty years later he found one for the Revolution, expanding the classical realm of Jacobite allusion and royal authority already entered by others such as Lord Maitland, whose 1691 part translation of the *Aeneid* for Mary of Modena touches on some of the points Dryden was to develop. And develop Virgil the former Laureate does, from the very first lines:

> Arms, and the Man I sing who, forc'd by Fate
> And haughty *Juno*'s unrelenting Hate
> Expell'd and exil'd, left the *Trojan* Shoar . . .
> His banish'd Gods restor'd to Rites Divine,
> And setl's sure Succession in his Line.[7]

The political situation has changed: where 'Astraea Redux' is explicit, Dryden's *Aeneid* deliberately cloaks its politics in translation, as later Jacobite writers were to do in typology, cipher and allusion. In this way, too, Dryden fashioned a new metaphor appropriate for changed times: one of form as well as content.

A message is being delivered, nonetheless, even in the first lines of the translation. As James Winn observes, where Virgil's hero is forced to fly by fate (*fato profugus*), Dryden's is 'forced, expell'd and exil'd'. Similarly:

Virgil's Aeneas simply brings his household gods into Latium; Dryden *restores* 'His banish'd Gods . . . to Rites Divine', a phrase in which some readers surely read the hopes of the persecuted Catholics.[8]

5 Dresser, 'Britannia', pp. 30-31. The fertility myth was central in the iconography of departure and return. For a discussion of it, see Murray G.H. Pittock, 'Rites of Nature: The Rural World of Jacobite Politics', *British Journal for Eighteenth-Century Studies*, 13 (1990), pp. 223-37.

6 Valerie Rumbold, *Women's Place in Pope's World*, (Cambridge, 1989), p. 184.

7 *The Works of John Dryden*, v, ed. William Frost, p. 343; for Maitland's *Aeneid*, see National Library of Scotland, Dep. 221/62 MS 2/5; for a discussion of Dryden's opening, see James Anderson Winn, *Dryden and his World* (New Haven and London, 1987), p. 487.

8 Wynn, *Dryden*, p. 488.

The idea of 'restoring' of course, links the opening lines of Dryden's translation with 'Astraea Redux', setting up a recursive link both between the Virgilian texts and within history: Astraea is of course an image from a cyclical, typological historical tradition rather than a linear, incremental one: the shaping force of Dryden's translation is its intention of reiterating history. The restored Augustus of 1660 has become the wandering Aeneas of 1690, who will, Dryden's alterations to Virgil help to prophesy, become Augustus once again. 'And setl'd sure Succession in his Line' does not appear in Virgil's text[9]; in Dryden's, it tells its own story.

In the first eight lines of Dryden's translation, there are three substantive changes to Virgil, all pointing to a Jacobite reading which can be continued throughout the text. Dryden himself hints as much, writing less than a year after the 1696 assassination plot:

> My Translation of Virgil is already in the Press . . . I have hinder'd it thus long in hopes of his return, for whom, and for my Conscience I have suffered, that I might have layd my Authour at his feet . . . [10]

Dryden here hints that, like Virgil, he would have liked to see the triumph of Book XII accomplished by Aeneas/Augustus (in the person of James II and VII) before releasing the volume. As it is, the poem must stand as a prophecy, yet unfulfilled.

In the preface to his translation, Dryden employs typological suggestion as a method of introducing us to the nature of his political comment, much as is done (though more explicitly) in *Absalom and Achitophel*. The replacement of the Jewish by the Roman people in Dryden's typology can indeed be read as the replacement of the manifest destiny of Anglicanism by the imperial Catholic church. The historical analogy used is a dual one: first it is suggested that the *Aeneid* itself was intended as contemporary political comment, and a comparison suggested between Dryden's own time and Rome in Virgil's age; then Dryden draws a direct comparison between the 1688 Revolution and the overt subject-matter of Virgil's text. Having suggested that 'the *Roman* People were grossly gull'd; twice or thrice over: and as often enslav'd in one Century, and under the same pretence of Reformation', Dryden returns to the *Aeneid* itself for the moral, in doing so pointing a stout finger at the usurpation of William of Orange: '*Aeneas*, tho' he Married the Heiress of the Crown, yet claim'd no Title to it during the Life of his Father-in-Law'. Hence William, who had done just this, is no

9 Ibid.   10 Quoted, ibid., p. 485.

true Aeneas, no true heir of the Brut myth. Yet in a sense he is *an* Aeneas (and Dryden was perhaps aware of William's use of British Trojan themes in contexts such as the 1688 invasion medal, portraying the Declaration of Indulgence as a Trojan horse). This status, undercut by elements in the preface and the emphasis of the translation, is acknowledged with protective ambivalence in features such as the portrayal of Aeneas with a hooked nose like William's in the text, or by assuring us that '*Virgil* . . . was no Arbitrary Man', though these find their counterweight in 'a group of engravings with altars, sacrifices, and divining scenes dedicated to Roman Catholics'.[11] The adjective 'Roman' here is another key hint found in Dryden's translation: the 'banish'd Gods' who will be restored by the true Aeneas will be restored to Rome, will be Roman gods. Augustus was, after 12 BC, pontifex maximus: so is the pope. The status of Aeneas is one which presages religious as well as political restoration. As in Dante's *Inferno*, in Hades are found the traitors who must be overcome so that restoration may succeed:

> Then they, who Brothers better Claim disown,
> Expel their Parents, and usurp the Throne;
> Defraud their Clients, and to Lucre sold,
> Sit brooding on unprofitable Gold . . .
>   (Dryden's *Aeneid*, vi, lines 824-30)

In Virgil, the brothers are hated, the parents are beaten; in Dryden, they are respectively 'defrauded' and 'expelled', as Stephen Zwicker points out.[12] Maitland here in fact goes one better than Dryden, with 'those who brothers for a crown disown'.[13]

Throughout the translation similar manipulation of Virgil appears, ramming home the parallels, constructing a metaphor. A mention of marriage rites becomes 'Succession, Empire, and his Daughter's Fate' (a reference to Mary's treachery); '*magnum bellum*' becomes 'waste' and 'change the state'. Dryden turns part of Virgil's text into a litany of treason and mutability. An ill fate was indeed to attend the attempts of James and his son to return home and begin a new Augustan cycle. A fresh exile awaited the young Aeneas Dryden had celebrated in 'Britannia Rediviva':

11 Dryden, *Works*, v, pp. 280ff; discussed in Zwicker, *Politics and Language*, pp. 66-67, 192; William J. Cameron, *Poems on Affairs of State: Augustan Satirical Verse, 1660-1714*, v, *1688-1697* (New Haven and London, 1971), p. 121n. For medallic iconography, see Noel Woolf, *The Medallic Record of the Jacobite Movement*, (London, 1988), p. 12 and passim.

12 Zwicker, *Politics and Language in Dryden's Poetry*, p. 200.

13 National Library of Scotland, Dep. 221/62, MS 2/5.

> Not Great *Aeneas* stood in plainer Day,
> When, the dark mantling Mist dissolv'd away,
> He to the *Trojans* shew'd his sudden face,
> Shining with all his Goddess Mother's Grace . . .

Here, trembling on the verge of blasphemy, can be read the status of the young James III and VIII as Aeneas, 'a pre-Christian type of Christ' in the sacred reading of Virgilian prophecy. In this typological equation, Astraean and Aenean/Brut myths combine: the 'Goddess Mother' is Mary of Modena, bearing the name of the Blessed Virgin, Mary Queen of Heaven: she is also Venus, mother of Aeneas. Hence she belongs both to the *Aeneid* and to the Fourth Eclogue, with its prophecy of the birth of Christ (or coming of Augustus). As Astraea, she is '*virgo spicifera*'; as the Blessed Virgin, she is '*Porta caeli et stella maris*' (Feast of the B.V.M., 31 May), '*aromatibus myrrhae et thuris*', 'aromatic with myrrh and incense' (Assumption of the B.V.M., 15 August). The Feast of the Virgin falls in the Stuart season of May/June, the dates of Restoration Day and the birth of 'Britannia Rediviva', James III and VIII, on White Rose Day, 10 June (Britannia herself, incidentally, had been portrayed as 'Mary Dolorosa' in a print of 1682, the Anglican Church under attack from Jesuit and Puritan alike). As '*stella maris*' Mary was a name appropriate for the mother of the exiled Aeneas, since Venus herself, Aeneas's historical mother, was both a star (planet) and born of the sea.[14]

If Dryden's *Aeneid*, along with his earlier poetry, shows a great power of developing and centralising metaphors concerning the Stuart dynasty, he was their best agent rather than their originator. As has been noticed elsewhere in discussion of *The Hind and the Panther*, Dryden uses the political fables of weaker writers and chapbook culture to create his own synthesis (indeed, *The Hind and the Panther* itself uses the *Aeneid* 'to raise issues of invasion and conquest . . . and political legitimacy').[15] In his use of traditional typologies and their popular expressions, Dryden was like Pope. Perhaps one of the most exciting approaches to these poets and their age available is one which ignores many of the distinctions between high, popular and folk culture: for the common cause of oppositionalism to the post-Revolution polity preserved and encouraged an alliance between the images of fugitive Jacobite literature and the great iconographies of poems such as *The Dunciad*.

14 Winn, *Dryden*, pp. 424, 431; Zwicker, *Politics and Language*, pp. 120, 202, 253; Dryden, *Works*, v, p. 348; Paul Korshin, *Typologies in England, 1650-1720* (Princeton, 1982), p. 5; Dresser, 'Britannia', 32.

15 Zwicker, *Politics and Language in Dryden's Poetry*, p. 153.

Typically, Dryden was by no means the only user of the *Aeneid* as a Jacobite metaphor, a position it was to occupy with great force far into the eighteenth century (though there was certainly an anti-Jacobite struggle to control Virgilian rhetoric from an early date (for example, in the battle for control of the seas), it is also revealing that by the early Hanoverian period Saxonicity rather than Trojan Latinity was being stressed, a move which in turn led into the triumphalist 'Anglo-Saxonism of most of the Protestant historians of the nineteenth century'). Contemporary verse sympathetic to the Stuarts was quite ready to find in William the anti-Aeneas suggested in Dryden's Virgil:

> To make the parallel hold tack,
> Methinks there's little lacking;
> One took his father pick-a-pack,
> And t'other sent his packing.[16]

The pun emphasizes the filial duty of Aeneas carrying his father from the burning town in contradistinction to William's treatment of his Anchises, James.

Perhaps one of the most interesting treatments of the *Aeneid* metaphor at this time is to be found in James Philp of Almericlose's Latin poem, *The Grameid*, which celebrates the 1689 campaign of Lieutenant General John Graham, Viscount Dundee. As its only editor, Alexander Murdoch, writes, 'Virgil has evidently been so thoroughly studied and absorbed by our author, that his parodies have often the freedom of spontaneity.' Besides the *Aeneid* the poem also has close links with Lucan's *Pharsalia*, and in its resulting categorisation of the 'glorious' Revolution as bloody civil war, undercuts Williamite apologia for consent and continuity.

'We sing the Scottish wars and civil strife', Philp opens, immediately laying the blame for such strife on the anti-Aeneas, William: asking 'does she [Britain] herself prepare to cut off, in fatal strife, the British race'? The word used is '*Brutigenum*', the nation originated by Brut. William, the anti-Brut (a real brute) promises a nation divided against itself, for the whole being of Britain depends upon its loyalty to the exiled native king. Brut's heir. Nor is James Brut's heir only, for shortly after this passage Philp uses the Scottish foundation myth to further emphasise the gravity of the situation: 'the mortal land and house of Fergus, fall by their own arms'.

The action of the poem focuses on Graham's own territory, 'the land of Angus', which in Latin is '*locus Aeneadum*', Aeneas being usually Scotticised

16 Ibid., p. 234n.

as Angus. The hero prepares the defend the cause of King James, as also does the Trojan King of France ('great Louis, in Hectorean arms'). Graham's allies, such as Glengarry, quote the *Aeneid* as they stand ready to defend their cause. Glengarry's own brother, in fact, bears the name 'Aeneas', while Cameron of Lochiel calls his men to fight for 'the sacred Caesar' in an attempt to restore 'the golden age' (that renewed by Astraea). Commemorating Restoration Day on 29 May, the Graham observes: 'I will perform this annual solemnity in honour of the peace-bringing Charles. He, arms being laid down, put an end to the civil war, and peace restored, brought round the Golden Age.' 'Brought round' is a noteworthy phrase, since on such a cyclical view of a second Restoration both Stuart hopes and typologies depended.

Charles's collateral descendant, James VIII and III to be, is the 'illustrious youth, the splendour of your great ancestors' for whose right the royalist forces fight. The Graham, the 'last Hector' of Scotland, as he was to be the last Brutus in a Latin elegy by Archibald Pitcairne translated by Dryden, defends Brut's people, the Trojans, and Fergus's people, the Scots, against 'the Dutch Prince' and his 'Belgic general' (Mackay of Scourie, a Scot as Philp well knew, but 'Belgic' in sympathy): 'Rather than that the illustrious James, the son of Fergus, the descendant of mighty ancestral kings should be sold for Dutch gold . . . who would not meet the flash of arms . . . '. 'Alas! bitter was the lot of the exiled Caesar', hero and leader of the Trojan people.[17]

This vision of a Jacobite Aeneas was an extremely powerful one, drawing as it did on ancient myths of native Britishness which still retained a considerable degree of credibility, and a greater one of vitality. In John Banks's *Destruction of Troy* (1679), the audience was addressed under the title 'London Trojans' (in the anticipation that they 'would identify with the events surrounding the fall of Troy . . . when Troy fell "its Remnant here did plant. And built this Place call'd it Troy-novant" '): the potent boost this kind of equation gave Jacobite Toryism in the capital and elsewhere was a significant one, especially given the foreignness of William and the Georges. (It was possibly not till the time of the Patriot Whigs in the 1730s that British Trojanness was significantly recaptured from a Jacobite context). Xenophobia was central to Jacobite typology, whether expressed through the *Aeneid* or otherwise: it is significant in this respect that English Jacobitism was

17 Hugh A. MacDougall, *Racial Myth in English History: Trojans, Teutons and Anglo-Saxons* (Montreal, New Hampshire and London, 1982), p. 103; James Philp of Almericlose, *The Grameid*, ed. Alexander D. Murdoch (Edinburgh, 1888), pp. xxiii, xxxvii, 1–2, 5, 10, 17–18, 20, 30, 37, 43, 47, 99, 102–3, 113, 133, 170.

markedly muted in Anne's reign, and that that queen identified herself from an early stage as 'entirely English'. For some writers, indeed, Anne's accession was 'The Golen Age' again, a 'second Restoration of the Stuarts': her sex, if not the number of her children, made Anne a suitable candidate for the role of Astraea; '*Saturn's* Days return with *Stuart's* Race', as one eulogist argued.[18]

Long before Anne's accession, however, the Williamites had perceived the force inherent in Jacobite adoption of the foundation-myth language, and those who opposed Dryden and his allies sought 'to build a Williamite myth by satire', also emphasising the right of conquest found in Virgil's epic and the exploits of Caesar and Augustus in first-century BC Rome. Richard Stone was among those to write in the latter vein:

> The Mighty *Julius* whose Illustrious Name
> Till now stood first in the Records of Fame;
> Who by his Courage kept the World in awe,
> Was but a type of the Divine *Nassau*.

Although this kind of argument was to gain gradual weight among reluctant Tories as the years passed, it was the satirical attacks on the Jacobite use of the foundation myths which proved most immediately effective, as in 'Mall in Her Majesty' (1689):

> Perkin ap Dada Prince of Wales
>   Shall be High Admiral,
> And if the Dutch dare hoist their sails,
>   He'll burn and sink them all –
> The only way to prove his right
>   To th' scepter or the rod.
> If be beshit himself by flight,
>   He's Jemmy's son by God . . .
>
> Then will begin that Golden Age
>   The papists long to see . . .

The mention of 'Golden Age' mocks Stuart dreams of renewal, while Dada (the papal nuncio) becomes the father of a Welsh Prince ('ap Dada') in order to Celticize and marginalize 'Perkin', used frequently as a name for James

---

18 MacDougall, *Racial Myth*, p. 24; Brinkley, *Arthurian Legend*, p. 118; Frank H. Ellis, ed.,   *Poems on Affairs of State*, vi, *1697-1704* (1970), pp. 449, 453, 465n.

the III and VIII in anti-Jacobite propaganda in reference to Perkin Warbeck, pretender to the throne in the reign of Henry VII, who himself had made such ample use of the Brut myth and its collateral imagery. The reiteration, in this and other poems, of the accusations of James III's illegitimacy shows how strong the Jacobite foundation myth case was: this crude slur was repeated ad nauseam as a major defence against hereditary right by what has been called 'a factory' for anti-Jacobite propaganda, to try and undermine the case that Aeneas Arthur Astraea patriot king readings of James's right possessed. The Jacobite opposition insisted again and again that the true illegitimacy was a constitutional, not a personal one:

> In times when Princes cancelled nature's law
> And declarations (which themselves did draw),
> When children used their parents to dethrone
> And gnawed their way like vipers to a crown . . .
> (Arthur Mainwaring, *Tarquin and Tullia*)

Mainwaring also used the cadences of the *Aeneid* when he chose, as in 'The King of Hearts' (1689):

> I sing the man that raised a shirtless band
> Of northern rabble, when the Prince did land.

Here the echoes mock their subject: William is again the anti-Aeneas, a poor imitation of the sacred king, not 'The Lords great Stuart . . . our second Brute' who 'shall three in one, and one in three unite', the unity of England, Scotland and Ireland compared to that of the Holy Trinity.[19] Just as the Greek attack on Troy in Dryden's translation unroots 'the Forrest Oaks' (Dryden had already used the oak as a symbol for Charles I's martyrdom in his 1649 elegy on Lord Hastings), and destroys 'The marks of state, and ancient Royalty' (Dryden's *Aeneid*, ii, line 612), so Pope, in the *Epistle to Burlington* and *Windsor Forest* mocks the state of things in the guise of describing them: the 'growing Honours' of the 'tow'ring Oaks' promise a reversal of the desolation of William III, the second Conqueror; the 'stately Hind' that stalks 'O'er Heaps of Ruin' now promises a restoration of the 'ravish'd . . . Fanes' of faithful Catholicism in the future (in this context, the early Williamite emphasis on an iconography of shattered oaks and flourishing orange trees ensured a strongly pro-Stuart symbolic value for the oak

19 William J. Cameron, ed., *Poems on Affairs of State*, vii, pp. 28, 30, 46, 84; Korshin, *Typolo-gies*, p. 118; Brinkley, *Arthurian Legend*, p. 8.

into the eighteenth century). Pope speaks here to Dryden's typology in the *Aeneid* ('His banish'd Gods restored to rights Divine') and in the *Hind and the Panther as* Dryden himself spoke to Mainwaring's, and in his libretto for Purcell's *King Arthur* may have created at least in parts a Jacobite anti-text to set against Nahum Tate's libretto for *Dido and Aeneas*.[20]

Jacobite typology was thus perpetually extending its use of intertextuality in diverse and allusive ways which provided an ever-developing counter-argument to the satire and de facto claims of Whig propaganda. This was effective to the extent that the Jacobite reading of the *Aeneid* came culturally to prevail, as is evident in works like *Aeneas and his Two Sons* (1746) or the particularly popular *Ascanius, or the Young Adventurer* (1746). It seems to have become ingrained to the extent of being a standard code of allusion, as in the letter of 9 April 1743 from the Rev. Forbes to Oliphant of Gask, which speaks of 'the kind providence of Heaven . . . so remarkably preserving Aeneas & his Two Sons' from 'the late illness, or rather Contagion, that has been raging with so much violence on the other side of the Water', or in the famous quotation from John Daniel, where Aenean and messianic images are linked:

> The brave Prince marching on foot at their head like a Cyrus or a Trojan Hero, drawing admiration and love from all those who beheld him, raising their long-dejected hearts, and solacing their happy minds with the happy prospect of another Golden Age. Struck with this charming sight and seeming invitation '*Leave your nets and follow me*', I felt a paternal ardor pervade my veins, and having before my eyes the admonition '*Serve God and then your King*', I immediately became one of his followers.

Daniel tellingly closes his account with the leitmotif quotation of defeated Jacobite gentlemen, '*Fuimus Troes*'. The quotation of Dryden's translation was used to illustrate the nature of political change and its illegitimacy, as for example in Mary Astell's *Moderation Truly Stated*, where the Puritans are likened 'to false Greeks bearing gifts', and Dryden's translation is the means used to identify the language of their duplicity.[21] Williamite difficulty in using the Virgilian categories can perhaps be seen in a high cultural context in the 1690s, in the verse of Matthew Prior:

20 Winn, *Dryden*, pp. 47ff; Dryden, *Works*, v, pp. 391, 398; *The Poems of Alexander Pope*, ed. John Butt (London, 1977), pp. 197, 202; Woolf, *Medallic Record*, pp. 22ff; Robert Etheridge Moore, *Henry Purcell and the Restoration Theatre* (London, 1961), with a foreword by Sir Jack Westrup, discusses the libretti; the suggestion in the text is my own.

21 T.L. Kingston Oliphant, *The Jacobite Lairds of Gask* (London, 1870), p. 100; 'A True Account of Mr John Daniel's Progress with Prince Charles', in Walter Biggar Blaikie, ed., *Origins of the 'Forty-Five and other Papers Relating to that Rising* (Edinburgh, 1916), pp. 168, 224; Ruth Perry, *The Celebrated Mary Astell* (Chicago and London, 1986), pp. 193-95.

> If Namur be compared to Troy;
>   Then Britain's boys excelled the Greeks:
> Their siege did ten long years employ;
>   We've done our business in ten weeks.[22]

Here Prior, whose writing was unashamedly Williamite, does not attempt to usurp the story of Aeneas for his hero but inverts its moral categories: Britain is no longer Troy but Greece, a new typology which in different form would carry itself through to 1914. Even in an overtly foundation myth poem such as 'Carmen Seculare', Prior draws no direct equation between William and Aeneas, and in 'An Ode: Humbly Inscribed to the Queen, on the Glorious Success of Her Majesty's Arms' (1706), he says only, rather vaguely, that from 'boasted Brute . . . Tudors hence, and Stuart's offspring flow . . . ' It might be reading too hard to note of the word 'offspring' that Anne's children were dead and that there was only one living Stuart offspring to whom the term was appropriate: James III. But Prior did, after all, fall under suspicion for his role in the 1710-14 Tory administration, which had between half and three-quarters of a mind to bring the exiled Aeneas home.[23]

The Jacobite version of the *Aeneid*'s message was one well-known in Pope's circle. As F.P. Lock points out in *Swift's Tory Politics*: 'Arbuthnot, writing to Swift in November 1714 . . . borrowed Panthus's lament for Troy . . . to express his sense of the passing away of the age of Queen Anne:'

> fuimus Troes, fuit Ilium et ingens
> Gloria Teucrorum: ferus omnia Iuppiter Argos
> Transtulit; incensa Danai dominantur in urbe.

Once again the '*fuimus Troes*' mantra is intimately joined to the fortune of the Stuart dynasty. Nor was Arbuthnot merely borrowing classical typology: he was writing in what he must have known to be established code, not least because one of his brothers had fought with the Jacobite forces at Killiecrankie and later served as an agent for James III.[24]

---

22 Matthew Prior, 'An English Ballad on the Taking of Namur by the King of Great Britain, MDCXCV'.
23 *The Poetical Works of Matthew Prior, with a Memoir and Critical Dissertation by the Rev. George Gilfillan* (Edinburgh, 1858), pp. 51, 107-24, 175; Rumbold, *Women's Place*, p. 241, for Prior and Jacobitism. For the Greek typology, see Richard Jenkyns, *The Victorians and Ancient Greece* (Oxford, 1980).
24 F.P. Lock, *Swift's Tory Politics* (London, 1983), pp. 68-66; Maynard Mack, *Alexander Pope: A Life* (New Haven, 1985), p. 191.

Pope was to write in this code in greater detail. His vision of Caryll in autumn 1715 as an Aeneas returning to his inheritance was unusually timely given the season's political events, but it was only one of many allusions Pope was to make which, like the poetry of retreat itself, conflated personal virtue with the language of public politics. As Howard Erskine-Hill notes: Pope concludes the *Epistle to Burlington* with 'an unmistakable allusion to Dryden's version of the *Aeneid*, Book VI, in which Anchises foretells to Aeneas the destiny of Rome': Rome's 'Imperial Arts, and worthy thee' (Dryden) becomes Pope's 'These are Imperial Works, and worthy Kings', and this is only the culmination of a general echo of the whole conclusion of the prophecy in the preceding lines.[25] Dryden's 'thee' is Aeneas: Pope's 'Imperial Works' are, as has often been pointed out, those which George II did not do. Of course he did not: for he was the anti-Aeneas. The true 'Kings' of Pope's last line are those who do such works, true Aencases, the Stuarts of the prophecy of lines 173-76 in the *Epistle*:

> Another age shall see the golden Ear
> Imbrown the Slope, and nod on the Parterre,
> Deep Harvests bury all his pride has plann'd,
> And laughing Ceres reassume the land.

Fertility, rather than Timon's waste, is, as I have argued elsewhere, a central image of Stuart restoration: the golden age which a returning Astraea will bring, accompanied by the fertility of Ceres (and also with the gardening order of both 'Slope' and 'Parterre'). Pope is here practising intertextuality not only with Dryden and Virgil (and Horace also, as Howard Erskine-Hill points out), but with himself in *Windsor Forest*, where 'O'er sandy Wilds were yellow Harvests spread' 'And Peace and Plenty tell, a STUART reigns' among the 'green Retreats, / At once the Monarch's and the Muse's Seats' (and interestingly the 'ruin'd Temples' of the earlier poem are transformed into the 'Temples, worthier of the God' which will 'ascend' in the restored fertility of the later Epistle). Deep kinship between rural retreat (particularly the quasi-sacramental *locus ameoenus*) poetry and pro-Stuart feeling pervades. Did not the topographical poem itself grow out of a Royalist response to the crisis of Civil War?[26]

The Dunciad, of course, is Pope's ultimate statement of the Jacobite Aeneas. The poem itself not only makes extensive use of parallels with the

25 Howard Erskine-Hill, *The Social Milieu of Alexander Pope* (New Haven and London, 1975), pp. 72, 324; Pope, *The Poems*, pp. 594-95.

26 Erskine-Hill, *Social Milieu*, p. 325; Pope, *The Poems*, pp. 195-96ff.

Aeneid (notably of Book VI 43 per cent of references in the 1728 *Dunciad* suggesting increasing gloominess on Pope's part), but also is itself almost an anti-*Aeneid*: 'The Action of the *Dunciad* . . . is the removal of the Imperial seat of Dulness from the City to the polite world; as that of the Aeneid is the Removal of the empire of *Troy to Latium*.' Dulness's 'good old Cause' (the phrase deliberately remiscent of the self-description of the Cromwellian/Puritan side in the Civil War) is that of the 'Saturnian Age of Lead', the reverse of the golden promises of Astraea, 'redeunt Saturnia regna': the return of what Jacobite writers were calling not 'pius Aeneas', but that 'Godlike Man' of 'Another Maro's . . . pen', Charles Edward Stuart:

> See how Hereditary right prevails!
> And see Astraea lift the wayward Scales!

It was in paraphrase of such hopes that William King spoke repeatedly the word 'redeat' in his famous 1747 oration, and in his own *Anecdotes* used an episode from the *Aeneid* as a starting-point for discussing Sir Robert Walpole's administration. Here as in retreat poetry and the practice of such as the Man of Ross, high and popular/folk cultures were united. *The Dunciad* can be read as a great annotation of what fugitive Jacobite writers were saying: a defence of their dispossession against the official scribblers of the Whig state.[27]

To discuss *The Dunciad* as anti-*Aeneid* in detail requires more space to do justice than is afforded here. The structures of the poems, as Douglas Brooks-Davies notes, are paralleled, *Dunciad*, Book I, following *Aeneid*, Books I and II; Book II following *Aeneid*, Book V; and Book III, *Aeneid*, Book VI. *Aeneid*, Books VII to XII, feature less, perhaps because the fulfilment they prophesy does not come to pass, perhaps in order that 'we do not actually see the "foreign Prince" take possession of Latium.[28] Cibber is compared to Mezentius, the bad king of Virgil's poem; 'Books and the Man I sing', ironically opens the 1728 *Dunciad*; the games mock the sacred rituals of *Aeneid*, Book V, thus becoming 'a mock-commemoration of . . . George I';[29] Cibber is 'the young Aeneas' of *Aeneid*, iv, line 290; and the deliberate echoes, mainly from the less optimistic books of Virgil's poem, are a perpetual reminder of the discontinuity of tradition in this modern

27 Pope, *The Poems*, pp. 345, 351, 722, 728; Erskine-Hill, *Social Milieu*, pp. 16-17; Alexander B. Grosart, ed., *The Towneley MSS: English Jacobite Ballads, Songs & Satires* (n.p. privately printed, 1877), pp. 62, 67; Frank McLynn, *Charles Edward Stuart* (London, 1988), pp.

396ff; William King, *Political and Literary Anecdotes of his own Times* (London, 1818), pp. 25-29.

28 Douglas Brooks-Davies, *Pope's Dunciad and the Queen of Night* (Manchester, 1985), p. 51.

29 Ibid., p. 55.

epic, leading of necessity to mock-epic: where is the golden age, where are the household gods of an older religion and tradition, where is Aeneas, where is kingliness, where is the king? In 1743, Pope was writing the 'Fragment of Brutus, an Epic' of the origin myth: its fragmentary state is a metaphor of the 'Great Anarch's' victory: 'The Patient Chief, who lab'ring long, arriv'd? On Britain's Shore . . . with fav'ring Gods' was never to come, the winds staying Protestant. *Aeneid*, Book VI, had been used as overt Jacobite propaganda (in defiance of attempts to fling it back in their faces) in a 1708 medal celebrating the abortive rising of that year: but Anchises' prophecy was never to come true in the case of the Stuarts.[30]

If *The Dunciad* is Pope's great serious anti-*Aeneid*, *The Rape of the Lock* is his earlier version of the same motif, where the central metaphor of the siege of Troy, 'the fatal Engine' (Dryden's description of the Trojan horse) is matched to a pair of scissors, and where the vision of Hector's ghost is the appearance of the 'watchful Sprite' Ariel to Belinda/Aeneas. But the theme of 'By Force to ravish, or by Fraud betray' is one, again borrowed directly from Dryden's *Aeneid* ('fraud or force') which, though heavily cloaked as it is in zeugma, contains a disturbing series of political images. For just as the Trojan horse conceals its destructive purpose, so the zeugmatic levelling of 'Counsel' and '*Tea*' in Queen and ruling class generally conceals in its belly the world where 'Wretches hang that Jury-men may Dine'. Refreshment is linked to government: justice, like counsel, occupies the space between personal indulgence. Is this the 'day ordain'd to be the last' of Troy, that its inhabitants are celebrating, before 'Dunce the Second reigns like Dunce the First'? For all its unease, the zeugma of the poem makes yokefellows of the ideological polarities Pope would later keep apart. Whatever the rhetorical distancing involved, however, there is a consistency in the use of metaphor. Pope's 'Arma virumque / Hannonaie qui primus ab oris' was more than a dig at Marlborough's campaigns in Hainault: it was an encoded poetic language which penetrated Pope's whole oeuvre. In 'Messiah: A Sacred Eclogue', the images of Dryden's 'Britannia Rediviva' reappears in a poem which owes its form to Virgil and prophesies a returning fertility:

> Waste sandy Vallies, once perlex'd with Thorn
> The spiny Fir and shapely Box adorn . . .

---

30 Pope, *The Poems*, pp. 349, 836; Brooks-Davies, *Pope's Dunciad*, p. 88n.

Fir trees are still known as 'Charlie trees' among English Catholic families to this day: their presence on an estate was a sign of support for the Stuart cause.[31]

Just as Pope and Dryden spoke to each other and to others a political language rooted in Virgil's epic, so also a wide circle of writers used this central metaphor for Stuart exile which tradition had provided, and Dryden had centralised. Alexander Robertson of Struan, major general in the prince's army in 1745, translated *Aeneid* Book V; William Hamilton of Bangour, a gentleman-volunteer in the Lifeguards under Col. David Wemyss, Lord Elcho, translated *Aeneid*, Book X, with its study of bad kingship in the person of Mezentius; and interestingly enough, their nineteenth-century annalist J.C. O'Callaghan describes the deeds of the Irish Brigades with reference to Dryden's *Aeneid*. They were, in a sense, central military exemplars of its metaphor, their exile compared to that of the Trojans:

> An age is rip'ning in revolving fate,
> When Troy shall overturn the Grecian State,
> And sweet revenge her conqu'ring sons shall call . . .
>
> The banish'd Faith shall once again return,
> And Vestal fires in hallow'd temples burn.
> (Dryden's *Aeneid*, i, lines 386-88, 398-99)

This comment on the Irish Brigades' mission once again echoes not only the language but also the themes of Dryden: 'The banish'd Faith' is Roman Catholicism, kin to the 'banish'd Gods' and 'ravish'd . . . Fanes' discussed earlier. Other episodes in the Brigades' history were also paralleled with Dryden's translation: among them the Trojans requesting asylum from Latinus (*Aeneid*, Book VII) with the post-Limerick flight to the service of Louis XIV. On the other hand, the Williamites are seen as 'the nightly wolf' who 'roams . . . about the fold' (*Aeneid*, ix, lines 66-73).[32] In these kinds of allusion the symbolic story of Aeneas was functioning not just as the embodiment of the plight and ambitions of a dispossessed dynasty, but as a totalising metaphor of dispossession affecting a far broader range of people: it was transmuting itself into a metaphor for a state of exile from political

31 Pope, *The Poems*, 192, 222, 224, 231, 287.
32 Alexander Robertson of Struan, *Poems* (Edinburgh, 1749), pp. 301-44; Nelson S. Bushnell, *William Hamilton of Bangour: Poet and Jacobite*

(Aberdeen, 1957), p. 10; John Cornelius O'Callaghan, *History of the Irish Brigades in the Service of France* (Glasgow, 1870), pp. v, 66, 584, 603 and passim.

justice in general; a fundamental typological challenge to the premises of liberty employed by the Whig state as the ground-rules of their argument against so-called 'arbitrary power'. 'Popery and Slavery' was the Whig chant: but it was the 'Papists' (among others) who were the slaves, not the enslavers: and as a result, their argument for liberty was based on dispossession, a dispossession the premises of 1688 were forced to ignore, and on occasion still ignore.

As I have argued earlier in this essay, the Williamite and Whig side was not finally able, despite the efforts of Richard Blackmore and others, to reduce the Aeneas myth to the services of their side of the argument. Indeed, the developing status of the myth as a total metaphor for political dispossession, a tale of Trojan 'outs' overcoming their exile, led to its apparently deep absorption into the practice of Jacobite culture on a broader level than has hitherto been discussed. Its implications were recognized by non-Jacobite writers, in discussing 'the EXILE' (Aeneas/James), and in songs such as 'Young Perkin' ('The Stroler' [To the tune of, *Aeneas Wand'ring Prince of Troy*']).[33] The 'lost lover' lyrics, so popular on the Jacobite side, themselves 'derived from Virgil's *Georgics*', while Charles Edward himself may have leant in the direction of self-identification with Ascanius. In Scotland, Gavin Douglas's *Aeneid* was brought out by Robert Freebairn 'with a glossary . . . by Ruddiman', a long-standing Jacobite, as part of the patriotic response to the Union.[34] Writers like Gray and Thomson remained conscious of the potency of the foundation myth in political argument: Gray's quotation of Dryden's 'Form Divine' in his discussion of Elizabeth I is apt, but Dryden's lines are more so:

> But next behold the Youth of Form Divine,
> *Caesar* himself, exalted in his Line . . .
>
> (*Aeneid*, vi, lines 1077-78)

This was the 'Glorious Youth' of Jacobite intertextuality, Charles Edward. Gray had no sympathy with that reading of 'redeat' and the returning Astraea: but he knew the language he was speaking in application to the former Astraea, Elizabeth. After all, among his contemporaries: 'there are many Gentlemen now in *Great Britain* and *Ireland*, who have been in *Italy*,

---

33 Brinkley, *Arthurian Legend*, pp. 150ff; *Aeneas and his Two Sons* (London, 1745/6), p. 39; *A Collection of State Songs, Poems etc.* (London, 1716), p. 107.

34 Paul Monod, 'For the King to Enjoy His Own Again' (unpublished Ph.D. thesis, Yale University, 1985), pp. 80, 117-18; David Daiches, *Robert Fergusson* (Edinburgh, 1982), p. 14.

many who have had opportunities of being personally acquainted with *Aeneas* and his Family . . . ' This alternative reading, this alternative reality, remained a persistent sore under the skin of literature, as under that of the body politic, until at least the accession of George III.[35]

At about that time, as has long been agreed, political Jacobitism entered the last phase of its long decline. But as a literary typology, an ideology of nostalgia, it endured in transmuted form. As Frances Yates once suggested:

> Perhaps Astraea never really quite leaves; rather she has to go underground in the iron ages; and the privileged golden ages are those in which she has no need to hide. The Return of Astraea must always be a *renovatio*, a renewal or rebirth or rediscovery of the past through which a new future is created.[36]

The historicity of the Brut myth was being demolished, and as a result its vitality was almost exhausted, even had it not been linked with a fading cause. The Golden Age, in the terms that Dryden had used in 'Astraea Redux', or Pope in the *Epistle to Burlington* or *Windsor Forest*, would never return: but its underground life, its persisting exile, would continue. The length of its continuance is beyond this essay's scope: but anyone familiar with the Virgilian model will meet it again in the pages of Macpherson. In *Fingal*, as Fiona Stafford points out, Crugal's appearance is like that of Hector's ghost, a parallel underlined in the notes, and the use of Virgil's Troy rather than Homer's in Ossian poems underlines the sense of doom:

> In *Fingal* . . . the choice of Virgil's 'fortia facta patrum' ('the brave deeds of the forefathers') as a Latin tag has ominous undertones. The words come from the gold plate at Dido's banquet in *The Aeneid*, i, line 641 – presage of the death of Dido and the ultimate ruin of Carthage.[37]

Virgil, that is, perhaps mediated through Dryden: for as Stephen Zwicker observes, in Dryden 'we are meant to feel the active malignance of gods who in Virgil are detached or indifferent'.[38]

The 'exiled hero and the loss of paradise', Macpherson's great theme,[39] has, as I have argued elsewhere, Jacobite overtones: and one way he sought to convey that central theme was through its existing central text, the *Aeneid*. It was no coincidence that the theme was also the central one of Jacobite ideology:

35 *The Poems of Gray, Collins and Goldsmith*, ed. Roger Lonsdale (London, 1969), p. 197; *Aeneas and his Two Sons*, p. 40.
36 Yates, *Astraea*, p. 214.
37 Fiona Stafford, *The Sublime Savage* (Edin--

burgh, 1987), p. 147.
38 Zwicker, *Politics and Language in Dryden's Poetry*, p. 203.
39 Stafford, *The Sublime Savage*, p. 178.

Then far upon the northern hill,
My hope shall cast her anchor still,
Until I see some peaceful dove
Bring home the branch I dearly love:
   And there I will wait
   Till the waters abate,
Which now surround my swimming brain,
   For rejoice will never I,
   Till I hear the joyful cry,
That the king enjoys his own again.[40]

---

40 James Hogg, *The Jacobite Relics* (Paisley, 1874), song 1.

7

'Lord Burlington is Here'

Jane Clark

The eighteenth-century visitor to Lord Burlington's 'new house' at Chiswick entered though a doorway presided over by a bust of Augustus. He was then greeted by an imposing portrait of Charles I and his family, framed in bunches of grapes, symbol of Christ's blood and of the Divine Right of Kings. Facing that royal family portrait across the octagonal Saloon was a portrait of the young third earl of Burlington with his three sisters. The children are accompanied by a greyhound, symbol of loyalty, while one of the girls holds a pug, symbol of courage and fidelity, also of secrecy. The other girl holds a basket of spring flowers, out of which has fallen an outsize hyacinth that lies prominently on the floor,[1] one of the many references to rebirth legends that adorn Chiswick. This programme is perhaps one of the most vital clues towards answering the questions raised by an attempt to study the surviving contemporary papers relating to lord Burlington. The impression gained from these papers is that the restoration of Augustus, bringing with it the rebirth of true, ancient values, in the form of the House of Stuart, as inheritors of the Divine Right of Kings, was the aim of Lord Burlington throughout his life. It would be naive to expect to find direct or explicit references to this loyalty to the Stuart cause. In any subversive movement the leaders, for the most part, remain in darkness. The case for Lord Burlington's Jacobite loyalty is made most convincingly by the fact that it is possible to explain everything in these terms, whilst a Hanoverian loyalty leaves far too many questions unanswered.

Little has so far come to light about Lord Burlington's childhood. His mother, widowed in 1704 when her son was ten years old, came from a royalist family, the Noels. Despite the vast extent and value of the Burlington estates, she evidently found difficulty in meeting demands for

1 Michael Pearman identified this flower. My thanks are due to Dr Toby Barnard, Howard Colvin, Dr Eveline Cruickshanks, Peter Day and Richard Hewlings for constant help and advice and to Howard Colvin and Ruth Smith for reading and commenting on this essay.

payment of her husband's debts: 'We have noe hopes of Lord Burlington's Debt; my lady upon sight of a Bond said she wod pay noe more Debts, having paid fully thirty thousand pounds since her Ld. died.'[2] Like the later debts incurred by her son, which involved the sale of some of his Irish estates, something that would have horrified his great grandfather, the first earl, it is difficult to account for them and one possibility is that money had been loaned to the exiled Stuarts. That this may be the case is strengthened by the fact that at Oxburgh Hall, remote Norfolk home of the Catholic Bedingfeld family, into which one of his daughters married, hangs a full-length portrait of the second earl, resplendent in Garter robes, an honour he never officially received. The only possible explanation for this portrait is that the coveted Order of the Garter was awarded to a loyal supporter, in gratitude for services rendered, by the exiled monarch. In 1688, when he was twenty-one, both his father, Lord Clifford and his grandfather, the first earl of Burlington, though unhappy about the Catholicism of James II, were equally unhappy about William of Orange wearing the crown of England and felt that it should be set on Mary's head 'and thence descend in its right course'.[3] In 1715, when his son, the third earl, was twenty-one, the crown deviated even further from that course, the usurper on this occasion not even possessing the advantage of a Stuart wife.

That the third earl was precocious is implied by the fact that he was a director of the Italian opera in London in 1710, when he was only sixteen.[4] That he was, two years later, regarded as suitable to share the responsibility of keeping the crown on its Stuart course is indicated by his presence on Skelton's cipher, now amongst the Stuart Papers at Windsor.[5] Skelton was one of the most influential people at the exiled court of Saint Germain and responsible for handling correspondence in cipher.[6] His cipher is a short list of key people and the young 'Lord Burlington' appears as 'Mr Buck'. It is undated but from the information on it it can be dated 1712, two years before the death of Queen Anne, a time at which her illnesses and the question of the succession became critical. At this time the idea of a Hanoverian succession did not appeal to her. She appointed the duke of Hamilton as her ambassador to Paris and it was rumoured that he would facilitate James III's return to Scotland. Jacobite hopes were dashed when Hamilton was killed in

2 *Verney Letters*, ed. Margaret Maria Verney (Edinburgh, 1930), i, p. 384, Pen Vickers to Lord Fermanagh, 5 April 1712.
3 Sir John Reresby, *Memoirs*, ed. James J. Cartwright (London 1865), p. 435, 3 February 1689.
4 *Vice Chamberlain Coke's Theatrical Papers*, ed. J. Milhous and R. Hume (Carbondale, IL, 1982),

p. 139.
5 RA, SP, box 5/20. All quotations from The Royal Archives, Stuart Papers, are given with the gracious permission of Her Majesty The Queen.
6 I am grateful to Dr Eveline Cruickshanks for this information.

a duel in November that year, an incident which aroused the suspicion that it was a political assassination.[7] The cipher was evidently drawn up on his appointment but Skelton has been forced to write 'dead' beside his name. It was not until May 1714, when the queen's illnesses gave cause for alarm, that Mr Buck eventually left, in something of a hurry, for the Continent. In a letter to William Kent, who was in Italy, Burrell Massingberd, a member of a Jacobite family,[8] wrote: 'If I had not been so unfortunate as to have been out of town from his (that is Burlington's) first resolution to travel to the time of his setting out I had been introduced to him.'[9]

Lord Burlington's Grand Tour is continually cited as an example of a typical cultural exercise, but a careful study of the accounts, which survive, does not bear this out.[10] It is perhaps helpful to remember the advice given by the great earl of Cork to his sons, the first earl of Burlington's brothers, when they set out on their continental trips. He told them not only to study art, which they could quite well do at home, but to study 'what forts and forces are in every place'.[11] The next generation of Boyles did likewise and wrote home 'impressed by fortifications, especially those of the King of France'.[12] In May 1714, with the queen's death imminent, the crown of Britain threatening to deviate from its 'rightful course' and with an invasion to restore the Stuarts being planned, forts and forces were of far greater interest than paintings and sculpture. From the third earl's account book it is clear that he had received similar instructions but, because of his carefully created image of aesthete and arbiter of taste, this has passed unnoticed.

Lord Burlington spent well over two months in the Austrian Netherlands and Holland, both hot-beds of Jacobite activity. Cultural entries during this time are almost non-existent but many more important items are recorded. 'Mr Buck' was shown round Bruges by soldiers and there is a payment to 'Two soldiers that stood sentry by My Lord's order' at a house at Ghent. He visited the duke of Marlborough, at that time living in 'a sort of banishment' in Antwerp,[13] which caused a flutter in the heart of the British

7 Noel Woolf, *The Medallic Record of the Jacobite Movement* (London, 1988), p. 67; Martin Haile, *James Francis Edward* (London, 1907), p. 129.
8 Paul Monod, *Jacobitism and the English People* (Cambridge, 1989) p. 330.
9 Quoted in Jacques Carré, 'Lord Burlington (1694-1753): le connaisseur, le mécène, l'architecte' (unpublished doctoral thesis, University of Dijon, 1980), i, p. 58.
10 Chatsworth, Devonshire MSS, Lord Burlington's Grand Tour Account Book 1714-15.

All quotations from this collection are given with the permission of the Chatsworth Settlement Trustees.
11 Nicholas Canny, *The Upstart Earl* (Dublin, 1982), p. 104.
12 *Calendar of Orrery Papers*, ed. Edward MacLysaght (Dublin, 1941), p. 340; the third Earl of Orrery to his grandmother the dowager countess, 5 November 1697.
13 Frances Harris, *A Passion for Government* (Oxford, 1991), p. 192.

representative, the earl of Strafford, who seems to have been confused with Burlington. Strafford wrote to the earl of Oxford saying that the visit had 'caused a report that I was gone thither, which I never shall'.[14] The duke of Marlborough was taking out one of his periodic insurance policies against a possible Stuart succession and he sent £2,000 to the exiled court at Saint-Germain in April 1715 with a further £2,000 in August.[15] Lord Burlington's call on the duke was also noted by the representative in Brussels: 'The earl of Burlington, who I told your Honour was arriv'd here, is at present with His Grace at Antwerp.'[16] Lawes also tells Secretary Bromley that the duchess of Marlborough, who was perhaps not so happy about a Stuart return, is in Antwerp, which means she was absent during Burlington's visit to her husband. The earl's arrival in Brussels on 2 June (n.s.) had been reported back in London,[17] but it was not until 11 June that he visited Marlborough so the timing could have been carefully arranged. Brussels was the home of the exiled Thomas Bruce, second earl of Ailesbury, an ardent supporter of the Stuarts, whose son married one of Burlington's sisters. Lord Burlington was expected back in Brussels before proceeding to Holland but in fact he went to Rotterdam by way of Mardyke.[18] This could have been in order to inspect the harbour there, which was of vital importance as an embarkation point in the planned invasion, the English having insisted on the demolition of Dunkirk. Mardyke was also under threat according to the conditions laid down by the Treaty of Utrecht but the French were, understandably, taking their time.[19]

'Mr Buck's' entourage must have been privy to his secret. It included the painter Louis Goupy, a Frenchman and a Catholic, who joined the party at The Hague before 23 June (n.s.), when there is a payment to him in the accounts. Later Goupy became a member of the household of Kitty, duchess of Queensberry. In addition to teaching her to paint, as he did the Burlington family, she used him as a carrier of letters she did not want to risk in the post. Sister of a leading Jacobite, Lord Cornbury, and of emphatically anti-Hanoverian sentiments herself, Kitty probably had a lot to hide. Goupy was clearly a man to be trusted. Another member of Burlington's party was Isaac Gervais, an Irish cleric (often erroneously thought to have been the painter Charles Jervas) who served the Boyle family with loyalty all his life. It is impossible to tell from the surviving

14 *HMC Portland MSS*, ix (1925), p. 402, 6 July/ 25 June 1714.
15 RA, SP 44/82.
16 PRO, SP 77/63, J. Lawes to Secretary Bromley, 11 June 1714.

17 Ibid., 4 June.
18 Ibid.
19 *Historical Memoirs of the Duc de Saint-Simon*, ed. Lucy Norton (London, 1974), ii, pp. 335, 408.

Fig. 67 The third Earl of Burlington and his sisters, by Kneller (*Devonshire Collection, Chatsworth*)

accounts which of the countless errands in the Low Countries Burlington
made himself. Throughout the whole tour there is no reason, except where
it is specifically stated, to assume that 'His Lordship' necessarily accompanied his servants. Several of these servants, and quite probably Burlington
himself, made visits to Paris during the first two months. It has to be
remembered that though James III was in Lorraine by this time, Saint-
Germain and Paris were the nerve-centres of the exiled court.

From Holland Lord Burlington's party went through Germany with
astonishing rapidity, which makes it all the more surprising that, as Jacques
Carré has noticed, he made a strange detour and 'buried himself' in the
Black Forest.[20] Like his forebears he may have wanted to see 'the only Stone
bridge over the Rhine' at Schaffhausen,[21] but it is possible that he had an
assignation with someone from James's court in Lorraine, even perhaps the
Pretender himself, in order to report on his activities in the Low Countries
and to convey vital information from England. This would be no more
unusual than Charles II interviewing members of the Sealed Knot at six
o'clock in the morning in the Tuileries gardens during his exile.[22]

Lord Burlington arrived in Rome at the end of September and immediately became ill. How genuine this was has to remain an open question.
William Kent in a letter to Burrell Massingberd is comic about it and says
the rumour is that Burlington's 'generosity to ye Doctor has ye occasion of
it'.[23] The doctor in attendance was none other than the pope's doctor, which
is odd at this critical time, when British travellers were severely warned
against having anything to do with catholics. Another doctor in Burlington's life at this time was Dr Alexander Sandilands, who travelled back
to Paris with him. The Sandilands were an ancient Scottish family. During
his confinement the ailing earl was visited by friars who 'brought my lord
flowers'. For the Roman clergy and aristocracy James III was a symbol of
the faith persecuted and they supported the Stuart rebellions as they would a
crusade. Added to which the Jacobites used monks and friars as messengers.
Another visitor was Count Gallas's 'confectioner's boy'. Gallas had been
Austrian ambassador in London and was a passionate supporter of James III.
He was at this time Austrian ambassador in Rome. It is perhaps difficult to
grasp just how hard it was for Jacobites to send money and messages, let
alone arms, to the strategic centres of the movement. No customs officer
would have dared search a wealthy and important Englishman, who had

20 Carré, 'Burlington', i, p. 58.   (London, 1965), p. 254.
21 See note 12 above.   23 Carré, 'Burlington', i, p. 59.
22 Hester Chapman, *The Tragedy of Charles II*

taken the precaution of deserting his family's traditional Tory position for that of the Whigs.

On his recovery Lord Burlington took a quick look at the sights and did indeed buy some pictures and other objects, like the porphyry vases that are still at Chiswick. He then rushed off northwards and spent five days in Florence and just over a week in Venice, brief stays indeed if the purpose of his tour was to complete his education. On the other hand he hired harpsichords in both these cities, brief though his stays were, which says much for his interest in music. Whether he played the harpsichord himself is never clear, either from his Grand Tour accounts or from any of the later account books. It is quite possible that he simply wanted to make the best use of the three musicians he had brought with him from Rome, the Castrucci brothers and Filippo Amadei. Amadei's nickname was Pepo, which has caused subsequent complications because the customs at Dover confiscated some of his instruments (a situation any musician is familiar with) and this incident has gone down in history as evidence that Burlington already knew Alexander Pope at this time. The accountant's handwriting is hard to decipher where the letters o and e are concerned so it has been assumed that the confiscated goods were presents for the poet.

For such a lightening tour of cultural centres it seems strange that Burlington spent a month in Paris. Some explanation for this may be found in the fact that his banker was Sir Richard Cantillon, an Irish Jacobite whose services he shared with Mary of Modena and the exiled court. His dealings with Sir Richard were frequent and the sums involved huge. He also met Sir Andrew Fountaine, but this is likely to have been a cultural rather than a political encounter. Lord Burlington was twenty-one on 25 April 1715 (o.s.). He managed to get home in time to celebrate his coming-of-age but the rest of his party did not arrive back until 2 May.[24]

During his short stay in Florence Burlington collected two bas-reliefs from Soldani. Who had commissioned these bronzes is not clear but Burlington ordered the two companions that Soldani had already started.[25] These bronzes are a set of the *Four Seasons*, dated 1715 and now in the Royal Collection. Two of them, *Spring* and *Winter*, bear inscriptions from the *Aeneid*, inscriptions which imply that they were a gift rather than a commission from Burlington himself. The inscription on *Spring*, 'Burlingtonus eris/ Manibus date lilia plenis/ Purpureos spargam flores' (the

24 See Eveline Cruickshanks above.
25 Bodleian Library, Rawlinson MSS, Letters 132, Zamboni Correspondence, Massimiliano Soldani Benzi to Giovanni Giacomo Zamboni 15 October 1716. I am grateful to Dr Lowell Lindgren for bringing this correspondence to my notice.

original being 'Tu Marcellus eris') is based on a moment of intense
unfulfilled political destiny in Virgil's poem, a moment that would have had
great significance for a Jacobite in 1715. Marcellus was a Roman General
who defeated the Gauls, killing their leader single-handed in 222 B.C. It was
also the name given to the child chosen by Augustus to succeed him, but
who was doomed to die when he was only twenty. At this moment in the
Aeneid (vi, lines 883-84) Anchises is looking into the future and relating
how, if only the child could escape his destiny, he would be as formidable a
soldier as Marcellus. Whoever gave or dedicated these bronzes to Burlington seems to be implying that in return for faith imperial flowers will be
scattered, in other words, a restoration will be effected. Spring was closely
associated with restoration in Jacobite imagery.[26] The inscription on *Winter*,
'Unum omnia contra tela' (Book 8, lines 447-48), which appears on the
shield being forged by the Cyclopes for a mortal warrior and placed directly
under Burlington's coat of arms on the bronze, would have had equal
relevance for a key Jacobite. Since the exiled Richard, Lord Maitland's
translation in 1691, the *Aeneid* had been adopted by the Jacobites as their
great political allegory.

At some time during his twenty-first year, the earl had his portrait
painted by Sir Godfrey Kneller. In the three surviving copies of this painting
the recently returned 'Mr Buck' proudly displays the Order of the Garter.
One of these versions hangs below his father, wearing the Garter robes that
he never officially received, at recusant Oxburgh Hall. It has naturally been
assumed that the Garter had been subsequently added to the third earl's
portraits, after he had been awarded the Hanoverian Garter by George II in
1730. But the possibility of both father and son being awarded the honour
by those they considered their rightful kings, James II and James III, should
be considered. It is well-known that the exiled Stuart Kings caused the
Hanoverians concern by the honours they dispensed. When the Old Pretender's half-sister, the duchess of Buckingham, visited him in Rome in
1731, one of her rewards was to be the Order of the Garter for her son but
this was to be kept a secret until the king had been restored.[27] James had
earlier said that he was against dispensing honours of this kind unless he was
either restored or making an attempt towards it, which was of course true of
1715.[28] Alexander Pope's wishing to 'condole with' the third earl of
Burlington on his reception of the Hanoverian Garter, something Pope and
all Jacobites considered a piece of mere tinsel, seems to strengthen the

---

26 I am grateful to Dr Murray Pittock for this
    observation.

27 Haile, *James Francis Edward*, p. 342.
28 *HMC, Stuart MSS*, ii, p. 487.

Fig. 68 The second Earl of Burlington, attributed to Kneller
(*National Trust, Oxburgh Hall*)

likelihood.[29] With hindsight it appears nothing short of lunacy to have family portraits that revealed treasonable loyalties in the house but, the fact remains, many families possessed portraits of the exiled Stuarts which they managed to conceal successfully. There were portraits of James III and his wife, Maria Sobieska, at Oxburgh.[30] The Stuart queen's portrait was one of the most potent symbols of loyalty. Sir Henry Bedingfeld also owned a magnificent collection of Jacobite glasses.[31] Lord Burlington paid frequent and prolonged visits to his sister and her husband at Oxburgh and was clearly very close to his Catholic relations. His nephews were educated abroad under pseudonyms, just as their father had been, their mother going for ten years without seeing her sons.[32] It seems unlikely that the family loyalties did not coincide. As for Godfrey Kneller, professionalism usually overrode politics and, like his great compatriot Handel, he would have worked happily for both sides with his eye hopefully on the Bank of England. No artist in his senses would have wanted to endanger his relationship with patrons like the Boyles. This is borne out by William Aikman, who, even after six years in London, told his cousin, Sir John Clerk of Penicuik, that he had 'as yet gott never a farthing from His Lordship for all I have done but this is not to be spoke of he continues very favourable to me and recommends'.[33]

One of the great mysteries of the 1715 rebellion lies at Londesborough, the Boyles' Yorkshire seat. Amongst the plaques taken from the family tombs, and now in the parish church, is an odd man out, the earl of Drumlanrig, who died in January 1716, aged eighteen. The earl of Drumlanrig was the eldest son of the second duke of Queensberry, whose wife was Burlington's aunt. The family legend maintains that the young man, who was somewhat strange, when left alone by his guardian at Queensberry House in Edinburgh, had roasted and eaten the kitchen boy.[34] The guardian had deserted his charge because he could not resist going out to discover the result of the negotiations for the Union of England and

29 *The Correspondence of Alexander Pope*, ed. George Sherburn, (Oxford 1956), iii, p. 111, Pope to Burlington, 22 May 1730. See Howard Erskine-Hill above.
30 *Oxburgh Hall Sale Catalogue*, John D. Wood & Co., 31 October and 1 November 1951, p. 34, lot 727; p. 32, lot 669. I am grateful to Dr John Maddison for this information.
31 Monod, *Jacobitism*, p. 135, n. 41.
32 Fountaine MSS, letters, Sir Andrew Fountaine to Isaac Gervais, 4 April 1748. All quotations

from this collection are given with the kind permission of Andrew Fountaine VII; Catholic Record Society, 6 (London, 1909), p. 165: 'Two of Sir Henry Bedingfeld's boys go under the name of Clay.'
33 SRO, Clerk of Penicuik Papers GD18, 8 February 1729. Quoted with the kind permission of Sir John Clerk of Penicuik.
34 Violet Biddulph, *Kitty, Duchess of Queensberry* (London, 1935), p. 68; a biography based on family papers.

Scotland in 1707. Even allowing for the precocity of children in the early eighteenth century this seems an unlikely act for a ten-year old. Several aspects of the Jacobite uprisings cast doubt on this macabre story. Cannibalism, particularly the devouring of children, was the bogey attributed to both Jacobite soldiers and Templars, between whom there is a connection, as will be seen when the rebellion of 1745 is reached. At exactly the time of the earl's death there were bloody skirmishes with the rebels in the north of England, in which people were killed. Many Scottish families had taken precautionary measures in order to be safe in either outcome of the succession, the eldest son renouncing the title and joining his rightful king while the younger took the title and prepared to toe the Hanoverian line. The 'Union Duke', as Burlington's uncle was called, was said by his friend the duke of Mar to have regretted his support of the Union towards the end of his life and to have been a loyal royalist at heart. For this reason Mar endeavoured to gain the support of the young third duke for the Stuart cause.[35] This younger son, husband of Kitty, Goupy's employer, was certainly the arch sitter-on-the-political-fence. It seems more than likely that his elder brother renounced his title like so many of his neighbours, but instead of exile he met death and clandestine burial in the family vault of his cousin's church. This is strengthened by the fact that Stevenson, who based his books on fact, in *The Master of Ballantrae*, when writing about a family to which this situation applied, chose the name Durisdeer. Durisdeer is the village next to Drumlanrig, where the Queensberry mausoleum lies.

The only evidence of Lord Burlington's activities during the rebellion that has so far come to light is of the part he played as lord lieutenant of the West Riding. This has hitherto been taken at face value and used to demonstrate his Hanoverian Whig loyalty. However, when Sir Walter Calverley, whose own sympathies seem to have lain with the Stuarts, relates in his diary on 7 October 1715, that Burlington invited the deputy lieutenants and justices of the peace to dine with him at the Swan in Leeds, where he proposed a toast to the 'confusion of the Pretender and all his adherents, and to all his open and secret friends',[36] the smoke-screen put up by the most important Jacobites has to be taken into account. A poem that lies amongst the papers of that very active supporter of the Stuarts, the duke of Beaufort, may account for the young lord lieutenant's behaviour:

35 *HMC, Stuart MSS*, v (1912), pp. 182-85. Mar to Queensberry, 7 November 1717.

36 *Note Book of Sir Walter Calverley, Bart*, Surtees Society, 77 (1866), p. 138.

> Our fathers took oaths as we take our wives
> For better or worse, and kept them their lives,
> But we take the oaths like whores, for our ease,
> We whore and we rogue, and we part when we please.[37]

Sir Robert Walpole was all too aware of the tactics of the clandestine Jacobites:

> No man of common prudence will proclaim himself openly a Jacobite; by so doing he not only may injure his private fortune, but he must render himself less able to do any effectual service to the cause he has embraced; therefore there are few such men in the Kingdom. Your right Jacobite, Sir, disguises his true sentiments, he roars out for revolution principles; he pretends to be a great friend of liberty and a great adviser of our ancient constitution . . . these are the men we have most reason to be afraid of.[38]

Leeds was a city with a strong Jacobite faction. In June 1715 the Leeds bell-ringers, who normally rang every Thursday night:

> put off their ringing till the next day, which was the Pretender's birthday, and then begun two or three hours before their usual time, and tho' some Whigs took notice of it to the vicar to be the Pretender's birthday, he said he knew nothing of it. Then the chief churchwarden was applied to and he said at his request the ringers put off their ringing from Thursday night till then to entertain some friends of his with a peal or two. However, they also continued ringing two or three hours beyond their usual time and the Pretender's birthday was certainly the cause of that day's ringing, as is generally believed tho' perhaps not generally to be made out.[39]

Understanding what really happened in the rebellions of 1715 and 1745 is made impossible by the fact that it is very difficult to know what and what not to believe. In 1713 Lord Burlington had made his first tour of his north country estates, during which he stayed with Lord Lonsdale at Lowther. In a much-quoted letter to the Tory earl of Oxford, Lonsdale is said to be 'in ill (that is Whig) hands.'[40] Lord Burlington, whom the writer calls 'a good-natured, pretty gentleman,' was said to be 'in the same hands.' This slender

---

37 Quoted in Eveline Cruickshanks, *Political Untouchables* (London, 1979), between list of illustrations and abbreviations.
38 J. Doran, *London in Jacobite Times* (London, 1877), ii, p. 73.
39 *HMC, Various*, (1913), p. 90.
40 *HMC, Portland MSS*, iii (1899), p. 343. A Carleton to the earl of Oxford, 1 October 1713.

Fig. 69 The third Earl of Burlington, by Kneller (*Devonshire Collection, Chatsworth, copy at Oxburgh*)

evidence is constantly cited to demonstrate Burlington's Whig position. However, later in the letter, the writer says of Lonsdale: 'I verily believe that with good management he might be brought off from the Whigs.' Certainly his behaviour in 1715 rather suggests this. In November the mayor of Kendal received a letter saying that Lord Lonsdale was at Appleby 'with a few Cumberland gentlemen, and some half-pay officers who had left Penrith and Lowther in the hands of the rebels'.[41] Sir Walter Scott describes Lonsdale's troops as 'a mere undisciplined mob, ill-armed, and worse arrayed' who 'did not wait for an attack either from the cavalry or the Highlanders, but dispersed in every direction, leaving to the victors the field of battle, covered with arms, and a considerable number of horses'.[42] This kind of passive help for the Stuarts was repeated in the rebellion of 1745.

In 1716 Lord Burlington voted against the repeal of the triennial Parliaments, an overt anti-Hanoverian act, the proposed septennial ones being instituted in order to strengthen the Hanoverian position.[43] It would have been unthinkable after 1715 for Burlington, whatever his loyalties, to have reverted to his family's traditional Tory position if he wanted to be near the centres of power, from which Tories were excluded. Many active Jacobites were Whigs.[44] In 1717 a group of Whigs that included Burlington and Sir Robert Walpole went into opposition. This division was greeted with glee by the Jacobites who talked about 'the Tories and their new friends, the disaffected Whigs'.[45] The four years in which Walpole's party was 'so incorporated with the Jacobites'[46] must have given the future prime minister acute insight into how the Jacobite mind worked. There was a renewed spate of Jacobite plotting, an invasion was planned and money raised. In September 1717 the duke of Mar, James III's secretary of state, who was in Louvain, received a breathless letter from the passionate Jacobite plotter, Fanny Oglethorpe written from Paris on 15 (n.s.): 'I have but time to tell you . . .' the note gives Mar a few pieces of vital information at the end of which is scribbled, as a postscript, with the ink running dry, 'Lord Burlington is here'.[47] Shortly after this Mar moved south to an unknown spot in the environs of Paris. On 9 October (n.s.), at the suggestion of Fanny Oglethorpe's sister Anne, he approached Burlington's cousin, the fourth earl of Orrery, who agreed to help the cause.[48]

41 *HMC, Le Fleming MSS*, 12th Report, appendix (1890) p. 355.
42 Sir Walter Scott, *Tales of a Grandfather* (London, 1933), p. 922.
43 *HMC, Stuart MSS*, ii (1904), p. 122.
44 *Letters of George Lockhart of Carnwath, 1698-1732*, ed. Daniel Szechi, Scottish History Society, 55, (Edinburgh, 1989), p. xiii.

45 BL, Stowe MS 232, Sir Hugh Patterson to Mr Callender, 8/19 November 1717; original in French.
46 Basil Williams, *Stanhope* (Oxford, 1932) p. 460, Newcastle to Stanhope 14 October 1719.
47 RA, SP 22/119.
48 *HMC, Stuart MSS*, v, pp. 122, 123. Orrery's reply p. 306.

Fig. 70 The third Earl of Burlington and his wife, by Aikman (*Harris Museum and Art Gallery, Preston*)

Burlington featured in a postscript to another letter at this time. On 10 September (o.s.) Robethon, George I's Private Secretary, who referred to the opposition party as the party of the Pretender[49], told Lord Stair, British ambassador in Paris, that 'Burlington goes to France.'[50] Robethon begged Stair to take any opportunity he could to smooth over the differences. Stair acted on this by talking to Lord Burlington. He wrote to Robethon on 16 October (n.s.):

> Lord Burlington has left here to return to England by Flanders. He leaves here well-disposed, he talked to me as an honest man who loves his country and who sees the misfortunes which we could cause by our stupid and ridiculous divisions . . . he promised me he would speak to his friends and point out to them the danger they place their country in by their bad conduct. He complained bitterly of the haughtiness and pride of the ministers towards him. I beg you that someone speaks tactfully to him as soon as he arrives and so maintains the good intentions with which he leaves here.'[51]

Robethon's reply shows a measure of Lord Burlington's importance in politics:

> I have just read your letter to Milord Sunderland, who will observe with care what you say about Milord Burlington. As he never comes to Court I don't know where our Ministers could have shown haughtiness towards him unless he expects visits from them that they don't have time to make. Be that as it may, they will treat him with the greatest respect and I will take care the King does so as well.[52]

The fact that the young aristocrat clearly had no intention of ingratiating himself with the new Hanoverian monarch is perhaps significant of other loyalties. Burlington had evidently intended to go to Italy, where James III was now in Urbino, in the autumn of 1717.[53] Perhaps because Mar had come north there was no need. An interesting glimpse of Lord Burlington's character at this time is afforded by an Irish relative who had been promised an audience with the earl but found it hard to achieve, 'for so few are admitted into his presence (except his particular intimates) that he seems more to affect the monarch than the subject.'[54]

49 SRO, Stair MS GD135/141, 11, n.p., Robethon to Stair, July 1717; original in French.
50 SRO, Stair MS GD135/141, 12. Robethon to Stair, 10 September 1717; original in French.
51 BL, Stowe MS 230, Stair to Robethon, 16 October 1717; original in French.
52 SRO GD 135/141, 12, 29 October 1717.
53 Lowell Lindgren. 'Musicians and Librettists in the Correspondence of Giovanni Giacomo Zamboni', *Royal Musical Association Research Chronicle*, 24 (1991), p. 32.
54 PRO, Northern Ireland, D.2707/A1/7A (Shannon MSS), W. Boyle to H. Boyle, London, 4 December 1718; I am grateful to Dr Toby Barnard for this reference.

Earl of Burlington

Fig. 71 The third Earl of Burlington, attributed to J. Richardson (*National Portrait Gallery*)

In 1719 James was in Spain, drumming up support for another invasion of Britain. His return to Italy was deferred many times but he eventually arrived back at the end of August. Some time in August Lord Burlington left London for Italy. His departure had also been deferred many times.[55] A convenient cover for this procrastination was at hand in negotiations for a Charity School.[56] On 15 August Lord Londonderry wrote to an unknown correspondent asking him to 'dispatch that affair of the sugars in the manner the bearer Mr Buck shall desire.'[57] The combination of 'sugars', swords in Jacobite terminology, and 'Mr Buck' raises suspicions, particularly when Lord Londonderry's arrival in Paris was reported by Lord Stair just before Lord Burlington set out from there for Italy.[58] Despite his apparent Whig position Londonderry was evidently sympathetic towards the Jacobite cause.[59] Swords inscribed J.R. were found in London after the discovery of the Atterbury Plot, the culmination of the planning begun in 1719.[60] The ostensible purpose of 'Mr Buck's' trip (the accounts of which have vanished) was, as a letter to Sir Andrew Fountaine shows, to study Palladio. On the other hand the letter casts doubt upon the amount of time actually spent on this pursuit:

Dear Knight,
I ought to ask ten thousand pardons for not having thanked you sooner for the favour of your letter, which I received the day before I left Paris, but I am sure, if you knew the constant hurry that I have been in, you would be so good to forgive me, I was forced to make my stay in Vincenza much shorter than I intended for the waters were so out that there was no possibility of seeing any of the villas at any distance from the town besides that I was forced to sleep in a chair, there being but one bed in the house and that so bad that no creature but a frenchman would have gone into it so that you will easily imagine to whose share it fell, the town is so poor that I question whether your letter could have procured me one, you must pardon me for bringing of it back again, for I own I took such an impression of the *Nobili* from the few with whom I was acquainted that I did not deliver it, here has been such violent rains that the road from Venice to this place looks like a sea, I left a great many passengers upon the road and I was the only one that ventured to come on, *Cosucci*[61] are so scarce since you

55 Chatsworth, Devonshire MSS, letters, R. Bruce to Burlington, 29 July 1719.
56 *Survey of London* xxxii, pt 2, 'North of Piccadilly', p. 540.
57 PRO, SP/35/17.
58 PRO, SP/78/165, Stair to Craggs, 9 September 1719.
59 Eveline Cruickshanks, 'Lord North, Christopher Layer and The Atterbury Plot, 1720-21', *The Jacobite Challenge*, ed. Eveline Cruickshanks and Jeremy Black (Edinburgh, 1988), p. 94.
60 PRO, SP/78/165.
61 Venetian dialect for trifles or bagatelles.

Fig. 72 The third Earl of Burlington with his wife and daughters, by Van Loo (*Trustees of the Lismore Estate*)

drained Italy that I could find nothing but some tables at Genova and some drawings of Palladio at Venice.[62]

On 9 September Stair had reported from Paris that Lord Burlington intended to set out 'in a few days for Italy'.[63] He next turned up in Genoa, where he met William Kent. It is impossible to deduce from Kent's letter to Burrell Massingberd, which was written in Paris on 15 November (n.s.),[64] the exact date of this meeting. It is possible that Kent was being deliberately confusing to protect Burlington. It should be remembered that both the families that sponsored Kent's Italian sojourn, the Chesters and the Massingberds, were Jacobites. Kent says he had taken twenty days to get to Paris from 'Geneva', which, even in those days, seems excessive. The probability is, especially when Kent's erratic spelling is taken into account, that he means 'Genova' throughout the letter, in which case he left Genoa around 25 October (n.s.). He says that Lord Burlington was 'going towards Vicenza and Venice to get architects to draw all the fine buildings of Palladio'. Burlington would, in this case, not need to spend any time at all in Vicenza studying the buildings himself. He left Venice on 1 November (n.s.), having been there 'ten or twelve days.'[65] In his annotated copy of Palladio's *I quattro libri dell' architettura*, which is dated Vicenza, 3 November 1719 (n.s.), Burlington mentions his 'second visit' to the city.[66] His first visit could have been a trip from Venice or a stop on his way to Venice, or even one made during his 1714/15 tour because though his entourage did not stop there then this does not necessarily apply to His Lordship. Whichever it was it is difficult to see quite why he had been in such a 'constant hurry' in 1719, if his sole concern was the villas of Palladio. He wrote his letter to Sir Andrew Fountaine in Turin on 6 November (n.s.) and arrived back in Paris on 20 (n.s.).[67] If, on his outward journey, he had taken the same amount of time to get from Paris to the north of Italy he would have arrived there around 26 September (n.s.); and if he met Kent in Genoa around 20 October (n.s.), as seems likely, what did he do with the missing month, since, to judge from his letter to Fountaine he did not use it to make a tour of the Palladian villas?

From circumstantial evidence music historians have always been convinced that he went to Rome to negotiate with the composer, Giovanni

62　Fountaine MSS, letters, 6 November 1719.
63　See note 58 above.
64　Lincolnshire Archives Office, 42MM/B/19A.
65　PRO, SP/99/62, Burgess to Craggs, 3 November 1719.
66　Chatsworth, Devonshire Collection, Palladio, *I quattro libri* ii, p. 6.
67　PRO, SP/78/165, Stair to Craggs, 22 November 1719.

Bononcini, whose services he wanted for the new opera company in London, the Royal Academy of Music. Burlington had attended rehearsals of his opera *Astartus* in Rome in 1715. This is clear from the libretto of the London revision which Rolli dedicated to Burlington. 'This is the very opera that your Excellency, on his first journey to Italy, honoured by his presence at the rehearsals, and which I directed at the Teatro Capranica'[68] If he did go to Rome in 1719, which seems likely, there could have been other reasons. James III, who on 1 September had married Princess Maria Clementina Sobieska, was at Montefiascone. Amongst the *Stuart Papers* at Windsor lies a letter from the king, which could lay the Palladian ghost for ever, if only it were not, for obvious reasons, so cryptic. On 15 October James had written to the duke of Mar who was in Geneva. As this letter was being conveyed by the duke's wife,[69] the king felt he could have 'the pleasure of writing without risk'. He is sending Mar a copy of a memorial he sent to England from Spain which:

> on the King of Spain's account I desired might not fall into any other hands but those of our three chief friends on t'other side, and for the same reason I desire that the particulars relating to his present situation may be only for yourself, for nothing but self-justification could have obliged me at that time to have put them in writing.

James goes on to say that he had 'before that memorial was writt informed my friends in England how matters went with us in Spain'. This is borne out by his letter to Francis Atterbury.[70] It appears from this correspondence that the 'three chief friends' were in a higher position of importance than the most obviously active Jacobites, most of whom were eventually found out or forced into exile. If, and many things point to the possibility, Lord Burlington was one of the 'chief friends' James was referring to, it could explain the true reason for the hurried trip with its delayed departure and the absence of information on this part of the voyage. An official representative of the supreme royalist aristocracy in England bearing congratulations to the King on the gravely important event of his wedding would be in accordance with the etiquette of the time. It could also have been another moment at which Burlington was awarded his Order of the Garter which would then have been added to his recent portrait by Kneller and it perhaps accounts for the payment to the artist for 'two copies of His Lordship's

68 Quoted in Stanley Boorman, 'Lord Burlington and Music', *Apollo of the Arts: Lord
   Burlington and his Circle* (Nottingham, 1973),
   p. 17.
69 RA, SP 45/51.
70 RA, SP 45/57.

picture' made on 9 January 1720.[71] Many visits to James escaped the eyes of the Hanoverian spies, that of the duke of Beaufort in 1726[72] and that of Lord Cornbury and the duchess of Buckingham in 1731,[73] to mention but two.

That Burlington was well known to James can be deduced from a letter to the king from the duke of Mar, written on 5 February 1719 (n.s.). At this time of optimism Mar, who was in England until 1715, was offering advice, James having left England as a babe in arms in 1688:

> When yr Majestie comes to be restored, alow me to informe you of one who In my humble opinion is one of the most proper to serve you as one of yr principal ministers. It is Mr Henry Boyle, unckle to the present Earle of Burlingtone and who is now call'd Ld Carleton . . . he is well worth gaining to yr interest wch I believe will be no difficult work.[74]

This method of identifying Carleton, who had already had a distinguished political career, whilst his nephew had done nothing above-board of note by that date, is perhaps significant.

Lord Burlington's arrivals and departures from Paris in both 1717 and 1719 were carefully noted by Lord Stair, who probably had reason to suspect him: compared with the numbers of Britons who went through Paris, relatively few make the reports, and those who do are often Jacobite-orientated. Perhaps the best portrait of this Scottish diplomat comes from Sir Walter Scott:

> His almost miraculous powers of acquiring information enabled him to detect the most secret intrigues of the Jacobites . . . Lord Stair was always able, by his superior information, to counteract the plots of the Jacobites, and, satisfied with doing so, was often desirous of screening from the vengeance of his own court the misguided individuals who had rashly engaged in them.[75]

On the very day that Stair had written to Secretary Craggs in London telling him of Lord Burlington's departure for Italy he wrote him another letter:

> A man who has ever given me the best intelligence from the Jacobites, that they look upon their affairs to be in a better fashion than ever they were in. He asked

---

71 Chatsworth, Devonshire MSS, Graham and Collier account book.
72 Francescco Valesio, *Diario di Roma* (Milan, 1978), iv, p. 670, 14 May 1726.
73 Eveline Cruickshanks, 'Lord Cornbury, Bol-ingbroke and a Plan to Restore the Stuarts', *Royal Stuart Papers*, 27, p. 2.
74 *Mar's Legacies*, Scottish History Society, 26 (1896), p. 245.
75 Scott, *Tales*, p. 838.

me if we were sure of the Regent? I told him yes. Then says he, we are much mistaken; for we are assured, from hands we think good, that many months will not pass without a rupture between England and France. I told him that was the silliest of all their dreams.[76]

It is tempting to wonder if this was the exiled king's over confident 'chief friend', about to set off on his architectural study tour. It has to be taken into account that if James had been restored, and this was by no means out of the question, and if Lord Burlington was indeed a 'chief friend', those who had an inkling of this would not have wanted to run the risk of forfeiting their estates on a restoration, any more than Jacobites wanted to run that risk at the hands of the Hanoverians.

Shortly after his return to England the young architect earl was invited by Francis Atterbury, bishop of Rochester and dean of Westminster, to draw up plans for a new dormitory for Westminster School. The fact that this project, which had provoked endless controversy, was entrusted to such a comparatively inexperienced architect has puzzled many historians. Atterbury, as official leader of the English Jacobites at that time, was desperately careful not to have any visitors who might arouse suspicion. What could be more convenient than to have his architect arriving at any hour of the day or night, carrying plans that needed to be discussed? And if Burlington was in fact one of the 'chief friends' that the King had mentioned in his letter to Mar, there would have been many more momentous, if in the event less permanent, plans to grapple with. At the precise moment of Burlington's 1717 trip to France Atterbury was sending money to the Jacobites on the other side of the Channel.[77] Burlington's own debts at this time were rated at over £23,000.[78] He overspent on the dormitory, which is in itself not surprising, but overspending was the cover for many surreptitious Jacobite financial transactions, where known Jacobites are involved suspicions are naturally raised.

The duke of Chandos, whose brother was Atterbury's archdeacon at Rochester, is known to have sent money to the exiled court at Saint-Germain in 1715.[79] In 1721 and 1722, at the time at which the Atterbury Plot to overthrow George I was brewing, he wrote many letters blaming his unfortunate son, who was on the Continent, for overspending wildly.[80]

76 *Hardwicke State Papers* (London, 1778), ii, p. 593.
77 *Memoirs and Correspondence of Francis Atterbury*, ed. Folkestone Williams (London, 1869), i, p. 332, Atterbury to Mar, 29 September 1717.
78 *Survey of London*, xxxii, 'North of Piccadilly', p. 446.
79 RA, SP 44/82.
80 Northamptonshire Record Office, Temple Collection, Chandos Letter Book.

Amsterdam was one of the great Jacobite centres for banking and the storage of arms and Lord Caernarvon had dealings with the important banker, Andries Pels, who was used by many Jacobites. In January 1722, Chandos felt compelled to tell Lord Burlington that, as his son has a mild attack of smallpox, his return will be delayed.[81] Belief in the young man's profligacy wanes when, still away in March, he goes to see Lord Lansdowne, one of James III's representatives in Paris and Lord Bolingbroke, the Stuart King's erstwhile Secretary of State.[82] Another traveller who arouses suspicion at this date is Bryan Allett, who makes several appearances in the diary of the non-juring bishop Rawlinson,[83] and who made journeys centred around Bologna, the city of James III's own banker, Belloni. From 1738 Bryan Allett was Burlington's rector at Londesborough, a living he occupied at the time of the rebellion of 1745.

After the failure of the Atterbury Plot the fourth earl of Orrery was committed to the Tower. Lord Burlington and his uncle Lord Carleton each paid £10,000 to bail him out.[84] Orrery, whose debts, like Burlington's, became enormous, paid £20,000 himself. However, the lesson was not learnt, as he subsequently became official leader of the English Jacobites in place of the exiled dean of Westminster.[85]

The composer Bonocini also suffered, it is often thought, as a result of the Atterbury Plot. Whether he had seen Burlington in Rome in 1719 or not, he arrived in England in October 1720 with a contract to work for the Royal Academy of Music. He immediately became connected with two leading Jacobites, the duchess of Buckingham, one of her half-brother James's main agents, and Atterbury. Bononcini was suspended from the opera in 1722. He was evidently also closely associated with Burlington because on 18 October 1720 (o.s.) Paolo Rolli wrote to Giuseppe Riva, Modenese representative in London: 'Bononcino is here already. My Lord Burlington had only just arrived in town when he went into the country for a fortnight and he told me that on his return he will have the house prepared for him.'[86] Bononcini was familiar enough with Lord Burlington to use Burlington House as a *poste restante* for on 24 August 1721 (o.s.) there was a payment 'for the postage of a packet for Signor Bononcini directed from Italy to His Lordship.'[87] The fact that His Lordship does not figure among the subscribers to the publication of the composer's *Cantatas* that appeared in 1721

81   Ibid., 3 January 1722.
82   Ibid., Dr Stuart to Chandos, 20 March 1722.
83   Bodleian Library, Rawlinson MS D1182, diary iii, pp. 1085, 1102, 1106; D1183, diary iv, p. 1520.
84   Lieutenant General Adam Williamson, 'Diary', ed. John Charles Fox, Camden 3rd series, 22 (London, 1912), p. 38.
85   Cruickshanks, 'Atterbury Plot', p. 103.
86   Quoted in Otto Deutsch, *Handel: A Documentary Biography* (London, 1955), p. 115.
87   Chatsworth, Devonshire MSS, Graham and Collier Account Book, 24 August 1721.

is not surprising since he always appears to have distanced himself from anyone who came under a Jacobite cloud (his relation Orrery being a notable exception); this may also account for his dropping of the architect James Gibbs. He may well have known of Gibbs' correspondence with the duke of Mar and his intention to visit Italy (seemingly as a Jacobite agent) in 1717.[88] It may even have been Burlington who discouraged Gibbs from going, particularly if he intended to go himself. The other Italian suspended from the Opera in 1722 was the poet Paolo Rolli, whom Burlington had met in Rome in 1715. Rolli, who had written a poem on the use of riches for the twenty-one-year-old earl in 1715,[89] was appointed librettist to the Royal Academy of Music at its inception in 1719. He was a man many people did not trust, almost certainly on political grounds. Whether Lord Burlington suspended his association with Rolli and Bononcini until the dust had settled is not clear, but Rolli was certainly a member of the Burlington circle again later on, when he taught the earl's daughters.[90]

After the failure of the Atterbury Plot there seems to have been a lull in Jacobite activities. The next phase began in 1725. Burlington's borrowings in the years 1725-32 were enormous.[91] By August 1726 James was trying to borrow money to finance another invasion and, true to form, Burlington left for France on the twenty-third of this month (o.s.).[92] Where he went remains a mystery because for the first time he does not appear in the diplomatic reports from Paris, though the poet Gay was evidently under the impression that he and Lady Burlington spent their two-month stay there.[93] It perhaps shows a measure of Burlington's power that not only his wife but his Catholic brother-in-law, Sir Henry Bedingfeld, went with him to the Continent.[94] 'Mr Buck' features on another Stuart cipher at this date, but this time as 'Lamb' or '2376' on Zeck Hamilton's cipher, which was with the duke of Ormonde in Spain.[95] Ormonde's secretary, Ezekiel Hamilton, was a protestant chaplain, who was also a freemason.[96] A shadowy figure, who may well be Burlington, flits in and out of Atterbury's letters at this time. He first appears in a letter from the exiled bishop, who was in Paris, to the Pretender, written on 16 September (n.s.): 'They that know Robert Walpole well, and come lately from England/ . . . '[97] This one sentence

88 *HMC, Stuart MSS*, v, pp. 24, 27, 48, 378.
89 Carlo Calcaterra, *I lirici del Seicento e dell'Arcadia*, p. 586.
90 Chatsworth, Devonshire MSS, letters, 25 January 1736/7.
91 Chatsworth, Devonshire MSS, Andrew Crotty's account book 1725-1732. I am grateful to Pamela D. Kingsbury for this observation.
92 Ibid., 23 August.
93 Sherburn, *Pope*, ii, p. 415.
94 Ibid., ii, p. 392.
95 RA, SP box 5/146.
96 Frank McLynn, *Charles Edward Stuart* (London, 1988), p. 532.
97 RA, SP 97/47.

demonstrates the need for a key Jacobite to be working with Walpole, rather than against him, in order to be of any major practical use to his king's cause.

In 1727 George I died and was succeeded by the prince of Wales, with whom he had always been at loggerheads, a situation exploited by Stuart supporters. Lord Burlington and his wife, who had never had much contact with George I but who had been far closer to his son, were immediately at the centre of the court. Lady Burlington had already been a lady-in-waiting to the princess of Wales and continued her position now her mistress was queen, while her husband was appointed a privy councillor in 1729 and captain of the band of Gentlemen Pensioners, the king's bodyguard, in 1731. In 1733 Burlington resigned from all his official positions. These resignations puzzled his contemporaries, particularly 'considering how much notice always was taken of him at Court.'[98] It may be that George II had gained an inkling of the captain of his bodyguard's true loyalties and was wise enough not to promote him despite former promises.[99] Whatever the reason, His Lordship was 'not very well satisfied with what was doing.'[100] A clue may be found in a letter from his wife, still a lady in waiting, hoping he might come and see her at Court: 'You have not been forbid it, on the contrary, I am very sure you are wished back again and hope it will happen some time or other to your mind, for it is impossible that the same thing can hold for ever.'[101]

After his resignation Lord Burlington repeated previous history by siding with the prince of Wales, whose relations with his father were as bad as George II's had been with his. The situation was once more exploited by the Jacobites, so much so that the prince was even referred to as a Jacobite himself.[102] Burlington's association with Frederick, prince of Wales, is perhaps best evinced by his connection with the Opera of the Nobility, a company formed in 1733 in opposition to Handel, and therefore the king, the king rather than Handel being the real object. Burlington was a director and his old friend Paolo Rolli the secretary. The chief patron and figurehead was the prince of Wales, who called the first meeting on 15 June.[103] There was always a political undercurrent attached to the opera companies in London, if only because so many of the people associated with them were Italian and Catholic. There seems, however, to have been no doubt about

---

98 *HMC, Carlisle MSS*, (1897), p. 114, Colonel the Hon. Charles Howard to Lord Carlisle, 8 May 1733.
99 See Eveline Cruickshanks above.
100 *HMC, Carlisle MSS*, (1897), p. 115, Sir Tho-

mas Robinson to Lord Carlisle, 24 May 1733.
101 BL, Althorp MSS, box B8, no date 1733.
102 Doran, *London in Jacobite Times*, ii, pp. 77 and 78.
103 Deutsch, *Handel*, p. 304.

the prime political significance of the Opera of the Nobility. The star of the company was the castrato Farinelli, not only a legendary singer but also an astute politician who was acquainted with the exiled Stuarts.[104] When he was later in Spain he interceded successfully with the king and queen on behalf of Jacobite exiles who, as freemasons, were threatened by the Inquisition.[105] Referred to as a 'Blazing Star' by Owen Swiney before he ever set foot in England,[106] this was not a comment on Farinelli's ability as a singer but a reference to the fact that he was a freemason.[107] Sir Thomas Coke, another director of the new opera company and another whose Hanoverian loyalties are open to question,[108] wrote sadly to Lord Burlington in 1736, saying that 'as a virtuoso' he had also 'subscribed to Handel, for which I have been severely reprimanded by my Brethren.'[109] This may well be a reference to the masonic proclivities of the directors of the Opera of the Nobility.

In 1728 Lord Burlington had been forced to begin negotiating the sale of some of his Irish estates.[110] The sales continued and ten years later, in March 1738, the dedicated Jacobite, Alderman John Barber, wrote to Jonathan Swift: 'My Lord Burlington is now selling in one article, nine thousand pounds a year in Ireland, for two hundred thousand pounds, which won't pay his debts.'[111] Burlington had been forced to borrow £22,000 from Hoare's Bank in January 1722,[112] when money was being raised before the Atterbury Plot, which was to include a rebellion in the north of England[113], while in 1725 he lent money to the duke of Beaufort,[114] who visited James III in Rome that year.[115] The timings of these transactions have a significant look.

Although from 1717 until at least 1730 a great deal of money must have been spent at Chiswick, it is difficult to account for Burlington's enormous

104 McLynn, *Charles Edward Stuart*, p. 321.
105 J. Heron Lepper, 'Freemasonry in Spain under Fernando VII', *Ars quatuor coronatorum* 61 (1948), pp. 212-237.
106 Elizabeth Gibson, *The Royal Academy of Music* (New York, 1989), p. 366.
107 The Blazing Star is a well-known masonic term but, for eighteenth-century continental usages, see Baron Tschoudi, *L'étoile flamboyante* (Paris, 1766), and Mozart's masonic opera, *The Magic Flute*, where the Queen of the Night is referred to as 'die sternflammende Königin'.
108 Coke is on Christopher Layer's 'List of Loyal Gentlemen in the County of Norfolk' sent to the Pretender in Rome in 1721, RA, SP 65/10.

For Coke as Jacobite see also BL, Add. MS, 38507, quoted in Jane Clark, 'Palladianism and the Divine Right of Kings', *Apollo*, April 1992, p. 224.
109 BL, Althorp box B8, 20 December.
110 Chatsworth, Devonshire MSS, Irish estate letter book, 1728-29.
111 *The Correspondence of Jonathan Swift*, ed. F Elrington Ball (London, 1914), vi, p. 72.
112 Hoare's Bank Archives, M/L 1718-43, fo. 33.
113 *HMC*, 15th Report, appendix vii, p. 227, Robert Bruce MP to his nephew, Lord Bruce, 15 May 1722.
114 I am grateful to Lucy Abel Smith for this information.
115 See note 72 above.

debt in terms of his building operations and picture collecting, when these are compared with the far more extensive activities of his less rich contemporaries. He had plans to rebuild Londesborough which never came to anything, possibly because of the 1715 rebellion which intervened.[116] He planned to go to Ireland in 1728 to see about rebuilding at Lismore and even dispatched his faithful gardener, Ned Mead, who had been in Rome with him in 1715, to restore the garden, but Mead died in Bristol on the way.[117] A month after Mead's death Burlington wrote: 'Being fully determined to see Ireland in some convenient time I am not for cutting down the park woods or grove till I see them at which time I can best judge whether it will be requisite to rebuild any part of the ruin'd house or not at Lismore.'[118] This plan also came to nothing. The alterations he did make to his existing houses and gardens and the building of Chiswick, which is a mere 70 foot square, and would be dwarfed if it stood beside Holkham or Houghton (which is 450 feet in length), cannot account for the debts that grew worse as the earl's life wore on.

The confident optimism shown by the Jacobites where lending money to their exiled king was concerned appears surprising today. Faith in his return is testified by Lord Cornbury in 1731:

> His Majesty will in his own hand give receipts for such money payable at his Restoration with interest at 5 per cent, and these receipts will be given in the name and dispos'd of in the manner to be mention'd to His Majesty in the several Letters the Bills come in; and the King won't have any difficulty to give interest at 7 or 8 per cent for any considerable sum of money that shall be advanc'd to him.

The romantic means by which letters about the amounts of money raised were to be exchanged at Waters's bank in Paris are spelt out: 'The King will send Mr Waters very soon the broken piece of gold with directions to keep all letters directed for Monsieur Joseph Harrold à Paris and for William Baker Esq. à Paris till some person produce the other piece that tallys with it.'[119] Instructions for paying cash in England are more conventional: 'It may be paid in to Mr Cantillon Bankers in London & Waters's Correspondent.'[120] There is one payment to Philip and David Cantillon in Burlington's surviving accounts but it goes without saying that any substantial payment intended for the exiled monarch would never be recorded.[121]

---

116 Chatsworth, Devonshire MSS, box K, Londesborough Papers, J. Thomspon to Mr Fletcher, 24 August 1713.
117 Chatsworth, Devonshire MSS, Irish estate letter book, 1728-29, 1 March 1728.
118 Ibid., 10 March 1729.
119 RA, SP box 5/177c.
120 Ibid.
121 Chatsworth, Devonshire MSS, Andrew Crotty's account book, November 1726.

From 1731 onwards plans that finally culminated, after many setbacks, in the rebellion of 1745 were continually in progress. That Lord Burlington's financial state was not to be examined too closely is evident from a letter from another trusted servant, who was also in Rome in 1715, Henry Simpson. In September 1735 he writes a heartfelt plea to his master 'not to expose the value of your Lordship's Estate to the Whole Country or to any person who may make sinister use thereof and turn it to Your Lordship's prejudice.'[122] The previous May Simpson had ended a letter: 'I have heard nothing from the other side of the water since my last.'[123]

In 1736 Burlington dismissed one of his other agents, Andrew Crotty. Crotty wrote a threatening letter to his master, saying: 'In my own defence I shall be forced to reveal many parts of your Lordship's affairs which I would avoid as by no means agreeable to your Lordship.'[124] What Crotty had done to deserve dismissal is not clear, unless Burlington suspected him of creaming off some of the rents into his own pocket. This was a perpetual grievance of many landlords and very often had some foundation, but where money was being siphoned off and lent to the exiled Stuarts there was, naturally, a deliberate confusion set up, so it was quite impossible to discover the true state of these accounts. The fourth earl of Orrery's enormous debts were blamed on 'the villainy of the Irish agent' which is clearly unfair though there may be an element of truth in it.[125] The accounts of Burlington's that survive today are far too incomplete to give a true picture of any aspect of his expenditure. Crotty had been a trusted member of Burlington's network, if network it was, in 1731. He wrote to his master from Paris on 14 November (n.s.):

'It was last Sunday before I had the Opportunity of seeing the King nor could I sooner unless I had gone to Rambouillet for there he spent the whole Week till Saturday night; whether the Cardinal [Fleury] has any views of shedding human blood in Europe I know not, but the King seems intent only on the blood of Beasts, for he killed in that Week three Wolves, three Boars & three brace of Staggs, & almost killed his horses and Attendants into the bargain.'[126]

An interesting sequel to this is that when Burlington resigned from his official positions in 1733, Fleury knew about it before the British envoy in Paris.[127]

122 Chatsworth, Devonshire MSS, letters, 10 September 1735.
123 Ibid., 27 May 1735.
124 Ibid., 1 March 1735/6.
125 John Duncombe, *Letters from Italy in the years 1754 and 1755 by the Late Right Honorable John*

Earl of Cork and Orrery (with life) (London, 1773), p. viii.
126 Chatsworth, Devonshire MSS, Letters.
127 PRO, SP/78/204, Waldegrave to Delafaye 27 May 1733. I owe this reference to Dr Jeremy Black.

That the authorities were suspicious of Lord Burlington is revealed by Lady Burlington, writing to her husband on 11 November 1731 (o.s.): 'nor do I think they have gained much by their curiosity who have thought it worthwhile to open our letters, for if I had any secrets to impart to you I should certainly not commit them to the post, especially since the receipt of your last letter which had plainly been opened.'[128] Burlington was then in East Anglia with the duke of Lorraine, who was visiting the duke of Grafton at Euston and Sir Robert Walpole at Houghton. The fear of letters being opened is a thread that runs through all the Burlington correspondence. This is a clear indication that the Government was suspicious of Burlington because warrants were only issued to the postmasters general to open 'suspected treasonable correspondence'. This was particularly strictly controlled in 1731 because in the previous year, in answer to criticism raised against apparent liberties taken in searching mail without warrants, the duke of Newcastle had sent explicit instructions to the postmasters ordering them to open nothing without authority from one of the secretaries of state.[129]

William Kent was, of course, well aware of this. The letters he wrote to both Lord Burlington and his wife during the rebellion of 1745 give no hint that either he or his patron were other than loyal to the Hanoverian regime. His opening remark, in a letter to Lady Burlington dated 31 August (o.s.), is typical of Jacobite correspondence, and can be interpreted in two ways: 'I cannot find you better news than to let you know that the King landed at Margate.'[130] On 17 October he told her that 'we are here in better spirits than in some weeks past, as great preparations are made and the zeal that people show and the troops that are marched into the north, I hope will in a little time put all right again.'[131] At this stage in the rebellion the Hanoverian troops were under the command of General Wade, whose 'extraordinary lack-lustre performance' is one of the great mysteries of the whole exercise.[132] It was not until the duke of Cumberland, George II's third son, was called in that there was any effective resistance to the Stuart army. 'Great preparations' to welcome Prince Charles Edward were indeed being made in London, particularly in the City, which was predominantly Jacobite. The lord mayor was Sir Richard Hoare, son of Henry, Lord Burlington's banker. Henry Hoare, builder of Stourhead, was evidently sympathetically inclined towards the Stuarts and had been counted on for support in the

128 BL, Althorp MSS, box B8.
129 Paul S. Fritz, *The English Ministers and Jacobitism between the Rebellions of 1715 and 1745* (Toronto and Buffalo, NY, 1975), p. 110.
130 Chatsworth, Devonshire MSS.
131 Ibid.
132 Frank McLynn, *The Jacobite Army in England, 1745* (Edinburgh, 1983), p. 197.

Atterbury Plot.[133] Both his sons, Sir Richard and Henry II (creator of the garden at Stourhead), seem to have carried on the family loyalties.[134]

Lord Burlington spent the entire period of the Stuart uprising at Londesborough, conveniently near his great friend General Wade. One of Wade's assistants was General James Edward Oglethorpe, called after his king, James III, and brother of Fanny, who reported Burlington's arrival in Paris in 1717 with such speed to the duke of Mar. Oglethorpe managed to bungle every order he was given (including those issued by Cumberland) and was court-martialled. Wade somehow escaped an enquiry himself, which is another of the mysteries that surround him. His London house was designed by Lord Burlington and was on the architect earl's estate. The general lived there rent-free from 1725 until his death in 1748.[135] That there was always collusion between the two men is suggested by a letter written when the fort of Inverness fell to the rebels during the '45. The writer says that everyone is surprised at the fort being taken so easily but that:

> Mr Wade is now blamed, who was the contriver of these forts that are not worth a Twopence and they seem to have had my Lord Burlington for the architect, rather as an engineer. They say there is a Venetian window in the curtain of one of them, and that of Inverness was so commanded by a hill near it, that from thence you may see a soldier buckle his shoe within the fort.[136]

Even if the remark about Venetian windows was made in jest because of Burlington's well-known Palladian tendencies, it does not diminish the possibility of the Stuart king's 'chief friend' being behind Wade's well-known and, to many Scottish Jacobites, puzzling leniency in the 1720s, when he was supposed to be rendering the Highlanders impotent. Burlington was building the general's London house at this time so it is quite conceivable that the Westminster Dormitory situation repeated itself and that the plans under discussion were not confined to doors and windows. 'General Wade's come to Edinburgh to proceed towards the further execution of the disarming act, which will be of no further consequence than what happened last year' is a fairly typical reaction to Wade's methods.[137] The famous roads, an exercise carried out by the general with unusual efficiency, would have been every bit as useful to a Jacobite army as to a Hanoverian one, possessing the added merit of being paid for by the usurper.

133 Cruickshanks, 'Atterbury Plot', p. 98.
134 Clark, 'Palladianism', p. 501.
135 *Survey of London*, xxxii, 'North of Piccadilly', p. 501.
136 Atholl, Seventh duke of, *Chronicles of the Families of Atholl and Tullibardine* (Edinburgh, 1908) iii, p. 223, Mr Maule to Duke James, 8 March 1746.
137 *Lockhart*, p. 282.

There are, as would be expected, no direct references to Burlington's involvement in the '45, but several cryptic references in the *Stuart Papers* demand consideration. In the spring of 1740 Lord Barrymore, who was connected to Burlington through his wife, went to France to elicit support for an invasion from Cardinal Fleury. On 28 March (n.s.) James III's agent, Lord Sempill, wrote to his king from Paris: 'Besides Lord Barrymore Colonel Bret [an agent who had just returned from England] hopes that a gentleman will be sent from the gentry of Yorkshire who are zealous for the King's preferment.'[138] Fleury had to be convinced that support was forthcoming in England before he would commit himself. In a letter to James's secretary, Edgar, written the same day, Sempill laments the disorganised and indecisive state of the English Jacobites, but says that 'if our Yorkshire Traders send one, as they have promised, in that case I will not doubt of such a supply of arms and foreign troops as shall determine other traders to enter warmly into our measures.'[139] Yorkshire was clearly of key importance in the plans, as it had been in the Atterbury Plot.

During the rebellion Lord Burlington's Yorkshire antiquarian friend, Dr Burton, played an important part. He visited the Stuart Prince at Lancaster and, it is thought, took him money.[140] He told Charles that if he had done what everyone expected and come down the east side of England, which was in fact what the prince had wanted to do but was prevented by Lord George Murray, he would have met many supporters.[141] In view of the fact that Yorkshire, and Burlington himself, were possibly the most important Jacobite elements in England, it may seem strange that communications were so bad. Apart from the understandable paranoia that was a perpetual barrier to communication between clandestine Jacobites, the invasion did not follow any previously laid plans. Princes Charles's headstrong behaviour horrified his cautious father, and probably Lord Burlington as well. The English Jacobites would not lift a finger without French support, for which Charles had been too impatient to wait. Since even in doing the wrong thing, in Dr Burton's eyes, he almost succeeded, if the prince had followed his preferred eastern route and fallen into the welcoming arms of his father's 'chief friend' and his accomplices, the history of Great Britain might have been very different. As well as Dr Burton, Lord Burlington had another connection with the prince. The earl got his wine from a merchant

138 RA, SP 221/109.
139 RA, SP 221/108.
140 McLynn, *Jacobite Army*, p. 148.
141 Ibid., p. 73.

in Edinburgh called William MacDougall[142] who played an extremely important part in the rebellion.[143] Wine barrels were one of the received methods of transporting arms.

The generally accepted view is that after the fiasco of the '45 Stuart support died out, except for a few romantically inclined members of the lunatic fringe. This was in fact far from the case. In 1750 Prince Charles Edward visited London where he met, among others, that steadfast and active supporter, the duke of Beaufort.[144] In October 1747 Lord Burlington was sent a sympathetic account of the Lichfield Riot. The accompanying letter, written from Lancashire by Thomas Johnson, begs His Lordship 'will please not to make use of my name, as I am in a public employment' but tells Burlington that he may be assured that 'this county is not much better' (than Staffordshire) and 'to many seemingly as ripe for rebellion as ever, that if our enemies should make another attempt to invade it may be of worse consequence than the last.'[145] The use of enemies in this context is an example of the problems met in interpreting any Jacobite correspondence.

At the beginning of 1749 Burlington received another letter, this time unsigned, from Paris:

My Lord, I should be asham'd evere to remember that I left England without paying your Lordship my respects, and receaving your commands, but for the Confidence I have in your goodnesse for my pardon. I know you are not ignorant of the Cause which induc'd me to it, from a most unworthy proceeding. Therefore shall say no more of it, But beg leave to take the opportunity of the season to present your Lordship, Lady Burlington, Lady Marquise, and Mademoiselle Violette, with my most hearty wishes of a happy new, and a long succession of many . . . The chief subject of discours here runs upon railing at the peace and such Epithets ar given to it as I dare not wright for the Bastile has had plenty of free talkers, but what has added to the general discontent, is the proceeding in the seizure of him they call Prince Edward, who was taken at the Opera door as he got out of his Coach, as possibly you must have heard, and ty'd hand and foot, and caried to the Dungeon at Vincennes. Cartouche [a celebrated French thief] and he were treated in the same manner, with this difference that the first was broke on the wheel, and the other sent out of the

---

142 Chatsworth, Devonshire MSS, Henry Simpson's letter book, 10 October 1741, 'Mr Macdougall has sent the wine'; Lord Burlington's green vellum account book, 16 July 1748, 'Mr Macdougall of Edinburgh for Hogsheads of Claret; 224.6.0'; John Ferrett account books, 'Mr William Macdougall,' 15 March, 19 July 1748, 17 April 1750, 17 February 1752, 17 February 1753, 31 January 1754.

143 *Memoirs of John Murray of Broughton*, ed. R.F. Bell, Scottish History Society, 27 (1898) p. 103.

144 McLynn, *Charles Edward Stuart*, p. 398.

145 Chatsworth, Devonshire MSS, letters, 10 October 1747.

Kingdom. This treatment is highly resented by all here, and most particularly by the fair sex, and the Poets have exercis'd their Vein upon it in strong satyre. I dare not coppy, but perchance some sample may come to your hands, by which you may give a guess at their sentiments. Such Afiches ar put up, as ar not safe even to read . . . I should thinck it a happinesse if I could be any was servicable to your Lordship here; my letters ar directed by Mr Waters junior. But I am sensible how little your Lordship cares to wright, a line from you is a favour I cant hope for.[146]

The fact that the writer refers to the prince as Edward reveals a certain intimacy[147] and Waters was the Jacobite banking firm in Paris. Clearly this is a Jacobite who had managed to flee England, possibly escaping from a sentence given after the rebellion. Violette was a Viennese dancer, who was sent from Vienna with an introduction to the Burlingtons from the Empress,[148] who later married David Garrick. She was adopted by Lady Burlington who became extremely possessive about her. After her benefit concert in 1747 the anti-Jacobite Lady Shaftesbury remarked acidly: 'I hear Violette, the dancer, had an extravagent full house. I hear the Duke of Richmond gave her sixty guineas for a ticket; the Duke of Devonshire fifty; and Lord Hartington took forty tickets at five guineas each. If this be true, their prodigality flows (I think) in a very irregular channel.'[149] Lady Shaftesbury's thoughts may well have had some foundation since benefit concerts appear, in some cases, to have been covers for raising money for the Stuart cause. The duke of Devonshire and his son, Lord Hartington, would have been horrified at their money going into this 'irregular channel', which perhaps demonstrates the wisdom on the part of the Jacobites in using this particular method of fundraising.

in 1745 Lord Hartington became engaged to Charlotte Boyle, Burlington's younger daughter. This betrothal caused the duchess of Devonshire to leave her husband, so strong were her feelings against the match, but her reasons for this rift are not clear from the correspondence.[150] Lord Hartington, though he proved a devoted husband, reasoned with his mother on the grounds that if his view had been to 'make such a Choice as might be advantagious to the family, it was a laudable one.'[151] Since Lord

146 Ibid., 5 January 1749.
147 I am grateful to Dr Eveline Cruickshanks for this observation.
148 E.J. Climenson, *Elizabeth Montagu 1720-1761: The Queen of the Blue Stockings* (London, 1906), ii, pp. 145 and 146.
149 *Letters of the First Earl of Malmesbury, his Family and Friends 1745-1820*, ed. (third) Earl of Malmesbury (London, 1870), i, p. 51. Lady Shaftesbury to Mr Harris, MP, March 1747.
150 Chatsworth, Devonshire MSS, letters, 6 and 7 January 1745/6, Devonshire to Hartington.
151 Ibid., draft of Hartington's letter to his mother, April 1748.

Burlington's enormous debts were famous it cannot have been on financial grounds. As early as 1737 Sir William Heathcote had seen a list of the earl's debts amounting to £169,000.[152] One possible explanation lurks in the background to this sad family situation which is that the Devonshires knew, or suspected (Devonshire was one of the 1717 opposition group), Lord Burlington's important link with the Stuarts.[153] Clearly in the very possible event of a Stuart victory it would be wise for a loyal Hanoverian Whig family to have an ally in one of the returned monarch's 'chief friends'. No one could be blamed for hedging their bets in 1745. And if, as was the case, the invasion proved a failure, the only objection to Charlotte, who proved a devoted wife during her sadly short marriage (she died in 1754), would be her father's debts and mortgages. The Burlingtons, on the other hand, were delighted with the match. After the wedding in 1748 Sir Andrew Fountaine wrote to Isaac Gervais, the Irish cleric who had accompanied Burlington on his first trip to the Continent: 'Our friends at Burlington House are now in great joy having married Charlotte their only daughter to the Marquis of Hartington, a young nobleman with the best character and the greatest hopes.'[154]

In 1741 Lord Burlington's other daughter, Dorothy had married a great grandson of Charles II, the earl of Euston, son and heir of the duke of Grafton. This marriage was a complete disaster. Dorothy was, by all accounts, 'an angel' but her young husband treated her with such ferocious cruelty that within a year she was dead. Since Lord Euston was, by all accounts, a very strange young man it seems odd that the Burlingtons consented to the match, particularly since they seem to have been devoted parents. All Dorothy's letters to her mother reveal a gentle and considerate character whose chief desire was to do her bidding. On one occasion, when a trap carrying the two children overturned, Dorothy was so keen to reassure Lady Burlington that she insisted that Charlotte 'liked it so well she wished for another.'[155] On another occasion she wrote: 'I found three new laid eggs today and I took them for you told me I might have what was laid while you was away. I gave one to my sister.'[156] At the time of her wedding Henry Pelham reported that Euston's bad behaviour had 'caused a dejectedness which I never saw before' in the duke of Grafton.[157] Pelham depended

152 HMC, Egmont MSS, ii, (1923), diary of the first earl of Egmont, p. 452, 12 December.
153 W.A. Speck, Stability and Strife: England, 1714-60 (London, 1977), p. 190.
154 Fountaine MSS, letters, 4 April 1748.
155 Chatsworth, Devonshire MSS, letters, 1 February 1738.
156 Ibid., 2 November 1736.
157 University of Nottingham Library, Galway and Newcastle Collections, MS G12777/7, Pelham to Richard Arundell, 9 October 1741.

'on the young Lady's good sense and temper to bring about that which hitherto has made no progress. For her sake.' he says, 'I heartily wish it, for I truly think I never saw so engaging a creature in my life.'[158] However, things went from bad to worse and a fortnight later Pelham wrote of the Burlingtons: ' I must say, I have never seen a more miserable family that theirs justly was, the Duke of Grafton the same.'[159] To start with Dorothy's parents behaved in an astonishingly insensitive manner. Lady Burlington, who was not an easy mother-in-law (even the well-mannered and good-natured Hartington later had trouble with her), took umbrage at her son-in-law's behaviour (he had forbidden her to go to his house) and refused to see Dorothy. The worried and patient Pelham 'at last' managed to persuade Lord Burlington that it would be 'cruel' not to see his daughter, 'who alone could not have offended.'[160] Upon their daughter's death the Burlingtons were inconsolable and broke off relations with the duke of Grafton at once. Lord Burlington had not spoken to the duke of Grafton for 'upwards of twelve months', Henry Simpson reported thirteen months after her death.[161] Observers were critical of Lady Burlington for allowing the wedding to proceed but Dorothy was, by all accounts, in love with this odd choice. It was said that Euston was in love with his brother's widow but no sympathy was accorded him on this account. Rumours of an affair between Lady Burlington and Grafton, which have been held up as a reason for this unfortunate match, are not born out by her copious letters to her husband. These rumours stem from Lord Hervey, who is renowned for being unreliable, particularly if he did not like someone. Lady Burlington may have been difficult but she was clearly a devoted wife, as rings out from all her letters. In the context of Lord Burlington's possible proximity to the exiled Stuart king, the disastrous marriage of his daughter to one of that king's relations demands attention.

Two of Lord Burlington's sisters married into traditionally Jacobite families. Elizabeth Boyle married Sir Henry Bedingfeld in 1719, while her brother was away on the Continent. Evidently Burlington already knew and thought well of Sir Henry but, perhaps because he was a Catholic, Elizabeth bravely took the precaution of eloping:

Dear Brother, As I have allways had the greatest proof of your affection and kindness to me when I was in your house, (for which I am most truely grateful),

158 Ibid.
159 Ibid., 22 October.
160 Ibid.

161 Chatsworth, Devonshire MSS, Henry Simpson's letter book, 30 April 1743.

so I must now beg the continuation of your favour since I have left it. I am married to Sir Harry Bedingfeld a person of whom you seem'd to have so good an opinion that I have great reason to hope I shall have the happiness of your aprobation, the assurance of it from your self, and the satisfaction of hearing you are in health is most earnestly wish'd by your most affectionate sister . . . when I receive the favour of a letter from you I beg you will direct it for me at Oxburgh Hall in Norfolk.[162]

Despite religious differences (Elizabeth did not become a Catholic) and the tensions caused by having to educate their sons abroad, this marriage was long and happy. Apart from the initial inconvenience of having her allowance stopped until her brother gave his consent to its being restored to her,[163] there seem to have been no problems between the two families.

Juliana Boyle married Thomas Bruce, third earl of Ailesbury, whose father was an active Jacobite living in exile in Brussels. Burlington was on excellent terms with this brother-in-law as well. It is tempting to wonder if he visited the second earl of Ailesbury on any of his continental trips.

Lord Burlington's servants also were of royalists families. His secretary, Richard Graham, and the family lawyers, William and Anthony Abdy caused no anxiety, as the more ephemeral relationships with James Gibbs and Giovanni Bononcini seem to have done, being old family retainers. However, Lord Burlington felt impelled to dismiss Graham in 1725, on the possibly genuine pretext that he had mismanaged his affairs,[164] but it may also be that the Graham family's Jacobite loyalty had become an embarrassment. Lady Burlington was cautioned about her lawyer by her son-in-law, now the duke of Devonshire, in 1756, three years after Lord Burlington's death:

I receiv'd the favour of your letter with Sir Anthony's enclos'd, and you may depend upon it that I shall at all times be most excessively glad to do whatever you desire of me, at the same time I am sure you will not take it ill if I speak my mind freely to you; Sir Anthony and his father's Principles have been a little heretofore called in question, and his Friends and the company that he has kept have been of that stamp for which reason the King may find fault with me for recommending him, and therefore in order to obviate that difficulty, if Sir Anthony will make an avowal (which I am persuaded he will have no objection to) to Your Ladyship or Mr. Arundell of his loyalty and attachment to the King,

162 Chatsworth, Devonshire MSS, letters, 28 August 1719.
163 Ibid., Graham and Collier to Burlington, 22 October 1719.
164 *Survey of London*, 'North of Piccadilly', xxxii, p. 447.

I give Your Ladyship or Mr Arundell full powers to make use of my name in his behalf.[165]

Lord Burlington's children were taught by Catholics. The poet Paolo Rolli,[166] the painter Louis Goupy[167] and the musician Adamo Scola[168] all paid regular visits to Burlington House and Chiswick. This may be accounted for in the light of their father's interest in French and Italian culture, but it may equally be that these three men, all evidently Jacobite sympathisers and possibly willing and trusted messengers as well, were in need of a legitimate excuse to visit the Catholic James III's 'chief friend', if a chief friend he was. But it must be emphasised, whatever the extent of Lord Burlington's loyalty to that King, like most English Jacobites, he would never have consented to a restoration if there had been any threat of an officially Catholic State. Lord Orrery was most insistent with James on this issue.[169] It is probable that in the enlightened eighteenth century the head of the Boyle family was prepared to accept the religious toleration that he showed amongst his family and friends. One of the closest of these friends was the Catholic, Alexander Pope, whose condolence on Lord Burlington's Hanoverian Garter was echoed by the earl's brother-in-law, the third earl of Ailesbury, whose father converted to Catholicism after his exile: 'My dear Lord, I received the favours of yours last night. In the first place all here wish you much joy of your Garter. Then to come to our other business . . . ' The other, and clearly more important business, was arrangements for 'rooms in the Woods' at Tottenham Park and for a house at Bradfield that Burlington was interested in.[170] Like Kent's letters in the '45, the remark about the Garter is capable of opposite interpretations. In view of the fact that the Order of the Garter was the highest honour a sovereign could bestow on a worthy subject, this is lukewarm congratulation indeed so, as with Pope, an ironic message seems to be the likely one.

In the absence of direct evidence concerning the English Jacobites, the symbolism they used is one of the most revealing sources. It has to be treated with caution but the repetitions and the cumulative evidence do

165 Chatsworth, Devonshire MSS, letters, 26 February.
166 Ibid., Paolo Rolli's Account 25 January 1736/7.
167 Ibid., Louis Goupy's Receipt, 5 December
1739.
168 Ibid., Adamo Scola's Account 5 July 1739.
169 *HMC, Stuart MSS*, vi, p.260.
170 Chatsworth, Devonshire MSS, letters, 23 May 1730.

contribute greatly to our knowledge of those involved in the Stuart cause. Because the Restoration of 1660 was successful and the royalist allegiance of the families concerned revealed, it is easier to be sure of the messages hidden in portraits, ceilings, gardens and elsewhere in this period. Where these same messages appear in the eighteenth century, more often than not a clandestine Jacobite loyalty is revealed or, as with Lord Burlington, suggested, by documentation.

In order to understand the values of the architect earl it is necessary to go back to Frederick, elector Palatine and his wife, James I's daughter, Elizabeth, the 'Winter Queen'. Their court at Heidelberg was a centre of Protestant learning; open-minded and enlightened, the elector encouraged every form of art and science. It was as a mission ordained by God, against catholic Habsburg repression, that Frederick misguidedly accepted the throne of Bohemia in 1619. His brief winter reign ended in the dark ages of the Thirty Years War, in which enlightenment did not perish but went underground. The religious ideals that Frederick and Elizabeth believed in so fervently had been gathering force for many years, fostered by secret influences moving towards solving religious problems along mystical lines suggested by Hermetic and Cabalistic influences.[171] Alchemy, astrology and scientific research played an important part.

After their defeat by the Habsburgs, Frederick and Elizabeth set up their exiled court at the Hague. Here refugee members of this movement, known as the Rosicrucians or the Invisible College of the Red Cross Brothers, were protected. Here also, after the execution of Charles I, flocked exiles from Britain, including the young Charles II. One of these exiles was a brother of the Calvinist-inclined first earl of Burlington, Lord Shannon, whose wife bore one of Charles's many illegitimate children.[172] Another of the first earl's brothers, the scientist Robert Boyle, was a member of a secret society in England during the Commonwealth, a society likewise known as the Invisible College.[173] Its members were involved in the Restoration of Charles II.

Another secret society working towards restoring the Stuart line during the Commonwealth was the Sealed Knot. Closely associated with this group was Elizabeth Dysart, later duchess of Lauderdale,[174] whose ceilings at Ham House are echoed by those of Lord Burlington across the Thames at Chiswick. Lady Dysart was a remarkable woman who, while working to

171 Frances Yates, *The Rosicrucian Enlightenment* (London and New York, 1986), p. 40.
172 Chapman, *Charles II*, p. 128.
173 Yates, *Rosicrucian Enlightenment*, p. 182.

174 Doreen Cripps, *Elizabeth of the Sealed Knot* (Kineton, 1975), pp. 43-49; David Underdown, *Royalist Conspiracy in England* (New Haven, 1960), p. 269.

restore the king, was nevertheless a close friend of Cromwell. When she travelled abroad, which she did frequently, she managed to confuse everyone so completely that she was accused by the very people she was supporting of being a Commonwealth spy.[175] It is useful to remember this when considering Lord Burlington's travels abroad. The subject of the ceiling painting in her White Closet at Ham House is the Liberal Arts, presided over by Wisdom, who raises her hand to Heaven.[176] God is represented by an all-seeing eye, symbol of every masonic lodge. The Liberal Arts became part of the Fellow Craft Degree in freemasonry.[177] The painting is surrounded by sphinxes, traditional guardians of the masonic Temple and the four Cardinal Virtues, all-important in freemasonry.

Lady Dysart was said to have the gift of second sight and was even thought to be a witch,[178] an accusation often levelled at Rosicrucians. In a remarkable portrait by Lely, also at Ham,[179] she stares into space as she touches a rose. For the Rosicrucians the rose was a symbol of secrecy[180] a meaning continued into the eighteenth century, when it was a symbol of feminine initiation into masonry.[181] It also had an alchemical meaning. The basket of flowers is held by a black servant who represents darkness, or hidden knowledge, a typical Rosicrucian or masonic image that continued at least until the days of Sarastro's black servant, Monostatos, in Mozart's masonic opera, *The Magic Flute*.[182] There is a masonic motto, *Lux e Tenebris*, light out of darkness. For royalist families involved in the Restoration of Charles II the black servant had another meaning. Sir John Hinton, Charles's physician, relates in his memoirs, that General Monk drank to the health of 'his Black Boy', a title perpetuated in the public houses of that name which were named after the King.[183] Monk is held by many people to have been a freemason, so whether the Black Boy was a symbol adapted to fit Charles, who was well-known for being dark and swarthy, or whether Charles was the cause of the masonic use of the symbol is not clear. What is quite clear is the fact that an early form of Freemasonry was employed by Stuart supporters whenever that family was in difficulty. A well-known poem written during Charles I's troubles in Scotland bears this out.

175 Cripps, *Elizabeth*, p. xviii.
176 Maurice Tomlin, *Ham House* (London, 1986), p. 37.
177 Nesta H. Webster, *Secret Societies* (London, 1924), p. 163 n. 1.
178 Cripps, *Elizabeth*, pp. 45–46.
179 Ibid., plate 5.
180 David Stevenson, *The Origins of Freemasonry* (Cambridge, 1988), pp. 97–98.
181 Jacques Chailly, *The Magic Flute: Masonic Opera* (London, 1972), plate 9.
182 Ibid., p. 105.
183 Sir John Hinton, *Memoirs* (London, 1689), p. 28.

For we be brethren of the rosie cross;
We have the mason-word & second sight,
Things for to come we can foretell aright,
And shall we know what mystery we mean,
In fair acrosticks Carolus Rex is seen.[184]

Second sight seems to have meant knowledge that is gained from secret or occult sources or, in practical terms, being able to understand the cryptic means of communication employed by clandestine Stuart supporters.

There is an equally striking portrait, by Aikman, of Lord and Lady Burlington, both staring into space. Lady Burlington is dressed as a Guercino Sybil and she is mysteriously pointing to a completely empty piece of paper.[185] The Cumaean Sybil, who led Aeneas into the Underworld, where the future of Rome was revealed to him, was very significant in the Jacobites' adoption of the *Aeneid* as their great political allegory. This use of the *Aeneid* began with the translation by a nephew of the duke of Lauderdale, Elizabeth Dysart's second husband, while he was in exile with James II at Saint-Germain. Guercino himself was well-versed in the symbolism adopted by early freemasons, his painting of *The Raising of the Master* is in the possession of the Supreme Royal Arch Chapter of Scotland.[186] Lord Burlington holds compasses, attribute of the Master of a masonic lodge,[187] over an equally blank piece of paper. The members of the Invisible College, including Robert Boyle, and the Sealed Knot used invisible ink in their communications and lived in perpetual dread of losing the recipe for disclosing their messages. Boyle's friend, Sir Robert Moray, one of the first documented freemasons, used it in his correspondence with the duke of Lauderdale.[188] White ink, as it was called, was also used by Jacobites in the eighteenth century, as, amongst others, Fanny Oglethorpe testified in the *Stuart Papers*.[189] It is more than likely that the prominently displayed blank sheets of paper in the Aikman portrait of Lord and Lady Burlington refer to this ink.

Just as Ham House reveals the undoubted masonic affiliations of the Dysarts and the Lauderdales, so Chiswick House reveals those of the Burlingtons. The third earl's architectural masterpiece completely baffled

184 Henry Adamson, *The Muse's Threnody* (Perth, 1774), p. 84.

185 John Wilton-Ely, 'Lord Burlington and the Virtuoso Portrait', *Architectural History*, 27 (1984); idem, 'Design and Practice in British Architecture', *Studies in Architectural History, Presented to Howard Colvin*, pp. 376-78.

186 J.S.M. Ward, *Freemasonry and the Ancient Gods* (London, 1926), illustration facing p. 134.

187 'The Trial of John Coustos by the Inquisition', *Ars quatuor coronatorum*, 65 (1954), p. 114.

188 Stevenson, *Origins of Freemasonry*, p. 170.

189 *HMC, Stuart MSS*, v, p. 100.

his contemporaries. 'A small cupboard stuck with pictures';[190] 'Too little to live in and too large to hang to one's watch';[191] and 'rather curious than convenient'[192] are only some of the comments the villa provoked. Its miniature proportions were the source of constant wonder and foreign travellers, particularly, were puzzled in comparing it to other stately homes. Perhaps the one comment that solves the mystery is that of Lord Burlington's friend, Sir John Clerk of Penicuik, who dined at Chiswick, in the old house where the family always lived, in 1727. He described the 'new house' as '70 foot square.'[193] Whether Sir John, as a fellow freemason,[194] was aware that the remark had a special masonic significance, would depend on the degree of masonry to which he had risen.

Freemasonry as practised in the early eighteenth century, with its roots in Scotland and its inextricable associations with the Stuart cause, was viewed with suspicion by the Hanoverians. After the failure of the Atterbury Plot to overthrow George I in 1722, and the Grand Mastership of the Jacobite duke of Wharton which ended in 1723, the Hanoverians clamped down on the Brotherhood in an effort to rid it of its Jacobite element. Craft masonry, that is the first three degrees, through which all masons were supposed to pass, became officially Hanoverian. At this point Jacobite masonry went underground though Jacobite masons were not expelled from their former Craft lodges. In order to establish an exclusively Jacobite branch of masonry, higher degrees were added, with their own rituals and ever more stringent oaths of secrecy.[195] The higher degree known as the Royal Arch, and others modelled on the ancient knights of the Crusades, the Templars and Hospitaliers, originated, it seems, at least as early as the restoration of Charles II, and were closely connected with already existing secret societies on the Continent.

In the masonic secret code instituted by the exiled James II at Saint-Germain Great Britain was the Promised Land and London Jerusalem.[196] The Jacobites were the exiled Israelites.[197] The Jews had been banished for seventy years when the benevolent monarch Cyrus invited them to return to Jerusalem and build the Second Temple. An important aspect of Royal

---

190   Chatsworth, Devonshire MSS, letters, Elizabeth Finch to Lady Burlington, 5 June 1735, quoting a remark made by the young duke of Cumberland.

191   Lord Hervey, quoted in Richard Hewlings, *Chiswick House and Gardens* (London, 1991), p. 37.

192   Sir John Clerk, quoted ibid., p. 36.

193   Quoted in John Fleming, *Robert Adam and his*

Circle (London, 1962), p. 26.

194   Stevenson, *Origins of Freemasonry*, p. 199.

195   J.E.S. Tuckett, 'The Origin of Additional Degrees', *Ars quatuor coronatorum*, 32, (1919), pp. 5-55.

196   Le Couteulx de Canteleu, *Les sectes et les sociétés secrètes* (Paris, 1863), p. 108.

197   Murray Pittock, 'New Jacobite Songs of the '45', *Voltaire Foundation* (1989), p. 31.

Arch masonry is an adapted version of the return of the Israelites under Joshua, at the invitation of Cyrus, and the building of the Second Temple.[198] The perennial hope of the exiled Stuart Kings was that the usurpers of their throne might be persuaded to act like Cyrus and invite them to return peacefully to their 'Promised Land'.[199] During the Commonwealth the first earl of Orrery, one of the first earl of Burlington's many brothers, suggested to Cromwell that he could bring the king back 'and retain the same authority with less trouble.' Cromwell replied that the King would never forgive him his father's blood. Orrery's answer to that understandable worry was: 'You are one of the many that are concerned in that, but you would be alone in the merit of restoring him.'[200] This persuasion, with the moral reward of magnanimity, was no more succesful with William III, Queen Anne or the Hanoverians than it had been with Cromwell. It may have been the true reason for Burlington's resigning from all his official positions in 1733. Possibly, as one of James III's 'chief friends', in his position of close proximity to George II as captain of the band of Gentlemen Pensioners, Lord Burlington hoped to persuade the usurper to invite the exiled Israelites to return and go back to his own lawful lands in Germany. If Chiswick was a symbolic Second Temple, built either as a homage to his exiled king or even as a palace on the lines of Greenwich (to which it makes many references) to welcome that king home, it immediately appears perfectly 'convenient'. It also makes the possibility of the architect earl being one of that king's 'chief friends' more probable.

Like the masonic ceiling of Elizabeth Dysart's White Closet at Ham, Lord Burlington surrounded his villa with sphinxes, two guarded the entrance and three the northern face of the house. God is represented at Chiswick not by an all-seeing eye as at Ham, but by Architecture, on the ceiling of the Blue Velvet Room. The figure on the original drawing for this ceiling is God the Father and Burlington has simply substituted His masonic role as Grand Architect of the Universe.[201] Architecture sits on a column (masonic symbol of stability),[202] crowned with a Corinthian capital, symbol of rebirth,[203] accompanied by three *putti*, the equivalent of the Three Boys in the *Magic Flute*.[204] The *putti* hold the symbols of Craft masonry, plumb-

198 Leslie J. Biddle, 'The Principal Characters in the Royal Arch Story', *Ars quatuor coronatorum*, 79 (1966), pp. 283-89; Keith B. Jackson, *Beyond the Craft* (London, 1982), p. 12.
199 For two examples, see Haile, *James Francis Edward*, p. 64, Mary of Modena to Queen Anne; RA, SP 45/52A, Mar to James III, October 1719.
200 Chapman, *Charles II*, p. 323.
201 Chatsworth, Devonshire Collection. I am grateful to Pamela D. Kingsbury for this information.
202 Chalmers I. Paton, *Freemasonry* (London, 1873), p. 121.
203 Hewlings, *Chiswick*, p. 12.
204 Chailly, *The Magic Flute*, p. 114.

line, square and level. Architecture holds compasses, attribute of the Master of a lodge.[205] The surrounding design is punctuated at regular intervals by plumb-lines, important in the Craft Installation of 'Antient' masonry,[206] the type to which Lord Burlington would have belonged. If, as seems probable, this room was a Craft lodge, blue is the appropriate colour. Blue was the colour of the Craft and Craft masons known as the Blue Masons.[207] This room, which is on the *piano nobile*, is approached from the ground floor by a narrow winding staircase of fifteen steps. Eighteenth-century tradition held that the floors of Solomon's Temple were connected by a cochlear winding staircase of fifteen steps, the sum of the significant masonic numbers of three, five and seven.[208] Such early traditions and legends as survive constantly raise the suspicion that they could have originated at Chiswick.

From the Blue Velvet Room the mason would make the logical progression to a higher degree lodge, the Red Velvet Room, red being the colour of the Royal Arch and higher degree masons the Red Masons.[209] The main theme of the Royal Arch ritual is that of resurrection and restoration. One of the components of the early Scottish masonry that came to England with the Stuarts was the cult of Hermes and the study of Hermetic philosophy with its 'striving for enlightenment and spiritual rebirth of mankind, based on secret knowledge and secret societies,' a legacy of the Rosicrucians.[210] The ceiling painting in the Red Velvet Room portrays the resurrection of the arts by Hermes. Architecture is represented by a fallen bust of Inigo Jones and painting by an oval portrait of William Kent, who features along with Burlington in the *Freemason's Pocket Companion* of 1736.[211] Kent appears to be having the red veil of the Royal Arch removed from his eyes. In the early days of the Royal Arch the 'passing of the veils' symbolised 'the enlightenment that came with masonic progression' or in alchemical terms 'the uncovering of the inner faculty of insight and wisdom;'[212] in other words the gift of second sight. In biblical terms the veils were connected with the 'sufferings of the Jews returning from exile' and with 'the mysterious veil that was rent in twain when the crucified Saviour passed through it.'[213] In Jacobite terms this is a reference to the exiles and to the 'Crucifixion' of Charles I. The masonic symbols of mallet, compass and square are

205 See note 187 above.
206 Bernard E. Jones, *The Freemason's Book of the Royal Arch* (London, 1957), p. 251.
207 J.M. Roberts, *The Mythology of the Secret Societies* (New York, 1971), p. 40.
208 Jones, *Royal Arch*, p. 143; George Oliver, *The Freemason's Treasury* (London, 1863), pp.

254–57.
209 Roberts, *Mythology*, p. 96.
210 Stevenson, *Origins of Freemasonry*, p. 85.
211 *The Freemason's Pocket Companion* (London, 1736), p. 11.
212 Jones, *Royal Arch*, p. 195.
213 Ibid.

all present. The painting is dominated by Hermes, who appears in the upper half, separated from the earthly bodies by a Royal Arch. Above the arch and behind Hermes is a rainbow. A masonic ritual of 1723 asks this question: 'Whence comes the pattern of an arch?' and the answer that should be given by the initiate is; 'From the rainbow.'[214] An arch beneath a rainbow is a common subject for early Royal Arch banners and these rainbows sometimes contain signs of the Zodiac. The signs of the Zodiac appropriate for Hermes, Virgo and Gemini, are present in the rainbow in the Red Velvet Room. This central panel of the ceiling is surrounded by other signs of the Zodiac with their Gods. The study of the stars was an important aspect of Hermetic philosophy and a key to secret knowledge. The Zodiac is present in many Royal Arch chapters, also on ancient banners and floor cloths. The image of Hermes was used throughout the eighteenth century as a masonic jewel.[215] Hermes is accompanied by two *putti*, one holding a jewel and the other a cornucopia, another masonic symbol.[216] Portrait busts of Burlington and Pope occupy the end panels of the ceiling. Pope's 'Universal Prayer' is quoted in the *Ceremonies of Pure and Antient Masonry*.[217]

In the centre of the ceiling is a star composed of eight equilateral triangles. This is possibly a composite reference to the Imperial Crown (Augustus) which was made up of 'eight plates,'[218] the eight-pointed Garter Star, and the sun, all-important in masonry. Elias Ashmole, one of the earliest known freemasons, described how this star, 'as it is usually called' was 'assumed' by Charles I, 'upon the Sun's appearance like three Suns, which suddenly united together into one, immediately before his fortunate Victory at the Battle of Mortimer's Cross, an occasion, which he thought himself much oblig'd to perpetuate.'[219] Charles as sun king, with his particularly close association with the Order of the Garter, became one of the mainstays of Stuart and Jacobite symbolism. Charles's portrait, with his family, hangs in the adjacent Tribunal, where another eight-pointed star graces the floor.

Burlington would have been well aware of Charles I as 'Mercurian Monarch' and of the association of the Order of the Garter with an Egyptian, Hermetic past.[220] His desire to possess the Inigo Jones designs for the Jacobean and Carolingian masques may have been as much for his belief in the symbolism of these great allegorical pageants as for his interest in the

214 Ibid., p. 38.
215 Ibid., p. 229.
216 Paton, *Freemasonry*, p. 444.
217 W.J. Williams, 'Alexander Pope and Freemasonry', *Ars quatuor coronatorum*, 38 (1925), p. 113.
218 Jacques Le Goff, *Medieval Civilisation* (Lon-

don, 1988), p. 269.
219 Elias Ashmole, *The Institution, Laws and Ceremonies of the Most Noble Order of the Garter* (London, 1672), p. 216.
220 Douglas Brook-Davies, *The Mercurian Monarch* (Manchester, 1983), pp. 89, 106-7.

draughtsman himself. It is possible to trace the symbolism of the ceiling in the Red Velvet Room to Carew's great *Coelum Britannicum* for which Jones did the designs. Here Hermes/Mercury is associated with 'a young man in a white embroidered robe/ . . . / holding in his hand a cornucopia filled with corn and fruits, representing the genius of these kingdoms'. When he descends at the beginning of the masque he establishes Charles I and Henrietta Maria as Gemini.[221] The climax of the masque comes with 'the prospect of Windsor Castle', seat of the Order of the Garter, which for Carew meant the Order of Hermetic reform, 'its members the stellified virtues who inhabit the eighth sphere of spiritual rebirth'.[222] Thus Hermes, as patron of the arts, of which the Stuart monarchs were the traditional guardians,[223] may be seen to be restoring this symbolic kingdom to its rightful heirs. The evident legacy from a Hermetic, Stuart past that manifests itself in Royal Arch symbolism may stem from Lord Burlington. As builder of the Second Temple, the aspect of Royal Arch masonic symbolism that he inherited from the exiled James II, was Burlington perhaps the mysterious 'Joshua of the Red masons?'[224]

All higher degrees of masonry are pyramidal and, despite Prince Charles Edward's deliberate obfuscation in 1777, James III and his son do seem to have been the 'Unknown Superiors'.[225] If Burlington was one of James's 'chief friends' he was possibly the 'Unknown Superior' in England, his identity being known to only a few carefully chosen initiates. Perhaps it is no coincidence that Royal Arch masonry is first mentioned at Youghal, where the Boyle estates in Ireland lay.[226] That this is as late as the 1740s is not surprising considering its Jacobite *raison d'être* and the secrecy that must have surrounded it. Equally significant may be the fact that Lord Burlington based his Assembly Rooms at York on Palladio's Egyptian Hall, while the Royal Arch Chapters of Edinburgh and Dublin, to mention but two, are Egyptian Halls. Once more, the architect earl may have left his mark on Royal Arch masonry.

Royal Arch masons and the Craft masons of the lodges that remained independent of the Hanoverian Grand Lodge rejected the changes in the ritual made in the 1730s and stuck to their 'Antient' constitutions. In 1744 'some of the Fraternity', that is the official Grand Lodge, complained that the secrets of the Royal Arch were being kept from them but the 'Antients' stuck to their independence. In the 1760s they began to relent and by 1766,

221 Ibid., p. 105.
222 Ibid., p. 106.
223 Ibid., p. 109.
224 F. de P. Castells, *English Freemasonry in its*

Period of Transition (London, 1931), p. 123.
225 McLynn, *Charles Edward Stuart*, pp. 532-35; Monod, *Jacobitism*, p. 303.
226 Jones, *Royal Arch*, p. 45.

thirteen years after the death of Lord Burlington, they were officially recognised.[227]

That Lord Burlington was an important mason is evident from the first edition of Dr James Anderson's *Constitutions of the Freemasons*, commissioned in 1721.[228]

> Then in our songs be justice done
> To those who have enrich'd the Art,
> From Jabal down to Burlington
> And let each Brother bear a part
> Let noble Masons' Healths go round
> Their praise in lofty Lodge resound.[229]

Anderson prefaces his *Constitutions* with a history of the 'Royal Art' of architecture from Jabal down to the earl of Burlington, 'who bids fair to be the best Architect of Britain (if he is not so already).'[230] Since in 1721, or even 1723 when the *Constitutions* appeared, there were far more deserving candidates for this honour than the twenty-seven-year-old earl who had very little in the way of literal architectural achievement behind him, it seems probable that Anderson, a Scot himself and son of the former secretary of the Lodge of Aberdeen, was using the word in its metaphorical sense. To Dryden, one of Burlington's 'favoured authors'[231] and Pope, both Jacobite sympathisers, and presumably to all Royal Arch masons who were by definition Jacobites, architecture implied civilisation itself,[232] which in its turn implied a restoration of Augustus in the form of the House of Stuart.

Anderson's history, seen through the eyes of eighteenth-century freemasons, is a mixture of fact and fancy, of history and legend. It stresses the importance of 'the glorious Augustus' who became 'Grand Master of the Lodge at Rome' and of his patronage of Vitruvius, the remains of whose buildings 'are the Pattern and Standard of true Masonry in all future Times.'[233] For Dr Anderson the Stuarts were of major importance. James I and Charles I being Mason Kings, were responsible for restoring the 'Augustan Stile' through 'the great Palladio and the glorious Inigo Jones.'[234]

227 R.A. Wells, 'Why the Royal Arch?', *Ars quatuor coronatorum*, 78 (1965), pp. 217-18.
228 James, Anderson, *Constitutions of the Freemasons* (London, 1784), p. 208.
229 Ibid., 1723, 'To be sung and played at the Grand Feast', p. 83.
230 Ibid., p. 48.
231 Richard Graham, *Short Account of the Most Emminent Painters, Both Ancient and Modern*, appended to the 1716 edition of Du Fresnoy's *The Art of Painting*; Graham's Dedication to Burlington.
232 Howard Erskine-Hill, *The Social Milieu of Alexander Pope* (New Haven, 1975), p. 323.
233 Anderson, *Constitutions of the Freemasons* (London, 1723), p. 25.
234 Ibid., p. 39.

Thus far in the history the ideals are those of Burlington as well. Anderson then dutifully goes on to praise William III and Sir Christopher Wren. How much the failure of the Atterbury Plot, which intervened between the commissioning of the *Constitutions* and its appearance, affected the work will never be revealed, but it is generally accepted, if unwillingly by some masonic historians who are squeamish about the Brotherhood's involvement in politics, that before the conspiracy masonry was predominantly Jacobite, which is why the Hanoverians made such repeated and determined efforts to regularise it. The man initially responsible for trying to divorce masonry from politics was said to be Wren,[235] which may explain Lord Burlington's hatred of that architect, particularly if he changed sides. Anderson's 'best Architect of Britain' was excised from subsequent editions of the *Constitutions*, both in the text and in the song, which is almost certainly significant. Equally significant is the fact that all the proceedings of Grand Lodge from its inception in 1717 to 24 June 1723 have vanished: 'This year [1720], at some private lodge, several very valuable manuscripts concerning the fraternity, their lodge, regulations, charges, secrets and usages, particularly one written by Mr Nicholas Stone, the Warden under Inigo Jones, were too hastily burnt.'[236] In this connection it is as well to remember that 1717–19 were the years in which there was a split in the Whig party and that both Burlington and Walpole were of the disaffected group. Walpole's masonic career is as shady as Burlington's;[237] he seems to have been a mason but he does not appear in the post-1723 proceedings. Both men would have had ample reasons to destroy incriminating records. After 1719 they obviously went their separate ways but these joint years of opposition may well have been the cause of the constant fear that letters were being opened which hung over Lord and Lady Burlington. Conversely, the masonic oaths that Walpole and Burlington may have taken at the same moment could have preserved Burlington from the fate that overtook his cousin Orrery, incarceration in the Tower.

1717 was the year in which the first building at Chiswick, the Casina, was planned. It was unusual in that it had three storeys, traditionally one of the attributes of Solomon's Temple.[238] Its proud young owner had his portrait painted at this time, standing in front of the unfinished building, holding compasses, 'whose signification is applicable to the Master,' explained John Coustos, a London mason at his trial by the Inquisition in Portugal in 1742.[239] It seems likely that the three-storey Garden Temple was a private

---

235 Oliver, *Treasury*, p. 25.
236 Anderson, *Constitutions of the Freemasons* (1784), p. 207.
237 *Ars quatuor coronatorum*, 37 (1924), p. 126.
238 Oliver, *Treasury*, p. 254.
239 See note 187 above.

lodge. Later, when he acquired the estate next door, Burlington built a wooden bridge over the serpentine river that flowed through his garden, leading to a new back door to the Casina. An old masonic tradition which became part of the ritual, presumably of the Royal Arch, held that on his return to Jerusalem with his exiled followers Joshua crossed the river of Jordan by an ancient wooden bridge.[240] Freemasonry for the Jacobites was not only a spiritual ideal dedicated to restoration, it was also, as it had been during the Commonwealth, a highly practical method of conveying messages and money about Europe.[241] With its back entrance the Casina was directly approachable from the new and lonely West entrance Burlington made, inside which the visitor was greeted by an obelisk in a circular clearing and a fir tree.[242] Fir trees were one of the signs recognised by Jacobite messengers,[243] and they seem to have been planted in close proximity to an obelisk, as at Stourhead, home of Burlington's banker Henry Hoare,[244] presumably a doubly certain message.

Another obelisk in a circular space, this time a pond, stood in front of the Ionic temple in the garden at Chiswick. Coustos explained the masonic symbol of the point within the circle: 'the Compass being placed with one of its points on the ground cannot fail in the correctness of the circle which the other point describes, thus also the Master should circumscribe his actions so that they be without fault, and thus complying set a good example to others.'[245] Coustos's confession 'contained elements which now are unknown to the Craft, but which, in an elaborated form, are present in today's Royal Arch ritual'.[246]

Eight unusual obelisk chimneys graced the roof of the 'new house', which was built after the garden temples. It was crowned by an octagonal dome. The number eight was used in Christian iconography as a symbol of resurrection for several reasons, one being because there were eight survivors from the ark after the Flood (important in masonry) and another because Christ's resurrection occurred on the eighth day after his entry into Jerusalem.[247] It is also perfectly possible that if Burlington saw Chiswick as the Hermetic 'eighth sphere of spiritual rebirth,'[248] a combination of

240 Oliver, Treasury, p. 243; Chevalier de Berage, Les plus secrets mystères des hauts grades de la maçonnerie dévoilés, ou le vrai Rose Croix (Paris, 1768), p. 113. Private Lodges, particularly among the Ancients, conferred a degree known as Passing the Bridge, W. Hannah, Christian by Degrees (Chulmleigh, 1952) p. 85.
241 See note 195 above.
242 Travers Morgan Planning, unpublished report for the Department of the Environment, 'Chiswick House Grounds: Historical Survey' (1983), i, p. 19.
243 Monod, Jacobitism, p. 289.
244 Clark, 'Palladianism', p. 225.
245 See note 187 above.
246 Jones, Royal Arch, p. 44.
247 Joanne Snow-Smith, The Salvator Mundi of Leonardo da Vinci (Washington, 1982), p. 61.
248 See note 222 above.

Christian and Egyptian meanings would not have seemed incompatible to him. The octagon was associated with The Holy Sepulchre and the Knights of St John of Jerusalem. The origins of the chivalric orders of masonry, to which the Royal Arch mason may progress, are obscure but it is clear that from its beginnings masonry had, again, despite the protestations to the contrary of some masonic historians, connections with the Templars and the Knights of St. John. These two rival groups are joined, with no pretence at historical accuracy, in the higher degrees of masonry.[249] Prince Charles Edward attended an 'encampment', as their lodges are called,[250] of the Order of the Temple of Jerusalem in Edinburgh in the '45:

> Our noble Prince looked most gallantly in the white robe of the order, took his profession like a worthy knight; and after receiving congratulations of all present, did vow that he would restore the Temple higher than it was in the days of William the Lion.[251]

There may be a connection between the white robe of the Order of the Temple and the 'young man in the white robe . . . representing the genius of these kingdoms' in Carew's masque *Coelum Britannicum*. Based on the works of Giordano Bruno, whose influence was felt in Rosicrucianism, which in its turn many authorities feel to be connected with the Templars, the complicated symbolism of Carew's masque possibly contains hidden allusions to the Stuarts' hereditary right as the Unknown Superior. If Burlington was the living Unknown Superior's representative in England these involuted possibilities should be considered.

The war against the Infidel was added to the already overburdened Jacobite/masonic symbolism: it is commemorated at Chiswick on the ceiling of the gallery by a copy of the painting in the Doge's Palace in Venice of the *Defence of Scutari*.[252] The Chiswick painting is surrounded by scenes at encampments which could doubtless be traced to some Templar ritual. Opening off the Gallery at either end are two small rooms, one octagonal and one round, probably a reference to the round Temple of the Rock and the octagonal Holy Sepulchre in Jerusalem, and the two orders of knights who guarded them. Once again the question arises: did this masonic fusion of the two great knightly orders take place at Chiswick, or was Chiswick the epitome of all previous masonic symbolism?

249 Jackson, *Beyond the Craft*, p. 48.
250 Ibid., p. 48.
251 Sir Robert Strange and Andrew Lumisden, *Memoirs*, ed. J. Dennistoun (London, 1855), i, p. 81.
252 This painting appears as *The Relief of Smyrna* in many references to Chiswick. I am grateful to Pamela D. Kingsbury for pointing out the error.

The two remaining rooms on the *piano nobile* are the Green Velvet Room and the Bedchamber. The plasterwork in both is astonishingly elaborate. In the bedchamber, with its tiny closet, oak leaves (all-important in Stuart symbolism since Charles II hid in Boscobel Oak), roses, Prince of Wales feathers and royal gold fringes abound; while in the Green Velvet Room, colour of eternal hope, an acorn nestles amongst the decoration on one of the two fine fireplaces. There was no kitchen in the 'new house' but there was a wine cellar. On the ground floor there was a Linen Room and another containing £2436's worth of plate. All the requirements of masonic ritual were at hand.

James I's self-appointed role as the British Solomon,[253] and his motto *beati pacifici*,[254] immediately enforce the tradition that the Stuart kings were indeed the hereditary Grand Masters of all masonry. For Jacobite masons the murder of Hiram Abif, the architect of Solomon's Temple, symbolised the execution of Charles I.[255] If the building of Solomon's Temple and the murder of Hiram Abif, which eventually became the Grand Lodge ritual for Craft masons after 1717, were symbolic of the earlier Stuarts and the first Restoration, it seems only natural that the building of the Second Temple should be adopted by the Jacobite masons working towards a second Restoration.

If Lord Burlington's 'small cupboard' was the symbolic Second Temple, its much remarked upon miniature proportions would have been no disadvantage. It would have been ideally suited as both a practical and spiritual centre of Jacobite operations. After the symbolic seventy years of exile it is easy to see why 'Joshua of the Red Masons', if indeed the architect earl was he, should choose to build his Temple 70 feet square.

It is perhaps impossible today to comprehend how an eighteenth-century royalist mind worked and it is a grave mistake to imagine that Lord Burlington's outlook was in any way comparable to our own. He inherited the outlook and the symbolism of his forbears, the values of the men involved in the Restoration of Charles II. The similarities between the attempts leading to the first, successful Restoration, and those unsuccessful attempts at a second Restoration, are illuminating. It would never have occurred to Lord Burlington, that given time and determination, a second Restoration could not be achieved.

Shortly after his 1719 trip to Italy, when he possibly visited the recently married king, William Kent painted the ceiling of the Saloon at Burlington

---

253 Graham Parry, *The Golden Age Restor'd* (Manchester, 1981), p. 21.
254 Ibid., p. 22.

255 Alec Mellor, *Our Separated Brethren* (London, 1964), p. 100.

House. Known as *The Banquet of the Gods*, this painting features a wedding couple who almost certainly represent Jupiter and Juno, symbols of royal weddings.[256] James III married Maria Clementina Sobieska at Montefiascone on 1 September (n.s.) and Burlington and Kent returned to England together at the end of November. Kent began work on the ceiling soon after.[257]

A pamphlet complaining about Kent's controversial altarpiece for St Clement Danes (unfortunately destroyed during the last war), in which the main figure was thought to represent Maria Sobieska, infers that Kent brought a portrait of the princess back from Italy with him:

> Who is the painter, and of what Principle? How long has he been from the Court of Rome, before he painted that Picture? And, whether he brought no Picture, or Resemblance of the Princess Sobieska over with him? You will not repent of what you have done, but when you shall further enquire after the Person who employ'd him, Whether he be a Protestant? Or, if he call himself so, whether his children are not sent Abroad to Popish Seminaries for Education?[258]

Kent's idea of the young queen appears to be present on the ceiling of Lady Burlington's Summer Parlour at Chiswick. She appears as a bust, being painted by a *putto*, watched over by a second *putto* with his fingers to his lips, a masonic gesture.[259] The bust bears a strong resemblance to the only remaining photograph of Kent's altarpiece[260] and to Hogarth's satire upon it. The same *putti*, who could allude to the young Stuart princes, Clementina's sons, occupy a panel at the other end of the ceiling. This time one of them sleeps, watched over by the other who affectionately hugs an animal that seems to have undergone some restorational metamorphoses, but which originally was, it seems certain, a pug. This is borne out by the frontispiece of the 1743 publication of *Le secret de la Société des Mopses révélé* (*Mops* being the German for pug), in which the pug is almost identical to the animal at Chiswick. Both these panels are in octagonal surrounds. The central panel in the Summer Parlour is a series of four charming views of ports. In female masonic lodges in France (which for the most part derived their ideas from England) the 'sisters' made fictitious voyages and talked of anchoring in ports.[261] The ports are grouped round a sunflower, equivalent

256 Sir James George Fraser, *The Golden Bough* (London, 1925), p. 151.
257 Michael Wilson, *William Kent* (London, 1984), p. 40.
258 *British Museum Catalogue of Prints and Drawings*, i, *Political and Personal Satires*, vol ii, p. 622.
259 Chailly, *Magic Flute*, plate 28.
260 *Artwork*, 25 (1931) p. 32.
261 *Ars quatuor coronatorum*, 24 (1911), p. 7.

of the eight-pointed star in the Red Velvet Room.[262] Owls peer from the corners of the ceiling, the owl being an emblem of Lady Burlington's family, the Saviles. Owls were also a Jacobite symbol, appearing in satirical prints where they imply that Jacobites are 'all of a feather'.[263] They also hoot in the satires on the Opera of the Nobility.[264] It is perhaps possible that the Savile owl was the origin of this political symbol. The fireplace that was originally in the Summer Parlour, but moved by the sixth duke of Devonshire to Chatsworth, displays a relief of Diana wearing her crescent moon, in her masonic role as Queen of the Night, Goddess of the Mopses.[265] Trivial though these female lodges may seem it is perfectly possible that the meaning of the pug in the Summer Parlour was as serious to Lady Burlington as the meaning of the pug held by Lord Burlington's young sister in the family portrait that faced the martyred Charles I and his family in the octagonal Saloon. Known to have been a secret masonic emblem in the eighteenth century, when satires on masonry revealed some of the signs and symbols, it seems likely that, as with so many of these messages, the pug had been a secret signal for many years.

The Black Boy was a masonic symbol at least from the time of the Commonwealth and Elizabeth Dysart's visionary portrait. A seventeenth-century portrait at Oxburgh of two children in Dutch clothes, presumably young Bedingfelds away at school in Holland, shows a black boy lurking in the shadows offering the children a bunch of grapes, a reference to the king and his Divine Right. Like the Black Boy, public houses called the Bunch of Grapes referred to the exiled Stuart monarch and appear in many satirical prints.[266] Not only Charles II, but also James III, was referred to in this way:

> My Laddie can Fight, my Laddie can sing,
> He's fierce like the North-Wind, yet soft as the Spring,
> His Soul was designed for no less than a King:
> Such Greatness shines in my Black Laddie.[267]

The Burlington's, like many families, did have a black servant, but the presence of the black boy who stands behind the family in their group portrait by Van Loo is not necessarily to be taken as a mark of affection. As well as being a good family likeness,[268] this portrait is a celebration of the

262 For illustrations of this ceiling see Clark, 'Palladianism', pp. 228, 229.
263 Cruickshanks, *Untouchables*, illustration facing p. 71.
264 Deutsch, *Handel*, p. 382.
265 Chailly, *Magic Flute*, p. 94.
266 I am grateful to Dr David Vessey for this information.
267 BL, Jacobite Tracts, C115.a.3., quoted in Peggy Miller, *James* (London, 1971), p. 264.
268 Walpole Society, 22 (1933-34), Vertue, 'Notebooks', iii, p. 96.

arts: architecture, painting, music and literature all being represented. This may be a literal reference to the family's skill and interest but it may also bear the same message as the ceiling of the White Closet at Ham, the ceiling of the Red Velvet Room, the closing lines of Pope's *Epistle to Burlington* and countless other mediums ranging from private letters to public buildings: the restoration of the king by Divine Right.

In a letter written from Berlin in March 1751 Franceso Algarotti, who claims to have eaten 'many dinners' with Pope and Burlington when he was in England,[269] tells the architect earl of Frederick the Great's interest in his architecture.[270] Algarotti's correspondence with that monarch is somewhat cryptic, which is perhaps not surprising since they are both widely known to have been freemasons. Frederick's interest in the arts was, like Burlington's, clearly genuine. He saw himself as a great Maecenas but in addition to his duties as a procurer of *objets d'art* for the king it is almost certain that Algarotti doubled as a political agent. It is equally probable that he ran the odd political errand for Burlington. In his letter to the earl he says that if Burlington responds to Frederick's requests for drawings 'the fine arts, so abused today, will rise again in proud flight.' By 1751 neo-Palladianism had made its point in the literal sense so it seems probable that Algarotti was using the term 'arts' in its Jacobite/masonic connotation. This is made almost certain since at precisely this time Frederick was making promises to help another Stuart invasion. Prince Charles had visited him a month before Algarotti wrote to Burlington.[271] Unknown to Burlington or Algarotti, Frederick was using the Stuarts as a pawn in a game.[272] If this last attempt by Charles, the Elibank Plot, was in any way master-minded by the architect earl, it is a testimonial to a singularly poor judge of human nature. The English Jacobites were duped by one participant after another. One of the men deeply involved in the Elibank Plot was Dr William King, who had long been one of the Jacobite leaders. His association with Lord Burlington is revealed in his *Political and Literary Anecdotes*, where he reports having dined with him in the company of Pope, Lord Orrery and Sir Henry Bedingfeld.[273] Even though this must have been at an earlier date because of the poet's death in 1744, the united sympathies of the guests and the fact that the purpose of the occasion was for the host to acquaint them 'with an affair that engaged our attention' suggest more than a purely social gathering. The fourth earl of Orrery's son, the fifth earl, was another leading Jacobite.[274]

269 I owe this information to Dr S. Kaufman. See also BL, Althorp MSS, box B8, Lady Burlington to Lord Burlington, n.d.
270 Chatsworth, Devonshire MSS, letters, 28 March 1751.
271 McLynn, *Charles Edward Stuart*, p. 400.
272 Ibid., pp. 400–14.
273 William King, *Political and Literary Anecdotes* (London, 1819), p. 12.
274 Cruickshanks, *Untouchables*, p. 38.

Interestingly, despite the débâcle of the final attempt at a Restoration, there were still Jacobites, including King, willing to rise in June 1753.[275] After this Burlington became too ill to do more than go to Bath, hoping for relief. In December he died. Whether there is a connection between the death of the Jacobite cause and the death of Lord Burlington may never be revealed.

In one of his letters to Frederick, Algarotti refers to 'the palace of Chiswick'.[276] This may be insignificant but it may perhaps be an allusion to its symbolic purpose. Pope, on the other hand, must certainly have been initiated into the secrets of Chiswick. When he wrote about 'imitating fools' in his *Epistle to Burlington* he surely did not merely mean the Philistines who misplaced doors and windows in their Palladian buildings but the unfortunate Hanoverian Whigs who imitated the latest fashion in architecture without realising they were jumping on a bandwaggon which might take them in the very direction they were at such pains to avoid.

Until very recently the only attention Lord Burlington has been paid is as an architect, with his interest in music and the other arts following behind like poor relations. Perhaps if the possibility is recognised that architecture for Burlington was a fulfilment of the prophecy of Anchises, inscribed on his bas-relief by Soldani, it will lead to a clearer picture of the man. 'A new Marcellus shall arise in thee' is how his favoured poet Dryden translated the original 'Tu Marcellus eris', If his life was a long struggle 'Alone sufficient to sustain the war', a fight to discharge a responsibility placed on his shoulders and inscribed on the shield of the twenty-one-year-old Mr Buck and to welcome the living Augustus at the door of the waiting palace, the door presided over by the king's classical namesake, a more complex and fascinating man has to be faced.

A few glimpses of this 'Unknown Superior' are to be seen through the chinks in the brilliantly maintained armour. In a letter to his wife who had reported some snide remarks about the garden at Chiswick, he says that did those who made them 'but know how case-hardened I am against all the forces of the *Dunciad* they would not throw away their time upon me'.[277] That His Lordship was liable to fly into a rage and to be somewhat ruthless is revealed by his servants. His steward Henry Simpson told his master that it was not legal to shoot some dogs that had strayed onto the estate at

275 McLynn, *Charles Edward Stuart*, p. 410.
276 Francesco Algarotti and Frederick the Great, *Correspondence* (Berlin, 1837), 13 December 1751.
277 Chatsworth, Devonshire MSS, letters, 16 September 1735.

Londesborough, whereupon the angry landlord replied that he knew it was not: 'but notwithstanding that he would have 'em shot and let him [the owner] take his remedy which would be an action at law.'[278] If 'Mr Buck' was in fact one of James III's 'chief friends' his life must have been one of intense worry and immense labour. Despite this, he evidently created the impression of indolence. In September 1745 the archbishop of York, keen to raise support against the rebels, not surprisingly, had trouble with Lord Burlington who did not attend the meeting the archbishop called in York.[279] The earl's letter was sent to Lord Chancellor Hardwicke by the Archbishop, because he was 'not quite pleased with it.'[280] Hardwicke returned it, saying he took 'the coldness and dryness of it to proceed from the indolence of his temper, rather than from any other motive. Men must be taken as they are made. For these reasons I have not spoken of it to anybody, and should think it best for your Grace not to do so.'[281] Despite the archbishop's efforts the 'gentry of Yorkshire', who were considered so vital in the negotiations with the French in 1740, were evidently living up to expectations. The frantic archbishop told Hardwicke a month later that the troops raised by

> the Gentlemen have been completed some time, and they have been in daily expectation of arms for them, which they say they had assurance from above were put on shipboard for Hull, but afterwards, for reasons of despatch and safety, removed into waggons, above three weeks ago. They have heard nothing at all of them since, nor have any sort of information where they are.[282]

Just before the York meeting that he did not attend, Lord Burlington had evidently been asking his great friend, Richard Arundell, who was in Allerton, about hiding places. 'I have enquir'd about Cock Walks, & am told that Farm houses remote from towns are the properest to send 'em to, of such I can supply you with eight or so, tho' I fear they will be in some danger from foxes'.[283] To those accustomed to substituting money for 'muslins', swords for 'sugars' and Walpole for 'the fox', to mention but three of the Jacobite code names, 'cock-walks' raise suspicions at this date and place. Arundell was, on the face of it, a perfectly conforming Whig but, like Wade, he enjoyed a rent-free house on the Burlington estate in

278 Chatsworth, Devonshire MSS, Henry Simpson's letter book, 28 July 1743.
279 Chatsworth, Devonshire MSS, letters, Jo. Wood to Lord Burlington, 28 September 1745. See also Eveline Cruickshanks above.
280 'Correspondence of Archbishop Herring and Lord Hardwicke', 15 September 1745, *English Historical Review*, 19, (1904), p. 537.
281 Ibid., 21 September 1745, p. 542.
282 Ibid., 19 October 1745, p. 722.
283 Chatsworth, Devonshire MSS, letters, 6 September 1745.

London.[284] One of James III's least satisfactory agents, a kinsman of Orrery's, Colonel William Cecil, who was apprehended by the Government, stated at his examination in 1744 that, 'Mr Arundel' had been present at one of the meetings of Jacobite conspirators.[285]

Lord Burlington appears on the lists of people willing to support the Stuarts in the event of a successful invasion that were sent to James in Rome in 1733 and 1743.[286] These lists are often thought to be over-optimistic estimates but as more comes to light about the underground stream of Jacobitism they may prove more accurate than has hitherto been believed. The 1733 list, drawn up by Lord Cornbury, includes thumb nail character sketches of many of the candidates. If Burlington was as important to the exiled king as so many factors in his life suggest, James may have been amused to read his testimonial: 'Has honour and spirit and good common sense, naturally indolent, very angry with the Court and Walpole and pretty proud.' Cornbury would, as an important Jacobite himself, almost certainly have been aware of Burlington's sympathy for the cause but not necessarily of Burlington's importance. It is also almost certain that James would not have told his son, Prince Charles, about this 'Unknown Superior'. Without the jealousies and factions that dogged the Jacobite cause, both in Britain and on the Continent, the inevitable paranoia and secrecy that made communication almost impossible, even between its most faithful supporters, would have ground all but the most star-favoured operations to a halt.

Lord Cornbury's character sketches also include Walpole, who was 'interested, ambitious, wanting courage, ill treated by the Duke of Hanover, fearing the Opposition'. Walpole had got wind of Lord Cornbury's journey to Rome in 1730 and was trying to find out how the land lay as regards a Stuart Restoration. From all the many references to his behaviour towards the exiled king at this time it is very difficult to see whether he was in any degree sincere or whether, as most authorities believe, he was simply attempting to find out about Jacobite plans. James, from the first to the last, warned his English friends, 'with what little effect', to beware of Walpole.[287] In November 1731, a time of intense Jacobite plotting, there was a mysterious house-party at Houghton, Walpole's Norfolk seat, at which an 'emergency' masonic lodge was held.[288] The star-

---

284 *Survey of London*, xxxii, 'North of Piccadilly', p. 501.

285 *Memorials of John Murray of Broughton*, ed. R.F. Bell, Scottish History Society, 27 (1898), p. 409.

286 RA, SP 162/124; 253/51.

287 Haile, *James Francis Edward*, p. 347.

288 Gilbert W. Daynes, 'The Duke of Lorraine and English Freemasonry', *Ars quatuor coronatorum*, 37, (1924), p. 107.

studded assembly included the duke of Newcastle, the earl of Essex, major-
general Churchill and the duke of Lorraine, who was in England on a
mission from Austria and in whose honour Walpole's house-party was
given. James Anderson has received severe criticism from masonic historians for his historical inaccuracy in reporting this and other meetings in the
1738 edition of his *Constitutions*. The likelihood is that he was deliberately
fudging the issue since the Houghton meeting was clearly a political
assembly. The lodge was summoned by Sir Thomas Coke, whose choice of
Norfolk lodge was not the obvious one of King's Lynn, but that of the
Maid's Head in Norwich, which had been constituted by Martin Folkes,
who seems to have had Jacobite loyalties. The Master of the lodge was
Thomas Johnson, probably the same Thomas Johnson who sent Burlington
the account of the Lichfield Riots. Johnson made Newcastle, Essex, Churchill and Coke's chaplain masons, presumably because these were the only
guests unbound by masonic oaths. The English Jacobites' 'Unknown
Superior' is not mentioned but he was indeed there as his wife reveals in her
letters.[289] The attitude of Austria towards the Jacobites was critical at this
time.[290] Lady Burlington's letters also reveal that Burlington was never
'indolent' at any point in his life. He may have been misguided and
politically inept, easily duped by Machiavellian figures like Frederick the
Great and Walpole, but he had quite amazing tenacity. He may have been,
like his king, a poor judge of human nature and like most idealists,
somewhat remote from the real world but he certainly was not lazy. The
image of indolence may partly have been cultivated to give the impression,
again not borne out by the correspondence, that his agents were able to run
rings round him. The detailed letters he wrote about his Irish estates in 1729
show a thorough and knowledgeable concern as well as a scorn for those
who did not do their job properly, one of which he termed 'a troublesome,
insignificant fellow'[291] He was evidently impatient of frivolous occupations
for in one letter his wife condoles with him because he has been obliged to
play cards. She feels it must be tiresome when 'one does not love it to lose
into the bargain.'[292]

   The often repeated idea that Lord Burlington abandoned Burlington
House and retired with his pictures to Chiswick on his resignations in 1733
seems to be based on one remark by Sir Thomas Robinson.[293] Burlington

289 BL, Althorp MSS, box B8, 2, 4, 6 November
     1731.
290 Jeremy Black, 'Jacobitism and British Foreign
     Policy, 1731-5', *The Jacobite Challenge*, ed.
     Eveline Cruickshanks and Jeremy Black
     (Edinburgh, 1988) p. 147.
291 Chatsworth, Devonshire MSS, Irish estate let-
     ter book, 1728-29.
292 BL, Althorp MSS, box B8, 6 November,
     1731.
293 *HMC, Carlisle MSS*, p. 125, Robinson to Lord
     Carlisle, 24 December 1733.

did indeed move many paintings to Chiswick and he may have wanted to give Robinson the impression that he was retiring from central activities yet from all surviving documents it is clear that life went on at Burlington House as usual. The Burlingtons were always referred to as 'the family at Burlington House.' Though the children spent their younger years at Chiswick, because it was deemed healthier, as they grew older they had lessons at Burlington House, harpsichords were tuned there, letters were sent there and plasterers were employed there. They all always talked about 'going to Chiswick.' In March 1750, when Prince Charles Edward was starting to make preparations for his clandestine visit to England, Charlotte wrote to Lord Hartington from Burlington House, saying she is just off to Chiswick and that 'Papa also goes but I did not chuse to go with him he goes and comes back so late.'[294]

The intentional ambiguity of the Jacobites whenever they did put pen to paper has misled even the most rigorous scholars, unaware of the hidden loyalties they were dealing with. Richard Graham, secretary to both Burlington and his father, whose family Jacobitism almost certainly made him the confidant of the Boyle family,[295] bears this out in his dedication to the third earl of his *Short Account of the Most Eminent Painters, both Ancient and Modern*, which he published with the 1716 edition of Du Fresnoy's *The Art of Painting*. Graham speaks of Burlington's father as a man 'whom our late King pronounced the Finest Gentleman in his Dominions.' This to a Jacobite was of course not William III but James II and the tribute might account for the proud portrait of the King's 'Finest Gentleman' in his clandestine Garter regalia at Oxburgh. Graham also applauds the third earl's 'Glorious conduct in the North upon the late unhappy disturbances' and the 'exemplary Moderation and Generosity which mov'd you to intercede for the Lives of those, against whom you stood prepar'd to hazard your own.' The probability is that had it come to a crunch the young lord lieutenant would have found some means of standing stock still whilst others worked, at his behest, like moles underground, to put as many spokes as they were able into the Hanoverian wheel.

The assessment of any clandestine activity depends in large measure on cumulative circumstantial evidence. In a doubly clandestine underworld like that of Jacobite freemasonry the accumulation of pointers and comparisons, of signs and symbols is likely to be the most that can be expected. Conclusive written proof is a bonus that seldom, if ever surfaces. As more

294 Chatsworth, Devonshire MSS, letters, 30 March 1750.

295 See the essays by Dr T.C. Barnard and Dr Eveline Cruickshanks above.

work is done on this, on the whole, neglected area of seventeenth and eighteenth-century history the part played by the second and third earls of Burlington may become clearer. When the third earl's possible role in this underworld has been considered it may transpire that neo-Palladianism, with its roots in the great Stuart architect Inigo Jones, was a symbol of the resurrection of ancient, Augustan values through the mediums of, as Anderson said in his *Constitutions of the Freemasons,* 'the great Palladio and the glorious Inigo Jones,' rather than of Palladianism for itself. If when the third earl signed himself 'Burlington Architectus' he was referring to architecture in its masonic , universal sense, and if he was one of the 'wise Jacobites' who 'continued to waste their lives and their fortunes'[296] on an ideal that was doomed to fail, his work as architect in its literal sense has left the world one of the most perfect embodiments of an ideal ever to be executed in 'the Palace of Chiswick.'

296 Cruickshanks, 'Cornbury', p. 10.

Index

(References to Figures are in bold)